T0365092

ONCE A SOLDIER

ONCE A SOLDIER

A BIOGRAPHY SPANNING NINETY YEARS, TWO WARS
AND FOUR THOUSAND HOURS OF FLIGHT TIME.

R. RENWICK HART

Once A Soldier
A Biography spanning ninety years,
two wars and four thousand hours of flight time.

iUniverse books may be ordered through booksellers or by contacting:

iUniverse
1663 Liberty Drive
Bloomington, IN 47403
www.iuniverse.com
844-349-9409

ISBN: 978-1-4759-9962-4 (sc)
ISBN: 978-1-4759-9963-1 (e)

Print information available on the last page.

iUniverse rev. date: 03/13/2023

PREFACE

Many of my classmates and friends responded to the first edition of this book. They were more than generous with their comments, some of which I will list here.

Bob Ord, Lt General, U.S. Army Ret.

Your book is more than a just book.

It is a fascinating history of your fascinating life over 8 decades, a life of great significance in accomplishments and admirable compassion for your fellow human beings.

Even though we have been together a lot these last twenty-five years and shared much of our professional and personal history, I still enjoy learning even more of your and your families' experiences. Thank you for the journey and for your friendship.

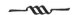

Leroy N Suddath, Major General, US Army

Dear Ren, the word is out that your book is a Block Buster, please send me a signed copy.

Three weeks later:

Ren – I received your book today and have already started reading it and am enthralled by it. This is a masterpiece; it captures one's interest from the get-go. Good on you! I do not know how my mother and father met one another and have often wondered and never asked while they were alive.

Best Wishes, Your friend, Leroy

Bernd Sawaski, San Juan Kosala, Mexico

It was a pleasure to read the true story of a professional soldier, with a great sense of humor. The book reads very well, is interestingly written, it flows! One does not want to put it away. It is a document of a time past and a guide for the future with sound and passionate letters to his grandchildren. It will be an enrichment for our family to read about your life!

It is a book I will read again! Very well done!

BG John "Doc" Bahnsen on March 28, 2017

"Once A Soldier" is a book about an Aviator, a Soldier, and Uncommon Common Sense. It is a superb story of a talented soldier who did it all his way. Many chuckles and surprises in a career that is filled with uniquely told anecdotes of how to get along with difficult commanders. Ren's flying experience makes you wonder how he survived all the close calls. His Vietnam flying duty in a top-secret unit will confirm America's ability to listen to our enemies' radio traffic. The cast of characters in the book include an unusual family, famous West Point classmates and a host of interesting people. Humor prevails in this well written summary of a man's life. Military buffs, and especially professional soldiers, will enjoy the exploits of R. Renwick Hart.

Major General Perry Smith

A book not to be missed.

Ren Hart has a real talent--he tells such great stories. Chapter One will grab your attention---his dramatic flying experiences are sprinkled throughout the book. But there is much more. I especially loved his stories of West Point in the 1950s, combat in Vietnam, and investigations of aircraft accidents. All this plus how to enjoy "deep retirement", advice to grandchildren, and so much more. Put this book. Just love it at the top of your reading list…not to be missed!

—⚯—

Ren, OMG…you are a great writer!!! Almost finished reading your book. Just love it! Truly a family treasure that will endure through the ages. Excellent 'lessons learned' in the appendixes. Your book is a masterpiece! The tremendous amount of work it took to compile, assemble, and publish, reflects great credit on your capacity on your capacity to hang with your project and polish the skills necessary to make it a most enjoyable and coherent story. Well done my friend. Simply outstanding work. Thank you very much for sharing.
Gary Weitz

—⚯—

Ren – You could not have focused better on what Judy, and I have been talking about, now that all our parents have passe., There is a gap in our knowledge of both the history and the reality of large portion of the lives of the ones we loved, who are gone. I have been up till one AM for the last two nights reading it!
Ian Mattox, Esquire

—⚯—

Ren – I recently borrowed a copy of your book from my neighbor and read it with great interest. For starters, let me tell you the book is terrific! You are indeed a modern-day philosopher. It was a light; quick and fun read and I was disappointed when I turned the last page and there was nothing more. I particularly enjoyed several parts – your early discussion of manners; the letters to your grandchildren, and the appendix of what you learned "in your first 80 years". And the interview notes taken from a discussion about your great-great grandmother Sarah was a classic of what America was like in the wild west days. I enjoyed your book so much that my wife Mary Beth downloaded it from Amazon to read on her Kindle and enjoyed it as well.
With Best Regards, John Stokes (Colonel, USA, Retired)

AUTHOR'S NOTE:

We lived in San Francisco, a block from West Portal Grammar School; a short walk for a twelve-year-old. It was 1944 and I certainly wasn't expecting my father to appear in the school yard during our morning recess. I hadn't seen him since he left for the Philippines two years earlier. Now he was in uniform, standing six feet two, in our school yard, with ribbons on his chest, gold braid on his hat and eagles on his shoulders. That appearance shaped my life; it was the epiphany that left me thinking: "That's what I want to be!"

Seven years later, the day after graduating from high school, I joined the Army. The Korean War was raging but my sights had long ago been focused on entering West Point. My father told me that West Point would be the best path for me to follow if I wanted a career in the Army. A year later, after basic training at Fort Belvoir, VA, I completed the Army's Prep School, entered West Point and faced the full onslaught of Plebe Year's Beast Barracks.

CONTENTS

PART III
A COLLECTION OF PERTINENT
EVENTS AND VIGNETTES

Colonel R. Ren Hart – 1977

FOREWORD

Too late in life we realize one never learns enough about their parents. It seems when we are young, and our parents are still around, there is no impetus to take advantage of available information about them. There is always time to ask questions about their youth or how they met one another. After all, they are there and can answer those questions any day. So, life rolls on, then one day they are gone and all those answers to questions you never asked are gone with them, FOREVER! Perspective changes.

Parents shape our lives in ways we never realize. When I was five, I would sometimes overhear my folks arguing. There were accusations of father's infidelity and in the vernacular of the times, having a "roving eye." In those days even one divorce was not only unusual but socially unacceptable. So, Father's four marriages were somewhat beyond the pale and an embarrassment to our relatives. Mother's reflections on all this are probably what led to my disdain for infidelity, which played a part in the conduct of my marriage. My parents ended their marriage in its eighth year, before I turned six, so there were many "blank years" when I wasn't with my father - years which might otherwise have made a difference in filling the gaps in what I know of my ancestors.

Throughout the last half of my life, I have wondered what my father's youth was like, his first wife, the details of his early days in college and the Army. Why didn't I ask his sister (my Aunt Helen), who lived some 30 years after his death? Now it is too late.

Having learned so little about my father and his side of the family, I decided to write my memories to ensure that my heirs would have the details of my life. Thus, I begin this epistle with the primary goal of leaving my children and grandchildren a written history of my life, as much as I can remember of our heritage and probably altogether more than they care about.

If perhaps my grandchildren, or their children, find something here they would like to keep, to remember, or put to use instead of learning it through the harsh experience of life, then my writings are worth the time and effort. My life has been a wonderful journey so far, a fascinating 90 years, and hopefully, now in the twilight of those years, there's still enough time left to tell you about it. As Sophocles noted, "One must wait until evening to know how splendid the day has been."

PART I

MY FIRST TWENTY-FOUR YEARS

CHAPTER 1

IN THE BEGINING

From my earliest memories, an interest in flying has always been a part of my life. This interest no doubt blossomed as a pre-teen during that period in the 1940's when those magnificent airplanes like the P 51 Mustang and the P 38 Lightning were controlling the skies during WW II. Later, the memories of real-life activities found their neurologic position of importance in the scale of life. Like the time I was taking a forensic scientist north to view the site and remains of a terrible highway accident in the vicinity of Redding, CA.

The flight to Redding was a three-hour trip from Monterey. I rented a Cessna 172 from the Navy Flying Club for the trip. My first stop was Palo Alto to pick up my childhood friend Bob, who was a PhD, Professor Emeritus in Nuclear Engineering and expert in matters dealing with "strength of materials". The second stop was picking up his attorney in Sebastopol, who was standing by when we landed at that little airport. With the three of us back in the air we headed north along Interstate Highway 5. A few miles South of Redding Bob asked if I would overfly the site where an RV had gone off the road, hit a ditch and burst into flames, severely injuring the occupants. It was Bob's task to determine why the RV had burst into flames. It was my task to fly us up and back and to render my lesser opinion on what had gone wrong. As a trained aircraft accident investigator, my ideas were of some value, but Bob was the expert in this field. We circled the accident site a couple times to get an overview and then continued north for a few miles before landing at the Redding airport.

It can get unbelievably hot in Redding, and this was one of those days when it was well over 100°F. Before leaving the aircraft to for our RV inspection, I arranged for the plane to be refueled with 20 gallons. With three large persons on board and the extreme heat, I was concerned about the weight of the aircraft when it came time to take off again. So, I decided to limit my refueling to 20 gallons, which is a little over three hours of flight time in that Cessna. With the fuel I still had on board, which would give me close to five hours of flight time going home.

After our examination of the RV wreckage, it was about 2 PM when we took off to head back to Monterey, a three-hour flight. Our return trip was uneventful, dropping off the attorney at Sebastopol and Bob in Palo Alto. As I prepared for takeoff from Palo Alto, I noticed the gas gauge was close to the E for both tanks. I had noted earlier that the gas gauge had been suffering from old age. The plane was over 30 years old, and years of sloshing fuel began to take a toll on the rheostat in the gas tanks. These older planes used a variable resistor, and over time the sending devices lose sensitivity in the mid-range and the gas gauge tends to read either full or empty. Now it was reading empty. With nearly 6 hours of fuel on board when I left Redding, I suspected the problem was in the sending unit, not the amount of fuel remaining. An experienced aviator determines the amount of gas remaining in the tanks through careful computation of fuel burn. I checked the Operator Handbook and noted the fuel consumption, at the altitude I was flying, was 6.3 gallons per hour. I was in good shape for the 40 minutes it would take to get home.

As I rose from the runway at Palo Alto and pointed the nose of my little craft toward the Santa Cruz Mountains, I was aware of but only slightly uncomfortable by, the near empty reading of my gas gauges. Then, just north of Watsonville, I noticed that the needles seemed glued to the empty position in a persistently motionless state. Should I land at Watsonville? Again, I checked my operator's handbook and computed the fuel remaining to be enough for over two more hours of flight at my cruising altitude and power setting. I motored on. As I arrived in Monterey's air space the controller delayed my landing for about three minutes for a larger aircraft. Now it was my turn. I lined up on final approach, slowed my speed and put down full flaps. At that point THE

ENGINE QUIT! As the saying goes, the propeller must be there to keep the pilot cool, otherwise why would he start to sweat when it stops? At that time, I was at about 500 feet.

Normally engine failure is not that big a deal for an experienced pilot; a bit distracting but well within the realm of one's ability to cope. At 5,000 feet above ground level, a 172 will glide in any direction for ten miles, so that gives you some 214 square miles of surface to pick out a suitable place to land. However, on short final, at 500 feet, with full flaps deployed, one's options become a bit thin and even thinner as you lose altitude while contemplating. And so it was, I began contemplating. At that point the pucker factor was not too high, so I pushed the transmit button and with the mike at my lips said matter-of-factly, "Monterey Tower, Navy 372 has a MAYDAY. My engine has quit, and I am going to land to the north." I was trying hard to be Joe Cool and not sound all up tight. It must have worked too well, because Monterey Tower did not recognize that there was a very real emergency going on just off the end of their runway. They replied, "Roger, Navy 372 is clear to land runway 28 Right." My thought process was WOW! I just don't have time to discuss this with them; I'm in survival mode. When I had put the flaps down and dropped the nose, the change in angle must have unported the last drops of gas. Things were getting worse in a hurry. Whereas I had been on a glide angle to arrive at the end of the runway (on the numbers), now without power, I am on a glide angle to arrive at the face of the cliff at the end of runway 28 Right. Should I take the flaps off to stretch my glide and try to make the airfield? To do so would initially cause me to lose some of my precious altitude. If I try to make the end of the runway and am short, I'm dead for sure. Statistics tell us that the tendency to make it to the airport after engine failure, is overwhelming. It takes a lot of discipline to lower the nose and accept the fact that you are going to make an off-field landing. Trying to make it to the field is all too seductive and often a fatal choice.

Turning away from the airport, I decided to keep the flaps down and try for a narrow road I see off to the right. It is perhaps two or three hundred feet lower than the runway, which gives me another bit of glide distance. Now I hear the plane in queue behind me on the radio. Seeing me turning and heading lower, he calls tower and confirms my transmission to Monterey, telling them that 372 has a problem and is headed for an emergency landing.

At that point I shut everything else out and am totally focused on my chosen landing area and looking for potential problems. No time to mess with further transmissions or restart procedures. My mind is racing: Is the road too narrow? Where's the wind from? Are there telephone poles defining unseen wires? Now committed to my landing area, I begin a self-talk. "How's my approach area look? Am I on glide slope? Oh crap, the damn oak trees are overhanging my road and that road is narrow, very narrow - just a one lane hardtop. I may need to snake it in under the canopy of the oak trees lining the road. Whoa, what if I catch a wing ...bad stuff! LOOK! There's a dirt road to the left, paralleling the hardtop and no trees. Take that! TAKE THAT! Line her up for the dirt road landing. There we go, straight down the approach line, no problems. Oops, the road turns into the trees ahead and it's not a road, its tank trail! Need to land short. Slow her up, slow her up. OH MY GOD, there's a berm in the road right where I'm going to touch down on that tank trail. No wonder it's all churned up. Get past the berm. Now back on the yoke, more, MORE. It's all the way back." Whoosh, the plane sinks into the powdery dirt just beyond the berm, rolls 200 feet and comes to rest. No crash, no dents, no damage

There are sirens in the distance but the first to arrive is the *Herald* Newspaper reporter and photographer. The next one to pull up is the Federal Police from Fort Ord, then the fire engine and some folks from the Ryan Ranch buildings. I stepped out of the plane, not believing it was over. What a day! Whoa, all those years of practice forced landings paid off after all. I also learned a valuable lesson: The plane descends much faster with a dead engine than it does when the instructor pulls the throttle back to idle. A spinning prop on a dead engine will cause as much drag as would a parachute of the same diameter, nearly doubling one's descent rate.

But that little event came later in my life.

Chapter 2

Early Memories

My earliest memories are of frolicking barefoot in Hawaii at age 3 or 4. We had moved from my birthplace in Columbus, Ohio in 1936 when Father, a career Army officer, was reassigned to Schofield Barracks, Hawaii. Mother and Father found a lovely home in Honolulu on Royal Circle Kahala, an upscale residential neighborhood on the edge of town. Kahala is a short street leading down to the beach and ending in a cul-de-sac with two or three homes on the circle overlooking the beach. We were one house up from the circle, close to the ocean, so Brother Harry and I spent much of our preschool time on the beach and living like native Hawaiians. We routinely ran barefoot across the sand never realizing it was hot until one day we saw tourists hopping around like they were on burning coals. We were finally introduced to shoes when starting kindergarten.

Memories of those early days are scarce but happy. I do recall one room in the house ... the enclosed porch with a rattan sofa. This was the room Mother liked and we spent time there together. On this day I was amusing myself and suspect that I was being better behaved than usual, because Mother sat down to hug me and tell me what a good boy I was. She was effusive, and finally noted that I was her favorite. This made me proud and happy, although at some level this favoritism must have struck me as strange, since the memory of the occasion has lasted for so many years.

Other early recollections include a huge banyan tree in our front yard. In the morning it would fill with a hundred mynah birds who, at the crack of dawn, raised an unbelievable ruckus. We had a string running from one of the upstairs windows to several tin cans hanging in the banyan tree. When the cacophony from the mynah birds became intolerable, Father would jerk the string a couple of times and the birds would scatter. I also remember walking home from preschool, playing on the beach with our parents nearby, our trip to the black sand beaches of Hilo, and our two rabbits caged in the back yard. There are also vague memories of a big party at our home, which I now presume was a party commemorating Father's promotion to major in about 1938. For three years my brother and I lived in this home, on this idyllic island finally leaving in 1939 for our next phase of life. However, before I go there, let me say a few words about my Mother and our heritage.

CHAPTER 3

MY MOTHER

Mother Circa 1928

Mother, Sacha (Alexandra) de Ciccolini, was born in Brussels on 23 October 1907. Her father was a marquis and rather wealthy, so her family had social recognition and position which was also accorded her. How different that is from the way most of us enter this world. I mention this because heritage can be a big factor in the formation of one's life; at least in early perceptions of what you are and who you are. However, if you are born into money, position and status, there is often little impetus to achieve. Perhaps that is why most of our family's wealth disappeared in two generations. So, although we are from a proud heritage, my childhood never had the trappings of money. That is partly due to my being a depression baby (no one had money in the early 30's after the great Depression of 1929) and partly due to the circumstance of divorce. When parents divorce, finances become thin. That partially explains why, in our household, nothing was wasted. Lights were turned off when not in use and we learned to conserve. All our basic needs were met but the frills were few and far between. Perhaps that's why, by age twelve, I was eager to have a job delivering newspapers in San Francisco to earn a few dollars. I earned $20 a month, a small portion of which went to pay family bills. This thrift set the tenor of my life; sort of a "waste not, want not" approach.

Though she was born in Brussels, Belgium in 1908, Mother's home was Nice, France. She was named Alexandra de Ciccolini but always preferred and used the shorter Russian version of her given name, "Sacha.". Her early life in southern France was during that period when Nice was transitioning from a fishing village on the Mediterranean to an international play spot. Her older sister, Lilly, was a lovely but frailer girl who died at age 7 from the typhoid fever that was sweeping through Europe in about 1917.

When Mother was 12, she attended a private Catholic school in Nice as a live-in student. She referred to it as a convent and was not very happy under the discipline and restrictions imposed by the nuns. By the age of 14 Sacha was fluent in French, English, Italian and Dutch, displaying the linguistic accomplishment expected of upper-class Europeans of the time. Because her English was pretty good, she was assigned a roommate who had just arrived from Norway who did not speak French but had a working familiarity with English. Soon they became close friends. When Mother was 15, her Norwegian roommate asked her home to Oslo to spend the summer. After that, Mother was off to Oslo every summer with her roommate, whose father, Mr. Plateau, was a wealthy businessman who, among other holdings, owned a large brewery in Oslo.

Mother was not a happy camper at her strict Catholic school. There was no chance for dating or meeting young men, and the regimentation ran counter to her free spirit. To some degree she also felt abandoned and betrayed by her parents. When Mother was 16, Mr. Plateau's wife died. So, it is no wonder when, the following summer, again visiting Oslo, she accepted Mr. Plateau's offer to marry. When they married, Sacha was a slender and lovely 17 while Plateau must have been in his late 40's. Marrying him was a chance for Mother to get out from under the strict routine of the seminary and start a life of her own.

Within two years Plateau succumbed to an illness and Mother became a widow at age 19! Most of Plateau's estate remained with his children, but Mother had been taken care of in his will with a small stipend. She also retained possession of her engagement present; a large painting Plateau had purchased from the widow of the curator of the Louvre Museum in Paris.

As an aside, I should note that this painting, purportedly by the Master Correggio and dating to the late 1400's, is still in our family. It is entitled "Leda and the Swan" and depicts the seduction of Leda by Jupiter in the form of a swan—a bit of Greek mythology which was perhaps being acted out by Plateau in his offer of marriage?

Now a widow at 19 and not wishing to return home to Nice in the role of a daughter, Mother left Oslo for Paris in 1927 and enrolled herself in a finishing school there. Her school included creative art and design as well as the art of being a lady! Mother had a strong affinity for the arts. One of her designs she later had made into French provincial chairs which still adorn our San Francisco home. She also had a lovely singing voice and enjoyed playing the piano. I suspect these talents were honed at her school in Paris.

On weekends she would horseback ride in the Bois de Boulogne. This eventually led to her meeting the handsome young army officer who was destined to be her next husband and my father. Horseback riding would also be the cause of her losing a kidney while in her 30's from an earlier injury she sustained after being thrown from her horse. In the early 1940s the injured kidney was removed. I was nine years old but never had the impression this extraordinary operation was a big deal. Mother was gone for a week or so and then matter-of-factly returned to the business of Mothering. Sometime later, when I saw the scar which stretched more than halfway around her waist, I better understood what she must have gone through. Mother was strong of constitution and mind and the kidney experience was soon left behind.

It is interesting to note her many distinguishing talents and character traits, which are showing up in bits and places in her progeny. Like her granddaughter Laura, Mother was a "know no fear" type of person, unusual for women of her day. Her singing voice seems to live on, not only in Laura but in her great-granddaughter Janine Alexandra. Mother had a flash temper which appeared out of nowhere and was particularly demonstrated when dealing with my brother and me. She would get mad at Harry mostly and start yelling at him and it seemed that the more she yelled the madder she got. I was careful to stay in the background during these tirades. More notable were her Mothering instincts—very protective, and there was absolutely nothing she wouldn't do for her children. This too I see in my daughter Laura with her children.

Sacha fought a continuing battle with her weight. It was her opinion (which may be correct) that having only one kidney was part of her weight problem. She was a great cook, given totally to experimentation as she created delights for her family—usually fattening, always good.

Her love of nature, animals, and the great outdoors was apparent throughout her life and in line with her warm-blooded, loving nature. In her later years, she doted on her cats, who had manipulated her into tasty cooking liver tidbits and other delicacies. Of course, Mother had spent a lifetime expressing her love through her cooking, so now, living alone, this was a natural follow-on. Mother was also a great sports person. She played a mean game of tennis, was a swimmer, a hiker, and enjoyed skiing. It's wonderful to see these talents spring forth in her granddaughter Laura. Mother also loved to play the piano, tried her hand at art and appreciated good music.

In the early 1960's she married her longtime companion and our surrogate father, Harold R. Lomo. Harold was great with Harry and me and responsible for much of what turned out right with us. He was born in Norway at the turn of the century and died in his sleep in San Francisco in his mid-70's. They had shared many wonderful years together exploring the back roads of northern California in his old Graham sedan.

After Harold's death in 1965, Mother moved to Sonoma. She had often talked of living in Sonoma and was very happy there except for an occasional complaint during the spring hay fever season and the summer heat. Her condo was just above the Sonoma Square and near enough for her to walk to the market. Sacha was a great walker, partly because she never learned to drive but mostly because she enjoyed the outdoors and the exercise. In my teen years we spent many a weekend hiking the trails of Muir Woods, which I learned to enjoy. On occasion I spent time teaching her to drive but it was not something she was particularly eager to learn at that point of her life.

When I returned to San Francisco in 1976 for an assignment to The Presidio, Barb and I would visit her in Sonoma relatively often, usually when coming and going from Lake Tahoe and a few specific trips in addition. In her later years our visits seemed to mean a great deal to her. My last visit was in early December 1990. I came alone to spend a couple of days. Her happiest moments were when she had visits from her boys! I will never forget that when I left, she mentioned she had been out of aspirin for a couple of days. Unknown to me, it was probably the aspirin that was keeping her from the stroke she suffered two days later. The fact that I was not proactive in ensuring she had some aspirin before I left continues to linger as a sense of guilt. I suspect that when one loses a parent, misgivings of all sorts are a common emotion which surface and need to be dealt with. In my case, it was "Why didn't I spend more time with her, why didn't I give more of myself when we were together, why didn't I delay my departure long enough to insure she had aspirin?"

The morning of her stroke she had evidently gotten up to make a cup of coffee before getting dressed to go to her choral group practice. When she didn't show for her group, one of the ladies came looking for her after practice. She found Mother lying on the kitchen floor, unconscious, with her coffee spilled. The doctor said it was a massive stroke and she would not recover. The two or three hours she lay unattended had resulted in irreparable damage.

For the next two months Harry and I visited her in Sonoma every day, either he or I or both at the same time but she did not recognize us. Sometimes we would meet at her condo and work on renovating it before going over to the hospital. It was extremely disturbing to me to see her lying in bed, immobilized by a straitjacket to keep her from removing the tubes. After about 6 weeks, when it was apparent she would not recover, I made the very difficult decision to have her released from the straitjacket and unhooked from the nasio-gastric feeding tubes. It is very hard, almost impossible, to take the steps to let a parent go. I could not have made that decision if it weren't for some penciled notes she had made expressing that it was her desire to not be kept alive with feeding tubes or other unnatural measures. I was surprised and relieved when the doctor and nurses applauded my decision to let her go.

With that decision, the hospital could no longer care for her under Medicare, so it was necessary for us to move her to a full-care facility. We decided on Hillsdale Manor, a few miles south of San Francisco, where

R. Renwick Hart

Barb's parents had been and where she would be close to Harry and Anita. It was not unexpected when she contracted pneumonia a short time later and in February 1991 died.

I shall always miss Mother and Harold greatly and even today, hardly a day goes by without my thoughts returning to her. Her ashes are at "Cypress Lawn Cemetery" in Colma, in a marked columbine, not far from Harold'

CHAPTER 4

FATHER

Colonel Harry Lee Hart, Father, 1951

Father was an impressive man. He possessed those attributes of character, honesty, and integrity which are so essential to success in life, and certainly in the Army. When I was in grammar school in San Francisco (West Portal School), just a block from our home, father was away at war. I had not seen him for nearly three years. It was a school day, and I was playing in the schoolyard during our 6ᵗʰ grade recess, when I saw Father approaching. It was in 1945 and he had just returned from the Philippines. Standing tall in his uniform, his six-foot two height was accentuated by his officer's garrison hat. The eagles on his shoulders, the medals, the warrior returned from the Pacific; I was deeply impressed. His presence demanded respect and admiration and it was at that point of my childhood when I knew what direction my life would take, must take. I would follow in his footsteps. Over the years, those aspirations never wavered.

Also, father was a gentleman. When I was a boy of ten or eleven, exiting an elevator with him, he observed with some disgust that a man in the elevator had failed to remove his hat. He went on to explain to me that a gentleman always removes his hat inside and when in the presence of ladies. Also, that it is particularly unacceptable to remain covered at the table when dining; odd, the things that stick with you and shape your behavior. Even today, when I see someone sitting at a table inside for lunch or dinner, still wearing his baseball hat, I must stifle my urge to pass him a note informing him of his gross behavior. I feel insulted by crudeness and having to share a dining experience with someone so ill informed.

Almost all manners spring from showing respect or consideration for others, so it is with some reluctance that I see America slipping away from these social amenities. In my youth, I read that a man does not address a lady first and does not extend his hand to a lady to shake hands. The privilege of "being recognized" rests with the lady. Such amenities as seating your lady, holding the door for her, walking on the curbside of the sidewalk (a residual of the horse and buggy days when the roads were potholed, and carriages would splash for days following the rains) are all slipping away as society "crudes down" and women go to war.

Today, when a lady arrives at or laves the table, I still like to stand and help her be seated (unless I am tucked away in a booth). Usually, such amenities are appreciated by the recipient, though certainly can be misinterpreted as an affectation to appear gentlemanly. It is important to show your children and grandchildren the utmost respect in that regard so that they may better judge their date's level of refinement and respect. Things that were totally gross in my day have now become commonplace.

But there is also another aspect in observing manners. Manners tell a story about how the individual was raised, what sort of stock they came from. Table manners are particularly revealing and not necessarily restricted to the realm of snobbery. Parents who come from parents whose parents knew better will demand that their children eat with some decorum. Parents who were abandoned at youth, or uncared for themselves, will not know to pass decent manners on to their children and so are marked as "lesser" by a social class that knows better. That class most often will include those who rise to positions of influence, and understandably would prefer to promote those under them who share the same values. So having a knowledge of what constitutes proper manners will be of value for a few generations yet. Father was born in Utica, New York on 23 December 1893. His mother, Annabel Lee, was one of nine children and married Harry Caley Hart, a "railroad man," said my Aunt Helen. Lee, as he was called, had three younger sisters: Lorna, who died at age 12 in 1908; Mary Lee, who died in 1918 when she was 16; and his youngest sister Helen, who lived until 1995. They were a handsome family; both Lee and Helen were tall, attractive people, as I presume were their two sisters who died so young. Father never spoke of his deceased sisters, Lorna and Mary.

In the early days of the 1800's there were two main Lee families, the Northern Lee's, from which he descended and the Southern Lee's, made famous by Robert E. Lee, the Confederate Army Commander (and graduate of West Point). Father grew up in New York and attended Cornell University for two years before joining the Army to "fight the Kaiser" in WW I. He was in the SAE fraternity and like many young men, in their first experience away from home, he placed more emphasis on his social life than his studies. He told me during that time, he contracted mononucleosis from a weakened condition as a result of "burning the candle at both ends" (i.e., courting the ladies!).

It was about 1915 and there was much patriotic fervor then, with young men anxious to join the war effort. With two years of college, he was eligible, more than eligible, for Officers' Candidate School (OCS), which he attended shortly after joining the Army.

OCS is a very demanding officer training course condensed to three or four months, designed not only to prepare a soldier to become an officer but also to separate out those who could not take the rigorous mental and physical training. Upon completion of this training, Father was commissioned a Second Lieutenant of Cavalry (as was the famous General Dwight D. Eisenhower, who in the same year, 1915, graduated from West Point).

His first assignment, after some basic Cavalry training, was as a Cav platoon leader. His unit left almost immediately for France by ship with his platoon of men and horses. Upon arrival, his Cavalry Troop commander gave him some French francs and told him to take his horses and men and find a place for them to stay until further orders. Fortunately, Father was fluent in French and was able to find a farm to accommodate his platoon. During this period, he lived in the farmhouse with the Rioux family. There he met the family's daughter, Milieu, and even though she was older than he, he courted her and asked her father, General Rioux, for her hand in marriage. About that time the war ended, and he brought his new bride back to the US, where they lived for a short while before divorcing. Even though his service in World War I lasted only a few months, he was awarded the Bronze Star.

Because he was fluent in French, he was selected to serve, for a brief period, as an aide-de-camp to General Pershing while in Paris. Father was a fine horseman and for several years, in his off-duty time, enjoyed polo. Eventually he changed branches and joined the ranks of the Quartermaster Corps. In the late 1920's he was again sent to Paris to attend the French Quartermaster School, which in those days was in an aging brick building complex known as des Invalides, which had at one time been a prominent hospital in Paris.

This was also the year Mother was attending her finishing school in Paris and on occasion would enjoy horseback riding through the park. It was on a spring Sunday, during this Paris tour, that the dashing young Cavalry officer was horseback riding in the Bois de Boulogne and spotted a comely young thing riding her horse on the trail ahead of him. He rode faster to get a better glimpse of her, but as he came alongside, her horse was startled and galloped out of control. Now the young cavalry officer spurred his stallion forward to catch the runaway horse and rein him in (as well as the damsel in distress!).

The young widow was of course swept off her feet and by early 1931 they were married. Shortly thereafter they left for America for his next assignment in Washington, DC. On 29 October 1931 their first child (my brother) was born at Walter Reed Hospital and named Harry de Ciccolini Hart. Father was by then a captain and remained a captain for an amazing 19 years, as did Dwight Eisenhower and all those officers commissioned at the beginning of WW I. After that war, as the Army became smaller and the economy slowed into the great depression of 1929, promotions came to a near halt. It wasn't until Germany begun attacking their neighbors, starting what was to become WW II, that promotions began again. By that time father had transferred from the Cavalry to the Quarter-master Corp. He would joke that in the Cavalry there were fewer horses than horses' asses.

Father's progeny, like Mother's, also carry many of his attributes. His grandson Lee bears a distinct resemblance in features and build, and both are about the same height of about six-foot one inch, but Lee reflects more of his grandfather than just his name and physical resemblance. He also shows the same quiet dignity, apparent calmness, and clear thinking which distinguish him. Father was the kind of man you wanted to be with, he commanded respect and appeared in control. After his death in April 1954, one of his associates told me that in his early Cavalry days he was nicknamed "Light Horse Harry Lee," borrowed from a colorful pre-Civil War officer who was Robert E. Lee's father. I was told by one of his peers, that Father was the only man he ever knew who always sat at attention.

1932 Father and Mother in Washington
DC at a costume party

Father's second marriage to my mother gave way about nine years later when he met and married his third wife, Lavon. In 1943 she gave birth to my half-sister, Nanci Lee, who also carried the genetic Hart lines similar to her Aunt Helen. His marriage to Lavon ended in divorce in about 1948.

His fourth and final marriage was to Marguerite Dapogny, a special person who was a GS-9 comptroller, about ten years his Junior, whom he met while stationed in Korea in 1948.

CHAPTER 5

I ENTER THE SCENE

Mother and Father were married in France in early 1931. In September of that year Father was transferred to Washington, DC, where brother Harry was born at Walter Reed Army Hospital. His next assignment was to a quartermaster depot in Columbus, Ohio.

We were living in Columbus when I was born in April 1933. My mother lovingly referred to me as "her Easter Bunny." She had one son and was ready for a girl now but had to settle for yet another man child. I was named after two of Grandmother Annabel's brothers, Uncle Rufus and Uncle Renwick, both of whom had achieved much in their lives. I was told that Uncle Rufus was the man who brought electricity to Iowa, but as life's turns would have it, in his retirement he was electrocuted when stopping to fix a neighbor's porch light. The story is that the neighbor lady called Rufus over as he was walking by to tell him that her porch light wasn't working. To check the circuit (the quick and easy way), Rufus touched the socket with his finger. Normally this wouldn't be much of a "bite," but with the porch still wet from the rain the results of his "quick test" were shocking, sufficiently so to kill him. On the other hand, Uncle Renwick lived to be 103. He was 101 years old when I visited him with our family in 1969 in Iowa, blind but we still enjoyed a game of ch3a together.

When I was two, we left Columbus, Ohio for Hawaii (1935). I do not have any memories of Columbus and have never returned. Also, I have no recollection of our move to Hawaii but do remember something of our home in Honolulu on Royal Circle Kahala.

By 1939, Mother's marriage was coming apart and she made the decision to take her two sons back to Nice for a visit with her mother while father finished up in Hawaii before his next assignment. I don't remember our trip through the Panama Canal, but I understand from brother Harry that we went by ship from Hawaii to New York with plans to continue to Europe. However, at that time the winds of war were blowing, and the Germans were starting to attack British ships in the Atlantic. I suppose Germany's invasion of Poland along with the general turmoil from the threat of war, caused Mother to cancel her European plans. We returned to San Francisco, where Father was now to be assigned.

In San Francisco, Mother received a letter from Bonnie which was a request asking what the relationship between father and mother was. The letter confirmed what she had suspected, and their divorce followed. The burden of the divorce did not fall heavily on me. I suspect that was because I had so little interaction with my father in our early years and because an older sibling (by 18 months) tends to buffer such an event. At that time, we were living in an apartment on Van Ness, near Fort Mason.

After the divorce, Mother gathered her two boys and headed to southern California to spend a summer in La Jolla in a leased home . . . the place came furnished and with a police dog named Sir. It was our first dog. I was very impressed with having a large police dog as part of the family and think I have been impartial to police dogs ever since. We also raised a chicken at the time, and it was quite an ordeal when it came time to take the bird to the butcher. I was relieved when I wasn't expected to eat my pet! Later we moved back to San Francisco for the fall school semester in 1939. In 1940, while I was at the Parkside Grammar School in San Francisco, Father and his new wife were assigned to Fort McDowell, on Angel Island in the San Francisco Bay. Harry and I would later join them there.

My early wanderings looked like this:

- 1933 April 3d: Born in Columbus, Ohio.
- 1936 Summer: Royal Circle Kahala, Honolulu, Hawaii (kindergarten at Punahou School).

- 1939 Summer: Departed Hawaii for New York, by ship, spent the summer in San Francisco on Van Ness Avenue.
- 1940: San Francisco and Fort McDowell on Angel Island.
- 1941: Fort Lewis, Washington and 31ˢᵗ Avenue, San Francisco.
- 1942: 257 Kensington Way, San Francisco.
- 1948 Lincoln High in San Francisco
- 1949: Osaka American School in Japan.
- 1950: New Cumberland High School, Pennsylvania.
- 1952: Anacostia High School, Washington, DC.

Father's new wife, Lavon (Bonnie) Price, was a buoyant, smart and pretty secretary Dad had met on the job (I presume) in Hawaii. Arriving at Fort McDowell as a major, he was soon promoted to lieutenant colonel and lived in a row of officers' quarters at one end of the island. These quarters were still standing in 1998—the last time I visited Angel Island.

Harry and I lived there for a portion of 1940 and 1941. There were so few youngsters on the island that grades one through six were held in a little church which was used as a one-room grammar school during the week and a church on weekends. The church, where I attended my first-grade class, accommodated the entire grammar school grades one through six, all in the same room. I remember it mostly because, when I was goofing off in writing class one day, the teacher had me write a word a hundred times. At age seven that was heavy duty and a memorable punishment.

I am sure that Father's two over-active boys must have taken their toll on his new wife, but my memories were of a happy home and good relationship. Living on that small island was a most unusual experience. Every day the ferry boat came to the island with passengers, food and equipment, stopping first at Alcatraz to discharge water, prisoners and supplies. It would then continue to Angel Island to disgorge passengers and supplies.

At that time, Fort McDowell was used as a staging area for troops being assigned to Hawaii and the Pacific. Our PX and commissary were located down the hill not far from the ferry boat landing. It is interesting that I should remember talking to a soldier near the PX while waiting for Dad and Bonnie to come out. He told me that his pay had just gone up from $18.75 a month to $21. Strange the things we remember but it gives you a point of reference of what the cost of living was in those days, shortly before WW II. Today, a private in the Army earns well over a thousand dollars a month.

In 1941, a few weeks before the Japanese bombed Pearl Harbor on that fateful Sunday of December 7, Father was promoted to full colonel and reassigned to Fort Lewis. We had already returned home to Mother and were living in a rented house on Van Ness Avenue in San Francisco. I don't know the court-ordered custody arrangements but from time-to-time Father would take custody of us. So, after a year of living in San Francisco, Harry and I left to join Father and Bonnie in Washington State. I'm sure Mother was ready for some much-needed relief from the relentless vigor of her two growing boys. When we arrived at Fort Lewis we enjoyed the benefit of living in the relatively large quarters made available to colonels. I attended second grade at nearby DuPont Grammar School, where Harry was in fourth grade.

The buildup for the war was now in full swing and temporary barracks were erected not far from our quarters. Brother Harry and I soon learned that we could earn a few dimes by visiting the barracks across the way from our home and shining shoes. Of course, when Father found out he put a stop to that. In those days, the wooden barracks buildings had rifle racks at the end of each bay. The rack was usually unlocked and on occasion when I was in the barracks shining shoes, I would take the liberty of handling the rifles…quite a thrill for an eight-year-old. These were the early years of WW II and Fort Lewis was a beehive of activity and training. Father had long hours at his job and our family times were few and far between. After the school year Harry and I again returned to Mother in San Francisco.

In another two years, MacArthur's promise in the Philippines of "I shall return" was fulfilled as U.S. Forces took back the Islands from the Japanese. Father was now reassigned to Manila, and we had moved from the downtown area of San Francisco to the Sunset district on 27th Avenue, where I attended third and fourth Grades at Lawton Grammar School.

CHAPTER 6

MY BROTHER AND SISTER

Brother Harry was born on 29 October 1931, two weeks after Mother's 22nd birthday. Although conceived in France, he was born at Walter Reed Army Hospital in Washington, DC. Our early relationship together was somewhat difficult, with only 18 months difference in our ages and the usual problems that arise when the new sibling starts getting all the attention. As we grew older, I caught up with him in size and began to hold my own physically in our squabbles. This changed the balance of power and helped improve our relationship, even though we fought often and hard. Our vigorous and frequent physical engagements no doubt had some effect on my willingness to engage in contact sports later in life and in developing confidence in my physical strength.

When we were old enough to be in school, we were separated most of the day, but I don't think it was until high school that we stopped fighting with each other. Still, as early teens, we had occasion to stand side by side in beating back some kids at the beach who were trying hard to pick a fight with us. In San Francisco in the 1940's it was not unusual for young men to pick fights with someone they didn't even know, in the vernacular of the time "to choose someone out." And so it was that one day at the San Francisco Beach two thuggish-looking guys about our age came up to Harry and me, saying, "Man, we choose you!" I suspect that in most cases this sort of aggression would build a bit of macho in the aggressors when it frightened the others to move on. But scrapping was a way of life for us, and the aggressors lost a bit of their macho that afternoon.

Early in 1948 Father was married for the fourth and last time, to Marguerite ("Cooks") Dapogni, a very special person who was a GS-8 comptroller at 8th Army Headquarters in Seoul, Korea. Cooks was unable to have children but was delighted to embrace Father's unruly teenage sons. So, when Father learned in December 1948 that he was being reassigned to Osaka, Japan, Harry and I were requested to join Father and Cooks. In April 1949 we boarded an Army transport ship headed for Japan.

Harry was two years ahead of me in school, so we seldom shared time together in our high schools. He had attended Lincoln High with me in San Francisco, and we were together again at Osaka American High School for the few months we were in Japan. The books, courses and subjects we faced at Osaka HS were totally different than the curriculum at Lincoln High, and our grades suffered accordingly. Then, when in the summer of 1949 Father took command of the New Cumberland Depot in Pennsylvania, Harry and I enrolled at New Cumberland High, our third high school in two years. I was a Junior, and he was a senior.

When Harry graduated, he started college at Penn State. To supplement his income, he joined the Pennsylvanian Air National Guard. His sojourn at Pen State was cut short when his unit was activated and sent to upstate New York. After his discharge he graduated from San Francisco State College, married Anita, and lived in the Bay Area for the next 45 years. In 2003, they sold their Belmont home and bought a lovely three-bedroom home with swimming pool in Indian Wells. Today he still lives in Indian Wells, with his four collector cars but is now alone, having lost his wife of 54 years in 2012. His only son, Jeffrey Ciccolini Hart, is married to Julie and they have continued the Hart line with two beautiful children.

Fortunately, in our later years we have developed two points of intersection in our lives; cars and Lake Tahoe. Being very much an antique car buff, Harry annually made a pilgrimage to Pebble Beach for their world famous Concours d'Elegance, held every August. Our other point of intersection was Lake Tahoe, where we both owned condos and during the summer months. often enjoyed spending time together. Harry Lived in Belmont, CA for many years with a vacation condo in Palm Springs. Eventually, he sold his Belmont home and condo, and moved to Indian Wells, just south of Palm Springs where he died in early 2022 at age 90.

—m—

Sister Nanci Lee Hart was born 30 July 1943 at Palm Springs, California after Father and his wife Bonnie left Fort McDowell on Angel Island and were assigned to what is now known as the Desert Training Center. A site near Chirico Summit, between Indio and Desert Center, was selected as the headquarters of the Desert Training Center (DTC) and called Camp Young. It was the world's largest Army post and at that time was commanded by Major General George Patton. Nanci's mother liked to relate her story of the time she danced with General Patton! Father and Bonnie were at one of the Officers' Club dances which they frequented and it was on one of those occasions that Bonnie danced with the general. Nanci says, "Since Mother was pregnant with me, I guess I danced with him too."

When Father left the Desert Training Center he was assigned to the Philippines until the end of the war in 1945. During that time Nanci and Mother, Bonnie moved to North Hollywood, California. By then, my mother and Nanci's mother had become good friends and Bonnie invited Harry and me to visit her for a few weeks in North Hollywood. That was our first meeting with our new sister Nanci, and I remember how enthralled Bonnie was with her baby daughter.

In 1946 Father was reassigned to Fort Mason in San Francisco. One of Nanci's earliest memories was of going to preschool there. General DeWitt was commanding and Nanci fondly recalls that from time to time his limo, with flags flying, picked her up for school, along with his son who was also in preschool. During that time Harry and I were young teens living in San Francisco, so we often were able to visit Father, Bonnie and Nanci at Fort Mason.

In 1948 Father was reassigned to Korea on an unaccompanied tour and it was there that he met Cooks, who would become his fourth and last, wife. When Nanci was six, her folks were divorced. Then she, her mother, her grandmother and Cousin Don Price all moved to Sacramento when Nanci was seven. By the time she was 14 they had moved again, to Carmichael, on the edge of town in a home with five acres. Cousin Don had moved away and gotten married. While in high school, she spent much of her weekend time becoming an accomplished horseback rider.

At sweet 16 she met the first love of her life, Lieutenant Benjamin G. Manceau, who was stationed near Sacramento at Mather AFB as a navigator on B-52 strategic bombers. At 18, when Nanci graduated from high school, they were married. They were blessed with their first baby, Michele Diane, when Nanci was 19. A year later, Ben applied for pilot training and was assigned to Williams AFB in Chandler, Arizona.

When he graduated from flight school their first assignment was to Otis AFB, Cape Cod, Massachusetts. Michele was 4 when Nanci became pregnant with baby Suzanne. Ben was sent off to Greenland on an unaccompanied tour, so Nanci headed home to mama, who was then living at Lake Tahoe. Suzanne was almost a year old when Ben saw her for the first time. Their next station was back in California at Beale AFB, where Dan flew reconnaissance aircraft, RC121's. Their third child, Daniel Scott, was born there in 1969. From there it was on to Castle AFB, near Merced, California, where Ben was a flight instructor for the KC-97 Tanker. They remained there until Ben's retirement as a lieutenant colonel in 1979.

In 1980, they bought their retirement home in Loomis, California, a few miles east of Sacramento and invested in the ownership of three service stations which featured the new concept of combining gas stations with a car wash. Loomis was a great place for their kids to have a stable home life and attend high school without continually moving.

In 2012 Ben died of a heart attack but Nanci continues to live in their Loomis home where, for about 10 years, she raised and trained American Paint horses before she became interested and successful in her current interest of raising, training and showing thoroughbred dogs. Fortunately, since Brother Harry and I both own condos at Incline Village, we often had the pleasure of visiting with Nanci in our travels to and from Lake Tahoe. After all those years of growing up in different households from our sister, it is nice to have a few years left to catch up!

Unfortunately, in 2021 Harry's health caught up with him and I lost him late that year after he had reached age 90.

1945

CHAPTER 7

THE EARLY YEARS - 1942 +

In 1942, brother Harry and I returned to San Francisco from our year's visit with Father at Fort Lewis, Washington. I was then nine years old. We lived in a rented home at 31st Avenue and Kirkham. Lawton Grammar School was nearby and since Mother did not drive, we walked or took the streetcar everywhere we went. It was a short walk to school and not far to the Golden Gate Park. Mother was a full-time mom and had only a limited income from alimony and her small inheritance. In her conservative European manner, she was very careful with her spending and use of utilities. Our home was located in the Sunset District, which was one of the last areas in San Francisco to be built out. To our west was mostly sand dunes but homes were springing up as the residential area pushed toward the ocean.

The city was in a war-time transition. There were still vendors going by our home with horse-drawn trailers carrying the ice for the ice box or selling fruit, and a wagon with knife and scissors sharpening equipment on it. But the pace of life was booming, and the shipping industry was in full swing. Homes then were about $5,000 in that area but it was a good neighborhood with nice surroundings.

It was hard for mom to be raising two boys by herself, so our visits with Father provided some respite for her and the necessary male role model for her growing boys. But Father was gone during those war years of 1942 to 1944, which were marked by the daily testing of air raid sirens and periodic drives to collect newspapers and tin cans for the "war effort."

Additionally, the war was being brought home to our insulated nation in our day-to-day activities. We had blackout curtains on the west-facing windows, and these were used during practice air raids to reduce the city's visibility from the sea. Also, the streetlights were painted black on the west side for the same purpose. The effectiveness of these practice air raids, and blackout efforts was never put to the ultimate test, but they did serve to carry home to the civilian populace that our country was at war.

These things had little impact on us as children . . . or at least on me, the younger. I was too young to be threatened by it and Mother was a gutsy kind of person I never knew to show fear. When parents don't transmit fear, children don't learn to be afraid. Therefore, Harry and I grew up with no phobias or fears of the war, the dark, or thunder, earthquake or whatever. Life in San Francisco was good for us. While living on the avenues, we spent much of our fun time at Golden Gate Park, sometimes playing tennis, sometimes at the playground, sometimes with a picnic. On a good day I might catch a garter snake slithering through the undergrowth in the park. The slippery creatures were totally harmless and provided an interesting diversion.

Having little money for the expensive things of life meant much of our family pleasures derived from walks in the park or at the beach. Mother's divorce settlement left her with a paltry alimony of $60 a month and child support of $30 per child. Of course, that was in the 1940's, before post-war inflation took hold. Hamburgers were 10 cents each and a nickel for the streetcar. So, the $120 a month that she received was probably just enough to get by. There was no charge for most city and state parks and activities. For example, the Japanese Tea Gardens and various other botanical gardens in the 1940's and 1950's were available to the public without charge.

Memories of those days are rather selective. I do recall that on rare occasions Harry and I would get a quarter to go out for dinner at the corner café. Now it seems amazing that with our quarter we could get two hamburgers (a dime each, with lettuce and tomato) and still have a nickel for a glass of milk. It was the equivalent of today's six-dollar value meal at MacDonald's!

In the summer of 1945, my brother and I were off to North Hollywood to spend the summer months with our stepmother Bonnie and infant Nanci Father was in the Philippines fighting the war in the Pacific, which was about to reach a stunning conclusion. He and Bonnie had a baby girl in July 1943 and she, Nanci Lee, was now 2 years old.

That same year, 1945, Mother purchased a home at 257 Kensington Way. Harry and I were to spend the summer with Bonnie. Somehow, Bonnie and Mother had become friends; perhaps to facilitate Harry and I getting to know our baby sister? Mother made arrangements with Bonnie for us to spend a couple of months in North Hollywood with her while Mother made her move from 27th Avenue into her new digs on Kensington Way. Harry and I had not yet met our new half-sister, and I suppose our visit was a way to unite our families. It was a most enjoyable summer for us, doing things which were totally different from our life with Mother. There are several memories I carried away from that summer. I think it was the first time I began to realize I wasn't the center of the universe, since Nanci was Bonnie's primary focus. At home, I was Mother's primary focus.

Interestingly, we always seem to remember our exact location when a major, world-shaking event occurs, such as Kennedy's being shot in 1963 or the terrorist attack on 9-11. On 6 August 1945 an atomic bomb was exploded over Hiroshima. Three days later, a second bomb was dropped on Nagasaki. Within days the war with Japan was at a close. On this date we were in North Hollywood, with Bonnie and Nanci, in the kitchen finishing breakfast when the momentous announcement came over the radio that an atomic bomb had been dropped on Hiroshima, ending World War II which had started when I was eight and continued for four years. For me, it had lasted a third of a lifetime and now it was finally over.

With San Francisco's eternally cool weather, one summer Harry and I made our escape from the city and rode our bikes to a swimming pool we were familiar with in Marin County at the smallish town of Fairfax. It was a 20 mile ride each way and as young teens became a memorable occasion. Of course, it was difficult for a single mother to keep track of her two exuberant boys, so Harry and I had several unauthorized excursions.

CHAPTER 8

HAROLD RUDOLPH LOMO

On the walls of our homes are ten or twelve pieces of art created by Harold Lomo. The paintings have "H Lomo" in the lower right side and include a scene of Emerald Bay at Lake Tahoe and a self-portrait of Harold as a young man strumming his mandolin on the edge of a fiord in Norway. There is also a smaller portrait of me reading a book as a 15-year-old and a mosaic of a phoenix made from pieces of vinyl. Harold also made and framed a wonderful scene of a duck landing in a lake. That scene was woven in yarn. He was a man of great imagination and many art forms.

It was during the war years, after her divorce, that Mother met this wonderful Norwegian gentleman on the tennis courts in Golden Gate Park. For the next many years, she and Harold Lomo played tennis and dated. Eventually he became the father that Harry and I had been doing without for much of our lives. Harold filled those masculine spaces that growing boys must have to mature properly. He was a strong, athletic man, born in Hammar, Norway in 1891. He won his high school's ski jumping championship in a land of skiers, was captain of his high school soccer team, enjoyed strumming his mandolin and over time, developed into an artist of great imagination. Harold was from a simple farming family north of Oslo but somehow developed a deep understanding of life and a sense of logic derived from experience rather than higher education. And of course, in the European school system, graduating from high school in those days, was probably equivalent to an AA degree here.

When Harold was only a year out of high school a wealthy Norwegian gentleman, who was planning to tour the world, asked Harold to make the trip with him in the capacity of a valet; someone he could rely on to take care of the many details he would encounter on such a trip. In the spring of 1910, with relative peace in the world, they started their epic journey. His travels were extensive, taking him through Eastern Europe, Asia and other parts of the world. Eventually Harold landed in San Francisco where he parted company with the old gentleman. Then, in his early twenties and having already seen the world, he found employment at the Pacific Union Club, located atop Nob Hill. The PU Club (as it is known) is probably the most prestigious club in California and most certainly in San Francisco. His work there continued for fifty years.

Although not part of our heritage, Harold greatly influenced our lives in several positive ways. Harry and I had many a memorable time with Harold doing those things that Fathers and sons should do. He was an "outdoors" person and passed on to us his love of nature with our hikes in Muir Woods and following the trails around Mount Tamaulipas.

Several fond memories I carry were from our trips to the High Sierras when he taught us to ski as young teens. I recall one winter he took me Camping in the vicinity of Nyack Lodge, now a wide spot in the road a few miles west of Donner Summit on Highway 80. I was about 13 at the time, which was several years before the Highway 80 freeway over the mountains was constructed. We hiked into the woods through deep snow on a beautiful sunny afternoon with our packs and a lightweight two-man pup tent. Harold talked of his cross-country trips through the deep powdery snow in Norway. To break trail, they would take turns as lead so the exhausting task of making a path through heavy snow would be shared by all. That day in the Sierras, we did not go far. In a small clearing Harold showed me how to take the bows from the fir trees which we placed on packed snow to form a base over which we placed the tent and sleeping bags. Between the altitude and the day's activities, sleep came early. That night, the wind blew, and the snow flew as a good blizzard rolled over the Sierras. I think it was the longest night I ever spent but an enjoyable one that I never forgot. I guess one night was enough for both of us, because when the blizzard stopped, we packed out and joined Mother at the lodge.

He did not earn much at the Pacific Union Club but was liked and respected there as their head masseuse. While he had money each month, he took the greatest pleasure in buying things for the family and taking us out. He was always generous to a fault. It was as though money had no value for him. Its only value was in the spending of it. This was actually a wonderful attribute, though certainly not one to get rich on. Fortunately, Mother did have some money from her family; mostly stocks she inherited from her Father, so with that and a very conservative European way of living, we had a pretty good life. When Mother bought our home on Kensington Way in San Francisco, Harold moved in and helped with the mortgage and other expenses. But it wasn't until April of 1963 that Harold and Mom were married.

Harold died in his sleep in 1972 while Barb and I were stationed in Germany. A couple of years later, Mother moved from San Francisco to Sonoma, buying a condo not far from the Square. Sonoma was an area she and Harold had always loved. With Harold's passing, a beautiful person is gone and the worst part of it is, with no progeny or siblings, his life will go unknown and when I am gone, unremembered. Fortunately, his paintings and art will live on and as long as they are appreciated, his memory will be honored.

Here is a painting of me that Harold made when I was 14.

CHAPTER 9

THE MID YEARS - 1945

At the end of August 1945, Harry and I returned from our visit with Bonnie in Los Angeles to San Francisco and the home Mother had bought herself for $5,000 at 257 Kensington Way in the West Portal District. It was not a large home but of the old San Francisco style; stucco, flat gravel roof and bay windows. It had two bedrooms with a view of the ocean and a split bathroom upstairs, in a nice residential area. Downstairs was a bedroom and bathroom for Harry and me. Harold was handy at everything and with just the basic tools of hammer and hand saw, he set about building a recreation room, bathroom and laundry room downstairs. The more difficult installations, such as plumbing and windows, were finished off by a contractor. I'm sure the home that Mother paid $5,000 for then, would sell for well over a million today!

West Portal Grammar School was only a block away, and I readily walked to and from my 5th grade and sixth classes each day for the next two years. The new guy in school always has a few weeks of finding his way with new friends and so it was that I migrated to someone who also needed a friend. Bob Anderson was an only child and lived a couple of blocks away. We were both without our fathers at the time (his was with ARAMCO in Saudi Arabia) and we seemed to have a lot in common. I guess that is why our friendship endured for these many years, as it does today some 75 years later.

6th Grade, West Portal School, San Francisco

When I was 12, I finished sixth grade at the West Portal School and the following fall entered Aptos Junior High. I was a big guy for my age and by the time I reached 13 I was close to six feet tall. I think that helped me avoid many a scrap in the city schools. But my frequent battles with Harry had me well prepared to handle any aggressors should the occasion arise. I knew most of the kids in my grade but there was another good-sized lad who decided to challenge me. I presume the "bully boy" was eager to exert his dominance. The expression of the time for starting a fight was "to choose someone," or "to choose him out". I was not a feisty person but out of self-respect I couldn't be a shrinking violet. I accepted his challenge and told him we would meet after school. There was no quarrel; it was clearly a bully hoping to intimidate the new guy. I did not like the idea of going against an unknown opponent but when school was over, with some trepidation, I headed to the designated spot for our battle. To my great relief he backed down and never showed. I don't recall ever seeing him again.

Also, about the time I started Junior high, I had my first chance to earn some dollars delivering the *San Francisco Call Bulletin*, an afternoon newspaper. My paper route brought in about 20 dollars a month. It took me an hour a day to walk the twelve long blocks, making delivery to a hundred or so customers. The route started at the firehouse on Portola

Drive, about two blocks from where we lived on Kensington Way. Each day the stack of newspapers was waiting for me on the corner and needed to be unbound and stuffed into the canvas carrying bag I wore over my shoulders; fifty papers in front, fifty papers in back. As I walked, I rolled the newspapers, tucking each one into a tight roll and throwing it at the door of a home. With a tightly rolled paper and a good arm, I could usually hit their front porch from the sidewalk, about 50 feet away. Each toss of my paper was a challenge to hit the front door. Delivering papers was a great job for a youngster. The two-mile walk every day developed my legs and a good throwing arm. Early on I learned a sense of responsibility and routine. At the end of each month, about 6 PM, when people were likely to be home, I would set out to collect the monthly subscription fees of $3.50 per customer. About a third of my customers would give me a 25-cent tip. But some of them would not answer the door to avoid paying and others would ask me to come back. I would usually need to walk my route about three times in the evening to get all the money owed. It only took four customers not paying their bill to cut my earnings in half, so I was also learning about money, people and persistence. A side benefit of the paper route was that my two best friends lived near the end of my route on Juanita Way. Sometimes I would stop and spend a little time with Al Sturges but nearly always I would enjoy 15 or 20 minutes with Bob Anderson. Bob, like I, was primarily raised by his mother since his dad was gone during the war. He always had lots of interesting things at his house which my family couldn't afford; a large chemistry set, model airplanes with small motors and stuff like that. And of course, on occasion, there were cookies and milk! Years later I lost track of Al, but Bob and I have remained friends throughout our lives.

As a single parent, mother had her hands full dealing with my brother and me, so the paper route also served the purpose of keeping me out of trouble after school. Of course, there is always trouble to be had and if a 13-year-old couldn't find it, no one could. So, it wasn't long before Harry and I found what could best amuse us. We learned that we could take two bolts and screw them together into one nut to make a sort of firecracker. We filled the chamber formed by the bolts and nut with match heads from those large self-lighting kitchen matches. Using a knife, we would scrape loose the red and white stuff that comprised these quick light match heads. Then we would carefully tighten the bolts to finger tight. Now, when the bolt was dropped to the pavement the impact would set off the match heads with a satisfying bang, usually blowing the bolts out of the nut.

In time, we became bored with our match head popper, and it was time to upgrade to a more exciting bang. From our chemistry set we learned that all we needed to create a decent gunpowder, was sulfur, potassium nitrate and carbon. To our delight, most of these ingredients were available at the hardware store for garden use or at the local drug store. We also learned we could make fuses by soaking a piece of string in a solution of potassium nitrate. When the string dried it would burn like a fuse. I am not sure who came up with that one, but it worked like a charm.

Now the challenge was putting together our bits of knowledge to make the mother of all firecrackers. We experimented with various and sundry containers, finally arriving at a small piece of pipe. Our short piece of pipe was then loaded with the black powder, tamped and the ends sealed with a good wad of paper. To fuse it, all we had to do was file a groove into the pipe and then complete the hole with a nail or drill.

Our nitrated string burned slowly enough to give us plenty of time to take cover. The explosion which followed was indeed a delight to behold! Since the net result was to blow the wadding out the end of the pipe, the next escalation would be to find threaded caps to seal the ends of the pipe. Before long it was ready, great excitement and anticipation! When our little bomb went off with a resounding CRAACK, we knew we had arrived. Where to go from here?! Obviously, bigger pipes would mean bigger bangs! We scoured the neighborhood for the ultimate pipe. The pipe we finally found had threads on each end and was about 10 inches long. We filled our pipe with the last of our black power, tightened the caps and set the fuse. We cut the fuse long enough to give us a couple of minutes to make our getaway.

But for proper results, this magnificent creation couldn't just be laid on the ground to go bang. No way. This baby had to achieve full actualization! Behind our home was an alleyway which provided access to the garages on our street as well as the street below ours. Across the alley from the back of our house was a garage belonging to people on the block below us. We were able to wedge our pipe between the drainpipe and the wooden siding of the garage; it was a nice tight fit and we wondered if it would bother the drain- pipe. We lit the fuse and high-tailed it up the stairs to our bedroom, which overlooked the alley and that neighboring garage.

The explosion which followed fulfilled all our boyhood dreams but when the smoke lifted it was clear that we had indeed underestimated the results. The drainpipe was ripped from the wall and lay crumpled and shredded in the alleyway. And there on the side of the garage was an embarrassing two-foot hole where it had disintegrated the wood. I learned later that the pipe had blown itself all the way through the garage and was imbedded in the opposite wall. Our neighbors of course knew it wasn't the two lovely boys living behind them, or did they? We were embarrassed enough to call our bomb making quits while we were ahead. Today, I imagine that such antics would be good for a few years in the penitentiary!

In those days, Junior high schools did not have much in the way of sports programs. However, in the 9th grade one of my school friends, Dick Checchi, invited me to join the after-school soccer team that his father was sponsoring. Soccer was practically an unknown sport at that time in California but the growing Italian contingent in the city was pushing the sport forward since it was so popular in their native Italy. Because it involved body contact, it was my kind of game and I learned it eagerly. We had uniforms and played against other organized teams that were not a part of the school system. Soccer was a great sport, and I am lucky that I learned it early but football was still my greatest love.

Academically I was a mediocre student. I was expected to do well but never received pressure to perform. Math was enjoyable, history and English were a bore and I proceeded through the Junior high grades with mediocre scores on my report cards. I did well in PE and shop and don't recall ever getting an F in any class. I was 15 when I completed the 9th grade at our local Junior high (Aptos) and graduated.

That summer the family took a rare vacation together. Mother and Harold were great adventurers and left no corner of California and Nevada unexplored. In the summer of 1948, after my graduation, we headed to the foothills of the Sierras for a few weeks, spending part of the time at a resort called Hobergs. Hobergs and Siegler were two popular resorts, each bearing one of their names. We had a grand time there for a week; it was my first exposure to resort life with swimming pools, tennis courts, outdoor dance floor and evening entertainment. I remember the special entertainment for one of the evenings was Bill

Crosby, Bing Crosby's' brother. His singing was not exceptional, but his name carried him through. There was also a costume contest one evening at the outdoor dance floor and Harold, with his artistic flare, decked me out as the "Pinecone King" with all manner of pinecones and forestry hanging from whatever I was wearing. I was a bit nonplussed when I turned out to be the winner of that modest event. It was an enjoyable summer which left me with many happy memories.

When Father returned from the war he was assigned to San Francisco at Fort Mason and Harry and I again joined him for the summer. We were young teens then; 15 and 16 and it was during this period that Father and Bonnie were divorced. Our home on Fort Mason was on a horseshoe-shaped row of large brick homes where the senior officers lived. We were there during the summer and some weekends and spent the rest of the time with Mother at 257 Kensington Way. In front of our house, at Quarters 42, was a large grassy area inside the horseshoe-shaped street (it is still there if you are ever in the area). I was 15, growing fast and getting interested in sports. We often played tackle football with other kids in the area but without any protective equipment. And so it was, one afternoon on that grassy area in front of our house, about eight of us had a rousing game of tackle going. I made a flying tackle at his legs and suddenly had a big pain in my shoulder, cracking my clavicle (collar bone) in the execution of (what must have been) a perfect tackle. It was right in front of our house and when I came inside, a visiting aunt assumed it was a dislocated shoulder and applied a good jerk to reseat it! I suspect that what had been cracked was now broken. Letterman Army Hospital was about two miles from us at the Presidio and before long I was wearing an interesting cast which formed a figure 8 holding my shoulders well back. After about 5 weeks I felt pretty well healed and was working my shoulders against the tension of the cast. That I managed to tear the cast in two pieces miffed the doc when I went in to see him, but he did not put me back in another cast and the collar bone healed as it should.

CHAPTER 10

MY HIGH SCHOOL YEARS

In 1948 I graduated from Aptos Junior High School and entered my sophomore year at Lincoln High in San Francisco. In my day, high school in San Francisco began with the 10th grade. I had no inkling when I started my first year at Lincoln that I was destined to attend a total of four high schools in the next three years. I had been looking forward to Lincoln; my brother was in school there and most of my classmates from Junior high had come with me. Some had been friends for years.

Football had always been my favorite sport and at 15, I was already 6' 1" and 175 pounds, so going out for our high school team was a natural. I had played sandlot and playground football for years and enjoyed it greatly, so was eager to be on the HS football team with several of my buddies from Junior high. I was surprised by the heavy workout the coach put us through the first few weeks, gradually moving into tackling, blocking, running, throwing, and catching. I had sore muscles for the first month. Although fairly tall, I was not too keen on running, which I guess pointed me towards being a lineman. Eventually, the coach put me at right tackle, which was fine with me. I enjoyed the contact honed from years of wrestling and fighting with my brother. And as noted earlier, I had already broken my collar bone two years prior while playing sandlot football in front of our Fort Mason home, so the rough and tumble was not new to me.

About two weeks before our first game we were going through tackling practice when I experienced a severe pain in my leg below the knee when tackled. It was a minor injury but involved enough pain for Mother to take me to Letterman Army Hospital for x-rays. They found an unusual cyst on my right leg, just below the knee, so kept me in the hospital for further examination and x-rays. From the x-rays, the cyst looked more like a little bone spur and perhaps it was?

In those years, when a military dependent entered an Army hospital the Father was informed, so it wasn't long before I got a call from my dad in Japan. His call was quite a surprise, because I hadn't known him to exhibit this level of Fatherly interest in the past. I think the fact that I was the son of a senior colonel who was calling from Japan probably contributed to the good care I received. They put the leg in traction for a few days. The bone spur started diminishing and after about a week, I was on my way home and back to school.

During the few days I spent on the ward at Letterman Army Hospital I learned a bit about life from the older soldiers there. Of the 18 or so patients on our orthopedic ward, half of them were there because of motorcycle accidents! That was quite a lesson in and of itself. Also, it wasn't long before I learned the extra interest, I was getting from the ward boy was associated with his homosexuality. And then there was the time the guy next to me was having the pins in his leg removed. Suddenly, from behind the blue curtain the doctors had drawn, came a blood curdling scream the likes of which were such that half the ward was levitated. Of course, there was also much "man talk" going on around the ward, quite an eye opener for a lad of 15. Altogether, I was four weeks recovering from the knee problem and was glad to get home and back on the team for the remainder of the season.

High School in Japan

In January of 1949 Father requested that my brother and I join him and his new (fourth) wife in Japan. By March we were packing for a mid-semester departure and the great adventure of crossing the Pacific to join Father in Japan. I would be 16 at month's end and Harry, 17, was now in his senior year. We filled a footlocker with all our earthly teenage goods and boarded the Army Transport Ship *Republic* at Fort Mason in San Francisco. The crossing would take us about 13 days on that little ship, but little did we know it would seem more like 13 weeks. The Republic was an older, smallish Army transport, and of course the Pacific Ocean is anything but pacific. Two days into the trip we encountered a storm that I am sure would send the staunchest sailor retching to the railing.

When the storm hit, we were pounded day after day by heavy rains, high seas, and high winds. I was astounded to see the ocean 30 feet above the deck as we dipped into the trough of the waves. By the second day, we became grossly seasick and Harry and I spent several days totally wiped out in our cabin, heaving, and losing weight. Harry came out of it first but I continued sick in lessening degrees for the remainder of the trip. Trying to eat dinner on the dining deck and looking at my soup sloshing around was guaranteed to bring on the nausea. At one evening meal an especially large wave broadsided the ship. As we pitched violently, I held on to my chair, which was anchored to the floor (as were the tables). However, the rope holding the chair to the floor anchor gave way and I went careening across the dining room until I caught my balance. The storm was so severe that at times the stern lifted out of the water, and you could feel the whole ship shudder as the props cavitated. Eventually a part of the ship's rudder was broken but we were able to continue on.

In our cabin, we had a record player with us and some of our favorite 78 RPM records. Interestingly, we played those Stan Kenton recordings so often that, for many days after our trip, I could sense a slight feeling of nausea every time we listened to a Kenton record. The morning our ship neared Japan, after 13 very rough days, we hurried to the main deck for our first sight of land. We were really looking forward to being off that seasick ship. As we stared at the horizon, a distant dot began to take the shape of a mountain. Soon we could see the magnificent, snow clad, Mount Fuji floating on the horizon. Its perfect symmetry, suspended between ocean and sky, was breathtaking. What a way to be introduced to this new land particularly after that horrible trip across the so-called Pacific. Not only was Fujiyama a most awesome sight but it was also a symbol that the voyage from hell was almost over.

As the ship docked in Yokohama Harbor, Father and our new stepmother were there to meet us. She said we were to call her Cooks, her nickname. She won me over immediately with her ready smile and sharp appearance. Cooks had been a civil servant for many years and had met Father when they were in Korea. Although she had been raised a good Catholic, her first marriage came apart after several years of trying to survive life with an alcoholic husband. That her divorce caused her to be excommunicated from the church was a great sadness for her, but she continued to attend mass when possible. In time, she became an important part of my life. She was Dad's fourth and last wife.

Father was now a senior colonel in the Quartermaster Corps. He was known as something of a straight shooter and disciplinarian, so was often placed in positions of command. This time, he took over as commander of Kobe Depot. The depot covered several acres and included a rambling area of stored equipment, much of which was war materiel residue. It also was the supply conduit supporting many of the units and personnel in Japan. Because his position had been previously occupied by a general officer, Father also assumed the quarters that came with the job. The house was a superb Japanese home, built in the western style. We had a six-acre compound with swimming pool, small lake and two acres of sculpted Japanese gardens. The home had three floors and included four maids, two houseboys, a gardener and a couple of cooks. It is surprising how nicely one can live under such circumstances! The third floor was a game and observation room with large windows all around and a billiard table in the middle. The second floor was split level with the servants' quarters below. Harry and I had a comfortable room in the west wing. The maid assigned to us was our age and had instructions to keep our cookie jar full! Of course, we had hoped for more than that, but Kaseko was a demure, moon-faced country girl whose kimono and obi were as light and bright as the morning sun. What a treat to watch her bow and carefully place our milk and cookies on the ornate chest. As she left, there were three more bows while backing out the door with a soft "Kombowa.".

Our Home in Ashia, Japan 1949

The household staff all wore the old style, traditional kimonos and obi's, with split-toed socks and getas on their feet. They were respectful and courteous. Their dress was in accordance with their age. The young women wore bright colors, and the shades darkened to matched their aging years. We were impressed by these very polite, demure people, the bowing and the hissing (an audible sucking of air through their teeth to convey that they were not breathing on you) to show the respect we hadn't earned.

The Japanese had a long history of warlords conquering and consolidating their fiefdoms. When a new warlord conquered a region, full and complete obeisance and respect was expected and received from the populace. This history is what set the tone for their behavior toward the American occupation forces. When I returned to Japan twelve years later, I found there was little to nothing of these customs left. In 1949, it was a time and era from another world and now gone forever.

We were in our Ashia home only a few days when I discovered we had a very special record machine, part of a radio/phonograph combination. It was in our living room, which overlooked the gardens and swimming pool. The intriguing thing about this circa 1948 machine was its complexity. It could handle a stack of perhaps 12 of the old, brittle 78 RPM records; the ones that were about ten inches across and would shatter like porcelain if dropped. The most interesting part of its operation occurred after the last record played and the two arms, shaped like a small forklift, would rise from the bottom, slip under the stack of records, and lift them from the platter. Then another arm would come down from above and hold the stack of records snug while the whole thing rotated and came back down on the spindle to play the other side. I have never seen anything like it before or since. As soon as our stack of Stan Kenton records had been unpacked, we introduced them to this complicated Japanese machine. The machine played the several records in sequence and as we gathered around for the grand finale when the stack is picked up and turned over, we watched transfixed as the records were forklifted up and the arm came down. Then it happened - the descending arm never stopped, and we gazed in horror as it continued through the middle of the stack, crushing every record into several pieces. Perhaps those who had lost the war left a booby trap for us?

Our Ashia home was about 20 miles from Osaka, where we attended Osaka American High School. Each morning, Harry and I would walk the two or three blocks down the hill to where the electric train (the Shinkansen) would stop. During the morning school run, one of the cars on the 8:15 Japanese train was designated for American school children. But on one occasion we were late for the American car and had to catch the next available Japanese train; one which did not have an American car. The Japanese were a bit surprised by our presence and our size.

Harry was about 6' 1" and I was 6' 2". Most of them were about 5 feet tall, so the contrast must have been astounding.

After we sat down on the wooden bench which ran the full length of the car, we were approached by a middle-aged Japanese gentleman who, with some hesitation, ventured to sit next to us. Bringing out his small Japanese- American dictionary, he said, "Excoosa me, I only speak pidgin English", followed by a big smile. Next, he asked, "How is your mother?" As I responded he added, "How is your father?" I awkwardly replied that they were fine and presumed from his opening questions that the proper manner of introduction in Japan is to inquire about one's family. With the amenities out of the way, he asked, "Excose me, how long are you?" I said 6' 2", and he asked, "In meters?" I told him, "About 2 meters", and by then it was time to get off the train. I guess as teenagers we were well isolated, because other than trading cigarettes for merchandise, this was the only modest conversational event with the local citizenry I can recall. Even though we were then still only four years from the atrocities of WW II, my impression of the Japanese was one of a dignified and very civilized people. It was my great fortune to live among them for a short time.

Our high school had relatively small classes with about 15 students per room. The little chair-desks were obviously built for the Japanese student and my 6' 2" frame did not take kindly to them. In fact, the first chair I was assigned to came apart as I stretched, much to the amusement of the class. Our transition mid-semester from a large, standardized San Francisco school to this country school environment with different books and curricula was difficult. I somehow survived the next seven weeks till school ended but Harry did not fare as well, with multiple F's on his final report card. Although our life in Japan was good, the combination of new friends, a new mother, and being in a strange and different country was a bit heavy on Harry's transition.

Osaka was an industrial city and Ashia was one of the bedroom villages on the outskirts of the city. Parts of Osaka had been heavily bombed, and the twisted steel girders in some of the bombed-out factories were still in evidence four years after the war had ended. Life in that war-torn country was not easy for the Japanese and the village routine was third world in most aspects. In the rice fields, the mama-sans carried their "Honey Buckets" suspended from a pole that went across their shoulders. There were also ox-drawn tanker carts carrying this human fertilizer. The early morning routine on the small farms surrounding our estate was to move the "night soil" from the homes to the fields. The resulting olfactory assault, when we first arose, was particularly offensive when the wind was heading our way.

Japan's agrarian life was in stark contrast to the busy, productive hustle of city life. In the countryside automobiles were a rare sight. Most of the light trucks and autos in Ashia were wood burners. With gasoline is short supply, wood was heated and the fumes from the heated wood were used to power the vehicle. During the initial stages of this process there was a tremendous amount of smoke given off from the heating box as they stoked the flames but once they got the contraption running it wasn't much different from a regular gasoline engine. The cool mornings were marked by an inversion which held a thin layer of smoke rising from the stoked vehicles.

In the cities, traditional kimonos were beginning to give way to western garb. On the street corners were new-age entrepreneurs selling brightly colored scarves, cigarette lighters and all manner of trinkets. The Japanese gift for miniaturization and detail was readily apparent in their merchandise. The cigarette lighters were engraved with American flags, unit logos and dollar bills. We learned early on that one of these beauties could be obtained with the illegal trade of a few cigarettes from a pack we bought for ten cents. On the black market our ten-cent pack of cigarettes was good for about 400 yen, about what a dollar could be exchanged for.

To make our way in this illegal boyhood activity it was necessary to learn a few critical words of Japanese such as "how much?" "too much" and "where is?" We soon learned the oriental art of negotiation with a counter offer of half the initial price. An indefinite grunt, a shake of the head and starting to move away would usually end the negations in our favor.

We had a great life in Japan, but it was not to last. In May of 1949, four months after our arrival, it was determined that Father had colon cancer. He was 58. We were to leave as soon as possible for Tripler Army Hospital in Hawaii for his further evaluation. A week later we were evacuated from Japan by military air. It was a notable trip home for us as we hopped from island to island. Our first stop was Johnston Island. It was about three miles long, with a maximum elevation of 7 feet. The most interesting thing on the island turned out to be the baby albatrosses. These were large awkward birds that had not yet grown feathers to enable them to gracefully soar the seas. Their clumsy waddling around and the mottled appearance from their downy feathers earned them the nickname of Gooney Birds.

Our next stop on the "flight which never ends" was Guam, a considerably larger island and the scene of some of the heaviest WW II fighting in the South Pacific. I remember as a child the newsreels of our troops clearing the caves of Japanese holed up in the cliffs of Guam during WW II. The enemy was forced out of the caves with flame throwers and the newsreel showed some of them on fire leaping into the sea. Seeing the cliffs on that side of the island as we toured Guam seared that part of the trip into my memory. The next day we landed on Kwajalein Island where we refueled for our last leg to Hawaii. It was another 6-hour flight by DC-3 (also nicknamed the Gooney Bird) before we would land at Hickam AFB, Hawaii. The DC-3, in service since 1939, was a grand old plane but the drone of its two engines in the unpressurized passenger compartment became mind numbing; a pre-jet aircraft experience, not recommended for long trips.

We spent about a week in Hawaii while Father was admitted to Tripler Hospital for observation and tests. It was determined that the operation should be performed at Walter Reed Hospital in Washington, DC and arrangements were made for our departure to San Francisco. This last leg from Hawaii would be in a MARS Amphibious Aircraft. These flying boats were the largest amphibians ever made and were part of that era. In the 1940's, the Navy at Treasure Island in San Francisco Bay, operated a tower to control the landings and takeoffs of these behemoths. Below is a photo of the "Caroline Mars," which was lost on 5 May 1950 off Diamond Head in Hawaii. One of her engines caught fire and though the pilot put her down on the water and a rescue crew on a boat tried to help, the fire spread rapidly, and the aircraft destroyed itself in a spectacular explosion. Fortunately, there were no serious injuries in the incident.

What I remember most about that flight from Hawaii in June of 1948 is that the flight took us an interminable 14 hours; 14 hours of those droning, 3,000 horsepower engines, before reaching San Francisco. From there, Father continued on with Cooks to Walter Reed and Harry and I spent the summer in San Francisco with Mother.

CAROLINE MARS

High School in Pennsylvania

In the summer of 1949, after his colectomy, Father took command of the New Cumberland Depot in Pennsylvania and plans were made for Harry and me to join him. By late August we were on our way to be with Father and Cooks. New Cumberland Depot was a Quartermaster Depot which also included the New Cumberland Disciplinary Barracks. The Disciplinary Barracks was a prison for those men sentenced to prison terms of greater than two but fewer than 15 years. Most of them were serving sentences for AWOL or desertion during WW II.

The commander's house was a grand old brick building of two floors, three bedrooms upstairs and one down, which was originally the servant's quarters. Behind the house was a separate garage with a drive parallel to the street. Coincidentally (or by design?) the name of our street was "Hart Place."

Down the street from our house, just a few blocks away, was the Post Chapel. In the Army, the default religion is Presbyterian or Episcopalian, and in those days, it was expected that the military community would attend church. Father never missed a Sunday. One day, when the family was leaving for church, I was a little slow getting ready. I came running out the front door just in time to see Dad and the rest of the family driving away. Life had been different with Mother. Now I was learning that with Father, things better happen when they are supposed to happen, not when it suited me!

Having completed my sophomore year at Osaka American High School, I was now a Junior at New Cumberland High School. Harry had a more difficult time than I in his transition to Osaka and New Cumberland High and so had to repeat the semester. He was now in his senior year at New Cumberland. This was our third HS in less than two years, and it took its toll on our learning. I was doing well in my math and science classes but wasn't learning much in English and history. Fortunately, my history teacher was also the football coach, and I suspect that it was his policy to not give his football players anything less than a "B". I am certain I had been delivering "D+" work!

Football, or any sport for that matter, is an important adjunct to high school life. At the end of my Junior year, I had my first real job, working for the government. I was 17 and Harry 18. We both had started dating and found it awkward not to have a car. If that were to change, we would need to earn some serious money. As commander of the New Cumberland Depot, I suspect it was not too difficult for Father to find us employment on post. The lowest conceivable rung in the Civil Service is a GS-1 Laborer. That was us. We would earn the fantastic sum of $1.25 an hour, before deductions. Of course, that was in the days of twenty cents a gallon for gasoline. By contrast, today the minimum hourly wage will buy about four gallons of gas.

Our place of work was at an outdoor storage area in the "out back" on post, where there was row after row of WW II, surplus army trucks of several varieties. The work team I was with was reprocessing "Brockway Bridge Trucks", a behemoth of a machine with ten large wheels. These wheels were about 8 feet high and attached to their hubs with 8 large lug nuts. The trucks were being stored on blocks and would perhaps eventually find their way to third world countries or some other remote use. Our job was to remove the wheels, grease the bearings and then replace the wheels. The job was not too exciting, but we needed to learn to get along with these very blue-collar types who at first thought we were spies when the word filtered down that our father was the commander.

It was good work for husky teens and by the end of summer, my dollar and a quarter an hour would be enough to buy the highly prized auto of my dreams. A side benefit was that the work helped develop young muscles and sculpt a heretofore soft body. I remember one of the older workers we called "Old Dutch.". Most of these guys were "Pennsylvania Dutch" and some had a strange way of speaking. One day, when I asked the team leader where Old Dutch was, he said, "He's on his off, his off is all tomorrow!" In their vernacular he was saying, "He is on his vacation, (off time) and his off time is all over tomorrow." I guess that set me back enough that I always remembered it. Another character we worked with was a black guy they called "The Preacher". But The Preacher was always talking about his conquests after each weekend. So eventually I asked him how it was that, as a man of the cloth, he was leading such a debauched life? He said, "Son, the Good Book says, "'tis better to sow thy seed in the belly of a whore than to cast it on the ground for the insects to feed upon." I'm still looking through the Bible for the phrase. It's certainly not in Romans.

—∿∿—

My First Car

And so it was, our hot summer days in Pennsylvania passed with work and fun, completing about three trucks a day; that's 30 wheels and 240 lug nuts off and back on. By the end of summer, I had huge forearms from twisting lug nuts day after day. Each month I earned about $200 but by the end of June did not have quite enough to buy the 1939 Plymouth coupe (with rumble seat) that was on the lot for $300. I was getting hungry for a car and my folks sensed an opportunity here. Harry and I had been smoking cigarettes for a couple of years, much to the disgust of Father and our stepmother Cooks. Cooks was a very sharp and personable lady who did a magnificent job of managing two, mostly out of control teenagers. She suggested that, if I quit smoking, I would not only save the quarter a day I was spending for cigarettes but also, they would kick in matching funds to boot. To top it off, they would give me an advance of enough money to round out what I needed to buy the car. That did it. I quit smoking and in early July, bought the car. What a prize (see photo). I now had a way to date and to get around!

I wasted no time arranging a date with Helen, my semi-steady. After the movie we "parked" way out, on a dirt road, in an area where teens of the day would go to make out. When we headed home later that night, I was going a little fast in the Plymouth (probably due to an increased heart rate) and failed to negotiate a sharp turn that didn't show in my headlights on that dark dirt road. As I left the road, I went across a ditch, through a fence and into a corn field before I got us stopped.

But by that time my poor date was on the floorboards, and I was feeling highly incompetent. That was my first and last accident as a teenager, very scary. No one was hurt but I had quite a time getting us out of the cornfield and back on the road. The following morning, I surveyed the damage. I was lucky. No severe body dents, only some scratches. However, the impact of the ditch bent the rear axle and broke most of the leaves in the leaf springs, in the rear suspension. Thus, ensued my first automotive repair experience. The mechanics of getting things apart and back together was no problem but finding the parts was a pain and it was several weeks before I was back on the road.

Me, in front of my 1939 Plymouth

Of course, all the costs associated with operating my car were borne by me, so following my summer work, I had to have various jobs to pay the bills. For a while, Harry and I were "bag stuffers" at the local grocery store and I was still earning my "no smoking quarters," which wasn't bad in those days when 21 cents would buy a gallon of gas.

It wasn't long, though, before my newfound mobility and freedom got me in trouble. It was after a Friday night dance. A few of the guys decided we should head out to the old quarry for some skinny dipping and to spend the night. I asked Harry to tell the folks I would be back in the morning. When I got home the next day it really hit the fan. I guess I was testing the envelope and Dad was making it quite clear that at 17, the envelope wasn't very large. They decided that an appropriate punishment would be two weeks confinement to post! That really wasn't too bad though, because on post we had a swimming pool at the Officers' Club, a theater, the PX and a recreation building for the enlisted men. I also learned one evening, when further testing the envelope, that the gate guards had been instructed to turn me around should I venture out the gate!

Harry, who was now the proud owner of a 1937 Dodge convertible, had to be pressed into action to fetch my date for me the following weekend and then take her home. Fortunately, he didn't have far to go, because there was also a lovely young lass from Haiti, Missouri, visiting her aunt and uncle on post not too far from our quarters. It was not long before I was totally swept off my feet by my first summer love and her southern accent. Strong stuff when you are young, totally absorbing and when the summer ends, nearly always heart wrenching. My first job, a taste of independence, a car, summer love and undeserved popularity. What more could a young man hope for, heading into his senior year?!

I was crushed when my love went back to Missouri. When I saw her again a year later, I was still in love, but she wasn't! I wrote my first (and last) poem of remorse!

To see beyond sight, to hear beyond sound,
To smile when depressed, to perceive the profound?
No, think not the thoughts, feel not the pain,
When all is lost, strive not to regain.
For the grass must grow and the rain must fall and,
man cannot walk before learning to crawl.
So, if this be life and life there must be,
Then who am I to harness the sea.

Fortunately, there were three other young ladies I was quite interested in during my senior year and that helped salvage my wounded heart and ego. In that little town of New Cumberland Pennsylvania,

I was something of a curio. I suspect that Army Brats become socially more adept when thrown into new situations, and this was already my third high school. Then, too, I was the son of the New Cumberland Depot Commander (the depot was the biggest industry in town), world traveler, first string football, over six feet tall, and president of our "home room". So, there were a lot of external forces at work for me, most of which I didn't deserve but they certainly worked to my benefit in establishing myself socially in this new school.

Ah yes, and those many youthful memories of being a jock when a senior in HS. One of my better friends was a football teammate, Jack Quick, our left end. He was selected as our football king and his twin sister Joanne was our football queen. I had my eye on Joanne but was going steady with Helen, whom I was also taken with. As I look back now, I can see that Joanne came from a better family than Helen and was more on my social level. But you don't really understand or know that sort of thing in HS as you blunder into various relationships. In a small town like that the girls, to my great chagrin, were very circumspect. We had some super make out sessions but never the Full Monte. Eventually, I had a date with Joanne, but if the date isn't warm and fuzzy you can't go for the "goodnight kiss" on the first date, so then it was hard to follow up. I guess we didn't really hit it off. However, Joanne would again enter my life about three years later.

At the end of that summer, Father had orders to take command of Cameron Station in Washington, DC. It was decided that I would stay a few more weeks with a fellow football player to finish off the football season at New Cumberland before heading to Washington. Harry had already graduated and was now at Penn State. I really enjoyed my football. I guess all that fighting with my brother led to the point where I liked the body contact. Right tackle certainly was not a glory position, but I enjoyed tackling and at 196 pounds and 6' 2" I can understand that they wanted me to finish the season. I remember one play when the opposing team's ball carrier was headed for a touchdown. I was angling cross field to catch him but just when I was about to close on him, he found some extra speed and began to pull away. I lunged, reaching and watching his right foot leave the ground as I slapped it hard. As planned, it was enough to cause him to trip. They didn't get the touchdown and we won the game. The next morning there was a picture of me in the paper, flying through the air, parallel to the ground reaching for him,

"Hart makes shoestring tackle, saves the game." Ah, yes...wee bits of glory floating my way.

Anyway, I was going to finish the season by staying with Jack Messic (our team Center), until Thanksgiving. But to my chagrin, after two weeks I found out he was gay when he made a move on me! After that incident, I left New Cumberland as soon as possible for our new location in Anacostia, a suburb of Washington, DC. Gone were my hero days as I started in as an unknown at my fourth high school in three years, following Lincoln High in San Francisco, Osaka High in Japan and New Cumberland High in Pennsylvania. With the football season over and the other seniors in their last semester and enjoying friendships formed over several years, I was a total nobody. I felt it but didn't feel bad about it. It was just the way it was nothing personal. They had their friends and I didn't, but I still had my car.

In a few weeks I found a new friend, Jim Carpenter, who was the son of a Naval officer. We became pretty close but mostly after school. I remember one Saturday, cruising around with Jim in my '39 Plymouth, we saw a van parked on the side of the street and the driver waving us over. This guy had a van full of soap that he was selling. He was an amazing salesman! As we pulled up, he handed us a bar of soap and started extolling its virtues and wanted 50 cents for it. To turn him off and be on our way we dug up our 50 cents. WRONG! He now offered three bars of soap for $1. The logic was that "if we are willing to part with a half dollar for one bar of soap, certainly one dollar for three makes eminent sense." The hook was set. Before I could get the one dollar all the way out of my wallet, he was bringing out more soap so that I could have seven bars for $2. Would you believe that. $21 and a trunk full of soap later, we were totally out of money and on our way again. The soap was worthless. Easy lesson learned early.

By the end of the semester, my very special 1939 Plymouth coupe with rumble seat developed a bad crank shaft. I pulled the engine apart and replaced the babbitt in the connecting rod that had gone bad. Now it needed a tune up and then I would sell it. I took it to the garage for the tune up and when I got it back, there was the rod knock again. What a disappointment! I had spent many hours and quite a few dollars fixing that problem. With a little more chutzpa, I could have insisted that the repair garage was at fault, but I knew in my heart that my repair was only a short-term fix, since I had already been told by a mechanic that it was going to take a new crank shaft to cure the problem. Sadly, I took it to a used car lot and got a hundred dollars for it. The next day, when I went by the lot, it was on a pedestal with a sign, "Our special for the week: $300." I guess that was my second heartbreak but no poem this time; graduation was only a week away.

I had wanted to be an Army officer ever since the 5th grade when my father came to visit me, back from WW II, surprising me by showing up while I was playing in the schoolyard during recess. I was impressed with his six-foot two stature, in uniform, with medals and the eagles he wore on his shoulders. His "Garrison Hat" added another two inches to his height and the bill was be-speckled with the golden embroidery known as "scrambled eggs". There are "formative events" in everyone's life; events which tend to direct our later life, unbeknownst to us but which reside in our subconscious. Father's visit that day was such an event in my life and greatly shaped my future; I was destined to follow in his footsteps.

Later, in my high school years, I asked Father how to become an army officer. He said the best way is to go to West Point. In my high school years, I never lost sight of wanting to go to West Point. I took all those more difficult math and science courses which would prepare me for the Academy. But the biggest hurdle for entering West Point was the "appointment." There were all types of appointments for our nation's three military academies (now four with the Air Force Academy); the Congressional, Presidential, and the Regular Army appointment. By virtue of Father's being a Regular Army Officer (as opposed to Reserve or National Guard), I was born with the entitlement to compete for a Presidential Appointment. But the problem with that was the Presidential is highly competitive. There are thousands of Regular Army officers with sons who want to go to West Point but only the eight or ten scoring highest on the entrance exam would get in each year. I needed better odds than that. Father suggested I join the Army so I could qualify for one of the ten or twelve appointments available to Regular Army soldiers each year. That would give me two shots at an appointment, but it was necessary to have served a year in the Army to qualify for that. This forced my decision on what I should do. On 10 June 1951, I graduated from Anacostia High School in Washington, D.C. I was 18 years old and stood six feet, two and a half inches. The next day I was sworn into the Army as a private E-1, at Fort Meade, Maryland. My teenage life, as I had known it, had just ended. I suspect there must be a correlation between achieving maturity and enduring hardships. Living under austere conditions, close supervision, discipline and being thrown together with people you don't know, don't trust and don't like, in unfamiliar circumstances, was a very maturing experience. No longer any privacy or time for myself to do what I want, and suddenly needing to do exactly what I was told and when I told to do it, was a total sea change in my life. Going from the warm loving comfort of home and apple pie to the shouting indifference of a drill sergeant, is an epiphany like no other I can think of. Yet, it was something I volunteered to do and would somehow make the best of it. It was step one in my plan for a career as an Army officer.

CHAPTER 11

FROM HIGH SCHOOL TO BASIC TRAINING

My first seven days, after being sworn in, were spent at the Fort Meade induction center: shots, uniform issue, haircut, KP, and a battery of Army Placement Tests. By the end of the week, I had qualified for Corps of Engineers basic training and off I went to Fort Belvoir, Virginia, just south of Washington, D.C. Father was commanding Cameron Station in Washington at the time, and I suspect he was closely monitoring what was happening to me. Perhaps he even influenced my assignment to nearby Fort Belvoir for basic training? Basic was a real shocker. I had always seen the Army from the privileged perspective of a high-ranking officer's family member. Now suddenly I was the lowest of low. "You deah young sojer, when ah is speekin, youse will be as quiet as a mouse a pissin on cotton. Now be at ease. You man, ah said to be at ease. Now gimme 10 pooshups." "Sergeant, this isn't right, that wasn't me speaking." "Young sojer, youse doan say what raght and what wrong, dese here stripes say what right and wrong. Now gimme lebenty-leben pooshups." "Yes, Sergeant." Our drill sergeants were mostly African Americans, low on leadership and education and at some level were not particularly keen on a "whitey" with a high school education.

The training was tough in that 90+ degree, high humidity, Virginia summer. We were at war in Korea and these trainers were determined to ready us for the worst. In those days of the draft, there was no need to win the hearts and minds of the recruits, just run them through the grist mill before the next load arrived. I vowed that one day, when I was in charge; there would be some big changes in this process. In addition to our suffering poor NCO leadership, we were of course living in those horrible, roach-infested, World War II wooden barracks. At the end of our building was a large room with toilets, showers and sinks. You can imagine my chagrin when first discovering ten or twelve toilets lined up against the wall without any partitions. And of course, you would have to sit there in front of God and country while, seven feet away, other guys are lined up shaving or in the open bay showers. It took a lot of getting used to. Our training went for at least 12 hours most days and after a 15-mile forced march in three hours, in heat that would kill a snake, we still had a full day ahead of us. We would finally get back from training about 5 PM and have a crack at the showers but by that time the hot water had long been used up by the drill sergeants who got there first. The evenings were spent getting our equipment in order and boots shined for the next day. I was 212 pounds going into basic training. At the end of the first six weeks, I was down to 190 and still eating everything in sight.

One recollection of our training is the day our Drill Sergeant had about fifteen of us sitting in a semicircle under a tree. He was explaining the various types of security necessary when in combat, explaining that there was internal security, out post security and security patrols. When the Sergeant saw the man next to me asleep, he called on him and asked, "What kind of security would you use Pvt Jones?" On a sudden, uncontrollable impulse, I whispered to the groggy trooper, "Social Security", which was, of course, what he replied. There was subdued laughter. I think the devil made me do it.

KP duty was something of a horror. We reported for duty at the mess hall at four in the morning to get things ready for the 6:30 mandatory breakfast. We had about six KPs and our shift went until eight in the evening. There were several jobs to be meted out. You might be the pots and pans guy, or the tray guy scraping the trays and putting them in the rack, or setting the table or peeling hundreds of potatoes, etc. Two of the worst jobs were cleaning out the grease trap or being on the garbage detail.

That day I was a bit unlucky. I got the garbage detail: "You deah young sojer. You come with me. You see dese heah garbage cans?" I looked down to see a stench-filled can of meat and bones that had been putrefying for a day or two in the heat. It looked alive! My eyes got wide, and my mouth dropped open. The mess sergeant said, "Now yo job is to separate de meat from de bone!" I involuntarily reeled back from the awful smell and the horrible prospect as the Drill Sergeant shouted, "GET YO HANDS IN DEAH. NOW GET 'EM IN!" And so, it went for ten weeks; the rite of passage, the coming of age, the making of a soldier in 1951.

At the end of our eternal first six weeks of basic training we were to have a three-day pass. Father and Cooks were living in Alexandria, Virginia, not far from Fort Belvoir and would be picking me up for the weekend. That morning we had our final barracks inspection - beds taut, boots shined, all belongings folded and displayed; lots of work. The Drill Sergeant, I didn't get along with, came through to inspect before we could get our pass. I was yet to learn that getting along with the boss was more important than how well you performed. "You deah, young sojer, youse will stay here." Yikes! My three-day weekend at home gone! Well, nearly. Evidently Father had come to the Orderly Room in uniform and the appearance of a full colonel there, at that time, was equivalent to the resurrection of Jesus Christ. Full colonels, at that level, are God-like! He requested I be fetched. "Yes Sir! Right away Sir! Will that be all, Sir?" I was "fetched" immediately and we left for the weekend with my new appreciation of RHIP (rank hath its privileges).

Our training was in two phases, Basic Combat Training (BCT) and Advanced Individual Training (AIT). By the time I completed AIT, my application for the Army's West Point prep school had been approved and I received travel orders to attend the "U.S. Military Academy Preparatory School" (USMAPS), at Stewart Air Force Base, New York,

—⚂—

USMA Prep School, Stewart AFB, Newburgh, NY, 1951

It was early September when I reported to USMAPS at Stewart AFB in Newburgh, New York. The change from Fort Belvoir was heaven sent! Still the WW II barracks but in better condition and with more space between the bunks, no harassment and a cooler, more temperate climate. Also, at that time, I was promoted from Private E-1 (lowest of low) to Private E-2 (next lowest to low) and was now earning the awesome amount of $78.50 a month! If I were to gain entrance to the Military

Academy, I would need $300 to pay for my initial issue of uniforms, so I started saving $50 a month.

It was academia. We had seven hours of class a day and relatively no homework. We had a complete review of all our high school higher math, advanced algebra, geometry, and trig. Our English classes were dedicated primarily to writing and studying the classics. We were tested nearly every day to get us used to the testing process. The questions were taken from old West Point exams covering Math, English, History and IQ-type questions concerning spatial relationships. We also had a pretty good football team. I played right tackle, but we had another soldier by the name of Bixby who beat me out for first string (but didn't make it in to the Academy!).

There were nearly 200 of us at the Prep School and it was there that I forged some of my closest friendships, many of which were to last over 70 years and continue to this day. My best of friends, Bob Arnold was a debonair, devil-may-care chap, nearly a year older than I. He was originally from Connecticut but entered the service from Texas, where he had spent the past several years. He, I and friend, David Gibson, became close, we spent most of our weekends together and got into most of our trouble together too. Somehow, our problems always seemed to arise in conjunction with our quest to find suitable young ladies to spend our time with. Such was the case at a Lady Cliff College dance we attended, just outside the gates of West Point, in the town of Highland Falls.

Always an instigator, Bob had brought a bottle of vodka along and when his subterfuge permitted, he emptied the entire bottle into the punch bowl. According to Bob, this punch bowl suddenly became very popular among the heretofore less interested nuns. We danced and drank and eventually escorted two of the young ladies to their room. The four of us were making out when Bob got a little boisterous in his courting conversation. Suddenly there was a loud banging on the door and a demand that the door be opened immediately. With nowhere to go, I forthwith rolled under the bed with Bob close behind me; a ridiculous situation of the two of us hiding under the bed (like a slapstick comedy). The door was opened to admit the night watchman, and of course he saw our shoes, which we had failed to hide and immediately looked under the bed. Bob was first in the line of fire. The watchman grabbed the shoes and started throwing them at Bob and yelling, "Get out, get out of there!" and Bob saying, "I will if you stop throwing those shoes at me." A very embarrassing moment as we crawled out from under the bed!

A couple months later we decided we would go in together to buy a car. I think it was David who found our set of wheels for $300. I cashed in two months' savings for my $100 and we made plans for a forthcoming weekend trip. We decided we would make the 100-mile trip to Connecticut to visit some old family friends of Bob's. I guess Dr. and Mrs. Ferris had been neighbors of the Arnolds at one time and Bob was interested in renewing his acquaintance with daughter Fawn Ferris. We had some difficulty getting away from the base, since as soon as we started our car there was an electrical short, of some sort under the dash, exuding smelly blue smoke. Fortunately, our friend Sal, who was seeing us off, stepped forth to solve the problem. His unorthodox solution was to use several condoms to insulate the shorting wires. It was a successful solution and soon we were on our way.

We arrived Saturday evening about 5 PM after an uneventful trip. Dr. and Mrs. Ferris were expecting us, and we followed them into their dinette to join the Ferris's and their friends for drinks. In the center of the table was a bowl of nuts. Bob was holding forth with a story of our prep school life and reached for some nuts from the bowl. As he put his hand in the bowl, all conversation suddenly, almost audibly, stopped. Every eye at the table was focused on the condom draped across the back of Bob's hand! There was an inaudible gasp for what little oxygen was left I the room. He had stuffed a couple of Sal's "insulators" into his jacket pocket for further emergency use on the car. Now, as he pulled his hand from his jacket pocket, the darn thing had somehow stuck to the back of it, I presume from static electricity. Such an event, even today, would raise eyebrows but if you can imagine the setting in the early 50's at the home of Dr. and Mrs. Ferris and their friends and their having a daughter of eligible age; well, it was a totally unacceptable situation. As Bob removed his hand from the bowl, suddenly, compulsively, everyone started talking at once while saying nothing but frantically trying to fill the silent void. The embarrassment was palpable and thickened as the guests rose to leave. Bob's face was ashen, it was as though it had died and was waiting for the rest of his body.

That evening, we were sharing a bed in the Ferris's guest room. My last memory before falling to sleep was Bob muttering his total embarrassment, that he couldn't face them in the morning, that he was going to get up and leave. I doubt that the Ferris's ever learned the condom was really intended for the car, not their daughter. I long remembered it as the most embarrassing incident in my young life. But for Bob, his discomfort was painful for me to see.

Our school year lasted about nine months, from the beginning of September to the end of May. It was April when I got the word that Congressman William R. Williams, in my Father's hometown of Utica, had two appointments available for West Point and would be giving them, to whomever scored highest on the Civil Service exam. Twenty of us took the exam and I got one of the appointments. This was great news because, with a congressional appointment, the only remaining hurdles would be to pass the entrance exam as well as the medical and physical. Bob was also able to secure a congressional appointment. We graduated from Prep School in early June and entered West Point later that month. As far as I was concerned my career was launched but the real challenge was just beginning. David, who had maxed the SAT mathematics portion of the entrance exam, finally decided to go to Annapolis.

At Annapolis, the Midshipmen got to go home for Christmas. David never returned from his Christmas leave and eventually graduated from college and became a highly sought-after computer guru. Bob left West Point in his senior year after getting into a row with his Tac Officer. He later completed college at Rice University and became an aeronautical engineer working for Boeing. Our paths would cross again.

CHAPTER 12

WEST POINT

In 1776, the Western prominent in the Hudson was utilized as a fortress responsible for preventing British ships from sailing north. The granite rock, on which the fort was built, is of such fortitude that the glaciers which pushed through the Hudson Valley, millions of years ago, could not carve through it. This granite promontory, protruding easterly into the Hudson River, sixty miles north of New York City, describes the name of our nation's premier military academy, "West Point". What better foundation of strength, fortitude, and endurance could mark the origins of this great institution 220 years ago!

West Point, Looking South across the Hudson River - 2000

As cadets, we knew it as our "Rockbound Highland Home." As graduates, we think of it as a Mecca of honor and integrity whose standards demand the highest level of performance and dedication from those who lead our country's youth into battle. Its geographic seclusion imposed by river, rock and mountain is also symbolic of the physical and mental separation you feel as a young man when first entering the stone "sally ports" of the surrounding, forbidding, rock structures. These gray granite buildings jut upward from the Plain, their Gothic impact blending with the rock ramparts which rise as a backdrop behind them. When winter falls and the gray overcast seals off the sky, blending the cold penetrating wind with the monastic life of the new cadets, the full impact of one's seclusion begins to take hold.

During this "gloom period" (as the cadets called it), in the early evening just before the last light leaves the hills, you can sometimes hear the murmur of a thousand ghosts of graduates past, who gave their lives in a warrior's final sacrifice to their country. Their spirits have returned here to dwell in these buildings which these heroes inhabited as young men. Their ghosts watch over West Point and form a long gray line from the past to the present. They stand gripping hands and each of us now knows that one day we will take the hand of the last man standing so that the long gray line can continue into "the years of a century told." This "Long Gray Line" stretches in mute testimony through more than 200 years of tradition and every graduate knows the ghosts from the past are poised to rise up and roar their indignation should their standards of duty, honor, country be tarnished.

—ΩΩ—

The First 24 Hours

Our "Plebe Year" began with "Beast Barracks," a most unusual phenomenon; intense, total immersion, 110% supervision 16 hours a day, to continue for eight weeks of basic training. The process envelopes you as you walk through the sally-port, a large arched opening into the Central Area barracks. Here we were met by a First Classmen, immaculately dressed, standing unbelievably erect in his white, starched trousers, short-sleeved, dress shirt, gleaming shoes and a brilliant red sash denoting a cadet officer. This tall, trim, erect, cadet officer approached and greeted me with the command "YOU MAN, HALT!". That stopped me dead in my tracks. This guy was impressive. I'd never seen anything like it. Looking at the small satchel in my hand he commanded, "Drop that bag!" I put it down and he yelled, "I said drop that bag, not put it down! Now pick it up! Now drop it!" I began to get the picture.

Then, two more First Class cadets descended on me and in about three or four minutes, with very sharp commands and close supervision, these three cadets instructed me in no uncertain terms in how to stand how to salute and the proper way to address a superior. This shouting and demanding ordeal was going on throughout Central Area and in each group, we were told there are only three responses allowed when addressed: "Yes Sir, No Sir and No Excuse Sir." When it became apparent, after a few minutes, that I could respond to commands in a respectful and proper manner, I was told to report as follows: "New Cadet Hart reports to the First Sergeant of First New Cadet Company for the first time as ordered." After messing it up the first time I was told to try again. The next time I had it right, but the "Firsty" yelled, "dusquizzel, that's the second time you reported". After several times (as it was designed to do), I was ordered to report on a run to a cadet standing by the barber shop. More harassment prior to a five-minute, very short haircut. I was again ordered on a run to uniform fitting, a brief moment of respite with a tailor. As he proceeded with his measurements he looked down at my crotch and said, "You need to dress right!" A concept entirely new to me.

Finally, I am back in formation for room assignments and dress hat fittings. On the barrack porch (known as the "stoops"), were a huge pile of boxes containing our dress hats (known as "Tar Buckets. We were lined up in alphabetical order on the stoops and several Firsties were opening the boxes and fitting the hats on each cadet in line as they stepped up. In front of me was Bob Gould, who had an unusually large head. Most of the heads being fitted were size seven or seven and an eighth. Bob was an unbelievable 8! When he stepped up for his fitting, the hat they tried on sat on the top of his head like one of those little red hats the Organ Grinders put on their monkeys. I had to suppress a giggle. The Firsty brought out a larger hat, perhaps a seven and a quarter, which also sat way up on top of his head. Then came one an eighth larger, then another eighth. I was valiantly choking back my laughter but with every increase in size the pressure was building. Finally, as the eighth hat was tried on, I exploded in a gurgling, unmuffled, choking, snot producing upheaval. The Firsties were all over me like a blanket, yelling, demanding, commanding! "Dumbsmack, are you ill. I know you wouldn't be laughing at a classmate, suck your gut up, get your chin in. Who gave you permission to snot yourself? Give me 20 pushups dusquizzel" …and on and on.

For the entire day I followed all commands at a run and was given instructions on what to do and where to go, with a time constraint that could never be met. As the day wore on, the pressure mounted. Once our rooms and roommates were assigned, we received instruction on making our beds, maintaining lockers, and how to shine shoes and brass accouterments. For those of us who had been through basic training and at the Prep School, this was old stuff, but it was greatly compressed and of a higher level of expectations than during Basic Combat Training. I felt for those who had no prior military training. A few, who had come from protected, millennial-like environments, and had no idea of the full impact of discipline and demands they would encounter, picked up their bags and walked out.

My room assignment, with three other roommates, was on the fourth floor of a hundred-year-old stone building. One roommate, Ernie, I had known in Prep School, but we had lived in different buildings and did not know each other well. His Father was a 1917 graduate of West Point, the same year my Father was commissioned. As fellow Army Brats, we had much in common. Another roommate, Bob Gould, was not yet 18. He came to West Point directly out of high school. His Father was also a colonel in the Quartermaster Corps who probably knew my Father, since the QM Corps was not that large. My third roommate, Don Holleder, had also entered directly out of high school and had just turned 18. He was from upper-state New York and had been "preselected" to play football at the Academy. We were a disparate group of young men facing a sea change of life and a sudden necessity of getting along and living with each other under very close and arduous circumstances. It was going to take a lot of adjustment!

Our entering class of 676 men was initially formed into six "new ca-det" companies according to height. The cadets in my company ranged from six foot one to six foot three in height. We were four to a room but by the end of summer most rooms would be down to only three. As noted above, by the end of that first day, there were already a few young men who just turned around and walked out the gate, shaking their heads, muttering this was not what they thought they were getting into.

When mealtime finally arrived, we formed up for inspection, which left us standing at attention as our masters screamed their disappointment at the slightest thing, they found wrong. A thread on my shirt elicited a very loud, "YOU MAN with the rope hanging from your shirt, who are you dumbsmack?" Finally, we marched to our ten-man tables in the mess hall. We remained at attention until the command from on high 'TAKE SEATS". Three or four First Class cadets were seated at the head of the ten-man table The rest were plebes.

We were expected to sit at erect attention, on the first six inches of our seats, and receive the food as it arrived from the waiters and pass it to the head of the table. Our manners were closely scrutinized, and infractions were dealt with instantly. Disciplinary commands rang out through the mess hall: "You man with that huge bite on your fork, are you trying to choke yourself? Get your chin back. Sit up straight. Report to my room after dinner for remedial instructions." And on it went. This continued throughout the year, but most heavily during Beast Barracks. When Beast ended and the full Corps returned to West Point for the fall term, there were only three or four plebes at each table. Each plebe at the end of the table was assigned particular table duties to perform. But until academics started the heavy harassment continued.

At the end of that first day, after dinner, our close and continuous supervision continued into the shower area, where we stood at attention with our towel around our waist and our soap dish in our right hand. The First Classmen moved through our ranks correcting our posture; "Suck up that gut, get your chin back, WAY BACK!". After about a half hour of this harassment we formed a line in front of each shower stall. One of the First Classmen had a stopwatch and explained we had two minutes for our shower. At the appropriate time he announced, "Into the showers." A minute later he announced, "One minute," then "Ten seconds" and finally, "Out of the showers." In time we learned we could do a thorough job of washing in two minutes, to include a shampoo. After the showers, with towels back around our waists, the First Classman in charge stepped up to each Plebe for our final report of the day. "Sir, New Cadet Hart has showered, shaved and had a bowel movement this day." Under the extreme pressure, some plebes were constipated for days. We were then dismissed and repaired to our rooms to prepare for the following morning's inspection. Little did we know that unbelievable first day would be followed in the morning with the resounding blast of the reveille cannon at 5:50 AM! The concussion must have raised me off the mattress at least ten inches. And while still levitating from the shock waves, I was then assaulted by a cacophony of the "Hellcats" piercing my barely conscious mind. The Hellcats, consisting of fifes, drummers, and buglers, were aptly named and obviously took great pleasure in blasting us out of the sack with their teeth-chattering rendition of reveille. At that time, the "five-minute bell" started ringing and the designated plebe began calling the minutes: "Sir, there are five minutes till reveille formation. The uniform is fatigues. Five minutes, sir." As the last strains of the reveille bugle floated across the area, every man was standing tall and answering roll call. Three minutes later we were back to our rooms to prepare for breakfast formation and the associated inspection at 6:30, as the trying day began again.

One of the more memorable events occurred the second day at a company formation. The Cadet First Captain (known as "The King of the Beasts") had stepped into the spotlight for the first time and was standing on the stoops as we formed up in our designated ranks as "The First New Cadet Company". It was like facing GOD. He was immaculate, spiffy, shiny, tall, erect, handsome, confident and in-charge! About three minutes into his delivery, a large fly was buzzing in front of his face. It landed on his cheek, walked across his nose on to his forehead and flew away. He never twitched or moved while the fly was touring his face, just remained at attention and kept speaking!

When my class entered the Academy in 1952 the war was still on in Korea. Our generation was too young to have been called up for WW II, but we were about the right age for Korea. Being at West Point kept us out of that war but life as a Plebe was a tough substitute. It was a long year with no weekend passes; we even spent Christmas at WP. In recent years much has changed to make life at the Academy better, although perhaps not easier because academic requirements and competition have gotten tougher. In my day, everywhere we went outside of our rooms, we were at a posture of exaggerated attention with our chins pulled in and our chests popped up, and shoulders back. Having nearly three upper-classmen, for every single plebe, resulted in an overload of supervision. We also had continuous oversight by the Tactical Department, which was the ultimate authority for enforcement of regulations.

We were assigned to companies according to our height. My company, M-2, was comprised of half the tallest cadets (the other half were in A-1 in the other regiment). All of us being about the same height presented a uniform appearance at parades and reviews. But this also led to an attitude on the part of various cadets, depending on their groupings. The tallest companies of cadets were all 6' 1" or taller and were called "flankers" because in parades the tallest individuals were placed on the flanks of the formation. Flanker companies tended to be more laid back than the "runt" companies and consequently life was a bit easier for us. Usually, the runts had more to prove, and their "little man" complexes made life miserable for the plebes in those companies. Arguments to the effect that increased demands in the runt companies resulted in better officers or leaders did not prove out in later years. In about 1960 West Point discontinued this company sizing.

One of the tortures all cadets endure were the practice parades and Saturday parade formations. Parades usually started at 11 AM Saturday mornings and were over by noon but our preparations began hours before with special attention to our uniforms, shined shoes and glistening brass.

In the warmer months we wore white trousers. The trousers were heavily starched, so the pant legs were stuck together and had to be pried open to get your feet through them. The best way to handle that, without wrinkling the pant legs, was to use our bayonets to slice open the trouser legs, then after donning the trousers, not sit down until after parade. During the parade there would be fairly long periods of standing at attention or at "parade rest" for the award ceremony portion, after which the Corps of Cadets (about 2,000 men) would pass in review. On particularly warm days or long parades there would occasionally be a plebe or two who would pass out from standing in the sun at rigid attention as was expected of plebes. From time to time, without moving, a plebe would be called upon to tell a joke to break the boredom of standing so long. At most of our parades an upperclassman would call out at least once for a joke, so as plebes we always tried to have one in mind in the event our name was called. The jokes had to be short, funny and clean. On this particular day a voice called out, "Dumbsmack Wilson, let's have a joke." The plebe responded with, "Sir, for neither love nor money, can I find a joke which is both clean and funny!" A slight ripple of laughter rolled through the company, probably not noticeable from the reviewing stands across the Plain.

Beast Barracks continued through the summer. It was tough, with lots of exercise, inspections, parades, harassment and always moving at a run, never a moment to relax. We had two months to learn our soldier skills, the same sort of thing a soldier learns in basic training; rifle and pistol and the ability to strip the weapon into its parts and put it back together blindfolded. I suspect that roommates were selected based on previous service experience which would explain why Ernie and I were matched with two 17-year-olds. We learned marksmanship, first aid, guard duty, inspections, map reading and much more. It was basic training at Ft Belvoir all over again but this time with excessive supervision but good leadership! The last hurdle of Beast Barracks was a 20-mile march and an encampment. When finally, we returned to end our summer training there was a brief ceremony to accept us into the Corps of Cadets. At that time, our title changed from "New Cadet" to "Cadet." We were now ready to take our places in the Corps and begin the academic year but being a plebe would last till next June.

Initially we were assigned to classes in various subjects according to our academic prowess. The best students were in sections one through five. The worst students were in sections 15 to 20. We marched in formation to breakfast, then walked back to our rooms. We were allowed about 30 minutes after breakfast to get our act together and leave our rooms ready for inspection. After that we formed up and marched off to an academic building. Early on we were issued a slide rule, the absolute cutting edge of technology at that time, a "Keffler & Esser log-log duplex, decitrig slide rule" made of magnesium. This was a very fine and expensive item which enabled us to do all manner of mathematics and engineering problems, including geometric and trigonometric functions, square roots and multiples of pi. Today those functions are accomplished by simple calculators and computers with a higher level of accuracy but only a bit faster.

Of the four men in our room Ernie and I grew the closest. We came to West Point with prior military service and had known each other from Prep School. Our families lived in California and our Fathers were both retired Colonels, and we both had brothers. Our other two roommates had arrived directly from high school, having graduated only weeks before. We were all in great physical condition. Don was the total athlete, having lettered at high school in football, baseball, and basketball and being selected for the "All Eastern" teams in two of those sports. He was later to gain fame as our All-American end on Coach Red Blake's winning football team during our Second-Class (Junior) year in 1954. Ernie and I had many shared experiences and several mutual friends. We were destined to be roommates for four years and close friends until his death in 2010. Interestingly, we all had quite a sense of our own self-importance, perhaps because we were athletes and big guys who were not about to take any crap from each other. Our interactions were not without confrontations and disagreements. I guess that is part of the stuff that eventually forges lifelong ties. Don died a hero in 1967 in Vietnam. He was shot by a sniper as he rushed to the scene of a firefight to replace a fallen commander. Ernie retired after 20 years and died of cancer at age 78. Bob didn't make it through our junior year. He finished university in California and was successful in real-estate. After retiring in Palm Springs on a golf course, he later moved to a care facility and died in 2014.

As plebe life settled into an odd blend of academics, discipline and military training, we were also expected to participate in sports. "Every man an athlete" was the cornerstone objective of the physical training program. We were introduced to all the sports, receiving specific instruction in boxing, wrestling, swimming, gymnastics, tennis and golf. But in addition to our formal PT Classes, every cadet was required to participate in intramural or intercollegiate sports after classes ended in the afternoon. I had played football in high school, but college football is not something you try out for; it's a sport for which you are preselected. I had played a lot of soccer in Junior high, so when I wasn't selected for football, I went out for the intercollegiate soccer team.

As I previously noted, we were grouped into companies according to height and initially Norm Schwarzkopf and I, both 6' 2", were in the same company. I guess we knew each other particularly well from playing intercollegiate soccer together. He played halfback, I played fullback. I must admit, we were a rather formidable pair and I have always claimed that if it weren't for breaking my wrist during an early season game in my plebe year, I would no doubt have gone on to greatness. Norm, of course, did go on to greatness 30 years later, as a four-star general, leading the invasion forces against Saddam Hussein in 1990, operation Desert Storm.

Our practices were demanding but being on an intercollegiate team had some bennies. We ate at the sports table with other athletes, which meant no harassment at mealtime and a higher calorie diet with slightly better food. Nearly every weekend there would be a Saturday parade which sometimes we could avoid when there was a conflict with soccer practice. And of course, there was a trip or two away from West Point to play at other colleges. Here is a photo of our intercollegiate soccer team with Stormin Norman on my right.

Norm and I in the 2nd row from the top,
Norm the tallest, I am on his left.

I thoroughly enjoyed soccer and was pretty good at it but before the season ended, I managed to land on my arm and break a small bone in my wrist, (the navicular bone). The navicular evidently has a very limited blood supply and takes upwards of six months to heal. This ended my plebe soccer, as well as participation in most other athletic activities for the year. Since it was my right wrist, and the cast covered the knuckles on my hand it was very difficult to write. Fortunately, I knew how to type and had enough fingers sticking out of the cast to reach the typewriter keys. This allowed me to successfully complete the weekly English 1000-word essay assignment. Also, much to my relief, I missed the boxing instruction and the chance to mix it up with the gorillas in my heavyweight class (who averaged about 210 pounds).

For plebes in general, a trip to Philadelphia in December for the Army-Navy football game and one to New York for the Army-Columbia game, are normally the only times away from the Academy that first year. However, since Dwight Eisenhower was elected President in 1952, the entire Corps of Cadets traveled to Washington, DC to take part in his inaugural parade in early 1953.

Since our graduation in 1956, much has changed at West Point, so the atmosphere now is not quite what it was sixty-five years ago. Even as upperclassmen, we were not allowed to drink within 25 miles of West Point or on post. This policy was closely adhered to. As First Classmen, if we signed out on pass, our signatures when we returned meant we were honor-bound to have not gotten married or brought any alcohol back on post. We were not allowed to go into the adjacent town of Highland Falls except on weekend passes (very limited) and when on post, we were not permitted to order in food from off the post and have it delivered, as they do now.

One Sunday evening during the "Gloom Period" just after Christmas, our company had formed up and marched off for supper as usual. After being released from Washington Hall (the mess hall) to return to our rooms, there was quite a congregation on the stoops of a nearby company. A Tac Officer was in the process of writing up a First Classman for "unauthorized item in his room," specifically a quart bottle of beer. Evidently the cadet had been cooling his prized beer by submerging it in the sink with the water running. After covering the bottle with tap water, he left the cold water barely running at what he thought was just the right pressure so it wouldn't overflow, then left to go to dinner. However, after the entire Corps had left their rooms the water pressure went up, the sink filled too fast, and the water overflowed onto the floor, down three flights of stairs, across the stoops and all the way into North Area.

The Officer of the Guard saw it and reported it and of course it was traced to the originating room. That First Classman spent the rest of his days, until graduation, in confinement.

Down through the years, one of the more famous cadet escapades was that of the late John "Jack" R. Lovett, Class of January 1943, fondly known as "The Mole." Jack discovered an array of steam tunnels running under West Point and used his discovery throughout much of his stay at the Academy. Lore has it that he set up "alternate" sleeping quarters underground to periodically escape the rigors of cadet life.

Following his lead, there were other "Sequel Moles" who made the discovery from 1958 to 1960. It seems one sequel mole was visiting the office of the Post Engineer as part of his duties and procured a map of the steam tunnels. He later recruited some friends to accompany him as he explored the wonders of surreptitious underground travel at West Point. They found one could travel from their barracks buildings to the old gym and also up to the Cadet Chapel by concealed routes. During one of their nocturnal visits to the Cadet Chapel, a member of the Mole Contingent played a few bars of "Hail, Hail, the Gang's All Here" on the chapel organ before beating a hasty retreat to their bunks.

These latter-day Moles also directed their talents to above ground forays like disassembling the "Reveille Cannon" (the much hated cannon which was fired at reveille to awaken the Corps). One Mole task force member possessed an extraordinary mechanical aptitude which he used removing the breechblock from the reveille cannon, which he did, several times. After each episode, the breech block was hidden cleverly in plain sight with ever-increasing ingenuity. Once, it was used to chock the wheels of the Commandant's car in his driveway. Another time, it appeared mysteriously inside the refrigerator in the office of the 1st Regimental Commander. In yet another foray, the Moles removed all the furniture from the poop deck inside the Mess Hall and in their place, displayed the breechblock on a table. However, their ultimate success in hiding the breechblock was to place the misappropriated item in an ordnance display case on the third floor of Thayer Hall. It reposed there, among other bits of highly machined, case-hardened material, well lighted and gleaming, where it remained for several days before it was discovered and returned to the reveille cannon. The honor code demanded that a cadet not lie, cheat or steal…but borrowing was not an honor violation.

Of the many cadet pranks over the years, perhaps the most notorious was the brilliant and as yet unexplained feat of a group of cadets, led by Hugh S. Johnson, in 1903. The cadets somehow hoisted the reveille cannon, weighing several thousand pounds, to the top of the Clock Tower. The story of that event concludes with the post engineers spending most of a week figuring out how to remove it, finally having to dissemble a portion of the Clock Tower to get it down. Today there are no longer such pranks, since the reveille cannon is permanently welded to its mount.

—⚊—

For most of us, Plebe Christmas was the first Christmas we had spent away from home. There was a lot of unsupervised spare time during those 12 days, and a special Christmas dinner was served in the mess hall. At some point in our plebe year everyone had been assigned a "Plebe Poppa", an officer on the staff or faculty appointed to take a personal interest in his wards. My Plebe Pop was the eminent Colonel/Professor George Lincoln who was, at one point in his career, a presidential speech writer. He had three plebes assigned as his wards, but we had never heard from him until we were invited for Christmas dinner at his home. It was a nice gesture but his having never made any previous effort to meet us or talk to us before, made the occasion rather perfunctory.

We were to be at his home at 2 PM, and we figured dinner would be at 4 or 5 that evening, so it made sense for us to not miss the special Christmas lunch in the mess hall at noon. After totally overindulging at the mess hall until about 1:30, we walked to the colonel's home. To our astonishment, within minutes of our arrival we were sitting down to eat. After our huge mess hall meal, I wasn't ready to even look at another turkey for a week, let alone eat one and here was this great Christmas spread in front of us! I pretended to relish every bite but I suspect the Colonel and his wife had pretty well figured out what happened by the time the desserts were served. For us, what should have been a special occasion turned out to be socially awkward and physically uncomfortable. I often wondered if any other classmates ended up in that overstuffed condition?

During Christmas week we were allowed to have our dates come to West Point and there were some special dances and events which we could enjoy. In those days, first year cadets received only five dollars a month for spending money. Since that allotment was not nearly enough for a proper time out with your date, it was universally understood that our dates had to pay their own way if they were staying at the Thayer Hotel or if we went out to dinner. Fortunately, most activities which included sports events, dances and trips down to Flirtation Walk, were without expense. However, finding a place to "make out" was always a problem, particularly during winter when temperatures were often below freezing. If a TAC Officer came across anything more than hand holding, a cadet would be written up for PDA (public display of affection), which had a minimum penalty of about five demerits. But a more severe offense, such as "embracing young lady in the prone position", could easily earn about 20 demerits. At the end of the month, each demerit above 20 would result in one hour of walking the area or four hours of restriction to quarters on the weekend.

It was easy to earn demerits, given that we were subject to continuous inspections during the day. Every day at our reveille and meal formations we were meticulously inspected for shined shoes, haircuts, grooming, condition of uniforms, etc. Late arrival (even one second after the bell) would bring five demerits. And our rooms were inspected nearly every morning to ensure they were clean and orderly, with beds made and uniforms put away. Then there was also the opportunity of earning ten or fifteen demerits for violations of regulations. During the course of that first year, I probably earned myself eight or ten hours on the area. I suspect that was pretty much an average for most of us.

The punishment for honor violations was dismissal and disgrace. The violator was gone from the Academy within hours. An honor violation could be something as innocuous as letting your eyes wander to the solution on the board of the cadet next to you when writing at the blackboard during classroom recitations. Or it could involve not telling the whole truth in any matter. One cadet was dismissed on an honor violation when his Tac told him to destroy the dilapidated shoes he was wearing. The cadet had an even worse pair of shoes in his room and tossed those out. The next day when he was asked about his shoes he stated, "Sir, I have destroyed a pair of shoes." Although that statement was true, he was dismissed because the honor code demands honesty in "thought, word and deed" and he was attempting to deceive.

A further illustration of the honor system is a situation I got into as the "Charge of Quarters" (CQ) one evening as a Yearling. My specific duties were set forth in detail in the CQ instruction book. At Taps the CQ would proceed to the top floor and go from room to room asking for an "All Right" from each room. The CQ would call out "All Right, Sir?" as he reached each door. The expected response was "All Right, Sir," which meant the lights were out and all occupants were in bed. Normally there was no requirement to open the door if the CQ could be heard.

When I returned to my CQ desk after completing the All-Right check and was about to sign off in the CQ book that my duties had been properly performed, I noted the instructions called for a clockwise check of the rooms. On the fourth floor I had checked in a counterclockwise direction. It was of course totally unimportant whether I turned left or right at the top of the stairwell, but you could make a case for "not performing your duties in the manner prescribed." And of course, no one except me knew whether I had turned right or left on the fourth floor. That was a tester! If I reported it, it could result in hours of walking the area. If I didn't report it, I could live happily ever after. I reported the error, feeling relatively certain that any demerits I received for that "non-event" would be relatively minor. No such luck! I ended up with five punishment tours on the area. Of note, is that West Point's honor system is "non-toleration". It states that, "A cadet will not lie, cheat or steal, nor tolerate those who do". This is also true at the Air Force Academy where my grand twins attended, but not at Annapolis. At the Naval Academy (which I refer to as The Navel Academy), there is no "nontoleration" clause in their honor code. In fact, "Thou shalt not bilge on a classmate" is generally accepted. Perhaps appropriate for on board compatriots when at sea?

Probably the highlight of my 12-day Christmas break was a visit from a girl I had been dating in Washington, DC, before entering West Point. Dana was 16 and her folks were friends with my parents. We had been dating for about a year and I was falling in love (again). She arrived a few days following Christmas, just in time for our Christmas Hop (as dances were called at West Point). These events were formal affairs, complete with hop cards and music by an orchestra from the West Point Band. It was an "old world" occasion, with the cadets in full dress uniforms and their ladies beautifully attired in their ballroom gowns. When the hop concludes with the traditional playing of *Army Blue*, it basically signals the end of the evening, leaving only enough time to walk your date back to the Thayer Hotel, which was about a mile away.

Dana was my first date during plebe year and getting to know her again and being with her was very special. It had been a very long time since I had a date, and just being together, walking, talking and holding hands was great. I believe that was the first time we kissed good night, when we got back to the Thayer. And of course that led to some great make out sessions during the following two days. It was difficult to find an inside place where we could be together without the eyes of a Tac, but there was sufficient motivation that we were able to solve that problem. By the time she headed home on the third day, I was in love again. She would reenter my life that summer.

West Point is a foreboding place in the winter, with just enough snow to cover the ground but usually not enough to present a "winter wonderland." The temperatures are below freezing and the wind from the north howls off the Hudson at bone-chilling speed. For cadets, the only place for privacy was Flirtation Walk but in sub-freezing temperatures it was not the greatest place to take a date in the freeze of night. Sometimes cadets could be seen heading toward "Flirty" with their dates and a portable typewriter case. Of course, the typewriter in the case had been substituted by a blanket.

During Christmas break there would be an opportunity for visiting family or guests to have a meal in the mess hall. In my day, the Cadet Mess fed about 2,000 hungry young men at one sitting. Today, that number is over 4,000. It takes an amazing bit of coordination to get that many men fed in less than an hour. Our 2,000-calorie meals were closely supervised by the upper classmen during plebe year. We had specific duties at the table and perfect manners were expected. Our meals followed a pattern. One day it would be cereal and fruit, the next bacon and eggs, etc. On pancake days there was a large pitcher of maple syrup on every table. It was referred to as the "Sammy Pitcher." Eventually, when I inquired why it was named thus, I was told the story dating back to the mid-1800's when the maple syrup was kept in a large wooden barrel just outside the kitchen. Sammy the cat, who usually frequents the kitchen, had been missing for several days, and it wasn't until the syrup barrel was nearly empty that Sammy was discovered. There, at the bottom of the barrel, was their dearly departed kitchen pet, Sammy the cat, who had always been a bit too curious. From then on, syrup containers were known by cadets as "Sammy Pitchers." With 200 years of tradition, the good stories never die.

Food items also often acquired special names. Since we were seated at ten-man tables, the cube of butter was pre-cut into ten patties. For some reason the slicing machine always left one end piece of butter a little bit larger than the other nine patties. This end piece was referred to by cadets as "Big Butter." Of course, "Big Butter" was a highly coveted item and normally the head of the table would exercise his prerogative in this regard. On rare occasions, Big Butter would get past a few upper classmen, but it was destined never to reach the plebe's end of the table. It wasn't until Christmas, when the upperclassmen had all departed for home, that I finally attained my first chance at Big Butter. Big Butter was evidently of sufficient gravitas that it became an item of mention in one cadet's written rating in the cadet rating system. His evaluation of the cadet concerned stated what he felt was the ultimate derision, "This Cadet always takes Big Butter!"

Sometimes, under special conditions, plebes were authorized to eat "at ease." Such occasions were very few; for instance, when Army would win the Army-Navy football game. But if a plebe could provide a particularly good joke or other entertainment, he might also win the opportunity to eat at ease. On "prune days," a plebe could "qualify" for relaxing at mealtime for a week if he were able to consume a hundred prunes during the meal. When the announcement was made that there was a plebe who wanted to qualify on prunes, the routine called for two of the plebes to go from table to table collecting prunes for the great event. Of course, everyone was ready to give up their prunes for such a worthy endeavor. Once a hundred or more prunes were collected, usually in just a matter of minutes, the contestant would have at 'em. It was an accomplishment to which I never aspired. However, my roommate, Bob Gould, who was a big guy with a healthy appetite, decided to go for it. He not only got through the 100 prunes but found 12 more to consume before announcing, "Sir, please pass the eggs."

One evening I came up with a scheme to qualify for "eating at ease." Since childhood I had always enjoyed practicing a few basic magic tricks, so when my wristwatch finally died a natural death, I came up with a scheme to use the dead watch to qualify for eating at ease. Seated at the foot of the table, I asked the requisite question: "Sir, may I eat at ease?" "And how do you expect to qualify for that, Mr. Hart?" responded the table commander. "Sir, I have a magic trick. Please pass me your watch." With some hesitation and trepidation, the head of the table passed his watch down to me. I had my old, broken watch in the palm of my hand so that when I threw the napkin over his watch, I actually had allowed his watch to drop into my lap. The napkin was covering my old watch, which would still tick for a few seconds when it was moved. I let the upperclassman next to me feel the watch and hear it tick. Then, using the napkin as a sling, I began furiously beating it against the table and smashing at it with the bottom of my coffee cup. The head of the table was becoming more and more agitated and concerned as I applied the coup de grace by dipping the napkin-covered watch into a glass of water several times. While dipping with my right hand I recovered his watch from my lap with my left hand. Then I did the reverse switch, letting my broken watch fall into my lap this time and removing the napkin to reveal his watch. Of course, by this time the table commander was trying hard to maintain his cool, but his face had changed color and there was no doubt in his mind that I had done him a job. When his watch was passed back to him, he grabbed it, inspected it closely and held it to his ear to see if it would still tick. Finally, finding nothing wrong with it, he uttered, "OK, you can fall out, Mr. Hart." That was great! I was content to have been awarded the "eating at ease" but my real reward was my performance and watching the table commander go apoplectic while trying not to show it.

Our relaxing Christmas ended in early January when the upper classes returned from their vacations at home and academics began again. In January 1953, as every year at that time, the Corps of Cadets was facing what we called Gloom Period. It was a time of short days and frigid months with little relief from academics. We also had upstate New York's usual miserable winter weather to cope with. But there was a glimmer of hope rippling through the Corps, anticipation that we would be called upon to march in President-elect Dwight Eisenhower's inaugural parade later that month. If that rumor materialized, it would indeed lift some of the gloom from January. Before long we learned that the Corps would indeed be headed for Washington, DC and the big event.

Late Monday night, January 19th, the barracks at West Point were alive with activity as we readied ourselves for the trip to Washington by train. At about one AM, cadets started pouring out of their rooms into the darkness and forming into their companies. In about ten minutes the entire Corps of Cadets, some 2,000 men, began the march down the hill to the train station. The 34th president of the United States was to be inaugurated at noon the next day, and the Corps of Cadets would be leading the parade. At the train station, we picked up box lunches before boarding, then piled into our seats and almost immediately fell asleep for the remainder of the six-hour trip. When the train jerked to a stop at Washington's Union Station, we struggled into the aisles to get dressed in our long overcoats, white cross-belts, cartridge boxes, rifles, full dress gray, uniform caps and gloves. Then we loaded into buses for a short ride to our assembly area. We were deposited within sight of the Capitol on New Jersey Avenue and off-loaded into our company formations. The inevitable command came, "If you are taller than the man in front of you, move up." Each company mass was twelve across and about sixteen deep.

The Order of Precedence dictated our marching order; first the Corps of Cadets, then the Midshipmen from Annapolis, followed by the Coast Guard Academy. As usual, our First Regiment would lead off, with Company A-1 going first at the head of the Corps, Company M-2 at the rear of the Corps. All 24 companies would also be sized, with the tallest cadets in each company in the front rank on down to the shortest ones in the last rank. The effect of the sizing was to give the Corps of Cadets the appearance of all being the same size as they gradually went from tallest to shortest and then back to tallest.

In an aside, it is interesting to note that although the companies in each regiment are lettered A through M, there is no Company J at West Point, or any military unit. The missing J may date back to the Romans and is also missing from the street lettering in Washington D.C.

D.C. can get mighty cold in January and that Tuesday was no exception. It was a nice clear day, but the temperature hovered near freezing until mid-morning. By eleven AM we were ready to go but it was close to one PM before things got moving. The band started to play somewhere in front of us. We were brought to attention and given the commands, "Right Shoulder, Arms! Forward, March!" We turned onto Pennsylvania Avenue, made a left turn by the Treasury Building, and headed toward the reviewing stand ahead. We marched in total silence and perfect unison, in time with the heavy beat of the drum. As we neared the reviewing stand each man stood tall, eyes front, gloved hands aligned on the steel butt plates of our M-1 rifles. We aligned ourselves with the man alongside and stayed directly behind the man in front. Suddenly the company guidons rose and the command "Eyes, left!" rang out. We all saw our new president standing there with Mamie by his side. He acknowledged the salutes of the brigade staff as they passed. Then came the command "Ready, Front!" and in less than a minute the great event was over.

It seemed a long march to our release point. Crowds lined the back streets and clapped as the gray formations swung past. I heard someone say, "Look, they're all the same size." Finally, we received the commands," Company Halt, Order, Arms, Dismissed!" Rifles were quickly stored, and most of us headed out for whatever activity was planned for the evening.

At the time, my father was commanding Cameron Station and living in Bethesda, Maryland so my destination was home for a brief visit. Before midnight I returned to Union Station with hundreds of other cadets from all parts of the sleeping city. First Call was sounded, then the command to attention. Our tactical officers walked through the long gray ranks in front of the train, roll was taken and then came the command to fall out and board the train. We all immediately fell asleep for the ride home and the only thing anyone remembers of the trip back, was the five AM long, cold, half-asleep march back up the hill from the train station to our barracks.

The Long Gray Line

About the time we got back from the inaugural ceremony there was a rumor floating around that there was to be a movie filmed at the Academy. The story line would be that of a salt-of-the-earth Irish immigrant who became an Army noncommissioned officer and spent his entire 50-year career at West Point. Marty Maher was a legend at the Academy who started off with janitorial duties in the cadet barracks. He was still around during my first couple of years there, but I never met him. The film was to be entitled *The Long Gray Line...*

That spring the Hollywood producer, actors and crew could be seen filming various scenes around the Academy. The stars were Tyrone Power (playing Marty Maher) and Maureen O'Hara, his eventual wife. It was an exciting time for the cadets to see snatches of the filming going on in various places at odd times. There were a few unrehearsed scenes which occurred throughout the film, such as when Maureen O'Hara, in a moment of joy, grabbed a passing cadet and kissed him, with the film crew recording his great surprise. Early in the filming, when I was walking through Central Area, I was stopped by a First Classman, who told me, "You man, halt! Post over there and line up with the others for a film shot." As we stood at attention, a young Peter Graves, showing Marty around, appeared on my left with Tyrone Power (Marty Maher), who raised his pipe and pointed it a few inches from my nose, saying in a fine Irish Brogue, "By golly, they are in such a straight line you could shoot all their noses off with one shot!"

Years later, when the film was produced and first released, that particular scene showed up on posters in front of theaters all over the country. It wasn't until the turn of the century that I learned the existence of the poster and eventually was able to purchase it online. Of course, after that I always referred to Tyrone Power as co-starring with me in the film. Below is a copy of the poster with me on the right of Marty Maher, who is pointing his pipe at my nose. It was filmed in color and "cinematography," which was then the latest development in wide screen filming. Eventually, after several TV viewings, I purchased a cassette tape of the film but much to my chagrin it was not a wide screen reproduction and only an indistinguishable half of my face showed. Here is the poster of a scene from the 1955 release of *The Long Gray Line*:

The movie, *The Long Gray Line*

That first year of academics took a heavy toll of classmates, since we had lost perhaps 150 cadets from our starting number of 676. Our day began with the reveille cannon at 5:50 AM, followed by reveille formation ten minutes later at 6:00, Breakfast formation and inspection was at 6:30 AM and classes began at 8 AM. Our daily classes included English, math, chemistry, a foreign language and PE, usually about five hours a day ending at 3 PM. The time from 3 to 5 PM was filled with several scheduled activities, including drill and ceremonies, parade practice, intramural athletics and guard duty. Then at 5:30 PM was dinner formation and again inspection. Dinner was followed by study time in our rooms from 7 until 9:30 PM. There was no free time until the weekend. Occasionally the schedule provided a few minutes to catch a haircut, pick up laundry, and shine brass and shoes. At 10 PM the bugle played Taps and all lights were off before that last, mournful note was sounded.

But our week didn't end on Friday. Saturday mornings, classes went from 8:30 to 11:30 AM. After lunch, and about twice a month, we paraded in full dress uniform. The summer uniform included highly starched white trousers. We routinely used our bayonets to pry open the starched trouser legs to ensure the crease wasn't broken. Then, with brass and shoes highly shined, we reported for "Parade Formation" and of course, inspection. Our weekend free time began Saturdays after lunch, or after parade, if we didn't have guard duty, intercollegiate sports or demerit penalties to walk off on the area. Sunday was almost a complete day off but first we formed up for breakfast at 9 AM and then again at 10:30 to march to church before we could call the day ours.

Our classes were relatively small, ranging from 15 to 20 cadets. West Point's academic program called for every student to be tested every day in every subject. We had no concept of not completing an assignment. Without fail, we were expected to demonstrate assignment completion at the blackboard or by turning in a written assignment. Sometimes we had a spot quiz, usually in math, if not demonstrating our homework by standing at the blackboard solving problems. At other times cadets would be called on to recite or explain their solution to a problem. At the end of each six-week period, we were given a Written Partial Review, referred to as a WPR. At the end of the semester there was a "Written General Review, WGR." Those who did well on these tests would be moved up a section or two. In most subjects there were about 20 separate class sections. If you were very bright and did well, you would be in the first or second section. If you were "academically challenged" you would be in sections 19 or 20. The highest section, I ever achieved was third section physics. For the most part I was between sections 14 and 18. Those sections moved at a slightly slower pace and had less demanding problems to solve. This interesting concept, for the most part, kept everyone working at their max capability.

Perhaps the most notable difference between West Point and other colleges was the Academy's dedication to the "whole man" concept. We were being challenged academically every day, as well as physically, emotionally and psychologically. We were required to attend chapel each Sunday for moral development, were supervised at meals, had to participate athletically and behave responsibly. We were not allowed to drink alcohol and were obligated not to lie, cheat or steal, nor tolerate those who did. As this went on, day after day, month after month, year after year, it began to mold us into the men we were expected to be. Another big difference was that in college you needed to reach within yourself and find the self-discipline to complete your studies, or you may drop by the wayside and of course many did. At West Point, during that first year, you either did what you had to do or packed your bags. You knew that the option of walking away was always there but of course you toughed it out because that is what you signed up for and there was no way you would admit to yourself, your friends, or your parents that you couldn't hack it.

At the end of the first year there was a week of final exams. Each subject was covered with a final written review which lasted anywhere from 3 to 5 hours. If a cadet failed one or two subjects, they could retake the exam at the end of the week. If they failed more than two subjects or failed the re-examination, the cadet had to leave the Academy but could retake the exam at the end of summer to determine if they could repeat the year. Amazingly, the professors would stay up all night if necessary to assure the results of the exams would be posted in the morning. This was a leadership factor which falls under the heading of "Taking Care of Your Men". Unlike in many colleges, 2,000 cadets weren't left wondering and waiting to find out how they did on their final exams. I was astounded to learn that at most universities the results of the exams are mailed to the students, weeks or sometimes months later. The day after our exams the entire Corps of Cadets viewed their results on the walls of the sally ports. Listed there, on page after page, posted side by side, were the results of our testing and our new class standing in each subject and overall. For additional motivation, a copy was mailed to our parents and if a cadet was there by congressional appointment, a copy was sent to their congressman.

Grades and class standing were important, but the high point of Plebe year occurred during graduation week, known as "June Week.". That first week of June was crammed with ceremonies, parades, social and graduation activities. Toward the end, just before the graduation ceremony, was graduation parade, with full pomp and ceremony. After the opening portion of the parade the graduating class left their places in the ranks and lined up in front of the reviewing stand. At that time the Corps of Cadets passed in review, rendering a final salute to the graduating class while the band played the *Graduation March*. At the end of the parade, the Corps marched off the parade ground to their respective company areas for the "Recognition Ceremony." At this event, Plebe Year officially ended, and the plebes became a part of the upper classes and were recognized by a handshake. For the first time we were addressed by the upper classmen by our first names. Plebe Year, the great hurdle, the imprinting which lasts a lifetime, was finally over and for the first time in a year, we could leave the Academy for home and a full month of leave.

It had been a long year, one in which we were not permitted to leave the Academy even for Christmas or Easter, so understandably we were looking forward to, and making big plans, for our first great escape in a year; an entire month of summer leave! The memories of my Plebe year have lasted a lifetime for me, as I believe would be the case for all cadets who endured that experience. Graduation Parade and Recognition combined to create a glorious and memorable occasion.

I, and several other classmates, were planning to spend that summer month traveling to Europe. My close friend from prep school, Bob Arnold and I, would travel together and stay at my grandmother's home at Nice on the French Riviera. I had never met her. She had never been to America, and I had not been to Europe. Now I was 20, she was 79, and our meeting was long overdue. Bob and I decided we would travel by Military Air Transport Service (MATS) from an Air Force base at Patterson, NJ. The Air Force guys went out of their way to accommodate cadets with their summer travel plans, so we had no trouble catching a hop on one of the flights to Frankfurt. In those pre-jet days, our first stop was Newfoundland. Next was an overnight at Lages AFB in the Azores. The next morning our flight continued to Frankfurt, Germany. It was exciting stuff for me, being on my own in a foreign country for the first time.

About 5 AM, Bob and I got off the plane in Frankfurt, wearing our cadet summer uniforms. We had no idea what to do with ourselves, but Bob was never short on ideas. After making arrangements for a place to stay at the Rhine Main AFB BOQ, he picked up the phone and called the base motor pool. I am not sure what he said but before long our car and driver had arrived, and we checked into our BOQ room. An astounding bit of "chutzpah" for a young cadet, but it worked!

The following morning, we found our way into town and before long had located a local beer garden. By 1953, Germany had nearly fully recovered from the war and only a few buildings with bomb damage remained in the downtown area of Frankfurt. Across from the beer garden was a large building with doors on the side facing us. As we were preparing to leave the garden, the side doors of the building opened and 50 or 60 people dressed in coat and tie came out onto the sidewalk. Most of them were lighting up cigarettes and milling around. Bob and I were also dressed in coat and tie. We crossed the street, lit up our cigarettes and mingled with the Germans. After about another ten minutes a bell rang, and everyone started filing back into the building. Bob and I joined the crowd. Once inside, we could see it was an opera house. After everyone was seated, we took two unoccupied seats and waited to see what we had gotten into. Before long, Act 2 of "Madame Butter Flieger" began. The songs were in German, but we still enjoyed being there and were proud of our successful escapade in gaining entry.

After another night in Frankfurt, we caught a train to Paris and found a place to stay for a few days. While in Paris, we took in the sidewalk cafés on the Champs Elysees, Mont Maître, the Follies Bergère and the Eiffel Tower. After a year of celibacy, finding female companionship was high on our list of must do. Additionally, there were exciting places to visit, but our destination had always been Nice, where I had planned for us to stay for nearly three weeks with my grandmother at her home. This would be the first time I had ever met her, and it was time we got ourselves headed in that direction. The subway took us to the train station on the south side of Paris, where we pondered whether to travel by second or third class. First class was out of our league. Again, we settled on third class and saved a few francs. I was surprised to find that in third class we were travelling with the chickens and pigs. It was an interesting trip, with several country stops when farmers boarded with their small animals to make a short trip to market. The 300-mile trip, passing through Lyon and Marseilles, took most of the day. I had called Grandmother and told her of our arrival time in Nice. She arranged for her dear friend, Mr. Renouci, to meet us at the train station.

Seeing Nice and the Cote d'Azure for the first time was an impressive experience. The Alps Maritime rise abruptly behind the coastal cities and the Mediterranean Sea reflects the blue of the sky. It was calm and inviting. It wasn't hard for Renouci to recognize two Americans standing on the curb. His English was as limited as my French, but we managed to exchange a few words of introduction. Several blocks later, he stopped his car at a small kiosk on the waterfront to buy us an "aperitif", a heavy sherry-like wine mixed with a bit of soda water. As a non-drinker, I found it to be rather bitter. It was one of those drinks you need to develop a taste for. We then continued the last couple miles to my grandmother's home. The old chateau at 9 Route de Billet, on the edge of town, was surrounded by a ten-foot stucco wall with a large door-gate. Inside the wall was a garden of roses and cherry trees which had, for many years, been uncared for. In fact, the whole turn of the century home had something of the same unloved appearance.

Grandmother greeted us in the garden. All my ancestral genes sprang to attetion. Her English was excellent, since she had been born in England and lived there until at least a teenager. She showed Bob and me to our bedroom, where we would be sharing a double bed which got scant use by us, since we frenetically set about to cram enough fun into our next 18 days as possible to make up for a year's worth of confinement at West Point.

The next day we walked the short distance to Place Macina, where we caught the bus into town. It wasn't long before we found a USO Club (United Services Organization), created by President Franklin D. Roosevelt in 1941 to meet the morale needs of the servicemen and women during WW II. It was in downtown Nice and was organized to support the off duty needs of the 6th Fleet, headquartered there at the time. We attended one of the evening dances put on by the USO and found a couple of French girls our age who were willing to show us the sights in town. My new friend's name was Monique, whom I dated for the next several days. She was a trim, nice looking young lady and it was more than interesting for me to be with someone from a totally different culture. She worked during the day but the standard in those days was two hours off for lunch. So, we met nearly every day during her lunch hours. Sometimes we would enjoy an hour or more on the beach and go out in the evening. In those days the "bikini" was popular in France but had not yet been accepted in the US. Over time, we got to know each other. Being with a French girl was an interesting and delightful experience after the horrible rigors of plebe year. Needless to say, our make out sessions were the highlight of the year. Understandably, she gave me some wonderful lessons in the famous "French Kiss". I never asked her age, but assume It was somewhere between 18 and 22. There was never any thought of a lasting relationship. It was a summer fling which would end when I left to return to West Point. Before going out about 8 PM, we would go in to say goodnight to Grandmother. One evening she said, with her slight French accent and a twinkle in her eye, "You boys look very handsome this evening. I am sure you will have many conquests."

Our days passed pleasantly and all too soon, it was time to find our way back to Frankfurt to catch a hop to the U.S. When we boarded the plane, to our surprise there were several other classmates and friends. We traded stories of our first great taste of freedom and shared memories of that wonderful summer month.

CHAPTER 13

MY SECOND YEAR

It was the beginning of July when we reported back to West Point for Cadet Summer Training at Camp Buckner, on the shores of Lake Popolopen in the Adirondacks, a vacation-like setting just a few miles from West Point proper. Unlike our Plebe summer, here our trainers had built in time for fun. There were sailboats, tennis courts, dances and swimming, a great combination of fun and work. The summer would end with several days of festivities, competitions and a three-day visit of dates, ending with a dance and parade. There was much to learn and much to do.

With great pride, we had donned our new insignia, the helmet of Pallas Athena on a blue-colored shield; the blue indicating we were Yearlings. Summer training would be at a more advanced level than our previous Plebe summer. It would involve bridge building, firing weapons such as machine guns and rocket launchers, and negotiating difficult obstacle courses and night compass courses. Map reading, radio-telephone procedures, and squad tactics were also part of the summer curriculum. It closely paralleled the Basic Infantry Course required for newly-commissioned officers.

Our days were filled with field training activities but were limited mostly to eight hours a day and five days a week, which gave us time to enjoy the lake and get to know our classmates. There was also time to get in trouble. The challenge in previous years had been to surreptitiously throw the reveille cannon into the lake. To assure that wouldn't happen again, the commanding officer of the camp had the reveille cannon bolted to a concrete stand and a cadet guard posted on the cannon every night. Before long, the wily cadets figured that with the correct tool and about five minutes to work they could get the cannon unbolted. But the guard posited another problem. Finally, a plan was devised to foil the guard detail, which was relieved by a new set of guards every four hours. The routine was for the guard detail to march to each designated guard post, dropping off the new guards and picking up the old ones. The new guard would assume his post and the old guard would be relieved and march away with the guard detail. So, a fake guard detail was created and about seven minutes ahead of the scheduled relief, they marched to the cannon post and relieved the old guard with their own "cannon removal detail." As soon as the improvised detail left, other cadets sprang from the bushes, unscrewed the bolts and lifted the cannon from its mount. The following morning, when the cannon was discovered in the lake, the Colonel was furious but to no avail. His next action was to weld the bolts holding the cannon. As it turned out, that too was only a partial solution. It wasn't long before cadets found a way to paint the cannon candy-striped.

Our special summer at Lake Popolopen concluded at the end of August on a long weekend of fun events which included dates for the dance. I had planned to ask my Christmas love, Dana Dewey, to come up from Washington D.C for the occasion. I had met Dana at a "coming out" cotillion in D.C when on Spring Leave from the prep school and we had hit it off. We had a couple dates when I returned during the year to visit Father and Cooks. So, during our confined plebe Christmas at West Point, she was able come to the academy for a formal dance weekend which cemented our growing feelings for each other even though she was 3+ years younger than me, and in her last year of high school. We were able to get together again when she came to Buckner for the 4th of July weekend, and I asked her up for the big Labor Day weekend. But before our 4th of July weekend ended, her mother drove up from Washington and took her home! With her mother's intervention, our relationship had suddenly changed. She would now be attending the Labor Day weekend events with another cadet. I was crushed! It was never completely clear to me exactly what had happened but a few weeks earlier my mother had asked for Dana's address, since I had written to Mother telling her of my new love. I presume that Mother was feeling left out of my life and wrote Dana to tell her that indeed she, not Cooks, was my real mother. Dana's socially upward leaning mother evidently took this greatly askance and forbade her daughter to continue in the relationship. I was heartbroken when Dana arrived to be with another classmate for the events of the long weekend. Ah but true love cannot be so easily thwarted!

The opening event of the long weekend was a semi-formal dance. It was a magical setting, with the mess hall transformed into a dance pavilion on the edge of the lake. Cadets were all in their dress whites, the ladies in gay, semi-formal cocktail attire. Not all cadets attending had dates and before long, I swallowed my pride and asked Dana to dance. Within those three minutes it was apparent that we both still had strong feelings for each other and by the time the evening was over, I had supplanted her date. Dana and I spent the next two wonderful days together, sailing and enjoying our reunion. When her mother found out, she was prohibited from seeing me, nor did Dana ever come back to West Point. Summer ended and with a heavy heart. It was the 4th love of my young life so before long, having been there before, I was able to shake it off. The best recovery for a broken heart is to love again. I left Lake Popolopen to board the bus returning us to West Point and the beginning of the more serious activities of our second academic year.

Yearling year at West Point is a great year. I knew the routine and what was expected of me, and academics had not yet crescendoed into the complex engineering courses I would face the following year. We had lost nearly 20 percent of our classmates that first year, so our rooms and roommates were reshuffled. My old roommates Don Holleder and Bob Gould went to another room and Ernie, and I took on Mit Shattuck and Maury Cralle. The cast I wore for so much of plebe year was off my wrist, and I had settled into to a good relationship with my new roommates. Now, we had enough time on weekends to start dating and that was a major focus of our free time.

Ernie had been getting letters from Reader's Digest asking him to re-subscribe. The letters were always signed by "Carolyn Davis", the nom de plume still in use today by Reader's Digest. Then, one day Ernie decided to write this Carolyn Davis and invite her to West Point for a football weekend. By the time she wrote back (giving her real name) and accepting, Ernie had already arranged for another date. To solve the dilemma we decided that Mit, who was without a date for that weekend, would play the part of Ernie Wilson. That weekend I had asked Joanne Quick, my old high school flame, to come to West Point, so it would be up to Mit to pull off the sham. Of course, a simple explanation to "Carolyn" would have solved the problem but I guess the "date switch" had more intrigue for everyone. So, Mit became Ernie for the weekend. However, after a few hours of this subterfuge he found he was continually explaining to his date why people (who were not in on the scam) were not calling him Ernie. Finally the incongruity of the name change was becoming obvious and before the weekend ended the sham fell apart. His date didn't take the matter too seriously. She had come to West Point to meet someone she didn't know and to enjoy the football game and the dance. Her name wasn't Carolyn Davis.

I was a bit surprised that Joanne had accepted my invitation for that football weekend after three years of no contact. Perhaps she had better memories of our first date than I did. But we were both 21 and different people with three years of maturity. Joanne was in her third year of college somewhere in Pennsylvania and not yet involved with anyone. We had a grand time getting caught up and this time Saturday evening ended with an enduring make-out session. Sunday, after church, it was mostly goodbye time. We should have taken a stroll down Flirtation Walk but believe it or not, I didn't know where it was and graduated without ever being there. There was some kind of spark that occurred when I was with her. She was a well-shaped girl and taller than my other loves. I would guess about five foot eight We had a grand time getting caught up and this time Saturday evening ended with an enduring make-out session and the spark became a flame. After three days of being together I was very interested and her feelings towards me were the same. That summer when I was spending my month of leave with father and Cooks in Bethesda, Maryland, she came to visit for several days and that cemented her being my third love and, possibly a candidate for marriage.

The Army-Navy football game was always a big occasion, complete with rallies, bonfires, and heavy excitement. The entire Corps would be transported by train to Philadelphia. After the game, as upperclassmen, we were free to party it up around town and drink a few beers until it was time to board our train for the return trip to West Point. Missing the 11 PM formation at the train station would result in severe consequences. At 11:00 PM sharp we lined up, by company, in front of the thirty or so railroad passenger cars. The roll was taken. As we boarded our train, some cadets were in bad shape. Everyone slept on the trip back to West Point. At about 4 AM we were awakened to disembark. That march up the hill to our barracks, in the dark and cold of December, was a sobering experience. However, before being released to collapse in our rooms, there was a final roll call. One cadet was missing. Everybody agreed that he had been on the train during the trip, but nobody knew what had happened to him. The mystery continued all day Sunday, up until suppertime, when finally, our lost comrade came dragging in. He related how he had indeed been on the train and how he had found it necessary to answer the call of nature. He had found his way to the restroom and locked himself in. At that point, he was off to dreamland. When he awakened, the train was parked in a large and deserted freight yard in what turned out to be Buffalo, New York! The bus trip back had been long, painful, and filled with grim forebodings of the consequences. And his late arrival did, indeed, win him sufficient punishment to spend his next ten weekends in confinement. Being late was one of the unforgivable sins at West Point, and it didn't matter what the mitigating circumstances were; late was late.

The rest of yearling year was relatively benign academically. All our core subjects were basic to an engineering degree except for a language elective. My two high school years of French had pretty well carried me through the first two semesters at the Academy. But, in my third and fourth semesters of French, I was bogging down. I had moved up to the third section of physics (of 20 sections), but I was now in the last section of French and just hanging on. I somehow squeaked through the final exam and was more than ready to begin my summer vacation with my father and stepmother in Bethesda, Maryland, where they had moved when Father retired earlier that year. During my Easter vacation in the D.C. area, I had attended a half dozen "Debutante Balls," but had not met anyone I wanted to date. During the spring of the academic year I had, on a couple of occasions, asked Joanne up from Pennsylvania for a weekend. She was becoming my new love and later that summer she spent most of a week with us in Bethesda during my summer leave with my folks. She soon became my fourth true love. I had known Joanne for four years and I suspect we may have eventually gotten married were it not for my return to San Francisco the following Christmas when I met Barbara.

Cadet Hart (yearling) 1953

CHAPTER 14

MY THIRD YEAR & MY FUTURE WIFE

Barb and I met in December 1954 when I was a Second Classman (Junior)and came home to San Francisco for Christmas leave to be with Mother over the holidays. I had not been home for well over a year, since Father was close by in Washington, DC and many social activities, classmates and friends were also there. A couple of days after I got home, Mother casually mentioned that she was having a friend and her family over for drinks Christmas Eve, saying that they had two children about my age. Meanwhile, a girl I had been dating from Rutgers University called to tell me that she was in San Francisco and had come out from New Jersey on a lark with her girlfriend who was from the Bay Area. Knowing she was away from home, I asked her to join us for Christmas Eve. I was only half-way interested in her but since she was away from home it seemed appropriate to include her in our Christmas Eve party, to which she acquiesced. Mother also said OK to Cynthia's joining us for Christmas Eve, even though she had mentioned that she had asked a neighbor family and their two adult children to join us.

Mothers play such a big role in our lives. Mine was certainly not intrusive but her love and concern often found their way into my life. So, it was not out of character for her to have arranged our Christmas Eve gathering, purportedly for dessert and coffee with neighbors but actually so their daughter and I could meet. I did not connect the dots, that the real purpose was for "boy to meet girl", since this was of course years before my sensitivity training (a short course lasting through the first 40 years of marriage). In fact, had Mother's subterfuge not been so subtle, I wouldn't have asked Cynthia over that evening.

To my surprise, the neighbors' daughter turned out to be a first year college student at UC who was quite attractive and here I was with Cynthia, from Rutgers! I guess you could call it love at first sight. The chemistry was there and before the evening ended, the bits and pieces of her soul were touching mine. Our destiny was taking shape. *"She was a phantom of delight when first she gleamed upon my sight."* (Wordsworth). Unlike I, Barbara knew she was coming that evening to meet a blind date. So, when she found me already with a date she was rather upset and tried to ignore me. There I was, in this awkward situation of having a date when I was supposed to be meeting Barbara. And as luck would have it, Barb was someone I was immediately attracted to. But she was a bit miffed at the Cynthia situation and was holding back. When I spoke to her, she pretended that she didn't hear me, so her mother stepped into the breach, saying, "Why Barbara, I think Renny is trying to say something to you."

Barb claims her play at disinterest peaked mine. I might add that my being with another girl, might have peaked hers? I have always denied that but what do I know? Anyway, the next day I called her to arrange a date and explain the prior evening. It took eating a lot of crow and a handful of violets to get us back on track. Barb already had a date for New Year's Eve, so the best I could do was arrange to meet her around midnight as her second date of the evening. In another couple of days, it was time for us both to be back to school, she at UC Berkeley and I returning east.

At school, now a Second Classman, I was in the midst of the Academy's most difficult academic year. We were immersed in several demanding engineering courses; organic chemistry, strength of materials, electrical circuits (nicknamed "Juice" by cadets) and fluid dynamics to name a few. Fortunately, I enjoyed engineering and did well with those types of subjects. I understood chemistry well enough that I was spending time coaching my roommate Ernie after hours. However, my other roommate, Bob Gould, was really bogging down, about to succumb and wash out. One of the heavier courses we were taking was thermodynamics, which was primarily heat transfer, volumetrics, pressure and how they were related. Bob Gould and I were in the same section (classroom) in thermodynamics. One day when we filed in and stood behind our desks, the instructor ordered the usual, "Take seats," and then went to the blackboard. With his pointer he directed our attention to the sketch he had made of a large graph. He said, "Gentlemen, this is an adiabatic curve. What happens to the temperature of the gas when we go from this point of the curve (pointing) down to this point?" He looked at Bob Gould, addressing him erroneously as "Mr. Jones." Bob responded, correcting the instructor on his name by saying "Gould, sir." The instructor misunderstood and said loudly, "That's right, Jones, it's COOLED." And that, of course, was the only time Bob ever got a right answer in that class.

Barb and I were exchanging letters and two months later, in March of 1955, with Easter vacation approaching, I made plans to go west to see my mother and my new love. But, in early March '55, Father had been admitted to Walter Reed Hospital with the return of his colon cancer, under terminal conditions. I was now faced with the decision of going home on my Spring leave to see my mother and my beloved or spend the ten days in Washington DC. Of course, the call of love is very strong in the young and had grown stronger through our many letters and months of separation. I answered the primal call of love and went to San Francisco. When I returned to West Point from my Spring Leave, Father was gone. The long conversations we could have shared together, would never happen now. I was 21, he was 63 and it seemed that our conscionable life together could probably be measured in days, yet it was enough that I long ago aspired to be like him.

Now that father was gone, I carried the guilt of having made the Easter vacation decision to see my fiancée-to-be, rather than my father and for not having been with my father at his death. I suspect my stepmother did not tell me Father was dying because it was either not apparent or she knew it was important my studies not be interrupted during that difficult academic period. Now, sixty years later and with the perspective of time, I think that had I not gone to San Francisco to see my love, our relationship may not have survived the Berkeley competition for her nor my still warm feelings for Joanne. During those ten days of Easter vacation, we spent much of each day together and before I returned to West Point, we were pinned. The letters flowed; I was writing perhaps four or five times a week plus an occasional phone call, which in those days was very expensive.

The death of my Father was a heavy, emotional blow. I was not ready for him to go. It was only the week after I had turned 22 and we had not yet enjoyed being adults together. Walter Reed was a few hours south and I could have been granted emergency leave to go home if my stepmother had told me Father was dying. She did not wish to disrupt my studies and Father passed on without my seeing him.

When I was notified of his death I went home to Bethesda, Maryland on emergency leave for a few days, very upset that I had not gotten to see my father before he died. My stepmother was at loose ends. I took over the task of making funeral arrangements, choosing the casket and reaching the decision to bury him at Arlington National Cemetery. This responsibility was a bit heavy for a 22-year-old, but West Point had taught me to take charge, step into the breach and do what you must do. It was part of the transition from boy to man. The funeral service was brief. Father's casket was open, and he was in full uniform. He looked as I had remembered him, a handsome officer in his prime. My intense grief blurred other details. At Arlington, the *Funeral March* was played, and the caisson was drawn by two horses. Behind it came a saddled horse, boots reversed in the stirrups but no rider. The rider, my father, was in the caisson. At the grave site the casket was lowered, four riflemen fired three volleys and Taps was played by a far-off bugler. My Father was buried. I knew so little of him, only that he was the kind of man I wanted to be with. I was 22, he was 63 and it seemed that our conscionable life together could probably be measured in days, yet it was enough that I long ago aspired to be like him. He commanded respect and appeared in control. I miss him greatly but mostly I miss all the years which could have been and weren't.

That summer, when I came back to San Francisco on leave, I was carrying our engagement ring, a miniature of my West Point ring. We had discussed the type of ring I was buying, and Barb decided on white gold. My mother gave me Grandfather's tie clasp, which was set with a diamond in the center and several chips on each side. Barb's ring was set with the large diamond in the center, surrounded by the chips. The net effect of the setting was to make the three-quarter carat diamond appear much larger. I was impressed with the final product and anxious to consummate our engagement with this special symbol of our love. Of course, the occasion of my proposal for this grand event demanded a special ring ceremony! I also felt it appropriate that I first ask Barb's father for permission to marry his daughter. This part of the engagement was a bit uncomfortable for me but I finally ginned up my courage and asked her father if we could get married when I graduated from West Point. After a few questions, he of course said yes.

Once through that ordeal, I made a date with Barb for that evening and arranged to borrow my brother's car. Prior to picking her up, I hid an ice bucket, a bottle of Champagne, and a couple of glasses in the back seat. My plan was for us to first have a drink at the Tonga Room in the Fairmont Hotel, then drive to Mt. Tamaulipas. The Tonga Room in 1955 was "altissimo!" Our drinks had the little umbrella sticking out of the orange wedge and soon the lights flashed, thunder roared, and rain poured as a raft of ukulele-playing Hawaiians came floating across the water (on what I presume was at one time a swimming pool). At about seven in the evening, following our Tonga Room experience, we drove to the top of Mt. Tamalipas, arriving just in time to watch the sunset. Soon the pink glow faded into one of those clear California nights where the points of light on the distant horizon blend with the emerging array of stars. After a few well-tempered kisses, the stage was set for the right moment to pop the question. I don't remember the exact response but her "YES" certainly must have been a joyous one for both of us. Then out came the ring, sparkling in all its glory. I had decided on a white gold ring that was a miniature of my ring. The center diamond with the surrounding diamond chips had come from my grandfather's tie clasp. I placed the ring on her finger. Following her gasps of delight, I reached behind the seat for the Champagne and the two glasses I had stashed for the occasion. That was 67 years ago at this writing. I was 22; she was 19 and of course we lived happily ever after.

Before returning to West Point, we had several dates a couple of which were particularly memorable. On one occasion we went to the Fairmont Hotel for a drink before dinner to visit their newly constructed "Hawaiian Room" A swimming pool on the main floor had been turned into a cocktail lounge with tables surrounding the pool. Of course, all the drinks had little umbrellas in them. Suddenly, there was the sound of heavy rain and thunder and across the pool came a canoe with several Hawaiian musicians strumming Hawaiian music. Very impressive! When I returned 20 years later it was all gone.

Another memorable date was a visit to one of San Francisco's historic brothels which had been turned into a cocktail lounge named after the famous consort, Salley Rand. At the time she was a well-known burlesque dancer, renown for her ostrich feather and balloon dances. She had retired years before and died at age 76. At the time, the entertainment was a totally unknown, young man who was still in college at SF State University. He had a very unusually smooth voice that was impressive and thoroughly enjoyable. His name was Johnnie Mathis. Today, Johnnie is 86 years old, and still entertaining.

With only a year left at the Academy before graduation, we decided that Barb should come east to school at Christmas. Her folks went along with this, and our planning ensued. The University of Connecticut at Storrs was not too far from West Point, and we were able to finalize Barb's transfer there so we would have some time together for my last semester. I wanted her to see the Academy and get a glimpse of what the Army would be like. I also felt it was important for her to have some insight into the strange life we aspiring officers were leading at the Military Academy and for us to be together for the social events that take place during the final semester before graduation. Barb's parents acquiesced in our plans and arranged for her to come east by train in early January to arrive at U Conn before her semester began.

After summer leave in June, all cadets returned to West Point for two months of military training before beginning the next academic year. We members of the new First Class, "Firsties," were now in charge of the Corps. The photo below has significance in that Fred's father was a Major General in the Air Force. When he flew us from Fort Benniing to to the AF Base in Mobile he let me fly the plane. That's when I got hooked on becoming a p\pilot.

Fred Dent and I, Summer 1955

The remaining summer months would be directed at honing their leadership skills before beginning our last year of academics. Some of us would take charge of the new Plebes entering in July, acting as their cadre. Others would spend the remainder of their summer, training new Yearlings at nearby Camp Buckner. A select few would be chosen to go to various training commands throughout the Army to act as "Third Lieutenants" within those organizations, assuming positions as platoon leaders.

I was one of the 150 cadets selected to train the new Yearlings at Camp Buckner. Our first week was spent going over the training they would receive. I particularly remember our "log training" exercise. The logs were about 20 feet long, like telephone poles without the splinters. Four cadets were assigned to each log. I guess the concept was to build bodies as well as coordinated teamwork. On command the logs were lifted waist high, then over our heads, right shoulder, left shoulder, etc. Suddenly the voice of Colonel Julian J. Ewell exploded across the training field, "You man with the disreputable tee shirt, who are you?" Holding the log over my head had exposed a hole in my tee shirt which I did not know was there. It was the first of many encounters I had that summer with Colonel Ewell, who was famous for saving the day in WW II when his battalion of Screaming Eagles dropped into Holland.

But, despite the ubiquitous Julian J. Ewell, I managed to complete our summer training in good shape and we again began our academic endeavors after Labor Day in September.

Our football season was soon under way and Army's winning team provided great weekend relief from the weight of academics. By mid-fall, it was time for Firsties to receive the class rings we had ordered, and this provided one more element of proof that the long road to graduation was nearing an end. Trying on our new rings and comparing our stone selection with our classmates was and exciting occasion. That weekend was our Ring Hop, a formal dance to mark the occasion. For me it was a downer, my love was in San Francisco until after Christmas.

Following that, came yet another milestone; it was time to order our NEW CARS! I had a promise of $1,000 from my mother and another thousand from my stepmother Cooks, as early graduation presents, so that I could buy a car. There would be 480 new cars bought that month, and the agencies handling the sales were able to give us rock bottom prices for such a large order. After much poring over the options of which make and model to choose, I decided on a blue and white, six cylinder Chevy Bel Air with Landau top. It cost $1,879. Today, of course, the '56 Chevy is a classic, but mine is long gone.

The first Saturday I could get away, using one of the six weekend passes we were allowed as First Classmen, I drove to Connecticut in my new 1956 Chevy Bel Air. It was the earliest occasion we were allowed to use our newly purchased cars. We had not been together since Christmas, and I was greatly anticipating our Saturday reunion. Barb's dorm curfew required her to be back at 11 PM, so we had lots of time that Saturday to get caught up. I dropped her off before her deadline and went back to my visitors' quarters for the night. We could not be together again until 8 AM when the young ladies were allowed to sally forth from their dorm.

I set my alarm for what I thought was 7 AM and when it went off quickly arose, showered and dressed. Unbeknownst to me, I arrived at her dorm an hour and five minutes too early. The alarm had gone off at 6 and I hadn't noticed. The dorm was locked up tighter than a drum and no lights were on in the building. It was then I checked my watch and found that somehow, I was an hour off in my time. What to do? There was a still a couple of inches of snow on the ground, the sun had just risen above the horizon, and the temperature was around 30 degrees.

Waiting around for an hour until for the doors opened, was not an option. I thought to myself that perhaps I could somehow wake Barb and get her out of there earlier. I knew approximately where her room was, so decided that if I could gain entry to the building, I could awaken her and get the show on the road. It proved to be a classic case of fuzzy, and fallacious thinking gone awry.

The latticework on either side of the front door presented an opportunity to put my plan into action. It was just high enough for an agile 22 year-old to climb and thereby get onto the ledge that surrounded the second floor. My idea was to edge around the building on the ledge until I got to what I thought was her window, then do a tap, tap, tap. The lattice was strong, and the ledge was about a foot wide, so there was no problem in getting to the window at the end of the building. When there was no response from my window tapping, I decided to try the window at the end of the hall, go inside and look for names on the doors. Perhaps it was my inner child that guided me as I climbed through the second-floor window of U Conn's women's dorm at 7 AM that morning. From the ledge outside the hall window, I carefully lifted the window sash. As I stepped into the darkened hall, the lights went on and I suddenly found myself face to face with a very irate Dorm Mother. She asked, in her most accusatory tone, "Just what do you think you are doing?" It wasn't exactly a question and in my compromised situation, meaningful explanations seemed to go mealy as I spoke. My mutterings all echoed weak and evasive.

I later learned that one of the professors that icy Sunday morning was on his way to do some lab work when he spotted a tall young man making his way up the lattice at the lady's dorm. He called the House Mother, and the rest is history. Many words and several heartbeats later, after some successful convincing, I was finally off the hook. I think when my inner child began to shine through my innocence was apparent.

The next time Barb came to West Point, I gave her the keys to my new car so she would be able to drive to West Point for the social events and weekend get-togethers. We were together now almost every weekend. There was the "Hundredth Night Show," a cadet production marking a hundred days until graduation, many sporting events, visits to Flirtation Walk, and dances. Finally, my last week at the Academy arrived.; a whirlwind of events packed into what was called "June Week." There were parades, athletic events, dances, uniform fittings and all that had to happen in preparation for graduation. Barb's folks were due to arrive about the 3rd of June, and we were supposed to pick them up in New York City at the airport where they were arriving. But when that day and time came, we were caught up in a dozen things and the three- or four-hour trip to and from the airport was not going to be possible without missing some highly important events. We decided to send them a telegram, having seen in the movies how the American Express agent walks around calling out "Telegram for Mr. & Mrs. Rising." But of course, it didn't work that way and they never got the telegram. That was about 30 years before the advent of cell phones. They waited as long as they could stand and then made arrangements to find their way to West Point. Having left them in the lurch was, I think, one of the great guilt trips of my life. Every now and then one is torn between the overwhelming urge to meet personal needs or make the sacrifice to do what at some level we know is right. Eventually, I learned that when faced with such a choice I should ask myself, "Which is the harder, least desirable?" In every case, the harder choice will always be the right choice.

CHAPTER 15

I GRADUATE AND MARRY

On June 5th, Graduation Day, the entire Corps of Cadets marches onto the Plain and the 480 members of our graduating class take their positions by the reviewing stand while the remainder of the Corps passes in review to the strains of *Graduation March*, played only this one time a year and incorporating such West Point specific memories as *The 100th Night Song, Auld Lang Syne,* the Hellcats playing *Reveille, The Colonel Bogey March* and *On Brave Old Army Team.* It is a moving tribute to the graduating class. Our four years of trials and tribulations at West Point flash through the minds of every graduate as their backs stiffen and straighten. It is an unbelievable event, bringing those four long years to a close.

Company M-2 at out Graduation Parade

Watching the Corps pass in review at graduation. I am the second man in the front row, after Don Hollider on my right.

After Graduation Parade it was time to hustle over to Central Area to "recognize" the Plebes in our company and congratulate them on completing their first year at West Point, the most difficult year of their lives. The West Point bond is a camaraderie which takes form over time in the crucible of stress and pressure. You cannot survive the two months of "Beast Barracks" and a year as a Plebe without developing a special affinity and friendship for classmates, particularly with those closest to you. For the Plebe who has endured, it is almost a Stockholm Syndrome-type affection for his upper class disciplinarians. Recognition is the Plebe's official acceptance into the ranks of the upper classes and for the first time since admission to West Point, they will be addressed by their first name. It is also a most special occasion for the graduating class.

The plebes to be recognized are lined up in each company area, about 20 of them. We wended our way down the line, shaking hands and congratulating each man. The procedure takes about an hour and is followed by lunch in the Cadet Mess Hall. But on this occasion, fiancées and guests could join us for the meal. At our table were Barbara, her folks, and my mother. Barb's Father, Bellmont, had presented us with a honeymoon check for a thousand dollars, probably equivalent to $25,000 today. When I got up from our table, I left the check at my place, briefly unattended, which elicited a remark from Bellmont under the umbrella of our honor system for so long, it never dawned on me to safeguard it, nor was there any need or reason to but understandably, someone who lived in the real world would have thought me frivolous. Mother also gave me a thousand, so with the $1,000+ that I had saved in the past two years, I was in pretty good financial shape for our honeymoon.

After lunch we assembled for the final event, the graduation address by the Secretary of the Army Brucker. Upon completion of his speech, the graduating class of 480 cadets, filed on to the stage in one by one in the order of class standing. The Secretary shook our hands, and we were given our commissioning document and diploma. When the last man in the class, Jack Sloan, filed by there was a great uproar as all 480 hats were thrown into the air. The last man in the class is at least as memorable as the first man and therefore, "last man" is sought after by the academically, bottom 1%. At last, the trial of four years as Cadets was over and we would begin our lives as 2nd Lieutenants.

Graduation Day

My Mother, Barb, and her folks were seated together. After hugs and kisses all around, I went back to my room to change into the summer uniform of an Army officer and pin on my second lieutenant's bars and Infantry branch insignia in preparation for our wedding. Barb of course was at the Thayer Hotel getting dressed for the event. By the time we finished the preparations and reunited with our families there was barely time for our scheduled wedding at the Cadet Chapel that afternoon. There were perhaps 40 cadets scheduled for weddings at the various chapels on graduation day. We had drawn numbers to see who would go first and in what order. Fortunately, Barb and I were the fourth couple to be married that day at the Cadet (Protestant) Chapel. It was a great break having it early enough to still be able to have a reception at the Officers' Club and break loose in time to spend the night together for the first time. The Associated Press caught a picture of Barb going into the chapel on her Father's arm as the previous couple was coming out. Then, in a sequel photograph, they showed Barb and me coming out about 12 minutes later and passing under the drawn sabers of my company mates. It was one of those AP photos published in nearly every paper in the country. Six of my company mates had gladly volunteered to hold their sabers commending our marriage in the traditional army manner.

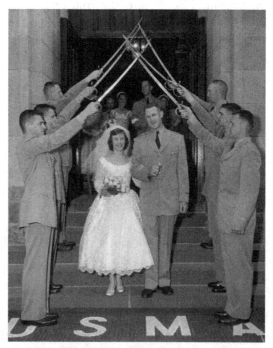

We Marry! Cadet Chapel, 5 June 1956

What a day! And we still had our reception at the Officers' Club to go. We probably had about 45 friends, classmates, and fiancées at the reception. My roommate of four years, Ernie Wilson, was my best man.

Barb looked as lovely as anyone ever had. The reception was a whirl of well wishes, cake cutting and Champagne which finally ended about 5 PM. We left for Cape Cod shortly thereafter for our first week of honeymooning. Since it was about a 300-mile drive, after a few hours on the road we stopped at a motel. Our ambitious honeymoon plans were to spend a week at Cape Cod and six weeks in Europe, then drive to Fort Benning in Georgia for my first assignment.

I had two months of paid graduation leave, my checks for a thousand dollars each, and a few more hundred I had saved from my cadet pay of $110 a month. Our new 1956 Chevy Bel Air was paid for, as was Barb's round trip plane ticket to Paris. I figured we had enough money for our two-month honeymoon. The next day we continued on to Cape Cod, where we spent nearly a week relaxing and enjoying the new experience of being man and wife, something we had looked forward to for a year and a half. About halfway through the week at Cape Cod, we signed up for a deep-sea fishing outing. There may have been other people on board that fishing vessel, but I don't remember them. Our captain steered us seaward and instructed us on the use of our drop lines, which had several hooks and a small lead weight. When we got to where we would do our fishing, we baited our hooks and dropped them over the side. It was amazing how many fish we were catching. Before long we had filled a small keg-size barrel with our catch. To get my line farther out from the side of the boat I swung the weighted line around a couple of times and let it fly. Fly it did but as the weight carried the hooks after it, one of the hooks caught in my thumb. It was buried far enough that the barb was also imbedded. The captain said the only thing for it was to push the hook on through and cut off the other end. That we did, using a rusty pair of pliers, to a successful conclusion.

My beautiful wife!

Returning to our honeymoon cabin with numerous fish and my sore thumb. I had never cleaned a fish, so we enlisted the help of a neighboring couple to show us how. We gave several of the 18-inch specimens to them in appreciation. After setting aside two for our dinner that evening, the remainder of the cleaned fish went into the freezer. Barb fried those dudes in butter together with frozen peas and potatoes to make our first home-cooked dinner together a great success.

Our honeymoon plans were rather ambitious, with the week at Cape Cod, then Paris, Nice and Tangiers. I would travel by MATS from Washington, DC, while Barb would leave the following morning on her commercial flight to Paris. I was still in touch with Dana's mother in DC and she offered to get Barb on the flight to Paris. I arrived at Orly Field the day before Barb and with the assistance of one of my mother's childhood friends, who lived in Patis, we arranged to be at Orly Field when Barb landed. I was 23, she was 20, quite a venture for youngsters! After a few days in Paris, we took the train south to Nice, where my grandmother still lived. Her old friend, Mr. Renuci, once again came through nicely, picking us up at the train station and delivering us to grandmother's home near Place Macina on the outskirts of Nice. He parked by the door-shaped gate in the eight-foot wall encircling her property. The plaque on the wall identified the home as "Chateau Bornala" at 9 Rue de Billet. It was a three-story, Mediterranean-style villa of pleasant proportions. In an earlier day, as "a mansion in the country," it did indeed deserve the chateau moniker. Now, however, the original property had been downsized and the structure needed attention. Grandmother's title of Marquise came with her marriage to the Marquis de Ciccolini and was from an era when the aristocracy of France had money, position, and power. Those times are mostly gone but even today titles are not taken lightly throughout Europe.

Grandmother was then in her late 70's and seemed quite ancient to us. At the turn of the century, some years after she had married the Marquis, they sold off the upper floor of their Monte Carlo villa and used those funds to build Chateau Bornala, with 20 acers on the western outskirts of Nice. Adjacent to her home was the servant quarters which housed her faithful maid, Maria. The main floor of the Chateau had a grand entrance and contained bedrooms, living room, bathrooms, and kitchen. In the living room hung the family tree tracing the Marquis' heritage back 15 or 16 generations. It now resides with my son.

This June day we sat in the garden sipping tea with grandmother. The air was warm and pleasant. I mentioned to her the impressive family tree in the other room, and she said, in her British accent, "My dear, my side of the family traces their lineage to before Christ." That tree and the heavy grandmother clock, now reside in my living room.

After the Marquis died in 1933, the same yar I was born, grandmother would from time to time sell off some of her acreage for additional money. The home, initially situated on about 20 acres of land, had at one time been a cherry orchard. Over the years, the city of Nice became squeezed between the Maritime Alps and the Mediterranean. It could only expand west, so the 20 acres kept increasing in value as she sold them off one by one and two by two. In time the area became known as Place Macina; quite built up and part of the city. Eventually, the old chateau's need for repairs became evident, and the building, like the garden and the aristocracy within, began to yield to the ravages of time.

In this regard, the garden was inviting but lacked care. The fading domain of once elegant surroundings. If one could look beyond the neglect of time and age, its landscaping revealed a hint of previous splendor. It was not hard to visualize the defunct fountain with an elegant spray of water. The path below, barely discernible under the encroaching weeds, had once meandered through the garden, no doubt as a centerpiece of the landscape. The statuary, seemingly out of place in the undergrowth, in an earlier day would have lent dignity. And the thinly covered arbor, with a thirsty vine framing the steps beneath it, hinted at a presumption of grace in a former life. Lavender and hyacinth at the border had somehow survived this benign neglect. Perhaps, like Grandmother, their roots run deep.

We passed our time there on the patio in the garden with pleasantries as we sipped our tea. Grandmother's servant, Maria, came with crumpets, which she referred to as "rusks." Maria, Grandmother's lifetime servant, was now also in her 70's, bustling about and mumbling. She had served Grandmother for nearly 50 years and had been rewarded with a small home on the property which now belonged to her. She still came down each day and spent a little time seeing to the needs of the lady of the house, to whom she referred as "La Marquise." They had become friends, even though the social gap remained. They conversed in Italian, but I sensed a lack of enthusiasm in Maria's having to help with extra people there.

After Maria had left us to fend for ourselves, I wandered into the garden among the several cherry trees which remained. The cherries were ripe, and I picked a bowl full to have with our "rusks" and tea. We had eaten nearly all the cherries when Barb and I discovered the last couple of cherries had a small hole in them. We opened the cherries to examine the reason for the hole and found a small larva inside, no doubt from the Mediterranean fruit fly. Since we had already consumed so many of the little fruits, I was hoping that these last two were the only ones with larva. Six or eight cherry trees were within easy picking distance. I went to the nearest tree to examine more cherries and indeed my worst suspicions were confirmed. Every single cherry had its own small hole. I frantically inspected the other trees, hoping that at least a few would be without protein. No such luck; absolutely every cherry had its telltale hole.

We saw Grandmother for the last time in 1966 at her rest home in Grass. Mother had come to France to get Grandmother's affairs in order and the old chateau was sold for not very much. Now, when I think back, I can still see Grandmother in the garden, enjoying the morning sun with herr tea and rusks. And of course, I will always remember those tasty cherries.

During our stay we spent some wonderful days wandering the area. We found a little shop in Ville France selling a very affordable "vin de cette annee," (wine of this year), and thoroughly enjoyed sampling our discovery. In 1956, in Nice, motor scooters were very popular. Not having a car, we rented a "Vespa" to see the local sights. Since Genoa was only a short distance into Italy, we set out early one day to visit that port city, stopping in route at a spa called Cap Istal. It was elegant, with a small swimming pool formed in a very large rock formation. As we wended our way back up the hairpin turns to the coastal road, I lost my balance as I came to a near halt making one of the tight turns and we tumbled into the upside of the hill. There were no hurts or scratches, but I was greatly chagrined and I guess that's why it is seared into my memory.

Genoa was a big disappointment. I'm not sure what we expected but it was a famous port city of Italy of very little beauty and a lot of industry. Before we headed back, we did find a beautiful church when we passed through an inauspicious doorway leading off an alley.

On one occasion, *Grand'Mere* arranged for her friend, Monsieur Renouci, to take the four of us on a wonderful drive up the Maritime Alps to a picturesque restaurant. Her gentleman friend had been in grandfather's employ and had borrowed quite a bit of money from the Marquis. When Grandfather was on his death bed, he forgave Renouci the debt and in exchange Renouci promised that he would look after grandfather's widow. From time to time, grandmother would call upon Renouci for his assistance. On this occasion she asked him to show us around Nice and to take the four of us for a trip in the French Alps, which loomed above that Mediterranean city. It was a delightful outing, however, in time, Renouci would prove himself to be a most despicable snake in the grass; a story which I will save for later.

We were in Nice for perhaps four weeks before leaving for North Africa, French Morocco, for a visit with my stepmother, who after my Father died had taken an assignment there at Wheeler Air Force Base as a DA civilian employee. Cooks had bought Barbara a round trip ticket from Nice to Tangiers as a wedding present. I was to get to Wheeler AFB by catching a flight from an air base in southern France. Cooks was to meet Barbara's flight when it landed in Tangiers but for reasons never explained, she failed to show. Barb was alone and on her own resources to find a place to stay and to contact Cooks. I was flying into Wheeler the next day and later was extremely upset to learn, after the fact, that Barb had been left to fend for herself in Tangiers.

We were to spend ten days or so in North Africa, which would be an interesting adjunct to our honeymoon travels. We were now on the fifth week of that journey after having spent three weeks with my grandmother in France. After a few days at Wheeler, we left Sidi Slimane in French Morocco by car, heading for Marrakech early in the morning. Cooks was with an Air Force colonel and the four of us were traveling to Gibraltar for the 4th of July long weekend. The main road was about one and a half lanes wide and lined with trees spaced about 50 feet apart. There was a donkey trail alongside the road, and on several occasions we passed someone on a donkey or camel moving leisurely along the trail. I was surprised to see that when a man and wife traveled together, the man was riding, and the woman was walking with a large bundle on her head; it was the Muslim way. Our destination for the evening was the El Minza Hotel, Marrakech's finest.

The El Minza was a large, pink-domed hotel of some elegance. Our room was pleasant, with a small veranda overlooking the town. We changed and went downstairs for dinner. The maître d' spoke English with a strong French accent. He rather swooped in on us with a flourish, as though he were greeting royalty, saying, "Bonsoir, monsieur/madam, eet ees our great pleasure to have you with us this evening." After a few preliminary exchanges my stepmother asked him if he would please order for us. I was amazed at how that seemed to put him into his element. He pondered in an exaggerated manner and then proclaimed his choices for each of us. He began, "Ah, pour la Madame, I would suggest le veau speciale, simmered in our red wine sauce; and of course, our pommes au gratin in order that we have ze proper balance. And pour la colour, to assure a presentation tres just, nous avon le baby spinach provincial, which I am sure you will enjoy. If this meets with Madame's satisfaction, I think you will find our vin du Portugal will provide the right ambiance."

And so, he continued around the table with each of us until we were totally enthralled. But of course, the dessert was the piece de resistance. For this he recommended the Cherries Jubilee! Their French cuisine, blended with Arabic flavors, was indeed wonderful, exceeded only by the size of my bill when we checked out the following morning. But the Cherries Jubilee was, in fact, a magnificent culmination of tastes which were presented with a fanfare, the likes of which I have never seen before or since. It began with the maître d' arriving first on the scene to assure we were ready to receive his munificence. Once this was accomplished and he had our rapt attention, he snapped his fingers over his head and in came a waiter wheeling the dessert preparation cart, followed by six servers and preparers. The first in line was the cart wheeler who, after positioning the cart, stepped aside. The next in line reached below the cart and brought up the large silver bowl of cherries, and then also stepped aside. The next server acquired and aligned all the ingredients to the right of the bowl of cherries and stepped aside. The fourth, a formally attired sous chef, added the ingredients in the proper proportions and assumed his position with the others. The fifth mixed the ingredients and when he was through, sprinkled liberal amounts of Grand Marnier over the creation. Now the dessert chef stepped forward, placed the concoction on a low flame and carefully blended the ingredients. Finally, with a bit of a flare, he lit a large wooden match and handed it to the maître d'. That worthy bowed to us, then took the match and touched it to the bowl of cherries which, in jubilation, burst into flame. While the whole was still flaming gently, the chef arranged a serving for each of us. One of the servers then stepped forth to deliver the final incarnation. Of course, there was a spontaneous round of applause but as I took my first bite of this coup de resistance, I wondered if that poor Arab woman I had seen on the road, struggling with her bundle, happened to be delivering cherries to the El Minza.

The next morning, following café au lait and croissants on our tiny veranda, we departed for Gibraltar, taking the ferry across to that historic southern protrusion of Portugal which for centuries had guarded the Straits. We followed the winding road which curved up the rock face of that fortress-like promontory. About halfway up, cars had stopped to see the "rock apes" which were seemingly everywhere, jumping, observing, and looking for handouts. They were a bit aggressive, so we didn't stay for long.

By mid-July 1956 we found our way back to Orly Airport in Paris and again travelling by our separate means (Barb commercial, I on space available), linked up in Washington, DC, where the Dewey family had kept our car for us. The following day we headed south to Fort Monroe, where we spent a couple of days before making our way further south, to Fort Benning for my assignment to attend the Basic Infantry Officer's Course; six months of classroom and field work. The honeymoon was over!

CHAPTER 16

THE FAMOUS DURWARD BELLMONT RISING

Before continuing with our arrival at Fort Benning, I need to say a few words about my new Father-in-law, Durward Bellmont Rising, because he directly and indirectly had a great effect in shaping my life, as well as Barb's and our married life together.

"Bellmont, with two Ls," he would say, had lots of quips and sayings for which he could have been famous. He could have been famous for having been the youngest Shriner ever at the age of 18 but his accomplishments were far greater than that. Born 22 December1899, he planned to span three centuries by living into year 2000 but died earlier than we expected, at age 89. During his life he Fathered two children, my wife Barbara and Richard Bellmont, her younger brother. When they were born, two years apart, both on January 3rd, he jokingly claimed it was "Standard Oil efficiency," referring to the company where he worked for 40 years. Although he had a doctorate in jurisprudence, his primary area of interest at Standard Oil headquarters, in San Francisco, was as a corporate purchasing and systems analyst expert. Chevron (as it is now called) Headquarters is still at 225 Bush Street in San Francisco. Every day of his 40 years there, Bellmont would walk a block to the Forest Hill Station to catch the streetcar which would take him downtown where he worked. There he would make decisions as to what equipment would be purchased by Chevron for use throughout the corporation. Before purchasing anything, anyone needed, it would first have to be approved by Bellmont.

At the peak of his career Bellmont was earning about $15,000 a year but his stock portfolio, which he had astutely invested over the years, was yielding even more than his paycheck. Investing was his primary hobby. He seldom sold a stock and told me, "Buy good companies and hold on to them." It was very sage advice and I lived by it for many years. In his investments he tried to buy issues which paid decent dividends and had good growth prospects.

At age 63 Bellmont suffered a heart attack and tried to shrug it off, but Marge insisted that he see a doctor. He was hospitalized and while under observation he had a second attack. After several days he was released with a regimen of several aspirins a day and a restrictive diet which he followed to the letter. After that life altering event, he retired in 1964 and he and Marge took a trip around the world that lasted six months and included every corner of the earth from Timbuktu to Machu Picchu. As he settled into his retirement routine in San Francisco, he often noted that he lived in the greatest place in the world. He stayed busy with his investments, his home, his family and his "efficiencies," declaring that he never worked a day in his life until he retired. It was his influence which got Barb and me into the stock market early on in our marriage. Even with my first paycheck a portion of it went into the stock market, in keeping with Bellmont's expectations. I do believe it was our early efforts of thrift and saving, which made Bellmont and Marge comfortable with their later gifting of $10,000 a year, to Barbara, which was the maximum tax-free gift authorized under the tax laws at that time. That little boost to our income, made a great difference in our lives.

Bellmont died in1992, a few years after a head injury he sustained when he fell while taking his daily walk. He left his heirs about two million dollars, fulfilling his grand plan that each generation should leave behind for their heirs more than they had inherited. He also said, "you'll make more money in real estate than in the stock market". It makes life a little easier for those who follow, so again, following Bellmont's lead, we too subscribe to that concept.

CHAPTER 17

BASIC INFANTRY OFFICER TRAINING

We arrived at Fort Benning at the same time as my 200 classmates who had chosen Infantry as their branch. Some were married, some single. As classmates, we had spent four years together at West Point, and nearly half of us had had a fifth year of camaraderie at the West Point Prep School before that. It was a great time of our lives, meeting up again with old friends and getting settled into a new way of life.

Nearly all of our married classmates were staying at the nearby home rental park called Camellia Apartments. The furnished 2-bedroom units were $90 a month and the unfurnished $60. My base pay as a second lieutenant was $220 a month but if we lived off post, we also received a quarters allowance of $110. Since this was a temporary duty station (less than a year) we also received an extra $120 a month. We had absolutely no debts, the car and ring were paid for, so our $550 a month was enough for us to live comfortably and still be able to drop $50 a month into the stock market, back when the Dow Jones average was about 400! Before long, we decided to buy a few pieces of furniture and move into an unfurnished unit to save an additional $30 a month. On weekends I would go to the craft shop on post to try my hand at making some furniture pieces. I always enjoyed woodworking and it didn't take long to turn out a bed frame, bookshelf and high-fi cabinet. Many of those basic pieces we used for years and years. We were always careful to keep our spending in close rein. In those days, when a nickel would buy a Coke, it would also buy a package of Kool-Aid, but the Kool-Aid would provide us four times the quantity of the Coke! Despite our thrift, we enjoyed a rich social life with our friends, exchanging dinner invitations and getting together for bridge. We were close with our many neighbors/classmates as we all entered life's challenge to do well and move ahead.

The Basic Infantry Officers Course (BIOC) lasted about six months and covered everything of a military nature we had learned at West Point but in much more depth and with a lot of time spent in the field on patrols and small unit tactics. Some of it was boring, most of it was interesting. I enjoyed the weapons training, rifle, mortars, machine guns, hand grenades and pistol. Our training with the M-1 rifle and the Colt .45 pistol ended with the qualification shootout and award of the Expert or lesser marksmanship badge. The 200 of us in BIOC decided on a 25-cent pistol pool, with the $50 to go to the winner and second place high scorers. I had always done well firing the .45 but never thought I was good enough to take our first prize for high score on the .45 pistol range. I also qualified for the "Expert Badge," which was almost as good as the $35 prize money which, in those days, was nearly a week's pay.

One of our more demanding exercises in BIOC training, was the 24-hour escape and evasion course, which required that we negotiate several miles of dense Georgia undergrowth and rugged terrain from late afternoon to the next morning. We were organized into two-man teams and using only a compass and map were to find our way through about 12 miles of Jungle-like terrain, with small creeks and heavy foliage, to a road where trucks were waiting to pick us up. It took most of the night and all our energy to reach our destination, cold, wet and dirty.

Graduation from the Course was something of a non-event, with everyone already looking forward to the next phase of their training. Most of us were slated to remain at Benning for parachute training, referred to as "Jump School," followed by Ranger training. Some of us would instead be headed to Flight School rather than the rigorous Ranger course. I tried for both, but the Army said, "No, only three schools in any one fiscal year."

BIOC ended for us in December and our graduation, followed by two weeks off for Christmas, was a most welcome event. Many of our bachelor classmates went home for Christmas, while those who remained at Benning were included in exchanging family dinners. We had three bachelors over for the occasion; my old roommate from West Point, Ernie Wilson, his current BOQ roommate and our classmate, Doug Williams and another close friend and classmate, Norman Schwarzkopf. All of us would go on to Jump School which would begin in early January.

CHAPTER 18

JUMP SCHOOL!

Jump School was an important career ticket punch. It was another hurdle which was demanding enough to give us a slight edge over those who had not qualified. There we were about to embark on the very unnatural experience of leaping from an aircraft! Our three-week program began with daily exercises and runs. Each day the exercises and runs became longer. To improve upper body strength, we were continually doing pushups and pull-ups. As we progressed into our training, each day started with exercises and runs. The idea was to wean out the less motivated and to toughen our bodies sufficiently to handle the inevitable transition from air to earth. In a parachute jump, you descend at about 19 feet per second. If you do the math that means you hit the ground, going about 13 miles an hour. If you don't do the math, you still hit the ground at 13 mph, but it feels more like 20 miles an hour! After a week of heavy exercise and five-mile runs, we started working on the correct body position for exiting the aircraft and contacting the ground. We began by jumping off a two-foot-high stand. The drill sergeants put us through our paces, learning every detail of the parachute landing fall - "the PLF" in jump talk. The instructor stressed, "Land on the balls of your feet, then roll like a rocker, making contact first on your calf, then your thigh, your hip, side and shoulder." The idea was for the impact to be absorbed consecutively rather than all at once.

Our next challenge was the 34-foot towers. A cable ran from the top of the tower to a post some 60 or 70 feet away. We would clamber up the stairs to the jump deck, hook our static line to the cable, stand in the door then leap out when commanded "Go" by the drill sergeant. It was breathtaking to drop some twenty feet before being caught by the static line; not unlike the thrill of a bungee jump. The first time out of the 34-foot tower took a bit of courage, since at that height one is fully cognizant of how damaging a fall would be. Of course, maintaining an air of bravado and nonchalance in the face of your friends and classmates is an important aspect of the event. As we vaulted into space, head down, arms grasping our reserve chute, we counted "one thousand one, one thousand two, one thousand three" and so on, simulating a parachute drop. The idea was that, during an actual parachute jump, if after five seconds your chute hadn't opened, you needed to look up, check for a canopy and if there was none, pull your reserve chute release. At the count of three, we were caught by the tether attached to a pulley and cable and then slid along the cable until meeting the ground. We made contract with the ground with a PLF, then detached our static line from the cable and got back in line for another jump. Of the 150 guys going through the training, there are always one or two who just can't bring themselves to jump out of that tower. Another few emitted an involuntary scream the first time they leapt from the door, leaving those of us watching feeling better about our own performances. The 34-foot tower phase of training was completed at the end of our second week.

The final phase of ground training would be the Coney Island-style parachute drop from a 250-foot tower. At Coney Island amusement park the parachute is tethered to the tower and floats to the ground guided by guy wires. At our tower, the drop was free fall, and hopefully floating away from the tower with the wind. There were four steel arms at the top of the tower, and on three of the arms parachutists would be slowly lifted to the top. The fourth arm, on the windward side, was known as the "dirty arm" and would not be used to avoid the chute's being carried by the wind into the tower. The worst part of the exercise was the contemplation phase while being slowly hauled to the top of the tower. Once released and floating free, all the anxiety was over. We each made three, free-fall drops before we were ready for the real thing.

To qualify for the coveted jump wings, we would need to complete five jumps. Now, the big day of our first jump from the C-123 aircraft, was upon us. Going out the door at 2,000 feet was breathtaking but not particularly courageous. You do what you have to do, what you are trained to do. Courage is oft born of necessity and yet we have choices to put ourselves in harm's way, or to go the other way. When our pilot activated the red light in the cargo area to alert us that we were nearing our jump zone, you could feel the electricity in the group. At the front of the plane, the red light flashed its warning, and the grizzled jumpmaster began his series of commands: "GET READY! STAND UP! HOOK UP! CHECK EQUIPMENT!" On the command "Hook Up" we hooked our nylon static lines to a cable that ran the full length of the aircraft. At the next command we checked our static lines and then the chute pack on the back of the man in front of us. We were ready to go!

When the amber light came on the jumpmaster barked "STAND IN THE DOOR!" He threw open the cargo door and the first man in line stepped into the opening, his hands on the sides of the door frame, wide-eyed but ready to lunge. Then the green light came on and the jumpmaster commanded "GO!" We began our jumper's shuffle, staying right up against the man ahead of us. One hand was on our static line, sliding it along the steel cable as we shuffled forward. The other hand was on the man in front of us to ensure we stayed close in the human chain. I well remember those moments. We are as one shuffling toward the door. I'm in the door, there is no hesitation as hands go to the door frame and I launch myself clear of the aircraft. The smash of a hundred and twenty mile an hour slipstream sucks my breath out. I began my count; one thousand two thousand three thousand... WHOPP! I look up to see an opened chute. What a beautiful sight seeing it billow open and knowing I would be floating and not plunging to the earth below. Anxiety gives way to relief and then that fantastic sensation of floating, floating earthward, quiet, peaceful. In less than a minute, 30 jumpers were in the air. With the other four aircraft, there were about 150 of us floating earthward. But at 205 pounds I seemed to be dropping faster than the little guys. In fact, the ground was rather rushing up at me and I was slightly oscillating. I reached up and pulled my forward risers to stop the oscillation. Our landing area was a large stretch of flat farmland relatively free of hazards. Suddenly I hit the ground and rolled into the PLF we had practiced so many times. My chute collapses around me and the first great event was over. What a thrill! All around, the other jumpers were also gathering their chutes and as lemmings, we headed toward the buses on a nearby road.

After our first jump it would take four more to qualify for graduation and the award of the parachutist's wings. The second and third jumps were only slightly less exciting. When dropping from the sky, the thrill is always there. Normally we would make one jump a day for five days to complete the final phase of our course. But on the fourth day the winds were too high, and we would need to make our final two jumps on Friday. Friday morning, we boarded our planes for the fourth jump. As I exited the aircraft, as usual I was floating down a little faster than the average guy and the wind had picked up a tad. As I neared the ground, I was swinging to and fro like a weight on a pendulum would do. I hauled down on my forward risers to dump a little air from the rear of the chute and reduce the oscillation. Perhaps that increased my drop rate and caused my contact with the ground to be a bit more robust than it should? Or perhaps I screwed up my PLF a bit? Whatever the cause, as I struck the ground, I heard a snap and my left ankle gave way. I gathered my chute and hobbled back to the bus as best I could with the rest of our "stick" to head back to the airfield for our final jump of the course. My old roommate, Don Holleder, was sitting next to me on the bus. I knew from his many years of athletics that he might have a feel for what kind of injury I had sustained. I told him what had happened and asked, "What do you think; it feels bad." He said, "Did you hear anything when you landed?" I said, "Yes, I heard a snap." He replied matter-of-factly, "It's broken." I asked him what he thought about my making my fifth qualifying jump. He said simply, "I don't recommend it."

What a dilemma! I was finally completing three weeks of rigorous parachute training and looking forward to graduation and going on to flight school. But I still had my fifth and final jump that afternoon to complete the course. I probably could not graduate and receive my jump wings with only four jumps completed. I wrestled with the question, "Do I make the last jump on what is probably a broken ankle, or do I report my situation, drop out of the program, and then have to repeat those three weeks of training?"

It was clear to me that one more jump on a broken ankle was the route of least resistance. It was not a hard decision to trade a few minutes of discomfort for three less weeks of it. Several minutes later we loaded up for the last jump. I needed to conceal my hobble, or they would pull me out. As the jumpmaster commanded "stand in the door" we shuffled forward. The green light came on and at the command of "GO!" the human chain began the parachutists' shuffle out the aircraft door. As I neared the door, I remember thinking, "Oh, hell, let's get it done!" and out I went.

On the way down I pondered whether I should try to land on only one leg or whether that might ensure an injury to that leg too. A minute and a half later I struck the ground, attempting as normal a PLF as possible. It went OK and was not as painful as I expected. We bused back to Benning, and I reported to the post hospital to have my ankle looked at. It was about 4:30 in the afternoon by the time I got there. The person behind the counter told me to have a seat and someone would be with me shortly. After a painful hour of sitting there like a good second lieutenant, I finally went back to the counter, where another person apologized that everyone had gone home and had not left word that I was waiting there with a broken ankle to be seen! I guess that was my first lesson in why not to be too passive in matters of self-interest.

Before long the emergency doctor had me in the x-ray room to get pictures of my ankle. It was decided that I should have a small operation, inserting screws to hold the pieces in place. In another couple of days, I was ready to leave the hospital with my new screws and cast. I decided that making the jump on a broken ankle had been a good choice, since I got credit for completing the course and was awarded my "Jump Wings." Before I was discharged, a colonel came to my ward and pinned my jump wings to my hospital robe. He said, "Congratulations, trooper! You made it!"

As for Don Holleder, a few years later, when we were in Vietnam, he was the operations officer of a brigade that included a battalion commanded by Lieutenant Colonel Terry Allen, son of the legendary WW II General Terry Allen. While Don was with his brigade commander in the air overseeing the action below them, during a heavy fire fight, Terry Allen was killed. The brigade commander ordered his ship to the ground so Don could get control of the situation. He jumped out and ran toward the heat of the battle and was instantly killed by a sniper's bullet. A tragic loss. I prefer to remember him now from his football days when he would use his speed to go deep for a long pass. In my mind's eye, the ball was high in the air as Don sprinted down the field to meet it. The two men assigned to stop him leaped up to block or intercept the ball. As six hands stretched upward for the prize, the two defenders reaching for the ball were now on their way down, while Don, with his perfect timing and the grace of a ballet dancer, was still going skyward to snatch the ball. It was a beautiful example of the talent which made him an All American. As MacArthur had said so many years earlier, "On the fields of friendly strife are sown the seeds that on other days and other fields will bear the fruits of victory." On the football field, as on the battlefield, Don did what came naturally. Courage? Perhaps, but then again, that's the kind of guy he was, doing what needed to be done.

By April, my ankle was not yet completely healed, so my orders to flight school in Texas were canceled and we remained at Fort Benning. I was assigned to the 29th Infantry School Training Brigade as a platoon leader. That four-month assignment was an interesting adjunct to my new career, since I was in charge of a particular segment of Infantry Advanced Training that involved the complicated procedures required of an infantry platoon in combat being replaced on the front lines by another platoon at night. My job was to receive the arriving platoon as though I was the departing platoon leader. When the new platoon arrived, I would have each soldier take over the foxhole of the soldier who was being relieved, show him where his field of fire was, and explain where the enemy was coming from. One memory of this "night relief" stays with me. I was taking a new soldier to his foxhole, but he didn't want to get into it. After a short discussion he said, "No suh, ah ain't getting in that fox hole. Dere might be 'no shoulders' down there." I said, "What are you talking about troop?" He said, "You know, suh, snaikes. Dere might be snaikes down in dere." Eventually I was able to get him into his fox hole.

PART II

THE NEXT FIFTY YEARS

CHAPTER 19

FLIGHT SCHOOL

It was mid-July when we arrived at Camp Garry Texas. Of course, Texas wasn't much better heat-wise than Georgia but with less humidity and with our window air conditioner we were a bit more comfortable than in Georgia. We moved in to our little two-bedroom bungalow On Field Street, in a housing tract which the Army had leased for their student pilots. It was basic. Up and down the street from us were about 20 other student pilots and their families.

By that time, we owned most of our meager furniture, the bed, hi fi, speaker cabinet and bookshelves, all of which I had made at the Fort Benning Craft Shop. The sofa, chairs, and breakfast table we had bought second hand. Life was simple; furnishings were basic. We were young and on our own!

Since all the officers on our street were there for the same purpose, it wasn't long before we had carpools formed to get us to and from Camp Gary, so Barb had use of our Chevy most days. We had all heard rumors about flight training, some good and some bad. Nearly all of my classmates had entered flight school a few months ahead of me, so I was in with a new group of guys, most of whom had not known each other before. It was a chance to make new friends instead of migrating to the comfort of old ones.

Camp Gary was a typical WW II air base which had been reactivated when the Army stepped up its aviation training program. It was in a dry, hot and dusty corner of Texas with a scattering of those old yellowing

WW II, wooden buildings, much like the ones that still survive today at several Army posts. The "Camp" designation means they were not authorized the same level of funding and facilities as a "Fort," which was readily apparent as we drove onto post for the first time.

I had been looking forward to flying for many years and now, as I walked into that old, reconditioned building with the "swamp coolers" whirring, I was ready to embark on a journey which would guide the rest of my life. I was ten years old when those magnificent WW II planes, the P-38 Lightning and the P-51 Mustang, were dominating the skies in Europe and the South Pacific. Now I would be learning to handle the controls of a real flying machine. Strange that I had always been interested in airplanes but had never before sought out a chance to fly one. I guess the cost and opportunity had just been way out of sight for a young man of my means. But now, in a few minutes, I would meet my flight instructor and the two other student pilots assigned to him.

Our instructors were all older, experienced civilian pilots under contract to the Army. Most had served in WW II in the Army Air Corps, which later became the U.S. Air Force. They would teach us the tricks of the trade. Evidently the Army did not have enough qualified Army aviators available to provide this instruction and thus had to contract it out. Our instructor, Mr. Soap, was in his early fifties but to a 24-year-old he seemed rather ancient. He sat us down at a table and briefly outlined our flying program. The discussion ended by his noting that one of the three of us would be gone, washed out, before training was over. The military flight training programs we hear about most are cadet programs where the young men are learning to be officers as well as pilots. However, we were officers already and therefore didn't have to endure the continual harassment that air cadet candidates received.

After about an hour of discussion, Mr. Soap took us out to the flight line and introduced us to the L-19 Bird Dog we would be flying. He said, "These are two-place, Cessna-built aircraft with tail wheels, commonly referred to as Tail Draggers. You will notice the seats are in tandem, front and back, not side by side as on most civilian aircraft." This may have been a holdover from early flying days when all single-engine military aircraft had tandem seating, perhaps to make for a thinner, faster fuselage. The cockpit arrangement during training put the student in the front seat and the instructor in back. The controls in the back were the same as the controls in the front seat but only the front seat had engine and flight instruments. Using the checklist provided, we preflighted the aircraft, with Mr. Soap explaining each step. "During your preflight inspection you must determine not only the amount of fuel in the tanks but that it is in fact aviation gas," he said. "Look at the fuel sample you've drained from the tank, feel it, smell it. What color is it? Low octane avgas is reddish. High octane has a blue tint. Remember that, it could save your life."

After the preflight, the other two students were left on the flight line to familiarize themselves with the airplane while Mr. Soap and I went up for my first flight in a light, single engine plane. This first flight was called a "Dollar Ride," probably an expression which dated back to the early days of flying when for a dollar the barnstormers of the day would take you up for a quick thrill. For me, this was indeed a thrill, the fulfillment of all my boyhood dreams.

In the next months we worked hard to learn all aspects of flight but there was always time for Mr. Soap to regale us with stories of his flying DC-3s over the Himalayan Mountains during WW II in support of our famous effort to build what was known as the Burma Road. Sometimes they flew in supplies, while other times they brought in planeloads of coolies to work on the air-field. His stories of flying "The Hump," as they called it, were always exciting. There was the time when, halfway through his flight, he heard a lot of commotion coming from the passenger area. He sent his copilot back to investigate and learned that their load of coolies was laughing like crazy and the passenger boarding door was wide open. They had just thrown out one of the guys. Another story I recall his telling us was that whenever they landed at the airfield in Indochina the coolies, who were working there repairing the bomb damage from Japanese attacks, would drop their shovels and run at the plane. It was their belief that, if they could come close enough to the whirring propellers, they could get the devil off their backs. But unfortunately, as he taxied down the runway, there would be an occasional "thump, thump-thump!"

At any rate, here I was in the front seat of an L-19, getting my first orientation flight. Mr. Soap explained to me that I should sit back and enjoy it, that this would be the only time I could just relax and look around. From there on out I would be learning to fly but today I was only a passenger. It was a short flight, perhaps only 20 minutes but I had the thrill of the high thrust, fixed pitch prop, accelerating us to take off, the feel of being in the air, and the sound of the roaring six-cylinder, fuel-injected Continental engine. It is interesting to note that, 60 years later, I am flying a larger aircraft (Cessna 182) but with the same Continental 470, 220 horsepower engine and always the same thrill every time I take off. Here is the L-19 "Bird Dog" Trainer in Texas.

The next day we were issued flight suits, a gray affair with lots of zippered pockets and a long zipper which went from below the waist to our collar. I felt official wearing my own flight suit with all the symbolism that went with it.

Flight school for us was a relatively laid-back experience. We would arrive at our instructor's table for flight training at 7:30 hours and leave our last aeronautics class at about 4:30. None of the training was a piece of cake but neither was there much pressure. There was much to learn in ground school and in the air and in the back of our minds we knew that only two-thirds of us were expected to win the coveted silver wings.

After our initial morning briefing on the maneuvers we would cover that day, Mr. Soap would take one of us up for about an hour of instruction. Meanwhile the other two would spend time in the cockpit of one of the L-19s parked in the tie-down area or in the briefing room studying the flight manual. We were expected to learn the preflight by heart, the starting procedures and to memorize the cockpit layout so that we could go through the entire emergency procedures blindfolded in the event of an engine failure. During our afternoon academic classes, we studied aeronautics, radio procedures, Morse Code, flight regulations, navigation, and meteorology. Much of our navigation studies covered map reading from the air and use of air navigation charts.

Our class was issued gold hats to reduce confusion with the several other classes that started every six weeks and to provide some cohesion and identification of one another. There were about 40 students per class and each class group wore different colored hats. There were people in blue hats, gold hats, and white hats, all training at the same time but having started six weeks apart.

Our table of three was a disparate group. Red Keville was a Transportation Corps officer, I was Infantry and Dick Connor was Artillery. Although we were all from different branches of the Army and different parts of the country, all of us were married and living on Field Street in the nearby town of San Marcos.

The first real hurdle facing us was our solo flight. We were expected to solo in 8 to 12 hours of instruction. As I recall, Red was the first to solo and with less than 8 hours. Dick was next with 8 hours. Seeing the other two complete this very important hurdle, I was beginning to get anxious about my status and recalled that Mr. Soap said early on. "Only two of you will graduate"! I had eight and a half hours and was wondering if I would be turned loose for my solo flight before the 12-hour deadline.

The day after Dick soloed. we followed our usual routine. I started the airplane and we headed out to one of the practice airstrips to work on landings. After my third landing, Mr. Soap told me to park the aircraft. I was taken totally by surprise when he got out of the plane and told me I was going to fly it solo!

Not far from where we parked was a wooden stand about 15 feet high that was used as a makeshift tower. It had a radio. He said, "I'll wait here while you take it around. Give me three good landings and call me on the radio if you have any problems." I had no idea that I was ready to fly that thing alone and his departure from the aircraft came as a total shock. I wasn't afraid of being alone but was really surprised that after only eight and a half hours of instruction he thought I could fly solo!

Takeoff was no challenge; full power, a little right rudder to counteract the torque of the prop and down the runway we went (the plane and I). As we gained speed the tail came up first and then, with a little back pressure on the stick, we are airborne. Wow, what a thrill to be in the air all by your lonesome for the first time! A strange sense of freedom wafted through my mind for a few seconds, followed by intense concentration.

I closely followed our usual flying routine of climbing to 500 feet straight ahead with 15 degrees of flaps, then turning right and continuing the climb to 800 feet. At that point it was time to take off the flaps and make my next turn downwind, flying parallel with the runway in the opposite direction. When I got a beam of the end of the runway, I completed the landing check (fuel pump on, mags on, 15 degrees of flaps, fuel selector) chopped the power, and began my right turn as I began my descent. At this point I had probably been in the air for less than 5 minutes and now it was time to make the turn to final and line up with the runway with full flaps. I was on my final approach, heading to the spot I wanted to land on and dropping fast but not as fast as I was used to with my instructor on board.

When I pushed the nose of the plane down my airspeed went up. As a consequence, the plane was a little fast and not quite ready to land when I was. With the back seat empty, the nose was a lot heavier than what I expected, and the wheels touched the runway heavily, and I bounced back into the air. Again, I pushed forward on the stick and again bounced into the air. This was getting embarrassing and I felt like "kangaroo man". I was concerned my instructor would be on the radio telling me to forget it, I wasn't ready. As I taxied back, Mr. Soap told me to give him two more, "good" landings this time, to complete my solo flight. In the next two landings, the plane was evidently tired of landing like a kangaroo, and we settled nicely onto the runway. The rest of the flight was uneventful. We headed back to Camp Gary with me on Cloud Nine. About 20 percent of our class never completed a solo flight. For me it was one of the greatest days of my life…maybe not as good as my honeymoon?

Our Basic Flight Training would end in four more months. Those of us who successfully completed this phase would go on to Fort

Rucker in December 1957 for Advanced Tactical Flight Training. Flying and studying and flying and studying, went on day after day, with the maneuvers becoming progressively more difficult. Every now and then we would lose another classmate who failed to pass one of the check rides at the end of a phase. I never felt like I was a great pilot, "a natural". I had to work hard at each new aspect of our training. Some guys seemed to just "strap the plane on" and become one with it. Nothing appeared to challenge them. In the civilian world of flight instruction, solo occurs for most at 30 to 35 hours. For us, it was 8 to 12 hours, or we washed out. In civilian flight training you can be a total klutz but with enough hours you will eventually get your private pilot certificate. Military pilots, on the other hand must demonstrate an aptitude for flight or they don't make it.

There were a few exciting times during our training. Toward the end of the course, we had a long cross-country flight of a couple of hours, which can be dicey when all you have to go by is a map and your compass. There isn't much terrain distinction flying over that part of Texas, just flat land with a rare river or railroad track that would show on our charts. So, calculating the wind velocity and direction became important. A few degrees off your heading and you would completely miss your turnaround point. It wasn't long before we learned those little Texas towns all had water towers and most of them had the name of the town on the tower. In a pinch, we could swoop down and see which town we were over.

Night cross-country flights were an entirely different story. If we had a full moon, there was plenty of light for young eyes properly night adapted. Our flights that first night had no moon, so off into the nothingness we went; each in his little plane, all alone. We wore parachutes at night because attempting a night landing after engine failure is highly problematic. The old joke goes, "If your engine quits, when you get about a hundred feet from the ground, turn on your landing light. If you don't like what you see, turn it off!"

By that time in the program, most of the weaker pilots had already washed out, so there were very few problems with our night cross-country. Out of the entire class, only one guy got lost and had to call for help. With our VHF radios we could contact the tower from many miles out. The procedure was to call the tower and request a "DF steer", a direction to fly. The tower would locate the lost soul with the direction-finding equipment when the pilot keyed his mike. Then they could give him a heading to fly to get home. During this night cross-country we were all closing in on home base when the silence was broken by a very concerned student. He didn't know where he was and called for a DF steer. His call started off with a Joe Cool tone but about halfway through the call his voice broke, revealing his fear. Of course, the next day he had to suffer the ignominy of everyone knowing he had been lost.

During this final phase of our training, we were practicing spin recovery. Our standard procedure was to initiate a two-turn spin at 2,500 feet above ground level. The airplane would drop about a thousand feet if the spin was properly executed. That would leave us about 1,500 feet above the ground. On this day I was climbing through 1500 feet when the instructor cut the power and said, "Give me a two-turn spin". For some reason he thought we were at 2,500. I unquestioningly executed the spin by pulling the stick all the way back into a stall and kicking hard left rudder. After two spins I started the recovery and suddenly felt all this back pressure on the stick as the instructor saw the ground coming up pretty fast. We had a couple of hundred feet to spare. The instructor said, "What happened?" I told him we started at 1,500 feet. At that altitude a poorly executed two-turn spin could be disastrous. I didn't know any better, but it was a scary moment for him.

By the time graduation day arrived we had lost 30 percent of our beginning class. During the basic phase we had accumulated about 120 hours of flight time but there was still a final check ride in our last week of school. It was of course the biggie. We three tablemates nervously made it through without a problem. I was ecstatic. But in that final check we did lose one more classmate.

By then it was mid-December. The plan was for us to report to Fort Rucker, Alabama, before going on Christmas leave. We would then return to start the Advance Flight Training Course at the beginning of January. For me, it didn't make sense to go east to Alabama with my family, sign in, then head west to San Francisco for Christmas. I asked the commander if I could take leave first, then report to Rucker after New Year's. He went along with that, so we had the movers load our meager furniture items for Rucker we headed home to San Francisco.

After Barb's birthday on the third of January, I left for Fort Rucker at Dothan, Alabama. Barb and our infant son would follow by air the next week, after I had arranged for our quarters, I drove to Phoenix the first night and in a couple more days arrived at Rucker. When I reported in, I learned my class had started their training before Christmas and I would need to join the following class of "White Hats." It was a shocker to learn I would again be thrown in with a bunch of guys I didn't know.

Army Aviation was still in its infancy and Fort Rucker was not entirely ready for the large influx of students who began to arrive. There were not yet adequate quarters for students and families and I had to choose between living off post or accepting what the Army labeled "substandard housing" in an area of the post known affectionately as "Splinter Village." If I chose Splinter Village, I would save about $60 a month on my housing costs and have the convenience of being on post. I inspected the shabby little quarters and signed for a small two-bedroom shack. It was about a thousand square feet of space on a foundation of stilts. It was gross, but we would be there for less than five months and everyone else was in the same boat. The most notable deficiency was the very thin walls made of "pressboard", with only a few bare light bulbs sticking out of the wall to illuminate the interior. There was some sort of oil-burning heater in the middle of the living room, fed by a rubber fuel line running out to a 55-gallon drum of diesel behind the unit. If the drum went empty or the fuel line clogged, the temperature could drop 30 degrees.

Barb would be joining me in a week, and I knew I better make the place livable before she got there. I had the furniture delivered the next day and got the carpets down, some curtains up, and things began to look better. But those bare light bulbs sticking out of the wall were sure to kill any hope of making the place look homey. My solution was to create angular cardboard shades to cover the bulbs and give us an indirect lighting effect. I painted the shades and used sand to pour over the wet paint to make a decorative pattern. It turned the trick and with a large bouquet of flowers standing on the entryway table, I was ready to greet my wife and son with a smile.

We enjoyed our months in Splinter Village and the ready socializing of our nearby neighbors and fellow pilots. Flight training was tactical, and more exciting now. We were learning to squeeze the last ounces of power from our little planes with short field takeoffs and landings. It was no longer a matter of learning to fly, it was a world of bush pilot techniques, of landing on unimproved fields and dirt roads that might be on a bend requiring us to turn with the road as we landed and took off.

Our night flying technique included landing on grass fields with landing lights off and only the headlights of a Jeep at each end of the field. We also practiced night tactical landings with a few small fire pots to mark the sides of the landing area.

There was seldom a day we would fly with our instructor when he didn't surprise us by turning off the engine and asking us to execute a forced landing. I would guess that in our nine months of flight training I executed well over a hundred forced landings, so many in fact that 40 years later, when I lost an engine coming into Monterey, I could still draw on the memories from flight school to execute a successful landing on a dirt road behind Ryan Ranch. But I covered the details of that event in the first chapter.

The weeks zipped by and before long it was early May and graduation day approached. Every now and then someone would fail a progress check ride but usually he was able to pass a retest after a couple hours of remedial training. However, the final check ride again took its toll of one man. Hard to understand how one could progress through 200 hours of flight training and still be singled out for rejection. From the class several months ahead of us; the class I would have been in had I not broken my ankle, word had filtered down that Don Holleder had busted his check ride and was out of the program. Evidently Don's flight instructor had asked Don to escort his nice who arriving over a weekend. Don was engaged at that time and demurred. The reason given for his washing out of the program was "hand to eye coordination"! A rather unacceptable verdict for an All-American End! Would he have been killed ten years later in Vietnam had he been in the air rather than on the ground? Most likely not. It is creepy to think that such a minor event on the road to greatness would cause your early death!

By graduation day we all had orders for out next assignment, some to Germany, some to Korea, others to special flight missions in South America and Alaska. I was quite pleased to be going to Fort Lewis, Washington, and looking forward to seeing what had changed in the 20 years since I was there as a child visiting my father.

Graduation was in the post theater. There were about 45 of us now suffering through the words of a guest speaker and then being called up to the stage one by one to receive a certificate, a handshake, and the coveted silver wings pinned to our uniform. That was a significant event and the start of a new era. Amazingly, I had now been in school nearly all my life, high school, prep school, college (West Point), Basic Infantry Officers Course, jump school and flight school! Now, in June of 1958, I was finally ready to begin my career with enough schooling, training and expertise to qualify for an advanced degree in "Military" (had there been such a thing).

It is interesting to note that when granddaughter graduated from her Air Force flight school (in the top third), the graduation events took the better part of a day, which ended with my pinning my army wings on her. I told her it was a temporary upgrade.

CHAPTER 20

FORT LEWIS, WASHINGTON!

We left Fort Rucker, Alabama, as a family of three and headed west. Our drive to Fort Lewis again brought us home through San Francisco to be with our parents, brothers and a few remaining friends for a short time. Our car did not have air conditioning, so we were glad to be leaving the south before the real heat and mugginess set in. I was like a horse returning to the barn, pushing on from town to town instead of making a vacation of the occasion and seeing the sights. In those early years, Barb was content to let me make the decisions and she lovingly went along with whatever I wanted. I was a long time transitioning from doing it my way to doing it our way. In later years I learned it was best to sometimes do it her way. When I write my first book about that transition, I shall call it "The Three Stages of Man," referring to my way in the beginning, then our way, and ultimately her way.

It was June 1958 when we arrived at Fort Lewis, where we checked into the transient officers' quarters and began to assess the housing situation. My classmate Charlie Saint and his wife Ann had arrived earlier and were established in quarters on post, which in those days, for lieutenants, consisted of a portion of old WW II wooden barracks that had been retrofitted with a kitchen and partitions for bed and bathrooms. They had an air of depravation about them. Charlie and Anne had us to dinner and with them we weighed the pros and cons of living in these old, substandard, makeshift quarters. We decided to see what we could find off post and began our search to buy a small home.

I was a first lieutenant now and was making about $400 a month, but we also received $120 flight pay, which gave us enough income to expand our options. Off post living would also be supplemented with a housing allowance of about $110.

A couple of miles from the Fort Lewis front gate, a new community called Lakewood was springing up. Two of my classmates had already purchased homes there and when we drove through the area it looked about right for us. We stopped by a home that was almost complete and asked the builder what it was selling for? "Fourteen five," he said, "and if you decide to buy it this week, I will be able to put whatever colors you want in the kitchen." That sounded mighty good to us, and we figured we might save a dollar, since there was no agent involved. Fortunately, we had already been careful to save what we could and had a few thousand dollars in the stock market we could use to make the 20 percent down payment.

At age 25, buying our first home was a huge step, and with no knowledge of what we were doing, I'm sure we didn't strike a very good bargain. But we stepped into the breach and never looked back.

We probably had 30 or more classmates stationed at Fort Lewis, which provided for a rich social life. We often got together for dinner and bridge with Charlie and Anne Saint. Those were busy, happy days. Charlie and I also shared a love for chess and decided we could probably set up a chessboard alongside our bridge table and make an occasional move when we weren't involved in bidding or playing a hand. That worked for a while but eventually the chess became so interesting that our bridge began to suffer, and the wives called a halt to our multi-tasking.

We also spent much of my off-duty time making that house into a home. There was no lawn, topsoil, or landscaping. I put together a simple drag from 2x6s to level the truckload of topsoil we brought in. With our one-year-old son riding the drag to provide extra weight and amusement for him, I harnessed myself to the apparatus with a heavy rope, like a mule to a plow, and off we went, back and forth across the front and back yards. In a few hours it was level enough to begin spreading the grass seed.

There was never a shortage of projects for us. The craft shop on post had all the tools and materials I needed to build a bed, headboard, speaker cabinet and bookshelves. It was basically a labor of love and a change of pace from the daily routine. By fall, we could finally call our first house "home."

When my leave was over, I reported into the 4th Aviation Company, which was part of the 4th Infantry Division. The company was commanded by a Major and had been growing dramatically as Army Aviation began to expand its role in the Army. We had about a hundred lieutenants and 25 aircraft in the company when I arrived. It was a bad situation. I would get about 20 hours of flying each month and the rest of the time there was little or nothing to do. How do you get a good efficiency report if most of the time you are just hanging out? I had about four classmates in the aviation company and several more in the 4th Division as Infantry Platoon Leaders. Classmate Dick Macken had arrived at the aviation company a few months ahead of me and evidently also recognized the "nothing to do dilemma". I spotted him rapidly walking through the company area with a clip board and asked him, "What's up?" He said, "Nothing but if you are moving fast and carrying a clip board everyone thinks you have something to do." It wasn't long after that I volunteered to take over the task of "Property Book Officer" in the supply room. The PBO was the guy who had to sign for all the property in the company; the aircraft, weapons, furniture absolutely everything. It all had to be inventoried, listed in the Property Book, and kept track of. It was a terrible job and a whole new world of requisitions and responsibilities in accordance with the "table of allowances". For example, each month we needed to requisition the supplies we used. We were authorized so many rolls of toilet paper per assigned personnel, per month; one amount for men, twice the amount for women. Different items were requisitioned from different sources. Some things didn't make sense like ordering the positive terminal for batteries from the Ordnance Corps and the negative terminal from the Quartermaster Corps. There was a procedure known as an "Inventory Adjustment" which allowed you to list an overage in one item for a shortage in a similar item to balance the books. Word had it that a Transportation Corp Unit had somehow lost a tugboat and adjusted their property book with an Inventory Adjustment Report listing a minus for "Boat, Tug" and a plus for "Boat, Gravy" which is the mess hall item for serving gravy. If you somehow had acquired an extra item, it could be listed as "found on post" by way of explanation. The Table of Allowances were an amazing compilation of everything an army needed to keep it alive and were derived from WW II data and adjusted over the years.

The demands on the PBO were unbelievable and had cut into the amount of time I could spend flying. Over time I lost some of the fine edge in my flying proficiency such as landing on short, unimproved field strips which lead to my only near accident in 55 years of flying.

—〰—

Who Can Land the Shortest?

For a young aviator with fewer than 500 hours flying time there is still much to master before he can consider himself "proficient" in the bush pilot type of flying we were expected to know. In those days, before helicopters dominated the battlefield, we were expected to fly much like the Alaskan bush pilot, landing on roads, open fields and unimproved strips. Also, our older tail-wheel aircraft required a more practiced hand than the conventional nose-wheel planes. But the extra effort to master those capabilities had to be matched by a higher level of pilot performance.

Most Army Aircraft of the 1950s and 1960s were tail draggers; the Bird Dog and the DeHavilland Beaver and Otter were all in that category. Those were the aircraft favored for short field, unimproved landing areas. But the "Plane du Jour", for most lieutenants starting out, was the Bird Dog. It was a great plane, because it's fuel-injected engine and high performance fixed-pitch prop could get you out of all sorts of trouble. And of course, if there were trouble to be had, young pilots would find it.

The trickiest technique for short field landings is to drop full flaps and slow the plane down to about 45 knots. The slower one could get the aircraft before touching down, the shorter the landing. To slow the aircraft as much as possible without falling out of the sky, we would raise the nose of the plane and add more power to keep from stalling. By the time we got to the runway we would be hanging on the prop, at nearly full power, nose high, on the edge of a stall. Once this technique was mastered it was possible to land in very short distances but staying proficient in this maneuver required continual practice. We would normally spend ten to twenty to 20 hours a month flying or practicing our short landing techniques. However, one month I had been heavily involved in straightening out our company's supply problems and had done very little flying. Finally, I found time to fly and fortunately that day we had unusually nice weather for Tacoma. I called operations and scheduled a Bird Dog for after lunch. The Ops Officer called back later and asked if I could take a crew chief with me. I told him that was fine. When I got to the flight line the plane, I was assigned had a large steel tube attached to each wing. The tubes were used to hold smoke grenades that the pilot could activate during air shows when a stunt called for leaving smoke trails.

The crew chief and I preflighted the aircraft. I noticed he also had his toolbox with him, which added another 40 pounds to our weight. Now, a bit on the heavy side with the steel tubes, mechanic, and toolbox, we taxied for takeoff and then headed to a field strip to practice some landings. About the time I arrived at the strip, my boss (another lieutenant) was in the air and called me on the radio and said, "Hey, Ren, let's see who can get into this strip the shortest." Of course, I picked up on his challenge. I really didn't care much for my boss, who also wasn't very popular with the other pilots in the platoon. Over time he acquired the nickname of "The Wedge" which, not coincidentally, is the simplest tool known to man. He was a cross between a dullard and a colonoscopy. So, there was no doubt in my military mind that I would put this guy to shame in short order. I said, "Sure, Dan, you're on." and turned the plane downwind to set up my first, winning landing.

On final I dropped full flaps and started to slow my bird down into the 5-knot headwind. My power approach had gotten a tad rusty. I was working hard with the balancing act between throttle and stick. The fact that I was carrying so much extra weight should have been part of my calculations for this event. Nor had I given any thought to the adverse effect of those heavy tubes. Not only did they add to my weight, but they also had a deleterious effect on the aerodynamics of the plane. So now I am lumbering down, feeling my way to the shortest landing known to man, when suddenly, fifty feet short of the runway, the plane dropped out from under me in a full stall. It simply stopped flying and took on the same aerodynamics as a rock. I immediately pushed the throttle full forward. Too late; too close to the ground.

All around the field strip the tall pine trees had been cut back but there was a heavy growth of Scotch Broom that had sprung forth from their exposure to sunlight. Beneath me the growth was six or seven feet high. I sank down into it with full throttle, a level attitude, and a quick prayer. I didn't have time to worry about getting hurt, which was less of a concern than the ignominy of bending my plane. We hit the ground with what is euphemitically called a "hard landing." Suddenly everything was obscured by the flying residue from the prop chewing through Scotch Broom like a columbine. I went on grinding through for what seemed like forever before the little Bird Dog again lifted into the air just as we reached the end of the runway.

I chopped the power and braked the plane to a full stop. Playing Joe Cool, I now exited the aircraft to inspect the damage. The tail wheel had acquired a new rakish angle. A piece of Scotch Broom was sticking out of the oil cooler. There were a couple of minor creases along the bottom of the horizontal stabilizer inflicted by the Scotch Broom stalks cut by the prop, but the plane would fly again. I reached into the cockpit, turned on the radios, and called the Wedge, who was still in the air. "Let's see you get in shorter than that," I laughed, while secretly wondering if I would remain a lieutenant the rest of my life.

The Wedge ordered me to not fly the aircraft out until he got our chief mechanic out to inspect the plane. While waiting for his arrival I walked back into the Scotch Broom to inspect the point of impact. I saw where the plane had hit, crushing the growth under it and cutting a swath for about 30 feet. To my chagrin, I saw where the left tire track had missed a foxhole by inches. Had the wheel gone into that hole, it would have ripped off the landing gear and totaled the plane and perhaps me. I also noticed, as I followed the tire tracks to where they ended when the plane lifted back out of the Scotch Broom, that there was a heavy log lying directly in its path. Had my little plane not become airborne again before it got to the log, it would have been a very bad accident indeed! Truly, that was my lucky day and the fourth time I cheated the grim reaper. Fortunately, the damage was light enough to be classified as an "incident" rather than an "accident" which means it didn't have to be reported to higher headquarters.

In those early days of flying, when we had too many pilots and too little supervision, there were a lot of fun times to be had. To maintain proficiency and build time we were able to schedule a plane any time for any purpose. Some days we would fly off to have lunch at Thun Files, several miles north of us. One day I took my plane south over the lush Willamette Valley and spotted a very fast train headed in the same direction. I dropped down to fly alongside of the engine to see what kind of speed it was doing. The engineer and I exchanged waves and I climbed back to a safer altitude. He was doing 90mph.

On another occasion, I took my bag lunch and 22 rifle, up the valley looking for a road to land on and do a little "plinking". I was flying low, maybe fifteen feet above the ground and headed for a large bush a few feet below me. To my great surprise, just before I got to the bush, about 15 or 20 birds flushed up, out of the bush. My initial reaction was to fly under them, which would have been disastrous at that altitude. And so, I learned that flying low had some unexpected associated dangers.

In December of 1958 the 4th Infantry Division was to conduct an amphibious landing exercise involving the entire division. The ground units went by ship. Most of our aviation company left by air for a little airfield at San Simeon, California, not far from the Hearst Castle. The concept of the operation was for the division to arrive by sea and fight their way over the Los Padres Mountains, ending up in Camp Roberts. A few days into the exercise, classmate Charlie Saint was fighting his way over the Los Padres Mountains with his rifle company. The division objective was inland on the east side of the mountains, near Camp Roberts. Our aviation company was flying missions to support the division's advance over the mountains. Among other things, we had a 24-hour radio relay mission to ensure units on the east side of the mountain could communicate with those on the west side.

One night, flying radio relay, I heard Charlie Saint's distinctive voice come over the radio. He was commanding a rifle company in the 4th Division. I noted that his call sign was Red Dog 6. By 3 AM, getting sleepy and bored, circling at 5,000 feet, I decided to send Charlie (my chess buddy) a message through the division radio relay net. Using the appropriate frequency, I transmitted, "Red Dog Operator, this is Sky Hawk 2. Message for Red Dog 6, over." On the other end a voice said, "Roger, Sky Hawk, send your message." "Message for Red Dog 6; Papa dash Kilo Four (P-K4). End of message, over." I had not said who the message was from, but I knew Charlie would recognize the chess notation for my usual opening chess move of pawn to king's fourth square. Several weeks later, when we were back at Fort Lewis, Charlie called me and said, "Damn you, Ren, I had been fighting my way over those mountains for three days without sleep and finally found a moment to catch a couple of winks when my radio operator shook me awake to tell me that I had to go to division headquarters to pick up a coded message. It took me an hour to get there and the only thing that stupid message said was P-K4! I knew who that was, and I'll get even!" Charlie and Ann were always fun to be with. Charlie's gone now but someday on that great chessboard in the sky, we'll finish the game we started 65 years ago.

Flying in the northwest is always a tricky situation in winter, with wave after wave of bad weather coming across the state of Washington. In those early years of Army aviation only about half the aviators was instrument rated but most of the younger officers like me, who weren't already qualified, were scheduled for instrument school at a later date. Until we were so qualified, we had to stay clear of clouds, either going under or over any weather systems we encountered. The bad part of flying into marginal weather is the unpredictable nature of weather systems. Forecasting weather has always been an inexact science, particularly 65 years ago.

That was the case on 20 December when we finished our Rocky Shoals Exercise and eagerly began preparations to get home for Christmas. We were to fly out in groups of three or four aircraft. I was the leader of one three-plane group. It would be a seven-hour flight back to Fort Lewis. We refueled at McClellan AFB, near Sacramento. I remember being at the operations counter filling out my flight plan and next to me was an Air Force jock working on his. He looked over at my flight plan with four hours in route, shook his head and said, "You Army guys are sure patient." I noted he was flying an F-104 to McCord AFB, next to Ft. Lewis. I asked, "How long for you"? He said, One hour"!

By the time we reached Portland it was 4:30 in the afternoon and getting dark. I was in the lead aircraft, with the other two planes following, when I called Portland Flight Service for their latest weather. Portland reported a broken layer at 5,000 feet, overcast ceiling at 7,000 feet north of the Columbia River, and deteriorating visibility. It was questionable whether to fly through, but we had been in San Simeon for nearly two weeks and Christmas was now five days away. Everyone wanted to get home in the worst way but here was this weather thing between us and home. I reasoned that, even though it was night, it wouldn't be too bad if we could stay below 5,000. I called the other aircraft and told them I was going down to 3,500 feet. I could see the stream of headlights from the cars on Highway 99 snaking north like a string of pearls. Off to my right were the Cascade Mountains. To the left of the valley was the Coastal Range. As we made our way north in the valley, between the two ranges, visibility was deteriorating. I let down another 500 feet and could see the lights from homes in the foothills but now the lights were above me. Suddenly that unpredictable nature of weather struck. I was inside a cloud and totally without vision of anything except the flashing of my navigation lights against the gray velvet blanket that engulfed me. I recalled a bizarre incident of the previous month when a flight of three helicopters from our unit got into bad weather not far from where we were. The first helicopter flew into a fog bank low to the ground, trying to maintain visual contact with the terrain. The pilot lost all visual and crashed. The other two helicopters went in looking for him and one after the other, the same thing happened. Three helicopters and their crews, all lost.

Once inside that cloud, I knew I was in deep trouble. This was the stuff that made pilots a statistic. The memory of my instructor's voice echoed in my head, "If you ever inadvertently fly into a cloud, immediately do a 180 and fly back out." I called the other two aircraft and told them my intentions. I was not sure whether I should turn left or right to avoid hitting the mountains on either side of the valley. I put the plane in a left bank and began my turn. My heart was pounding and palms sweating and now I could hear the engine RPM increasing. It was the beginning of the dead man's spiral; the maneuver that killed John Kennedy, Jr. several years ago. I raised the nose of the plane and leveled the wings as I completed my turn, relieved that I had not collided with the mountains but now concerned about the possibility of a head-on collision with one of the other planes. At that moment I popped out of the cloud, almost surprised to still be alive. I called the other aircraft and told them I was clear of the clouds, and we would be spending the night in Portland. Home and Christmas could wait one more day.

In flight school and for the first few years of flying, our total flying experience was in the Bird Dog, then officially designated the L-19 (the L standing for liaison). These light aircraft, made by Cessna, were in heavy use throughout the Army for some 20 years, until the mid-70s. By the late 50s I had almost 500 hours in the Bird Dog. My flying skills had gotten to the point where I could land on a curving dirt road by putting one wheel on the road and holding enough bank to follow the turn in the road. As the aircraft slowed for landing, the high wing stopped flying first and as you touched down, there was still enough rudder authority to stay with the turn of the road. One day I had just landed on such a road in the Yakima Training Area and was now taking off on the return flight. As I broke ground, I shifted my 216 pounds back a little and pop to my astonishment, the back rest of my seat broke off. My falling backwards, coupled with the acceleration of the aircraft, almost put me in the rear of the cockpit. Fortunately, I had enough presence of mind (unlike my normal state) to let go of the stick as I fell. Perhaps I instinctively knew I'd be dead if I held onto the controls as I fell backwards and pulled the aircraft into a nose-high configuration and stall. Fortunately, with proper take-off trim, the little Bird Dog was properly configured to climb and continued its upward path quite nicely without me during the few seconds it took to get myself reoriented in the cockpit. I've read of several fatal aircraft accidents that occurred when the seat lock failed at takeoff and the seat slid toward the rear of the airplane, but this was a new twist of fate. My next problem was what to do with the aircraft. I knew that if I returned to land the plane would be grounded and I would be stuck for the night in Yakima. But as things were, it was like trying to fly while sitting on a stool, no big deal but very strange indeed. It was about an hour and a half flight back to Fort Lewis. I decided I could sit on my stool for that long. As I rolled to a stop at Gray Army Airfield, I felt for the first time how lucky I was to have had a second chance. I had cheated death for a second time.

Later that year I was selected to attend a civilian instrument school in Oakland. Instrument training is rather intense, but I was glad to get back to the Bay Area and San Francisco, where I had spent most of my school years. Both our parents lived within two blocks of each other, so it was a great opportunity to be with our extended families again. Lee was now two years old. The three of us moved in with Mother at 257 Kensington Way for the duration of the six-week instrument course.

I was looking forward to flying the Cessna 172's they used for our training. It would be the first time I had flown a plane with a nose wheel, referred to as a "tricycle landing gear". As with flight school, the course was divided between time in ground school and time in the air. The written instrument exam consisted of 50 questions and the practical exam with an FAA examiner required flying several instrument approaches for an hour and a half. After graduation in February 1959, we returned home to Tacoma, and it was back to work as usual.

Instrument flying is the altissimo aviation experience. I compare it to a blind concert pianist. Like fingers moving across a keyboard, a pilot's eyes will dance across the instruments on the panel before him in what we call an instrument scan. Cameras have recorded airline pilot scans at an unbelievable thousand scans per minute. The brain then translates the information into control responses to keep the aircraft on heading, altitude, attitude and aispeed without seeing outside the cockpit. While this is going on, the pilot is expected to operate the radios and navigation instruments, changing frequencies and communicating with the controllers. It is indeed an orchestration that produces the beautiful music of survival. In rough weather this can be an exhausting endeavor, leaving one with sweaty palms and a puckered seat.

A qualified pilot will need to invest 60 or 70 hours of concentrated effort to achieve his instrument rating, then maintain proficiency with an hour or two of practice each month. For this purpose, we trained in a single engine plane that had a fully instrumented cockpit in the back seat. It was a strange hybrid Cessna (Bird Dog) that was created for instrument training. It had extra speed from the variable pitch propeller, and a completely closed off back seat with no windows. This was great for training because it forced you to fly entirely on instruments without being able to see out.

It was a wintry day in February when we decided to use the trainer in a flight to Portland. Air Traffic Control cleared us to 7,000 feet. About a half hour from Portland International we entered the overcast and called Portland for our approach instructions. It was then that ice began to form on our wings and prop. In these little aircraft, ice could be a killer. It distorts the shape of the wings, degrades lift, adds great weight and changes the prop from a rotating airfoil to something with the aerodynamics of a baseball bat.

As the ice began to form on the leading edge of the wings, we started losing lift. I added power to make up for the increased weight. But it wasn't just the weight of the ice we were fighting. It was mostly a problem of the ice destroying effects of the airfoil and reducing the lift produced by the wings. I raised the nose now and went to full power to stay at 7,000 feet but in our nose-high attitude we began to collect even more ice along the tail and belly of the plane. By this time our windshield was completely iced over, and our airspeed began to drop as our propeller lost thrust. Although we had ice on our wings, for sure there was sweat in the cockpit.

"Portland Control, this is Army 52799 at 7,000, request a lower altitude." "Army 799, Portland Control, unable at this time." "Portland we are taking ice and will be unable to maintain seven." "799, are you declaring an emergency?" Of course, Army aviators don't declare emergencies because they are always in control; right? But mostly, if I were to declare an emergency, regulations require a report in writing to the FAA within 24 hours to explain how one of my ilk could have gotten himself into that situation. "Portland 799 is not declaring an emergency, but we are unable to maintain this altitude and are coming down."

In bad weather, the controllers have their hands full directing and stacking air traffic. The last thing they needed was some little Army plane screwing up their act with a priority event requiring other aircraft to give way. "Army 799, you are cleared to 5,000, maintain heading and report intercepting the Portland ILS." "Roger, Portland out of seven for five, 799." As our little plane passed through 6,000 feet the ice began to come loose from the prop and the chunks were pinging against the clearing windshield. Next the ice gave way on the wings with strange sliding noises. I breathed a sigh of relief and leveled the aircraft at 5,000 feet. For a third time I had been given another chance; I would fly again.

By 1959 Barb was again expecting and we were looking forward to what we hoped would be a girl. As the date neared, we went through the preparations of buying a crib and making one of our three bedrooms more nursery-like. Finally in mid-November Barb's labor and the countdown began. Our first trip to Madigan General Hospital on November 18 was proclaimed "premature". By the time we got home her labor count confirmed that in fact our trip to the hospital was not premature and we headed back. By the time we got her into the gurney things were moving fast and off they went to the delivery room. In less than an hour we had a beautiful, eight-pound baby girl whom we named Laura Suzanne. I had chosen "Laura", Barb had chosen "Suzanne" and we felt like the luckiest couple alive.

A couple months after Christmas I received orders for Korea, to report June 1960. By then I would have been flying for three years and I guess the Army figured it was about time I learned to be an Infantryman again. It would be a one-year assignment, unaccompanied. It was a tough time of life to leave my wife and two little ones.

CHAPTER 21

KOREA

In general, during peacetime, career officers can expect one unaccompanied tour overseas every ten years. So, by early 1960, my orders to Korea were not unexpected. But leaving your family behind for a full year is indeed a hardship, especially for young couples. It also meant we would need to get our home in Lakewood sold and spend some time finding a place for the family to stay while I was gone. In those days, homes appreciated little or not at all, so we felt fortunate to have gotten our place sold for a couple hundred more than we paid for it and now, of course we had a bit of equity to use when buying our next home.

The Army paid our moving expenses and packing of our household goods, so what little we had accumulated made it an easy move. Using a month of accrued leave, we headed home to San Francisco to get the family settled in for the long year ahead. Most of May was spent living with our folks in San Francisco as we shopped furiously for a place to buy where Barb and the kids could live. Finally, we found a newly constructed home on Campana Avenue in Daly City that was selling for $18,000. It was a three-bedroom tract home in a nice neighborhood. Having just sold our little home in Tacoma, we were financially positioned to buy another in the San Francisco area but still needed to qualify for the loan. We made a partial down payment and completed the application process and were now awaiting approval and closing. Escrow seemed to take forever. Finally, I asked the real estate agent if we could have the keys so I could get some work done on the backyard. As the calendar closed in on my mandatory departure date, I was becoming concerned about getting the family settled before I left.

With eight days left before my departure, our furniture arrived from Washington and was now waiting disposition. I told the moving company to deliver it into our new home while still waiting for escrow to close. It was a gutsy thing to do, totally illegal but options by that time were running out. We had done a lot of work on the backyard, which was initially a pile of sand sloping uphill away from the house which needed landscaping. Barb and I spent several days transforming the sand mound into a yard, using 2x12 redwood planks to retain the upper part of the hillside. That left us about half the yard for grass and a concrete patio. Still without escrow closing, we called the cement company to bring in a few cubic yards of concrete for the patio. I had the forms down and ready for pouring. Barb's Uncle Lee was visiting so, when the cement truck arrived, we pressed him into action with me, bringing loads of cement from the front street to the backyard in wheelbarrows. Back and forth we went, while Marge stood in the pile of concrete inside the forms and leveled it with a hoe. We worked like beavers and finally the patio took shape. Altogether we spent two weeks making the house a home. I only had a few days left before I would need to leave for Korea. I decided there just wasn't enough time left to wait for escrow to close and still get my family settled. Our furniture was in the garage, and I was soon to leave. A few days after our fourth anniversary on June 5th, Barb drove me to Travis AFB. By then we were completely moved in and had landscaped the back yard but still no approval for the loan.

There was never a thought in our minds that loan approval might be a problem, having already purchased a home two years earlier and being in a better financial position now than then. I was a first lieutenant making about $500 a month, plus another $500 or so with flight pay and housing allowances. Barb talked to the agent about the closing and that we had moved in. Of course, he was flabbergasted that we had moved ourselves into the house before closing and called the loan officer. The mortgage company was evidently unaware that my total income was about a thousand a month and they were basing their decision only on my base pay of about $500 a month.

The next day Barb was seated in front of the loan officer, explaining our actual income and that there was no way we wouldn't be making the mortgage payments before spending a dime on anything else. She was convincing and a few days later, the papers were in escrow for closing. Escrow finally closed a few days later while I was in Korea.

—∞—

It was a very long flight from Travis to Korea. Now, as the C-141 aircraft circled Osan AFB for landing, a few miles south of Seoul, I had my first glimpse of the Korean landscape. It was liberally sprinkled with rice paddies and green hillsides. Exiting the aircraft, I was struck by the heat, humidity and ever permeating odor of the well fertilized countryside. My entire life was now in one large suitcase and a carry-on bag, which I loaded on the transport to our transient quarters and in-processing.

The next day I was on my way to the First Cavalry Division but without several pairs of socks that the houseboy had absconded with. The dirt road heading north was in pretty good shape, but the red dust billowed behind our jeep and floated above the road with every oncoming vehicle. As we slowed, passing through small, thatched villages, I had glimpses of the agrarian village life of a most rudimentary culture. I was amazed how third world this country was; a land where the ox was the primary piece of agricultural machinery and for the most part, the children ran naked in the summer heat.

Two hours later we arrived at the 1st of the 9th Cav Battle Group, located inside a link fence and barbed wire compound, spread across the side of a hill to the left of our dirt road. I was later to learn that this road was the Main Supply Route (MSR) leading north to the DMZ. As I looked up the hill at our compound, I was struck by its bleak general appearance, which would not have compared favorably to most prison compounds. The buildings were Quonset huts of varying sizes set on concrete pads. This was a compound you would expect to see in a war zone. In fact, we were a scant six years past the armistice between North and South Korea, having concluded a war which in three years cost our nation some 36,000 dead. This compound and its battle group, located 20 miles from the DMZ, would be our first line of defense if North Korea decided to attack south.

The gate guard saluted as we entered the compound and our driver turned left to the Headquarters Building. The main compound buildings were all located in the relatively level, lower part of the area. On the side of the hill above us were the officer quarters and officers' club. These Quonset huts were rounded, corrugated, tin abominations, sometimes placed side by side or connected in a line. Some Quonsets were large, some were small; all were ugly. The ones we lived in we called "hooches."

After meeting with the commander, I was escorted by another lieutenant up the hill to my quarters to get settled in. We followed a steep paved road up the side of the mountain. On the way up, he explained that this mountain was the highest terrain in the division sector. It was called "Easy Block" and was the key terrain our battle group would defend if attacked by North Korea. By the time we got up the hill to the BOQ area I was breathing hard, while my escort seemed to be doing fine. Six months and fifteen pounds later I too would be bounding up that hill. He opened the door to the 15x20 foot half-Quonset that I would share with another officer. There were two Army cots, two desks, two chairs and a diesel-fed pot belly stove. This was my hooch and would be my home for the next year.

My roommate was also a first lieutenant, Vincent McNamara, a fun-loving Irishman who over time would regale me with his tales of debauchery in the nearby village of Buedimae. Although I was no longer a religious person, the residue of my church years did not provide for the convenience of confession to expiate my sins to go forth and sin again. Whatever I did, or failed to do, would become an unforgiven part of me, and I was not prepared to be untrue to my wife live the way Mac did. Eventually, word of Mac's village exploits must have reached the ear of our battle group Catholic chaplain, which resulted in Father O'Malley's scheduling a visit with him. It was on an evening when I was at the photo lab working with black and whites, developing and enlarging. Later in the evening, when I got home, I asked Mac what the padre wanted to see him about. "Well," Mac said, "he wanted to know why I was missing mass and following that discussion the padre said to me, 'You know, Mac, eternity is a very long time. In fact, if a bird were to carry one grain of sand from Easy Block Mountain every year, the amount of time it would take to move the entire mountain would only be the beginning of eternity.'" Mac added, "And he left me with that thought."

—◌◌◌—

Being away from Barb was tough. It was our first extended separation. I anguished. Lee was three, Laura not yet one. I really hadn't bonded with them enough to have their absence bother me, but I was missing my wife terribly. I was twenty-seven years old, halfway around the world, with no hope of seeing my family for a year; it was a maturing experience.

For my first five months I was assigned to Headquarters Company as the Executive Officer (second in command). I was then a senior first lieutenant. My boss, the company commander, was a captain. The most notable trait of a good leader is that he is concerned with the welfare of his men. The most notable trait of my captain was that he took care of himself at the expense of his men. This guy really needed to know General Schofield's Definition of Discipline:

> *"The discipline which makes the soldiers of a free country reliable in battle is not to be gained by harsh or tyrannical treatment. On the contrary, such treatment is far more likely to destroy than to make an army. It is possible to impart instructions and give commands in such manner and tone of voice to inspire in the soldier an intense desire to obey. While the opposite manner and tone of voice cannot fail to excite strong resentment and a desire to disobey. The one mode or the other of dealing with subordinates, springs from a corresponding spirit in the breast of the commander. He who feels the respect which is due to others cannot fail to inspire in them regard for himself, while he who feels, and hence manifests, disrespect toward others, especially his inferiors, cannot fail to inspire hatred against himself."*

It was tough working for him. I hunkered down and did my best. Headquarters companies are ash and trash companies responsible for meeting the administrative and logistical needs of the battlegroup Headquarters. We had some bright soldiers, but their level of discipline was not at the same standard as in a combat company.

One of my great disappointments during the five months I was in Headquarters Company was a soldier I was appointed to defend in a special court martial. He was 28, a year older than I, somewhat old for a private but he had enlisted late in life. I guess he had problems adjusting. He certainly had problems with the Army, having been AWOL several times. On this occasion he had been gone for over a week. The MPs found him in Buedimae Village, a small town next to our compound. He was on a weekend pass to be with a Korean girl he fancied but didn't bother to return to post for duty on Monday. Because it was his third offense, this AWOL was punishable by special court martial. A special court is convened for moderately severe offenses, punishable by loss of pay, demotion and confinement for up to six months. In those days officers without any formal legal training could be assigned as the defense counsel or trial counsel (prosecution) in such courts. The jury would be composed of officers and sometimes NCOs and a senior officer would be appointed to preside over the case.

At the time, I was nearing my 28th birthday and had recently been selected for promotion to captain. I was appointed to present a defense for the soldier. A review of his records revealed that he had an IQ of about 165; it was the highest intelligence quotient of anyone in our battle group. I was impressed and determined to save this guy. After several long talks with my man, I was convinced he could be put to useful service in the Army if he were properly led and adequately inspired. I asked him if he could start soldiering if I were able to have him transferred to my unit. He assured me that his offending days were over, and he was ready to go to work.

By the time the court martial was convened I had thoroughly studied the UCMJ manual and was aware that his absence at roll call was prima facie evidence of his guilt. There was no defense. I explained to the court that this soldier had the highest IQ in the battle group and that to stash him away in prison for six months would accomplish no useful purpose. I asked the court to suspend his sentence and assign him to my unit, where I could accept full responsibility for his future conduct and productivity. Based on my display of confidence in him and my convincing the court that under my tutelage he would prosper, the court decided to remand him to my custody. I was very pleased with my legal prowess and looked forward to proving my confidence in him was justified. To my great surprise, the following morning he disappeared, never to be seen again. Wow! As a young Lieutenant, full of hope and conviction that I could make a difference in this man's life, I received my first dose of realism and a quick lesson in human nature.

That unfortunate event was in November. By then I was looking forward to receiving a week of R&R over the Christmas holidays. I had been gone from home for six months and looking back, I should have found a way to get home and see my family again. The separation was really tough for me and certainly no easier for Barb. But a lieutenant's pay was not adequate to bring a family of four together by commercial air halfway around the world. So, I took my week's R&R to Japan, where I could go by military air at no expense. I hadn't seen Japan since I was a teenager, eleven years earlier and was looking forward to renewing that experience.

I had made friends with Vin Hirsch, another West Point officer (Class of 1950), who commanded a rifle company in our battle group. He was a captain and easy to like. We had a jeep drive us to Osan Air Force Base, where we got a flight aboard an AF transport plane, known as a C-124 Globemaster and sometimes jokingly referred to as the Crashmaster. It was about a three-hour trip. We landed at an Air Force base outside Tokyo.

It was interesting now to see how completely that nation had recovered from the war-torn condition I had experienced there in 1949. Tokyo was a hustling, bustling city full of cars and well-dressed Japanese. We made our way to the military Hotel Sano near the Ginza, the primary downtown area of Tokyo. Our days passed doing such things as Christmas shopping at the local PX and visiting the Tokyo tower that the Japanese had constructed to be a few feet higher than the Eiffel Tower in Paris.

When I returned to Korea from R&R and somehow got through a rather lonely Christmas, we began preparations for a battle group command post winter field exercise involving only the battle group headquarters and supporting elements. Fortunately, the worthless captain who had been commanding Headquarters Company had rotated home. He was replaced by a grizzled 45-year-old captain who would retire after this assignment. Captain Posey had spent most of his career in Special Forces, well removed from direct authority. He was an innovator, a leader and totally immune from following regulations. I liked him. His unorthodox ways were not totally dissimilar from my own attitude.

The Korean Peninsula is given to wide swings of temperature. In the spring and fall it was not unusual for the warmest part of the day to be 50 degrees higher than the coolest. The summers were in the high 90's most days. The winter could be bitter when the freezing Manchurian air mass from the north swept over the country. Now, for our command post exercise, the earth was frozen and even at the warmest part of the day, temperatures would never reach much above zero. I was reminded of the stories of our troops at the Chosen Reservoir as the Chinese flooded across the Yalu and pushed MacArthur's forces south. Our men then were ill-equipped to face a Korean winter and had suffered greatly in those sub-zero temperatures.

Now, seven years later, I'm in the middle of a Korean winter and getting ready to move our headquarters into the field to train under almost the same severe winter conditions. It is one thing to be in cold weather, bundled as you dash from your car to your warm house. It is entirely another thing to be living in it, with little or no relief from the finger-numbing effects of freezing temperatures, 24 hours a day. Unlike our frozen comrades retreating from the chosen Reservoir in 1952, we were fully equipped with cold weather gear. My "Mickey Mouse Boots," as the soldiers were quick to label them, had two layers of rubber with an insulating air pocket between the layers. With two pairs of socks, there would be no frozen toes inside those things. We were also well layered with thermal underwear and outer, water repellent trousers, over our fatigues. Most of us had wool liners in our field jackets and over that a parka with a fur-lined hood. Our mittens were large enough to cover our gloves underneath. We were fully layered.

The battlegroup commander, a full colonel, had drawn a large circle on my map. As the Headquarters Company XO, I was responsible for selecting the field location for the battle group command post, somewhere within the circle. This meant finding an area that provided cover and concealment and a sufficient road network to provide ready access and resupply. High ground is also desirable for communications but not at the cost of cover and concealment. I also needed to locate an alternate command post for use in the event our primary location became untenable. We had a ton of tentage to put up and then camouflage. The Army had tents for everything; command post tents, mess tents, general purpose (GP) tents (large and medium). Putting these large tents up was not an easy matter. It took practice and coordination.

Meanwhile there were latrine pits to dig in the frozen earth and patrols to arrange in establishing our perimeter security. While that was going on we needed to set up elaborate communications by wire, radio and microwave. Wire needed to be laid, antennas erected, and the microwave towers located and aligned. Our signal detachment took care of that. We were setting up operations as though we were in combat. When all this activity was in full swing, I turned my attention to locating and erecting the four-man tent which would house the company commander, me and our other two officers. We had a small diesel stove for the tent. There was a hole in the top of the tent with a flap for the stove pipe to exit through and a gas line which ran under the side of the tent from a 55-gallon drum several feet behind. That night the temperature dropped several degrees more below zero and we would turn up the flame in our pot belly, gasoline fed stove. Sometime after midnight the top of the tent, where the stove pipe went through, caught fire. At that temperature it was easily distinguished but left a large hole making a warmer tent impossible.

About 6 AM we dressed and made our way to the mess tent for breakfast. The coffee was ready, the bacon and eggs were frying, and the field stoves were doing their job. But I noticed a strange thing happening on one of the grills. The eggs were frozen solid and were rolling around like billiard balls. Our cook would peel off the shells, put the eggs on the grill and they would just roll around until eventually they would start to melt and then settle on that flat spot. It was a bizarre sight. The breakfast, less than wonderful, would have been hot had it not been for the frozen metal trays. We learned a lot on that exercise, particularly how to stay warm at 20 below and still get the job done, unlike in 1950. Five days later we were back at Camp in the relative comfort of our Quonset huts.

In January 1961 I took command of a rifle company. Company E was the fifth company in the battlegroup and was being formed by pulling officers and men from other companies when our organization reorganized from a three-company battalion to a five-company battle group. Of course, when company commanders are levied to give up 20 percent of their people to form a new company, they aren't going to give away their best soldiers. So, my command was a bit shaky in the beginning until I could shape it and train it. It was a difficult command for me anyway, since my previous three years had been in aviation while other non-flying infantry officers were commanding platoons and learning the infantry ropes. Being selected to command a company of about 180 men was an important adjunct to my career. The other companies were all commanded by captains, one of whom was six years my senior.

Our primary company mission was to defend a portion of Easy Block Mountain, the highest terrain in the division sector. One day a month we would move, as a company, up the mountain. It was a steep and long trek, at least three miles of dirt road. When it rained, the road turned to red mud and the going was slow. Often, when we reached our positions on top of the mountain, the foxholes and other emplacements there had been pushed in and the sandbags slit. That was the handiwork of North Korean patrols coming south to harass us and gather information. We would repair the positions and begin work on additional areas. The destroyed positions were a reminder of the uneasy peace between North and South Vietnam.

Occasionally, the duty of "Officer of the Day" (OD) would fall to me. It was a 24-hour weekend duty that was assigned by roster. The routine required the OD to take charge of the compound, ensure the perimeter guard detail was properly conducted and solve any problems which arose. My name showed up on the roster about every four months. The worst part of the duty, for me, was to make the rounds in the local village. With the accompaniment of an MP, I was required to make at least one tour of our local village, Buedimae. I carried a fully loaded .45 pistol and wore a black armband bearing the letters OD. The adventure of walking through the village was never a comfortable one. Our young soldiers, some of whom had never dated before, would visit the village off duty, drinking and carousing with Korean prostitutes. I walked through the center of the village, on a dirt road too narrow to accommodate a jeep. I was not a welcome sight among the inhabitants or the troops, some of whom were drunk and a few on drugs. My job was to show a presence and let both villagers and soldiers know that Army discipline was close at hand.

Our young soldiers tended to sometimes confuse sex with love. So, the army provided some parental functions in so much as they needed command approval to marry a Korean National. I was the first line of defense in discouraging such frivolity. These young men, some only 17, may never have even been on a date before. The first time they spent the night with a prostitute they thought they were in love! Only once was I required to exercise my discretion in that matter when a young PFC requested permission from my first sergeant to see the company commander. The soldier explained to me that he was in love with a Korean girl from the village. I asked how old she was. He said 21. I asked him his age. He was 18. I asked, "Do you know how she has been making her living for the past six years?" He said that didn't matter to him. I did all I could to dissuade him, nothing worked. Finally, I said, "Permission denied! Come back and see me in four months." I never saw him again but am sure many years later he was thanking me.

During my tour in Korea as an Infantry officer, I also had to maintain my flying proficiency as an Army aviator. When not assigned to an aviation unit, aviators still needed to fly a minimum of four hours a month, some of which needed to be nighttime and some flying for instrument proficiency. I enjoyed getting up in the air to occasionally escape the routine of "Infantryman." The nearest Army Airfield was located about 20 miles south of us, near division headquarters. I would drive my jeep down to the airfield about twice a month to get my flying time. The night flying was always a bit creepy because there were so few lights in the countryside below and relatively few navigational aids to go by. So, for the most part, when flying at night, I made sure I was high enough to be well clear of any mountain peaks. In those days I smoked about a pack of cigarettes a day and a cigarette on my night flight was relaxing and enjoyable. On one particular flight it was a very dark moonless night and from seven thousand feet, I could see only one light on the terrain below. As I was watching the light to help maintain my bearings, I lit my cigarette and deeply inhaled. To my surprise the light almost immediately became very dim and hard to see. I learned later that nicotine has quite a deleterious effect on night vision, particularly at altitude. Smoking during night flights was something I would avoid thereafter.

Having spent most of my career thus far as an aviator, I had a lot of catching up to learn the ins and outs of being an Infantry commander. Without those several years' experience of being in an infantry unit, taking command of an Infantry company did not come easily. Our training routine began with individual training first, then the squads, platoons, and companies. Eventually we began to function as an effective company. At the end of the designated training cycle, about four months, the entire battle group would go to the field for the annual Army Training Test. The ATT was a three-day combat simulation exercise requiring company commanders to demonstrate the ability to maneuver their units in the attack, counterattack, establish a defense and conduct a night withdrawal. It would be a demanding three days with little time for sleep.

At "oh dark thirty" on a cold April morning we departed the compound for an 8-mile march to our assembly area. The description by Pearl S. Buck in her novel *The Land of the Morning Calm,* proved accurate as we moved past sleepy villages under the distinct layer of haze caused by early morning cooking fires and inversion restricting the smoke to about 30 feet above the ground. The huts all looked alike. The Korean equivalent of stucco was clay earth mixed with straw. At one end of their hooches was a chimney. At the other end was the cooking area. The heat from the cooking fire was drawn through small tunnels under the hut to the chimney on the far side, warming the floors.

We moved as Infantrymen in war, single-file columns on each side of the road with six to ten paces between soldiers. Our destination was a circle on an overlay I had received from group headquarters early that morning. There had not been time for me to conduct a route recon prior to crossing our line of departure. Now the cellophane overlay was affixed on my clipboard on top of my map. I was finding our way minute by minute, reading the map and making decisions about which way to go based on matching features depicted on the map to the terrain features. We had had a thorough course in map reading at the Academy, then again in the Basic Infantry Officers Course, plus many hours working with maps in aviation ground school. If there was anything I knew well, it was reading a military map.

Now, looking at my map, I saw that it indicated a small dirt road to the left, a few hundred yards ahead, leading into a valley and our assembly area but as we approached the road, I saw another road a hundred paces further on that did not show on my map. A dilemma. From our location along the ridgeline, it appeared that the two roads were headed off in different directions. The troops had been maintaining a good pace for the past two hours and this was no time for a wrong decision that could delay our arrival and add unnecessary distance to our road march. I called the column to a halt for a ten-minute break and a chance to solve my dilemma. The thought occurred to me about how much easier life was when my decisions affected only me. Now, on this road, I had a hundred and sixty troops behind me who depended on my knowing what I was doing. A wrong turn here and I would not only lose their respect but could become lost in the hills of the Korean countryside. There was no sure solution but studying my map, the second road appeared to be the more likely route. We mounted up and headed for it. An hour later, as the road crossed a stream at the base of a steep hill, exactly matching my map features, I knew I had made the right decision. Such were the joys of command.

In the assembly area we established a perimeter defense, distributed supplies and equipment and made radio contact with my XO, instructing him to bring the mess truck forward and arrange for the evening meal. As our luncheon C-rations were distributed I received a radio message to meet the battle group commander on a hilltop to receive the "Five Paragraph Field Order" that described all the details of the attack which would jump off in the morning. Standard procedures prescribe that each level of command use only one third of the remaining time until the attack or other operation to formulate his unit's plan of attack, leaving two-thirds of the time for subordinates to complete their portions of the attack plan. Therefore, as soon as I knew what my unit was doing, I called for my platoon leaders to meet me at a specified vantage point three hours later. That would give me sufficient time to determine my "concept of operation."

We began the exercise early the next morning with an attack five miles up the side of a mountain. After taking our objective, we began digging into our positions, expecting a counterattack. We were all totally exhausted when my radio operator handed me a warning order to continue our attack up the side of yet another mountain, even more daunting than the one we had just taken. I could scarcely believe we now needed to mount up and continue the attack. This sort of activity continued for an exhausting 36 hours without sleep. Finally, early the following morning, I told my XO I was going to catch a couple of hours of sleep. I guess everyone else was in equally bad shape because, when I awoke three hours later, my entire headquarters had seized upon this opportunity to zonk out. Incoming radio calls had been unanswered for some time. When the battle group commander finally contacted me, he had several choice words to express his displeasure.

Our exercise raged on for another 30 hours. When it was over and the march back to our compound was complete, the umpires finalized their critique and turned in their scores. I heaved a great sigh of relief as I learned that we had passed the Army Training Test; just barely.

In June of 1961 I left Korea to rejoin my family and end the longest and most difficult separation of my married life. It had undoubtedly been even more difficult for Barb, who at age 25 had to deal with raising two children, under the age of 5, shop, cook, clean, pay the bills and still stay sane. This responsibility had changed her dramatically. She was no longer dependent on me for decisions and emotional support. It was quite an adjustment for me to return to a no longer docile bride. And I guess, fitting me back into her life was a bit of an adjustment for her too. Before leaving Korea, my roommate. Mac, told me to be sure to get some green Jelly Beans before I got home. He said, "When you get to the front door and the kids rush out to greet you, you tell em, "Here, I got these for you", and you throw the jellybeans on to the grass. "It will keep them occupied for about an hour.

We spent the month getting reacquainted and making preparations for our departure. We decided to keep our home this time and we located a renter who paid enough to cover the mortgage each month. Before the end of June, I was promoted to captain, and we left San Francisco for Fort Benning and the Advanced Infantry Course.

CHAPTER 22

FORT BENNING AND THE ADVANCED COURSE

The Advanced Course brought our class together again with about 80 of my classmates who had also been selected to attend that six-month course. Army school time for me was a time to enjoy. For others, who felt the competitive need to move ahead, it was also a time for career progression. The three successive schools in the Army which are necessary for a successful career are the Advanced Course (for Junior officers), the Command & General Staff Course (for field grade officers), and the War College (for senior officers who have a shot at becoming general officers). Early attendance at each of these career-enhancing schools is an indicator of success. Within our class, those who had been selected for the Advance Course and when they attended, was part of the competition. The same was true for being selected for specific assignments such as Aide de Camp or command. I was fortunate to have commanded an Infantry company as a lieutenant and was surprised to learn that hardly any of my classmates had similar company command experience. This gave me a slight leg up and could influence my next assignment. Having command experience meant that I would be ready for the next step of being placed in a key staff position. That in turn would qualify me for early attendance at the Command & General Staff Course. With C&GS under my belt, the next step would be commanding a battalion and then high-level staff (the Pentagon or NATO).

However, early on in my career I learned that as an Army Aviator, I would likely sacrifice the opportunity of becoming a general. That was the devil's bargain; enjoy flying and the additional hazardous duty pay but forget being competitive. It was understandable. As an aviator, I would need to split my time between flying assignments and Infantry assignments. My career branch as an Infantryman depended on passing through specific command and staff career gates, which would be jeopardized if I were in flying assignments. Additionally, non-aviators held a certain degree of disdain for those who got to fly airplanes and received additional pay for it, while the Infantry guys were slogging it out in tough ground assignments.

There was one other factor which also militated against career progression for the Army aviator: The old heads in aviation were there because they did not want the additional responsibility and to make the effort required in a branch assignment. All they were interested in was flying; promotions were less important than being in the sky and being paid extra for it. Of course, the problem there was that the young aviator would not have good role models to follow, nor would he be receiving good efficiency reports from those who had never gotten a decent report for their own performance. It was certainly not the path to greatness. However, with the advent of the Vietnam War, which was essentially a helicopter war, the aviator finally became king.

Fort Benning is something of an Infantrymen's Mecca. It brought old friends together and provided the opportunity for new friends and to learn the latest weaponry and tactics. Our school attendees were all located in housing on post, small brick buildings with two bedrooms. For the most part we lived near our friends and having the same schedules, were able to carpool to class. We had a great social life with club parties, bridge games and golf. Aside from that, were weekend activities with our preschool children and my squeezing in the requisite hours of flying time when I could. Studying really wasn't my bag but I enjoyed most of our classes and had a little fun along the way, like the time our instructor asked me how I would employ the battalion radars we had been learning about. I said, "Sir, I would mass them for the attack and if they didn't kill the enemy, they would at least make them sterile, and we won't have to fight their next generation." He did not like my answer and asked me to see him after class.

About halfway through our course, we were asked to write an article for the Infantry Magazine; the best one would be selected for publication. Norm Schwarzkopf, who seemed to excel at everything he did, won the contest with his article entitled "The Burnished Helmet". The story was of a commander and all the difficulties and tribulations he encountered in his command. In the last paragraph, the commander came back to his tent exhausted and threw his helmet on his bunk with words which revealed he was a Legionnaire in the Roman Army. The article illustrated that the problems faced by commanders have stretched through the centuries.

During the 1960's, employing nuclear weapons on the battlefield was part of our training. The Advanced Course, at that time, included a special Nuclear Weapons Employment Course option which was established to train us in the proper use and application of tactical nuclear weapons. It was a fascinating, highly classified, six-week course which was an add-on to the Advanced Course for those who applied and were selected to attend.

For years our country had been testing nuclear weapons with massive computer programs to determine the effects of radiation and blast on the troops under various conditions and circumstances. Tables had been developed for each size weapon to enable us to compute the effects under every imaginable scenario, such as how large a weapon would be needed to cause a square mile of tree blowdown to create an effective obstacle or to stop advancing tanks. Or, what would be the effect of a 2-kiloton air blast on friendly troops if they were in their foxholes a half mile away. We even computed the size weapon necessary to create a crater in the Bosporus Strait, such that the lip of the crater was high enough to prevent ships from passing through the strait. Years of "computer detonations" produced extensive reference tables which enabled a qualified Nuc Employment Officer to choose what size weapon and delivery means were needed to accomplish any given tactical military objective. Upon completion of the course I was awarded a certificate as a "Prefix 5 Nuclear Weapons Employment Officer." Fortunately, my talents in that capacity were never utilized.

By the time the course was over, I had already received orders assigning us to Fort Ord, with helicopter school at Camp Wolters, Texas in route. It was May 1961, and we begin packing for our seventh move in five years.

CHAPTER 23

CHOPPER SCHOOL AT CAMP WOLTERS

In June of 1962 we arrived at Camp Wolters, Texas for a six-week assignment to the Army Helicopter School. Wolters was about three miles from Mineral Wells, Texas, in the northern part of the state along the Brazos River. It was a considerably nicer area than Camp Gary, which had been flat and relatively treeless. As we drove on to post, there was an extensive hard top area with about 30 H-23 Hiller helicopters neatly parked. From a distance, they looked like huge insects. Those were the choppers that were used in the Korean War and made famous in the TV Series "Mash". They were first generation coppers with reciprocating engines providing limited power. Unlike all other moving vehicles, the pilot sat on the right side. The reason for that was because, in flight, the advancing rotor blade developed more lift on the right side than the n the retreating blade.

Learning to fly a helicopter was really a hoot. In fact, most of my Army Aviation assignments were one great playtime sprinkled with occasional boredom balanced by moments of sheer terror. Our English professor perhaps best expressed what the Army was all about when he said, "When I was in Korea during the war, our jeep ran over a land mine. The blast blew the jeep into the air. and I landed in a bush, relatively unhurt. Where else can you find that kind of excitement!" There are a thousand stories that illustrate how this bargain has played out, almost always heroically and with many sacrifices, written in red on history's battlefields. As the old army ballad goes, what finer way to meet our maker than "to find a soldier's resting place, beneath a soldier's blow." But alas, I digress.

Since our helicopter class students were already pilots, it was expected that we would learn to master the helicopter with six weeks training. The interesting thing about helicopters is that they are dynamically unstable; like trying to balance a pencil on its point. Not so in an airplane that will continue to fly without control inputs. I was not use to a machine that would fall out of the sky if you ever let go of a control. When you release the controls in an airplane, it will seek level flight. I.e., it is dynamically stable. There is even a recorded event of an airplane being hand-propped by a pilot, coming to life with a roar and taking off without the pilot on board. The aircraft flew about until it ran out of fuel and then glided to a halt in a field, undamaged! However, in a helicopter, if you ever release the controls the beasts within will immediately cause the machine to plunge to earth.

Initially, learning to fly this thing and control the beast within appeared totally impossible. Your feet are on the rudder pedals controlling the tail rotor, one hand is on the cyclic stick, controlling the plane of rotation of the blades, the other hand holds the collective pitch control handle, which also incorporates a motorcycle-type throttle you twist to add or reduce power. At first you feel like a one-armed paper hanger. Once you have everything in balance, the beast will hover in one spot. But if you change any one of the five controls you are balancing, then you must alter the other four accordingly. Our first day in the chopper proved there was no way this thing would ever fly.

In the training area, there were perhaps 20 choppers with students and instructors, all trying to hover over their designated spots. It was a totally ridiculous scene as 20 helicopters, mostly out of control, are sliding sideways, forwards, backwards, and up and down. The instructors, of course, manage to exercise enough control when needed to avoid collisions. These random oscillations continue through the first couple of hours, then things mysteriously begin to settle down. Somehow the neural linkages between the brain and muscles take form and slowly, very slowly, you start to anticipate what the beast is going to do next. Eventually it goes from total craziness to rudimentary control.

The problem is that both feet and hands are all working to provide five different control inputs. As you add pitch to the blade to go up, you must also add throttle to provide the necessary power. However, as you add power, the torque increases, which means you need to get your feet going on the tail rotor pedals or you will start spinning in place. As you add right pedal to counteract the torque, it takes additional power to keep from settling back to the ground. But adding power adds torque, and the great juggling action continues without respite. Once you get the thing stabilized enough to hover, you can move the machine right or left, forward or backward by applying slight pressure on the cyclic stick to tilt the rotor plain. In time, somehow your brain begins to put it all together, just like the first time you try riding a bicycle or driving a car. You try and try, then suddenly you can do it. By the end of the first week, I had soloed and was off practicing maneuvers, landings and auto-rotations (the emergency action you must take if the engine quits).

After five weeks, when I finally became part of the machine, I had logged about 50 hours of flying. From then on, it's playtime, zooming down the riverbed below treetop level, popping up two hundred feet with a cyclic climb to practice an emergency landing by autorotation. Talk about fun! On one flight, my instructor was demonstrating the technique for autorotation at low level, in the event of an engine failure. He chopped the throttle about 20 feet above a dry riverbed at 60 knots. Then he flared the chopper, pulling back on the cyclic to raise the nose, gain altitude and increase rotor RPM. Unfortunately, he was a couple of feet too low, the tail rotor hit the riverbed and disintegrated. Without a tail rotor the chopper will begin spinning uncontrollably. But he was good enough and fast enough that he stuck the chopper on the ground before it could get spinning. That was a bit of excitement. Fortunately, he was at the controls, not me. Once on the ground, he embarrassedly radioed for a repair crew and a replacement chopper.

Finally, with about 70 hours of helicopter training, it is time to graduate with all the qualifications of an Army chopper pilot. But first, in the final few days before graduation, I must master "pinnacle landings" on a mountainside where there is only room for one skid as you hold the chopper steady: creepy stuff indeed, and a good test of skill.

Of course, the best was yet to come. Once assigned to a chopper unit I would be flying bigger, faster, more powerful machines with rockets and machine guns and 40-millimeter cannon. This was followed by instrument training, nap of the earth flying, and navigating at treetop level at a hundred + miles an hour. By the following year, Camp Wolters had been redesignated Fort Wolters and the helicopter training program expanded to the point where at the peak of the Vietnam War we were graduating 800 pilots a month. Eventually the helicopter became one of the finest weapons of war and was also instrumental in saving hundreds of lives by rapid evacuation of casualties from the battlefield. As Army aviation expanded, the Army began an Aviation Warrant Officer Program. At that point we had hundreds of captains and lieutenants flying helicopters or fixed wing aircraft, but most were destined to leave the service or be promoted to major, and colonel and those ranks dictated higher levels of responsibility than just flying. So, with the advent of the Warrant Officer program, we established a permanent flying cadre. Warrant officers would always be warrant officers and would form the basis for Army helicopter expansion plans. With Vietnam, it became apparent that aviation was the wave of the future. In a few short years aviation went from being the dreg of the Army to a much sought-after specialty. In fact, by the mid-60's, those colonels and lieutenant colonels showing promise were sent to flight school to get their wings and ride the wave.

By now our children were 5 and 3, probably not old enough to remember much of those quick six weeks before we readied for our next move. By the end of July, we loaded up and headed out of a too warm Texas, home to California and another phase of life after eight moves in five years.

CHAPTER 24

FORT ORD - 1962

This time on our trip west, we visited a few points of interest on our way to San Francisco. We were looking forward to a visit our parents before signing in at Fort Ord. After a couple of weeks at home, it was time to report into our new assignment. The Army was pretty good about moving families during the summer, when it was least disruptive for their school-age children. Lee was now 6 and Laura 4, so Lee would begin his first school experience at Fort Ord. Ord was a great assignment for us, since we would be only a two-hour drive from our parents in SF. Our move was a relatively smooth event since our two-week visit in San Francisco gave the movers sufficient time to deliver our household goods, and quarters were immediately available for us to move into.

I was looking forward to the challenge of fitting myself into a new unit, the 17th Aviation Company, and learning to fly a much larger airplane, the De Havilland Otter. This plane was one big dude and would require many hours of instruction before completing the transition to a more complex aircraft. During this transition phase, I was still flying helicopters and the smaller aircraft we had available. The Otter was the largest single-engine aircraft we had in the Army. It could carry a ton of supplies or 10 passengers and with full flaps could take off using very little runway. All my fixed wing flying to date had been in cockpits with the seat directly behind the nose of the plane. The Otter had a large roomy cockpit with the pilot seated about two feet to the left of the centerline of the plane. Having spent about a thousand hours in smaller planes the natural tendency when landing was to line up on the runway with the nose directly in front of you, which of course, in an Otter, would have the plane pointing to the left and putting the aircraft into a "slip". After about ten hours of flying with an instructor all those little wrinkles got ironed out and flying that big bird became much more comfortable.

It was my understanding that the De Havilland Otter, at that time, was the largest single-engine aircraft in the world but I've never confirmed that. It was, and still is, very popular with Alaskan bush pilots because it was happy to land anywhere it could find a few hundred feet of unimproved runway or dirt road. In those early days, before the helicopter became the preferred method of keeping battlefield supplies flowing and removing the wounded, the Otter was a wonderful workhorse that could be coaxed into remarkably small areas to offload men and supplies. It was the first utility aircraft the Army had and was therefore designated the U-1 ("U" for Utility). Its reliability and responsiveness won the hearts of those of us who flew it.

Shortly after qualifying to fly the Otter, I was attached to a new unit that had been formed with the mission of running airfield operations. The unit was known as an "AOD" (Airfield Operating Detachment). When fully equipped and trained, an AOD could run a division airfield, to include approach control, tower operations, weather and ground-controlled approaches (GCA). That summer, the unit was assigned to run the airfield at Camp Roberts during the Reserve and National Guard training periods. I had an Otter and a Beaver assigned to my part of the detachment.

After arriving at C ramp Roberts in late May, one of my first assignments was a request to fly the Beaver to Oakland for an emergency leave soldier. Classmate Dick Macken was on hand to fly with me and at sun-up we got the plane ready for the short trip. Camp Roberts can be remarkably cold in the mornings in April and May, so we were glad to complete our preflight and get the engine started. One of the first things we did was to turn on the "Janatrol Heater", a heating box fed by gasoline which is effective in keeping the plane warm. With the heater turned on we suddenly experience an unbelievable stench, and it got worse. The only solution was to turn the heater off and be cold. We discussed the problem and decided there must have been a rat or other rodent in the heating box that was being cooked. After we were airborne Dick lit up his usual stogie and I told him that the stink from that was worse than the burning rat. Other than the olfactory assaults, the flight to Oakland was uneventful.

The next evening, at dinner, the previous AOD Commander, Major Cochran sat down next to me with his tray and said, "Ren, don't you have an Otter at the airfield which we could use this evening to get our night flying time?" I said, "Yes, sir. Would you like to go flying?" He replied that if we were to fly it to Vegas and catch a couple hours in town before heading back, we could get all six hours of our required night flying time out of the way in one fell swoop! That sounded pretty good to me, knowing we would be back well before the general's flight which was scheduled the following morning at 8 AM.

We took off a little before 8 PM and headed for the Las Vegas Airport. We grabbed a taxi to the Strip and Cochran headed for the craps table. The problem was, I had no idea the major would get himself so entrenched playing the dice that it would take me hours to pry him loose. He had managed to win about six months' pay by 1 AM but by 2, when we had planned to leave, he had given nearly all of it back and was not about to leave without that pot of gold. It was another two hours before I got him out the door and into a cab. He was a few dollars ahead but nothing like he had been earlier. By the time our wheels left the ground it was nearly 5 AM and we had a three-hour flight ahead of us. After takeoff, while we were still climbing into the moonless darkness, he unstrapped his seat belt and said, "You take it. I'm going to catch some zzz's", and he headed to the back of the aircraft to lie down in the isle.

I struggled through my extreme drowsiness and got the lumbering Otter on course for our destination. At that point I was feeling a bit used and thinking that this guy was something of a rotter. I recalled there was an incident the previous year that could have foretold this situation. He landed one of our Beavers in what he thought was a dry lakebed in the center of the Laguna Seca Raceway. It took a few days and a flatbed truck to get the plane out of the mud. He knew he would never go beyond his present rank, so I guess he didn't have much to lose with this flight to Vegas. If we got back late, it was my problem.

By 7:45 in the morning I was at 8,000 feet, descending, when I saw the heavy ground fog covering the Salinas Valley. It lay like a blanket separating me from my 8 AM commitment. As I passed over the Paso Robles Omni, my Nav receiver told me I was only minutes away from the Camp Roberts runway. I continued my descent and contemplated my fate if I were late for the general's flight. As mentioned, it was scheduled for an 8 AM takeoff; it was now 7:50! I could visualize the possibility of my career coming to a sudden close. The fog appeared to be thinning in places and the rolling brown hills, typical of that area, could be seen rising through the layer. At a few minutes before 8 there were signs that the fog was beginning to break up and dissipate as the sun peeked over the mountains in the east and began to heat the morning air.

When I pulled off the power and started my final descent, the steady 2200 RPM engine drone changed to a quiet hum. Major Cochran, who had been sleeping behind me in the aisle, stirred awake. He was now sitting next to me in the copilot's seat. The Otter was a magnificent old Army aircraft with a prehistoric appearance like something out of WW I, but we loved it. I was bleary-eyed but the Otter knew what to do and responded to my control inputs in the same way that an old friend may anticipate what you are about to say. We knew each other well. I lowered the nose, hoping to catch a glimpse of the runway through the thinning fog.

Normally, if a flight was delayed due to weather, it was understandable and acceptable but in our case, I had taken the plane to Las Vegas on an unofficial Junket that should never have taken precedence over a scheduled operational flight. If I were not ready for the general at 8 AM, I could possibly remain a captain for the rest of my career.

At a minute or two after eight I could finally see our runway through the thinning fog, which had become thin and wispy. I lined up from the south, snaked the plane around some foggy spots and stuck it on the runway. I told the crew chief to get it gassed up and ready to go as I hurried inside to face the music. My operations NCO said, "Sir, the general's aide called a few minutes ago and said to cancel the general's flight." With a heavy sigh of relief, I knew my career was salvaged for another day and I chalked up one more of life's lessons.

Probably the most enjoyable flying memory from my Fort Ord days was a trip to Fort Carson, Colorado, to bring back a small H-23 helicopter. T As mentioned, the old OH-23 was underpowered and the two birds at Carson were practically useless in the thin air of that mile-high environment. The powers on high had, therefore, decided that those two choppers should be moved to Ord, where at sea level they would have better utilization. Another pilot and I were selected to fetch them. We flew commercially to Colorado Springs, where we were met by Army transportation that delivered us to the Fort Carson Airfield. Following a quick inventory of the parts and equipment which were to go with us, we preflighted the aircraft and got on board. I'll never forget cranking up the bird and trying to bring it to a hover. With full power, I could only get it about a foot off the ground and when I tried to turn, the extra power needed by the tail rotor caused it to sink back onto the grass. Then I remembered what the guy in operations had said, "Make all turns to the left." Right turns required additional power to overcome the main rotor torque and drain off just enough power to cause the ship to settle back to the ground.

By making three left turns I got the thing turned into the wind and very carefully tilted the rotor plain just enough to get it moving forward. I was skimming through the grass but slowly gaining speed. At about 20 knots the chopper reached "translational lift" and began to climb. Translational lift occurs when the bird is moving forward fast enough that the rotors begin encountering "clean air," or air that has not been churned up by the rotors. Turbulent or "dirty" air causes a reduction in lift, so it is necessary to transition through the dirty air to develop enough lift to fly away.

We climbed to a safe thousand feet above ground level and headed south to Arizona to go around the Rockies rather than try to get these underpowered birds over the 12,000-foot passes. In time we reached the famous Route 66 and turned west, following that highway. Since the OH-23 only held enough fuel to stay in the air for two and a half hours at 70 miles an hour, we needed to find a place to refuel every 140 miles or so. We were like grasshoppers, hopping from airport to airport, sometimes only flying for an hour or so.

We spent our first uneventful night at Williams, AZ; then continued west along Route 66, at about 1500 feet and to the right of the highway. There was a slight headwind, and it was annoying to see so many cars passing us as we flew against the wind. At some point in our journey, we needed to leave the highway and head south to refuel. After refueling, we again picked up a compass heading to the west and could see a large thunderstorm building ahead of us. It looked like the storm was headed north, so we turned slightly south to get around it. Before long, it was apparent we were on a collision course with what now appeared to be a humongous "thunder-bumper". We turned further south to avoid it. Eventually, we could see that it was just too large and moving too fast to avoid and we needed to find a place to set down. I spotted what appeared to be something of a grass runway just a couple miles ahead. As we got closer, we could see a ranch house at one end of the field and swooped down to land just as the storm approached. As soon as we got our rotors tied down the storm hit, and the rain began. I guess the rancher had been watching the scene from his window, because now he came out on the porch and waved us over to his house. We made a dash for it as the heavy rain began to pelt us. The rancher gave us a cup of coffee and we chatted for a bit, explaining we had flown considerably off course to avoid the thunderstorm and asked him for directions to Needles. He said we should go west until we came across the Colorado River, then follow that north to Needles.

In about a half hour the storm had moved south, so we thanked the rancher, untied our rotors and got back into the air. In about 20 minutes we came to the Colorado River snaking south through a deep gorge. Looking down at the rushing water and the beautiful sheer cliffs on each bank, there was no way I could resist flying that gorgeous gorge north to Needles. We dipped down to about 20 feet above the water and zoomed north. It was like flying a luge as we banked into the turns at 70 MPH between the steep sides of the canyon wall. It was an absolutely wonderful, picturesque journey up that gorge. It took a bit of concentration to weave around some of the tighter turns, and we needed to be alert for the occasional high-tension lines stretched across the canyon, most of which we could go underneath. As we neared Needles, we "pulled pitch" and popped up out of the gorge. A few minutes later I spotted the airfield. We planned to spend the night there and make our final leg to Fort Ord the following day. We hovered toward the gas pumps, not far from a small house where the guy who ran the airfield lived. In those days, helicopters were something of a rarity and we always drew a few onlookers when we arrived at an airfield. But this day, our onlookers consisted of cats; many, many cats. There must have been 60 or 70 felines of differing ages, colors, and sizes. As the gas guy came over to meet us, I asked, "What's with all the cats?" He said the lady who owned that home had just let them multiply and today she was in court while the SPCA was busily trapping the animals. By the time we got gassed up and found our way to the nearest motel, the temperature had reached well over a hundred. We hunkered down with the "swamp cooler" running full blast and planned our final leg home for the next day.

What a great trip! Three days on our own in our little chopper birds finding our way across country. That's the thing about the Army - always something new and challenging and almost always fun. But with Vietnam heating up, we knew it wouldn't be too long before Uncle Sam would call in his chips.

When I came to the airfield the following day, standing in the operations area was an elderly gentleman. He introduced himself as a retired staff sergeant and told me that he had recently lost his wife. He said her last request was to have her ashes scattered over Monterey Bay and could I help him with that? The regulation governing who is authorized to fly as a passenger in a military aircraft was not clear on this, but I reasoned that since a retired NCO was authorized to fly space available on Air Force transport aircraft, that I could justify taking him up. We arranged a takeoff time for that afternoon, and he went home to gather his wife's ashes. I had planned a short flight over the Bay in an H-13 helicopter. At about 3,000 feet over the Bay, I had him open his Plexiglas door so he could spread the ashes. I slowed the chopper down to about 20 mph; he took the lid off the container holding his wife's ashes and started pouring them out the door. To my surprise the rotor wash carried about half the ashes back into the cockpit some of which were now in my mouth and eyes. Of course, with the air blasting into the cockpit, the ash attack ended as quickly as it began with the only lingering effect being what was left in my mouth. As we headed back to Fritchie Army Airfield, I couldn't help but wonder just what part of his wife ended up in my mouth!

In the summer of 1963, I applied for and was accepted into the Army's Aviation Safety Program. I felt it was a good additional qualification to have. It meant I would be attending a 10-week aircraft accident prevention and investigation course at USC. Since it was a temporary duty assignment, the extra TDY pay made it possible to bring the whole family south. We found a small furnished rental unit close to the campus and moved the family in as I settled down to attend daily classes. It was our first up close encounter with the Los Angeles and

Hollywood area. Junior officers never quite have enough dollars to fully enjoy the opportunities of a big city, but the change of scene was good for us all and the course was generally enjoyable. I particularly liked the accident investigation portion of the curriculum and the field exercise of examining the wreckage of a De Havilland Beaver that had been pulled apart in a thunderstorm.

During my six weeks on the USC Campus, I twice ran into my classmate and friend H. Norman Schwarzkopf who was there for his masters' degree in Computer Information Technology. H. Norman (as we often referred to him) was always bigger than life. We had not seen each other since we had completed the Advance Course in 1962 and greeted one another like long lost brothers. In our "catch up" conversation Norm stated that he had been invited to play tennis at the Los Angeles Tennis Club that coming weekend, which evidently was quite a coupe since the club was rather exclusive. A couple weeks later, we again ran into each other on Krampus. In the conversation which followed I asked Norm how he made out with his match at the LA Tennis Club? He said, "They matched me with the president of the club, and we played two sets. I won 6-0, 6-0 but they didn't ask me to join the club!" I suspect, that for Norm, winning was more important than joining.

I completed our Aviation Accident Investigation Course a few weeks later with all A's, an unusual phenomena for me! When we returned to Fort Ord at the end of August, I became the company aviation safety officer. It was an additional duty over and above my flying requirements but also meant that I would be the principal member of any aircraft accident investigation boards convened in the California area. It wasn't long before I was called on for my first investigation of a fatal, Hiller helicopter accident occurring near Turlock, California.

In 1963 the Army had a flyoff between Hiller, Hughes, and Bell as part of their effort to determine which chopper would win the contract to become the next Army Light Observation Helicopter. The accident occurred in Delano, California, which was a smallish farming community about 200 miles from Fort Ord. I would be the Army presence on a high-powered board, constituted by DA. The Hiller was on a test flight and exploded midair. it fell from 6,000 feet, half burying the burned and inverted wreckage. When I arrived on the scene there appeared to be no recognizable features. The lighter parts had fallen from the chopper when it exploded and were scattered in an oval pattern for a mile across the surrounding fields. Because it involved one of the three helicopters being tested in competition for a large army contract, the accident received top priority attention. A team of six of us were staring at the wreckage but the charred remains revealed very little of value. Nver-the-less, we felt sure that eventually this wreckage would give up the secrets it held.

Several of our investigative team charted the location of the parts scattered in the field relative to the main wreckage. Then a small crane and flatbed arrived at the scene to lift the wreckage onto the lowboy. As the chopper body was slowly lifted from its crater, eager eyes scanned the burned hulk for any clues; nothing. Later we moved everything to a hangar at Edwards AFB to begin our reconstruction and analysis. The answer to the question, "What happened here?", would need to be pried from the wreckage and coaxed from the aircraft's records and history. Step one was talking to anyone who had seen anything.

A farmer reported two parachutes leaving the chopper. He raced his pickup truck to the near one and found Tom, the flight engineer, bleeding profusely from where his left arm and leg had been severed by the main rotor blade. He threw him in the back of the pickup and headed to the hospital. Tom was dead on arrival. Miraculously, Al the pilot survived. He would be our best source of information. Fortunately, he and the engineer were both wearing parachutes as required for test flights. When we spoke to Al, he related, "Everything suddenly went to hell. I had no control whatsoever; the stick was a wet noodle. I shouted to Tom to get out and I exited the aircraft as it exploded."

Examination of the wreckage revealed that the rotor mast had snapped; a catastrophic event which could only occur with extreme and abrupt force. One of the main rotor blades was grossly contorted and showed signs of blood and tissue where it had entered the cockpit and diagonally cut through Tom's upper torso. Did the explosion cause the rotor mast failure? Did a fire cause the explosion or did the explosion cause the fire? Most in-flight fires have electrical culprits. Electrical shorts often cause fires. When wires short, each strand of the wire will form a bead at the break. However, these wires melted into a glob at the ends, indicating the heat was external, not from the electrical overload. OK, so what caused the explosion?

As we reassembled the mangled parts, we noted the ruptured gas tank. Since the chopper's gas tank is located under the front seats, it now appeared likely that when the rotor blade entered the cockpit and cut through Tom, it also ruptured the gas tank. The fuel would atomize under this impact and the vapor would immediately combust from the hot engine.

Our theory now was, "When the rotor mast snapped, the blade entered the cockpit on the left side, slicing through Tom and rupturing the gas tank. The explosion followed." Now we needed to determine why the mast snapped. This was the hard part. While the lab examined all broken control linkages, our maintenance expert closely reviewed the aircraft's records. They revealed extensive work on the rotor head about 30 days earlier. Meanwhile, we recovered two important items from searching the field surrounding the crash site; the wire recorder Al was wearing and the aircraft's black box, which recorded its attitude. To read the taped record of flight from the damaged black box would require examination with infrared light. That process revealed the helicopter had made a violent right bank just before it exploded.

When the technicians were able to play Al's wire recorder for the investigators it provided details on the conduct of the test flight. His final words recorded on the wire were, "The nose of the helicopter is coming back through the horizon, now it is leveling off, it's falling to the right; GET OUT," he screamed, followed by a horrible swooshing crunch as the blade entered the left side of the cockpit and Al rolled out the right door. His recorded shout and the awful swooshing sound made the hair on the back of my neck stand up.

That afternoon the lab reported a "rod end bearing", on a push-pull tube, of the controls, had evidently failed from fatigue and from a bending moment. To determine what affect this control failure would have on the chopper, Hiller bench-tested a chopper at the factory. They found, when failing the rod end bearing, the weight of the bell crank was sufficient to activate full right cyclic with enough force to snap the rotor mast!

Evidently the threaded portion of the bearing had somehow been broken most of the way through and the last 10 percent, still connected, failed over time through fatigue. However, what caused the initial break? The chain of events had a few more links we needed to follow. The metallurgist informed us that the original 90% break occurred about 30 days before the final fatigue failure. This coincided with the maintenance data showing extensive work on the main rotor a month earlier. There was a small maintenance platform on the side of the chopper which could be folded out to stand on, when working on the rotor head. The control linkage (push-pull tube), attached to the failed rod end bearing, made a handy item to grab onto when hoisting oneself onto the maintenance platform! I could visualize a mechanic grabbing the push pull tube to hoist him up and after bending it, pushing it back into position.

The final piece of the puzzle was now in place. Someone had grabbed the push-pull tube when getting onto the maintenance platform and had cracked the rod end bearing about 90 percent of the way through. That set the awful sequence of events into action. We completed a thorough written accident report, and all headed back to our home stations. It had been about ten days that we worked on the accident before heading home.

Several months later, the Army Board selected the Bell chopper to be the next Light Observation Helicopter and named it the Sioux OH-58. The Army used that chopper for 50 years, and even today, with some modifications, it is in service with some police departments and other civil use.

—W—

The Night I Played Bobby Fisher

I had returned to my duties at Fort Ord in the 17th Aviation Company, mostly flying De Havilland Otters. It was October 1963 when I had read that Bobby Fischer was coming to McClellan AFB near Sacramento, to play a simultaneous chess match. He had signed on to play 60 boards at the same time. I had never played in a simultaneous but figured I might have an edge because he would be playing 59 other games at the same time! I had sent my name forward to be included among the 60 players. In those days, Army aviators were required to fly six hours at night each year to maintain their proficiency. It didn't matter where you chose to fly to meet the requirement. I could fly up there in about an hour and get some night flying time I needed. So going up to McClellan and back that night was OK and would give me a couple hours of night proficiency.

The match would begin at 7 PM. I landed about 6:30, tied down the De Havilland Beaver and walked across the tarmac to the hangar where the event was to take place. Inside the hangar was a string of tables arranged in the shape of a horseshoe, with chairs only on the outside of the horseshoe. When we were seated and the boards set up ready to play, the organizer introduced Bobby Fischer. He was tall, thin, introverted and dressed in a dark suit. A shy young man, he said nothing but nodded to the group when the introduction was over. At 21, he had already been a Grand Master for eight years! Now he stepped forward to the first board on his left, moved a piece and went on to the next board. The boards were set up alternating black and white from board to board. He moved down the line of tables at a slow pace, moving a piece at each board as he passed. I was playing white and would move first when he stepped in front of my board. I moved my king's pawn and he responded. I would now have to wait until he completed the circuit before I made my next move, since the rules of play were that you would make your move only after he arrived at your board. That way he could see the move and not waste time trying to figure out what you had played.

My senses were perhaps overly acute as I sat behind the chessboard waiting for the great man to arrive at my position and make his move. He was a youngish 21 years old, ten years my Junior, yet he had long ago astounded the chess world with his prowess. At 12 he won the Manhattan Chess Club Championship, probably the strongest chess club in the country. At age 14 he had beaten every contending chess master to win the US Open. And in another nine years he would defeat Russia's finest to gain the World Championship. But for now, as an International Grand Master, he would be facing the terrible onslaught of my favorite opening.

Chess requires a lot of energy, which is perhaps why it is classified as a sport. I've read that several years ago there was an experiment in which several tournament players were electronically monitored to determine what kind of physical effort was registered in the course of play. It was found that the increased heartbeat and mental effort during the game were burning calories at about the same rate as an athlete in a fast walk. On occasion, I have had opponents who began to sweat profusely, breathe more rapidly and get red in the face. However, there were none of these signs in my current opponent, who was effortlessly gliding from board to board.

As the simultaneous continued on, a few players resigned after blundering and losing a piece. By Move 20 there were only about 30 players still in the game, and Fischer was now completing the circle back to my board in much less time. Sometimes he would spend up to a minute in front of a player to solve a difficult situation but for the most part his play was decided in seconds. By Move 25 I was in trouble and to find a solution, needed the ten minutes it would take him to work his way back around to my board. Several weaker players had already succumbed to his mastery, so now he was coming by my board sooner. I could pass but then it would be another ten-minute wait. I found a plausible move as he was approaching my board and when he stopped in front of me, I hastily placed my bishop on the white square. His response was instantaneous and crushing as his knight forked my rook and queen. A few moves later I resigned. There were still a dozen diehards playing when I left the hangar. At least I had the flight home to look forward to.

The next morning there was a small article in the sports section of the *Chronicle* noting that Bobby Fischer had played 60 opponents in a simultaneous exhibition and had won 58 and tied 2. It was a good memory, and I could always say, "Back when I played Bobby Fischer . . ."

Fort Ord was a good assignment. It gave our kids two and a half years in one spot during the assignment turmoil that accompanied the beginning of the Vietnam conflict. And it gave me a chance to learn aviation and gain some maturity without getting into any career trouble. But it wasn't long before the Pentagon called and told me we would be headed to Germany. With my mother in France at that time, trying to untangle the financial remains of Grandmother's estate, I looked forward to seeing her again and visiting some corners of Europe we had not previously seen. In December of 1964 we packed our belongings, put our furniture in storage, and made plans for shipping the cat and the 1956 Chevy we had owned for nearly nine years. With heavy heart I sold the TR-3 which had given us so much fun on the Monterey Peninsula. We left December 18, with a stopover at Fort Dix, New Jersey, before boarding an Air Force Constellation for Frankfurt. We were about to embark on what would turn out to be the worst trip of our lives.

CHAPTER 25

GERMANY AND OUR TRIP THROUGH HELL! DECEMBER 1964

By December of 1964 my mother was in Nice trying to pull things together after her mother went into a rest home in Grasse, so plans for our reassignment to Germany in December would necessarily include a visit to Nice for Christmas. Never one to shy away from overly complex planning, I also needed to plan the details for shipping our cat, picking up a Porsche from the Stuttgart factory, and our departure by air to Fort Dix. To ship the cat, we first sedated her with a sleeping pill, then took her to SFO with us to get her on the way to Germany. Then the four of us boarded our flight to New Jersey. I joked that, by the time we saw her again, she would be saying, "Heil Meow." After we landed, I made arrangements for our night in the Transient Officers' Quarters at McGuire AFB, where we would be boarding the Constellation for Frankfurt the following morning.

Our children, now ages six and eight, were good travelers and well endured another night in a different bed as well as the inefficient processing before walking onto the tarmac to board our four-engine Air Force Lockheed Constellation. However, before we could get off the ground, our AF steward announced a problem with the oil filter. There would be a slight delay. For another hour the plane sat in the sun on the tarmac until all systems were go. We were facing a 12-hour flight which would overnight at Lages AFB in the Azores, then land in Frankfurt the following day, December 22. Our plans were to grab a rental car and drive to Stuttgart, where we would pick up our Porsche from the factory and our cat from the Stuttgart Airport. The five of us would then head south for Christmas Eve in Nice with my mother and grandmother.

About two hours out from Lages AFB, Barb nudged me from her window seat, saying, "That engine's on fire!" We called the stewardess over to point out the fire in the outboard engine, clearly visible in the dark night. I did not mention that in-flight fires are extremely dangerous; because once the fire gets going it is only a matter of minutes before the heat destroys the structural integrity of the wing. Fortunately, the procedures for extinguishing an engine fire were successful and we continued on with our remaining three good engines.

A couple of hours later, with the sun rising ahead of us and the Azores Islands in the distance, we began our descent for landing. But in addition to the usual pre-landing announcement, the pilot informed us that he was unable to get a green light indication that the gear was down and locked. When the landing gear is being extended, first the red light goes out and the orange light comes on, indicating the gear is in transit. When the wheels are down and locked the orange goes out and the green light comes on. We had only the orange light. That meant that either the gear could collapse on landing or that the gear indicator lights were goofed up. We circled with our three engines while the ground crew foamed the runway, and the stewards shuffled the passengers to put a male passenger with each family group. As we descended on final for our landing, everyone held their breath. Then the touchdown; would the gear collapse? After all the folderol and delay, the uneventful landing which followed was almost disappointing. But the best was yet to come.

We would not have a replacement engine until the next day. But even after the engine arrived there were problems. The Air Force routine was to get the passengers ready a couple of hours before takeoff time. So, for the next two mornings we were awakened at 4 AM and hurried to the field, only to learn that there was yet another problem to be solved before we could fly. By the third day we were all getting dingy-dingy as again we were awakened at four in the morning which, in San Francisco time, was about 10 PM the previous day. Jet lag, sleep deprivation, followed by this continuous early morning drill, is worse than the Chinese water torture but at last we were ready to fly.

In the "old days" the military had a particular knack for doing unexplainable, unreasonable things that resulted in the general discomfiture of its personnel. So it was in this vein that our flight landed in Frankfurt at 4:30 AM on Christmas Eve morn, when not even a mouse was stirring. Nothing was functioning anywhere and that included our sleep--deprived brains. The daunting task I faced was to move my little family of four and all our baggage from Frankfurt to the Porsche factory in Stuttgart, then try to pick up the feline fur person somewhere in that Christmas season locked city, thence to Nice for Christmas with Mother and Grandmother. Lord, I couldn't even see straight, much less plan this thing to a successful conclusion. The real trip from hell was just beginning.

By the time we picked up our luggage at Rhein-Main Air Base it was about 6 AM. We decided that Barb would stay with the children and luggage, and I would make my way to the civilian side of the airport to find a rental car. Unfortunately, when I arrived at the rental counter the sign said, "open at 7:30" and there was no way to contact Barb while she waited and wondered in those pre-cell phone days. When I finally got on the road with my rental VW, I had to negotiate my way back to the other side of the field via the autobahn. In no time I was on the autobahn doing about 90 miles an hour but unable to read the German signs, I was headed in the wrong direction with no place to turn around. My frustration was beyond description and of course Barb must have thought I had long ago perished.

It was about 9 AM before we were together again, loading luggage and children into the VW bug. Fortunately, I still had sufficient marbles left to call ahead to the Stuttgart Porsche factory and let them know I was on the way. My contact cautioned me that they would be closing at noon for the 14-day Christmas holidays but after I explained my situation he promised to wait for my arrival. It was after 2 PM when we arrived at the Porsche factory and went through a short checkout routine. Now we still had our cat to pick up at the Stuttgart Airport and the VW to turn in. I called the airport, found someone who spoke English and was finally connected to a person who explained to me that when we didn't show up as planned on the 22nd, they had to return the cat to Frankfurt, since they did not have facilities in Stuttgart to keep her. Good grief! We finally made the decision to forget the cat for now and continue with our grand plan to get to Nice by the next day, on Christmas.

But first we would need to turn in our rental car and find a place to stay. Barb would drive the VW and I would drive the Porsche to the rental car agency, then we would find a place to sleep and continue by Porsche in the morning. By the time we got on the road (on the shortest day of the year, I might add) a little after 4 PM, it was getting dark. With jet lag, sleep loss, culture/language shock and response-ability for the four of us, I was rapidly approaching the point of being dysfunctional. It was starting to snow, I couldn't read the street signs, and I didn't know where I was going (this was about 30 years before GPS) or where I was at. We pulled into a service station for gas and directions. Finally, struggling with the language difficulty, Barb had the good sense to ask the guy to lead the way across town to the car rental place. We gave him a few dollars and a half hour later had turned in the VW. The rental agent told us there was a hotel on the next block and we checked in there, totally exhausted. I thought I had made it clear to the desk clerk that we wanted a room with two double beds but when we got to our room it was with two singles. We were dead tired and not ready to try to explain again, so we took the room and made the beds into four singles by putting the mattresses on the floor and dropped into a heavy sleep.

The next morning, Christmas Day, we were on the way to Nice. The last town in Germany before Switzerland is Muehlhauser. We got off the autobahn there when we spotted a gas station with a restaurant. The only thing we could recognize on the menu was "Souppe." Below that was "Souppe mit aie." We figured souppe mit anything was better than souppe mit nothing, so we ordered that. When the soup came it had a raw egg floating in it but before long it was mostly cooked by the hot soup. Now we knew what an "aie" was, but the next problem came when it was time for us to pay the bill. In Germany they don't bring you the bill until you ask for it and I didn't know how to do that. Finally, I brought out my handy German American dictionary and looked up the word for "bill". It said "schnabel." I called the waiter over and asked him for the "der schnabel, bitte." He looked at me like I was short a few cards in my deck. I repeated myself and he went away shaking his head. Finally, I got the point across by making like I was writing a bill. Later that year I learned that schnabel does not mean a restaurant bill but a duck's bill.

We got our gas and blew through Switzerland at about a hundred miles an hour on their autobahn. Seven hours later we arrived in Nice in time to have a Christmas evening with Mother and Grandmother. Mother had arranged for us to stay in a pension (hotel with meals) for the week, which was really great. We very much enjoyed our café au lait and croissants and the ambiance of life in France.

On 4 January 1965 we four made our way north from Nice to report in for my assignment to the 3/12th Cavalry Squadron at Buedingen, Germany. But our first task was to recover our cat from the Frankfurt Airport. When we got to the airport and requested our cat, they brought it out on a string, and it was limping. They wanted about a week's wages to pay for the ten days they had kept the cat. I got angry and told them we had shipped the cat to Stuttgart, and they sent it back to Frankfurt and now they bring us a damaged cat. I said, "No way will I pay $135 for that cat. You keep the cat." At that Juncture they turned Justimere Cat over to us without charge.

My orders assigned me to D Troop, 3rd Squadron, 12th Cavalry, which was located in the village of Buedingen, ten miles north of Gelnhausen and about 30 miles northeast of Frankfurt. Initially there were no quarters available, and I had to accept the caveat on my orders that "Joint travel authorized with the understanding that officer will be responsible for dependents' housing on the local German economy." Within a couple of days, we found a nice apartment with German landlords (Herr Clipper and wife), whom we grew to enjoy in the coming months. The furnished apartment was on a hill above the Buedingen Castle. We wanted to put Lee and Laura into the local German grammar school but after much discussion, decided that total immersion into a new culture and language might be a bit much for them when added to the trauma of being displaced from their last school.

Our cav squadron was part of the 3rd Armored Division ("Spearhead"), headquartered in Frankfurt. The "Third Herd," as it was called, was commanded by Major General Walter T. "Dutch" Kerwin, a tough but good commander and a West Point graduate. Our cavalry squadron was also commanded by a West Pointer, Lieutenant Colonel Fuller, a man I liked and respected. The 3/12th Cav squadron was the eyes of the division. In combat they were forward of the 15,000-man division, moving and probing to find the enemy and make sure the division wasn't surprised, as well as providing essential intelligence on the location of enemy units.

One of the great innovations of the early 1960's was a helicopter unit which could, in turn, be the eyes for a cavalry squadron. That is an exceptional mission when you consider that a Cav squadron is respon-sible for a sector 3 to 5 miles wide in front of the division where it is patrolling, watching, probing and protecting through early warning. And in front of the Cav squadron is its' D Troop, flying the sector with its scout helicopters. D Troop, an Air Cavalry Troop, is composed of 200 officers and men and 21 helicopters. They are organized into three platoons of 6 helicopters each. The scout platoon has light, quick, small choppers, lightly armed with machine guns. The aerial artillery platoon has Cobra gunships with rocket launchers and 40mm nose-mounted cannon. And finally, the pioneer platoon with 6 Hueys, could deliver a platoon of infantry where needed. The three remaining choppers were for the commander to use as necessary.

The platoon leaders were lieutenants, the pilots warrant officers. The rank authorized for the troop commander in 1965, when I took command of the Squadron's D Troop, was captain. Later, in Vietnam, the position was upgraded to major. This recognized that an organization with 21 helicopters, some 26 officers and warrant officers and enough trucks and mechanics to keep it all running was a large and very complex outfit; probably more than a 32-year-old captain with 9 years in the Army should be expected to handle. A similar-sized Air Force unit would be commanded by a colonel.

At the time I took command in the summer of 1965, we were in the throes of phasing out our larger cargo helicopter, the CH-34, with its underpowered reciprocating engine. It was replaced by a new utility helicopter with a turbine engine, designated as the UH-1 Iroquois, which quickly became known as the Huey, a truly versatile and capable machine built by Bell Helicopter. The old CH-34s which we were phasing out had been around a long time and were much loved by their crews and pilots, so there was some reluctance in seeing them go. One afternoon I was walking the line of choppers which were being worked on by their crew chiefs. Some of the Hueys had arrived and some of the H-34s were still online. I stopped to talk to an older crew chief working on an H-34 and asked him which chopper he liked best, the H-34 or the Huey? He said, "Well, Suh, de Huey has a semi-rigid rotor system and de H-34s have a fully articulated rotor system." Then, using all the terms which describe the dynamic action of a blade in motion, he added, "When those blades are turnin, they's leading and lagging, hunting and searching, flipping and flapping and so ya know, suh, if they's any air out there it's gonna find it!"

I had been in command about ten months when I received a request from division headquarters for a Huey to pick up the deputy commanding general and take him to Grafenwoehr Training Area. We were a combat unit, and I normally objected to accepting requests for administrative use of our helicopters for transportation; it was not our mission. Division had its own flight section to ferry their command and staff personnel. However, this was a request to fly a general officer and could not be reasonably refused. The mission, to pick up the DCG at "Fliegerhorst Kaserne" in Frankfurt and fly him to "Graf," was a bit tricky, since the training area was located very close to the East German border and in those "Cold War" days, over-flying the border would be an international incident and possibly a career buster. I decided to send my executive officer, Captain Lincoln (who incidentally was also an attorney), because he was an experienced and mature aviator on whom I could rely on to make the right decisions.

His flight, which would normally take two hours in each direction, ran into unexpected head winds and after two hours, CPT Lincoln was still several minutes from the destination. Our Hueys had two and a half hours of fuel on board, which normally would have gotten them to Graf with the requisite 30-minute fuel reserve. However, with the headwinds he encountered, his 20-minute fuel warning light came on a few minutes short of his destination. He decided to land and called Graf to have them send the fuel truck to a specific location in route where he could land and refuel. The trip then proceeded without further incident and the general was returned to Frankfurt on schedule later that day.

The following morning, I was in my third-floor office at our Buedingen Caserne, signing papers, when First Sergeant Kurtz came into my office and said, "Sir, there is a helicopter landing outside on the soccer field and it has a 'two-star plate' on the side of the chopper. I think General Kerwin is on his way in to see you. He will want to know the status of our troop. We have 185 men present for duty, 2 on leave, 3 on sick call and 1 AWOL. There are 35 men at the motor pool and the rest are on the flight line." Unbeknownst to me, Sergeant Kurtz must have received a call from the command sergeant major at division warning him that the division commander was on his way to see us.

Within minutes of the generals' landing, he was on the third floor and Sergeant Kurtz called out "ATTENTION!" As I stood up from my desk the general came through the door. I saluted and said, "Sir, Captain Hart, Commanding D Troop." He perfunctorily returned the salute and asked, "Hart, what's the status of your unit?" Echoing Sergeant Kurtz, I said, "Sir, we have 185 men present for duty, 2 on leave, 3 on sick call and 1 AWOL. There are 35 men at the motor pool and the rest are on the flight line". He was surprised by my knowledgeable response and said, "Let's look at your barracks." We went downstairs where the troop was quartered. Sergeant Kurtz ran a mean operation; the floors were waxed and shining, every bunk was made up tight, and all the shoes under each bunk were lined up and shined. It was impressive. It is interesting to note that, if the First Sergeant had not wanted me as his commander, he could easily have used this opportunity to ambush me. The general was upset about the previous day's flight and was looking for anything that might be wrong to set the stage for giving me the ax! Sergeant Kurtz had saved my arse!

Unable to find even one thing wrong in the barracks, the general stomped out, saying, "Let's take a look at your motor pool." Sergeant Kurtz had alerted the motor pool. When we got there, everyone was busy doing something. General Kerwin asked, "How many people did you say were at the motor pool, Hart?" "Thirty-five, sir." We counted heads. There were indeed 35! He stomped out of the motor pool and said, "Let's go to the flight line."

At the airfield our helicopters were lined up just off the runway. We walked the line of choppers and counted heads; we counted the men in the maintenance shop and the operations. He asked, "How many men are supposed to be here?" I said, "One hundred and thirty-eight, sir." He said, "There's only 135." I said, "We have an avionics shop behind this building" and led the way there, not knowing if anyone would be in that little shack. I breathed a sigh of relief when I opened the door and Private Benson was in there soldering something. I could have kissed him!

When we returned to the operations building, the general said accusingly, "Hart, you told me you had 138 men on the flight line and we've only counted 136!" Up until that time things had really looked good for me and having recovered some of my confidence, I replied with what I hoped would be a disarming smile, "Well, sir, there's also you and I." He gruffly retorted, "That's not funny!" and then launched into the real reason for his visit.

"Hart, your people ran out of gas flying my deputy to Grafenwoehr. That is an unacceptable, and unsafe act." Finding some spine, I said, "Sir, Captain Lincoln did exactly the right thing. The unexpected headwinds meant he would arrive at Graf with less than the requisite fuel reserve. When the 20-minute fuel warning light came on he was only about ten minutes out. But rather than take any chance he called ahead for fuel. It was the safest action he could take, and I commend him." It was as if a light came on for the general. He evidently had a lot of smoke blown up his butt on how unsafe our Air Cav unit was and that we were just a bunch of "sky cowboys." Understandably our type of low-level "nap of the earth" flying sounded like a bunch of guys out having a good time zooming at tree-top level. But that was how we trained our pilots. It was the current doctrine for Air Cav units; fly low, pop up over the trees or hills, kill the enemy and drop back down again. And we were good at it.

Now, trying to regroup from the fact that he had most likely been misinformed, the general asked, "Well, then who is your safety officer?" Fortunately, I had completed the Aviation Safety and Accident Investigation Course at USC two years earlier and was able to respond with, "Sir, I am the safety officer for my unit." For some reason he liked that response and what could have been a career-ending inspection ended on a good note. I will always credit First Sergeant Kurtz for getting me through that day successfully.

A few months later, our cav squadron left for winter maneuvers at Grafenwoehr. This major training area was on the eastern border of what was then West Germany, across the Spessart Mountains in Bavaria. I was on my way there in the command helicopter, along with a few key NCO's, to establish an advanced party command post that would receive my troop when it arrived the following week. Captain Lincoln was in another Huey a few hundred yards off my left, in trail. The weather was icky, low overcast and a bit blustery. As we flew over the Spessart Mountains, we were forced to fly lower to avoid being in the clouds. Then, almost suddenly, we flew into a snowstorm that was moving south. It was necessary to fly even lower at that point to maintain visual contact with the ground. I slowed my Huey to about a hundred knots and turned on the windshield defrost and wipers.

Before long the snow became so heavy that it was building up on the windshield faster than the wipers could push it aside. I went lower and slower. Now the buildup on the windshield prevented the wipers from fully clearing the snow and the clear space I was looking through became narrower as the wipers became less effective. About that time, we were over the famous old Bavarian village of Rothenberg. The town is full of churches and each church has a steeple, one of which I was headed directly for. I dodged left and there was another steeple; they seemed to be everywhere. I slowed further and aimed between two steeples. In another few minutes I was past the town and looking for a place to set the chopper down. I picked the rounded knoll directly in front of me, flared, and stuck the chopper onto the clearing. I was not in contact with Lincoln anymore and was concerned about his status. In another half hour the storm had passed over us and we were again good to go. I called Captain Lincoln, and he responded that he too was now airborne after having been forced to put his Huey down in an empty parking lot in the middle of town. The rest of the trip was uneventful. I vowed that the next time I visited Rothenberg it would be by car.

Flying to Grafenwoehr was always a bit of a problem since it was very close to the East German border and any incursion across the border by U S Aircraft could become an international incident. The Soviets had even established homing beacons across the border with radio identifiers the same as our beacons in order to draw our planes across the border. These were known as "Mecoming Beacons". The previous December, my friend Dick Mackin was trying to find his way to Graff in a Bird Dog for the first time and became disoriented. Then it started to get dark. He desperately tried to find his way but eventually had to bail out when he ran out of gas. Unfortunately, he landed on the wrong side of the border and was picked up by an East German patrol two weeks before Christmas. When I spoke to him about the incident many months later, he said that they had him locked in a hotel and it wasn't until after New Years that he was turned over to the U S.

Germany was a great assignment and there was no better command for a young captain than that of an air cavalry troop. But the Vietnam War was raging and by 1966 we were well on the way to expanding our forces thereto over 500,000 troops. They needed pilots and choppers, and my troop was slowly being bled down, with first my pilots being reassigned and then my choppers. With less than 18 months in Germany, I also received orders for Vietnam and by May 1966, we were leaving Buedingen.

I had a month's leave to get the family settled in San Francisco. Barb's folks offered up their home to house the family while I was gone. I was particularly pleased with the prospect of the family living there where they would be secure and have the support of Barb's folks if something should happen to me.

CHAPTER 26

VIETNAM! 1966

When I was 8 years old, my parents had been divorced for three years and WW II was just beginning. Father served in WW I, WW II and during the Korean War. He was in the Army for thirty-five years and three wars, yet I know precious little of his service away from home. He died in April of 1955 at age 63, and of course the details of his wartime experience died with him. I will therefore spend a little more time on this portion of my life and the details of "my war," the only war I was in during my 31 years of military service although since I enlisted in the Army in 1951, I am also considered a Korean War Vet.

Going to war" is an exciting event in one's life and while the thought is exhilarating in one respect, it also carries the full panoply of feelings ranging from anxiety and concern to the worry of leaving loved ones behind. So, when Barb's folks offered to have our family live with them while I was gone, I was greatly relieved. I did not know what lay ahead for me in Nam, or if I would be coming home dead or alive but now, I knew my family would be in good hands no matter what. At West Point, one of my instructors noted, "From the moment you take the oath to serve your country, you are guaranteed a life free from poverty and hunger, a life where all your needs are met, if you work hard and do the right thing; you will always have a paycheck and a roof over your head. And your country asks only one thing in return; your life when that time comes." That was indeed the devil's bargain, one which my class of aspiring warriors all understood and accepted.

For me, having a home for the family was comforting and also meant we would be able to build our savings for whatever lay ahead. For Barb, the arrangement was not quite the slam dunk it was for me. Going home after 10 years of independent living would prove to have some rough spots but of course so would have being alone without the help of her parents.

With the family settled in, our household goods in storage, and the VW we had shipped from Germany now retrieved at port, we headed to Travis AFB in early June for my flight to Vietnam. It was a Boeing 707 contract flight which departed every day in conjunction with the buildup of forces in Nam. It was tough saying goodbye to Barbara and the little ones, but the real sacrifice would be on their side. When I said goodbye to Barb's Father, he said. "Don't be a hero". Rather sage advice when I considered all the wonderful classmates, I lost in a war that accomplished little.

Our flight to Saigon was via Fairbanks, Alaska, for refueling, a short two hour stop, just long enough to stretch our legs and gain an appreciation of where not to be assigned. From there we continued our "Great Circle" route for another seven or eight hours. Sitting next to me on the plane was an Air Force captain. He was being assigned to Tan Son Nhut Air Base in Saigon with the "Scat Back" Flight Detachment, where he would be flying the executive twin-engine Lear jets the Air Force used for their VIP flights. He told me I should call him if I ever needed to get somewhere "in country." This proved helpful some weeks later when I needed to hitch a ride to Da Nang, about 400 miles north. As we neared Saigon, all necks were craned, looking out the windows but there was nothing to see but Jungle and water. Finally, we touched down at Tan Son Nhut on the edge of Saigon.

My assignment was to a high-level intelligence-gathering organization within the Army Security Agency (ASA) with a cover name of the 509th Radio Research Group. Initially I was posted to the newly constituted 224th Aviation Battalion (Radio Research) which was part of the Group. As a junior major, my job was to be the battalion's aviation safety officer. That was a required position that had to be filled by a school-trained aviation safety officer, which I was. My job was primarily administrative, but I would also be spending several hours each week flying. Initially I needed to learn the nuts and bolts of flying ARDF (Airborne Radio Direction Finding) missions and to get checked out in the RU-8D, the Beach Queen Air, twin engine, which was configured for the ARDF missions. All of our ARDF aircraft were equipped with dipole antennae on each wing. The antennae were about six feet long and passed through the wings so that three feet stuck out above and three feet below each wing. Here is an excerpt from an article written by the **ASA** Veterans Association:

The 509th Radio Research Group, commanded three battalions and company-size direct support units assigned to all Army divisions. One of the 509th's subordinate battalions was the 224th Aviation Battalion (Radio Research), which pioneered in the introduction of Special Electronic Mission Aircraft (SEMA) to the battlefield. At the height of the war, the 509th radio Research Group commanded some 6,000 ASA personnel in-country. Meanwhile, the agency itself had greatly expanded, reaching a strength of 30,000 and attaining the status of a major Army field command in 1964.

The early days of Vietnam truly marked the beginnings of Army airborne signals intelligence. The Army's U-6 Beaver was one of the first platforms converted from a utility mission to take on intelligence collection efforts from the air. As a result, it was officially redesignated as the RU-6. This, in effect, initiated the process wherein most of the remaining Army aircraft which eventually became incorporated within this emerging fleet of signals intelligence platforms, were also redesignated with a reconnaissance or "R" prefix designator.

The RU-6A aircraft was a relatively simple and basis platform equipped with on-board mission receiver equipment for homing in on signals emitted by enemy forces. The data returned were only as accurate as the pilots' navigational skills. With no doppler/ inertial navigation system (INS) or global positioning system, the pilots relied on landmarks and dead reckoning to determine their known location from which to calculate the intercepts.

The single-engine companion Army platform, the RU-1 Otter, was similarly configured with personnel and equipment, as an expanded platform. But it wasn't until the introduction of the Army's RU-8D Seminole that a significant advance was made in the SEMA fleet and in the contribution these intelligence platforms were providing the theater tactical commanders. In addition to having on-board mission equipment similar to that found initially on both the RU-6A and the RU-1A, the RU-8D aircraft were equipped with the Marconi doppler navigation system. This required the copilot to manually plot the ARDF fixes (locations) to large pads of graph paper on his lap. (Masking tape was applied to the aircraft doors to prevent the plotting sheets from being sucked out of the aircraft.) Also, the RU-8Ds were equipped with blade antennas **in the wings, which gave them the capability to home in on a transmitter and fly a standard flight pattern to achieve the geometry necessary to obtain several lines of bearing (LOB).**

Although overflight of the actual target sometimes occurred, the procedure for flying the pattern for triangulating the target tried to prevent overflight whenever possible. Additionally, some of the aircraft were configured with radio fingerprinting to further enhance signal identification. The mission gear on board these RU-8D aircraft were known by the nicknames WINEBOTTLE, CEFISH PERSON, and CHECKMATE. These aircraft, with the on-board systems and crews, truly became the new workhorse of the Army's SEMA fleet primarily due to a combination of the improved mission gear and a newly introduced multi-engine capability, each contributing to expanding and improving the unit's mission coverage in several dimensions.

On 1 June 1966, the 224th Aviation Battalion (Radio Research) was activated under the command of the 509th RRG. It consisted of four companies:

The 138th Aviation Company (RR) at Da Nang in support of I Corps tactical zone of operation
The 144th Aviation Company (RR) at Nha Trang in support of II Corps tactical zone of operation
The 146th Aviation Company (RR) at Saigon in support of III Corps tactical zone of operation
The 156th Aviation Company (RR) at Can Tho in support of IV Corps tactical zone of operation

On 3 July 1967, the Radio Research Companys (Aviation) were assigned to the 224th Aviation Battalion (RR) to provide direct support to U.S. Military Assistance Command, Vietnam

*(MACV), flying six RP-2E aircraft from Cam Ranh Air Base,
Vietnam, on 13-hour missions.*

*The RU-8 offered advantages over the RU-6 Beaver. For the first
time, the 3rd Radio Research Unit had an all-weather capability.
With its ability to carry three crew members (pilot, copilot, and
intercept operator), the plane had enough room for navigational
equipment. Unlike the RU-6, a crew would no longer be
dependent upon visual landmarks to conduct operations.*

For all our missions we had two pilots and an enlisted "operator."
The copilot handled the navigation, while the operator in the back
seat dealt with the radio equipment, which at that time was pretty
sophisticated stuff. It was his job to tune and identify an enemy station.
He knew when it was time for the NVA regiments to receive reports
from their subordinate units. Also, he understood Morse code and was
able to determine from their call sign who was communicating with
whom. If it was a station of importance, or one that was listed on his
daily "hit list," he would flip a switch so that the Morse code could be
heard on our headsets. When we heard the signal, we immediately began a shallow turn while listening closely to the signal. As the aircraft
turned the signal became less audible. When finally, the wing antennae
were perpendicular to the target, there was no sound at all and we knew
the airplane was then pointing directly at the enemy transmitter (or
away from it). When these antennae were exactly perpendicular to the
signal, they would cancel each other out and there would be a "null,"
i.e., no signal reception. After the "null" we began our second turn in
the opposite direction so that our path in the sky was like a giant S. This
technique was known as ARDF…Aerial Radio Direction Finding.

The copilot's job was to keep track of exactly where we were on the
map at all times, no mean feat. So, when we heard the "null", i.e., when
we stopped hearing the signal, we knew the plane was online with the
station and the co-pilot drew a line on the map corresponding to our
heading and location. After the second turn he drew another line on the
map at the null. Where these two lines intersected was where the enemy
transmitter was located. For confirmation, we would make yet a third
turn and draw a third line, which again intersected close to the previous
intersection. The coordinates of that location on the map were then duly
recorded. This bit of aerial sleuthing enabled us to locate a regimental

or battalion headquarters within fifty or a hundred meters. The operator also knew which VC unit was transmitting and which was receiving. Our higher headquarters then evaluated this information to learn which enemy forces were moving and where. By comparing the information to previous ARDF reports they could determine the direction of travel. Our intelligence, gathered in this manner, provided by far the most valuable information of all intelligence activities in Vietnam.

For my first three months in Nam, I spent about half my time in the air and the other half on my administrative safety officer duties. We had four special operation aviation companies, scattered throughout Nam, with about 20 planes each. One company was located to our south in the Delta region. Another was collocated with us in Saigon at Tan Son Nhut Air Base. The other two companies were north of Saigon in support of II Corps. As the aviation safety officer, I would need to visit our outlying companies from time to time.

My first trip was to our Phu Bai Company, which was 400 miles to the north and difficult to get to. I called my Air Force acquaintance at the Scat Back Detachment and asked him what he had going north. In a couple of days I was winging my way to Phu Bai via Lear Jet at 400 mph! What a way to go compared to the low slow stuff we flew!

But coming back was a different matter. The only thing available was to hitch a ride with Air America, a CIA operation primarily supporting the Vietnamese government. The Air America guys were civilian contract pilots flying all sorts of aircraft. When I went to the local airfield to see what kind of flight I could catch back to Saigon, I saw that there was an old Twin Beech taxiing up to the terminal. After it discharged its load of eight passengers, mostly Vietnamese, including several chickens and a small pig. I asked the grizzled pilot if he were going to Saigon. He was. When he finished refueling the plane, he checked the manifest for his next load to Saigon. He said, "No problem" and noticing the wings on my uniform, asked if I wanted to fly "right seat" with him.

I said that would be great and we did the walk around together, which evidently passed for his preflight. I was somewhat astonished to note the cowl flap on the left engine was being held in place by a piece of the proverbial baling wire! It reminded me of the old WW II movies where the crash-landed plane was being put back together to get off the island. When I mentioned it he shrugged. I strapped into the copilot's seat, and he got the old beast started. The Beech C-45 Expediter, as it was called, had been used in WWII as a utility transport. In the early 50's it was upgraded to a command aircraft and used in the Air Force from 1952 to 1962. They were fine old birds, not too fast but reliable and stable.

We roared down the runway in Hue-Phu-Bai's 95-degree heat. With our full load of Vietnamese and a couple of chickens, I was relieved to see us finally lift off before the end of the runway in that hot, thin air. About a hundred feet into the air, my pilot turned to me and asked, "Would you like to fly it?" I was delighted to get my hands on that venerable old plane and replied, "I got it," which is mandatory pilot jargon used to avoid any doubt of who's in control. To my surprise, as I took the yoke and got my feet on the pedals, we suddenly veered left. I applied full right rudder to keep it straight and reached for the trim tab, noting it was already trimmed fully to the right. There was nothing for it but to stand on that right rudder. With my right leg already beginning to get tired, it was now clear why I had been invited to fly right seat. It was a two-hour flight but after an hour I was more than ready to give the controls back to the grizzled guy in the left seat, which I did before landing.

After about two months as the battalion safety officer, I was feeling I had made rather scant impact on the battalion's safety performance. In wartime, getting the mission accomplished always comes first and to have some officer running around insisting on matters of safety was just a pain in the neck for everyone trying to get the job done. I didn't want to be that guy. Also, as an Infantryman, I did not want to spend "My War" as a safety officer. I was desperate to find a job that was more career-enhancing and pondered how I could accomplish that. Then serendipity struck! I received orders to attend the PACAF Jungle Survival School, a short one-week course in Jungle survival training. It was a course I had requested, since flying in Vietnam was always dicey, with the possibility of going down in the Jungle. I had heard many stories about survival schools, mostly heavy stuff. But having an opportunity to attend the one in the Philippines at Clark Air Base was a welcome change from what I was doing, and I wanted this specific training in the event I should ever need it. I later learned it was a "gentleman's course," not one of those survival situations where all you get after three days of no food is a raw chicken. Also, this would provide a chance to break out of my current job. I explained my position to my boss, asking him to have me reassigned when I returned from the Philippines. He agreed and three weeks later I was headed to Clark for the survival course.

The first two days of the survival course were in the classroom learning about animals and plants in the Jungle, the snakes to avoid and the ones to eat. There were vines you could get water from in a slow drip once you hacked through them with a machete. There were tubers that were edible and some odd-looking fruits that grew in strange places. Machetes are great Jungle tools and we learned how to use them to build a quick shelter, booby trap or hammock. In the Jungle, bamboo will grow as thick around as a man's arm and on a weight to strength ratio, is stronger than steel. Being able to use it was important. Additionally, this phase of the course was building confidence that we could survive if we went down while flying over enemy territory.

On the third day we went into Jungle with a native guide who demonstrated the skills we had been studying. We each had a machete and can of Spam. We would supplement the spam by rooting up some edible tubers to go with it. We then wrapped everything in some large, heavy green leaves. This went into the ground with bamboo coals we had fashioned earlier. When you are hungry enough, everything tastes good.

With the learning phase behind us, we prepared for the actual escape and evasion part of the course. This was the heart of the entire training. If my plane went down in the Jungle, the concept was to make myself disappear for a day or two until the enemy search cooled down. Then I could make my way to a pre-designated area for pickup. To make this phase of the course realistic, we were to be dropped deep into the Jungle by helicopter. Pigmy natives known as "Negritos" would be used to track us down. The Negrito is a small, black aborigine whose tribes played an instrumental role in ejecting the Japanese from the Philippines in World War II. These little guys were only one generation away from cannibalism and with their loincloths and bones through their noses, it was creepy to have them tracking you down in the Jungle. To add realism and motivation, each of us was given three metal chits, like dog tags. If a Negrito were able to locate one of us in the next 18 hours, we were to give him a chit, which he could turn in for a ten-pound bag of rice. Their tribes were poor, so I mean to tell you, these guys were really motivated!

The chopper dropped us off about 5 PM in a small Jungle clearing. We had one hour to get lost before the Negritos were turned loose to find us. I quickly moved to the Jungle's edge and looked for the deepest, heaviest thicket I could find to crawl into. There was no doubt in my mind that I would survive this test without being found. Within 45 minutes I spotted a densely overgrown area of bush and vines and began to slither on my stomach under the growth. After about 20 minutes I came to an area where there was just enough room to sit up. I knew I had found a safe place for the night. I was there for perhaps 30 minutes before a Negrito child, about 14 years old, crawled up to me with his hand out for a chit! Well, at least I would complete this exercise with two chits in my pocket. It was getting dark now and I crawled out of my thicket and into the Jungle, looking for another hiding area. After about an hour I holed up again but there too I was soon approached for another chit. For a third time I moved out, now with but one chit left in my fatigues, which I again had to surrender within a few minutes of stopping. I had failed to evade capture and settled down for the night to sleep.

Two or three more times during the night I was shaken awake by chit-seeking Negritos. In the morning I took out my compass and map and headed for our safe area where the chopper was to pick us up. As the first twenty or so of the guys began to assemble in the safe area, we exchanged tales and discussed what went wrong. Nearly everyone had the same story. Evidently the Negrito "Mamasans" were on the hilltops watching the dispersion and directing their families by hand signals and calls in the directions we had gone. They had not bothered to honor the one-hour time lapse but had their menfolk on our trail right from the beginning. After all, how else would this great Jungle fighter have been caught!

Shortly after returning from Clark Air Base, I was reassigned to our next higher command the 509th Radio Research Group. The group commander, a colonel, was glad to have an aviator in his G-3 (Operations) section. I had already received my "Special Intelligence",

Top Secret clearance, which was required for assignment to the Army Security Agency (ASA). It was my first exposure to this level of intelligence operations. Specific projects were "code worded" so that, even though we were cleared for Top Secret, we only had access to the intelligence areas for which we had a code word. I was required to billet with other special intel people to reduce the possibility of secrets inadvertently slipping out during conversation or while talking in our sleep.

Our quarters were air conditioned and most of our meals were sit-down, served on tablecloths. I felt funny sending home my combat pay when my combat exposure was so little compared to the guys in the Jungles. For me, the tough part was being away from home and occasionally learning of a friend being wounded or killed. I truly felt that my wife's life on the home front, with our two children, Lee and Laura, ages ten and eight, must have been more difficult than mine. A couple of my Infantry officer friends who were flying were eventually able to talk their way into a transfer to a ground unit. If an Infantry officer has any hope of advancing to high rank, being in combat is very important on his record. I was therefore torn between the choice of advancing my own career by putting myself in harm's way and my duty to my family to stay alive and raise our children. My transfer to our next higher headquarters was a good compromise in this regard.

However, I did spend about 40 hours each month flying over those Jungles. Being in a single-engine observation aircraft, flying for hours over Jungles hiding an armed and hostile enemy a hundred miles from nowhere, took some getting used to. I always felt a little more comfortable on these missions when I was flying our twin-engine aircraft.

By December 1966 I had been in Nam for six months and so far, it wasn't as bad as my tour in Korea seven years earlier. Being older and of higher rank, conditions and circumstance were easier for me now. Also, I was flying on a regular basis, something most people have to pay to do, unless of course they are being shot at. My routine was to spend several days at my staff work and break it up flying missions for the 224th Aviation Battalion a couple of times a week. They were glad for someone to lessen their load and I was happy to get out of the office. Flying was always fun as long as one could avoid thinking of the consequences of engine failure. Life at two thousand feet was good, it was cooler and safer than being down in the Jungle. I could look down on the war below me with relative comfort and feel a sense of detachment. Ninety percent of all small arms hits occurred below 1500 feet, so my chance of being bothered by a bullet strike was rather remote. Plus, it certainly wasn't something one wanted to dwell on anyway. The North Vietnamese did not have anti-aircraft weapons in the south and the Viet Cong were not well trained at hitting a moving target. Yet, on occasion, one of our planes would come back with a bullet hole in the wing or tail. We referred to such a hit as a "golden BB"; that unlikely bullet which would find its way to a high-flying target. But during my tour in Vietnam, I never heard of one of our pilots being injured by ground fire. And only once during my 400 hours of flying over enemy territory did, I even come close to being hit by a golden BB. I had just started one of our 180 degree turns tracking a signal when I heard a loud CRACK from my right. When a rifle bullet, traveling above the speed of sound, goes past you, it emits a distinctive CRACK from the sound barrier being broken. I knew exactly what it meant but the event and threat were over as quickly as they occurred. My plane, moving at nearly three miles a minute, would not be available as a target for a second shot.

By early 1967 North Vietnam was sending thousands of troops and tons of supplies south, just across the border from South Vietnam, through the neighboring nations of Laos, Cambodia and Thailand in contravention to international agreements. The route they used was known as the Ho Chi Minh Trail. And what had indeed been Jungle trail in 1962 had become a veritable highway by 1967, with elaborate underground waypoints for vehicle maintenance and repair. It was estimated that, in 1966, North Vietnam moved 90,000 troops, plus sixty tons a day of supplies, down this route from North Vietnam to South Vietnam. During this period, our Air Force continued their round-the-clock bombing of the Ho Chi Minh Trail but with little effect in stopping the flow. General Westmoreland, then commander of U.S. forces in Vietnam, requested permission from the Pentagon to interdict this supply train with ground forces attacking across the border. His request was refused for fear of increased casualties and spreading the war into the neighboring countries. But this was such an important supply route for the enemy that many of our Airborne Direction Finding missions were dedicated to tracking NVA divisions as they moved south along the Ho Chi Minh Trail. At least we could track these units and learn where they were heading when they crossed the border into South Vietnam. The 509th was credited with providing a third of the intelligence available to ground commanders,

On one occasion, I had been in the air for over three hours in the vicinity of the Ho Chi Minh Trail and it was getting time to return to our airfield in Saigon at Tan Son Nhut Air Base. I told my "back seater" to shut down operations, that we were heading home. Just as I began a turn to the east, to my total astonishment I found I was turning directly into what appeared to be a load of logs falling from the sky above. As I veered away from the tumbling stuff, just a hundred yards to my right front, it suddenly became apparent that what was falling through the air was a long string of bombs which were now erupting on the earth below. Evidently there was a B-52, probably eight miles above me, unloading on a target below and nearly taking us with it. Those Air Force flights, code-named "Arc Light," were B-52 strikes on the Ho Chi Minh Trail. These AF bombing missions would often occur without any prior coordination with our Army units. Such was the occasion that day as I nearly flew into this string of bombs exploding below me. It was the only time I ever saw a bombing run up close and personal. It was an awesome sight! Of course, the success of an Arc Light mission is dependent on tight secrecy and so the information on that mission, if disseminated, never found its way to us. Likewise, it was highly unlikely that the cloak of "special intelligence", which enshrouded our missions, would have been lifted to inform the Air Force.

The next day, I am back to the office about 7 AM. My office is in a concrete, air-conditioned building with no windows and only one door. The door is heavy; made of steel and painted green. There is a guard standing by. The "green door" informally means it is a Top-Secret facility. Entry requires a "Special Intelligence" clearance card. As I pass through the green door, on the left is a room containing perhaps 20 teletype machines, with several clacking away receiving or relaying top secret material or messages from one general officer to another. These were referred to as "back channel" messages. Interestingly, the system was essentially a precursor of today's Internet. All telephone and teletype machine wires leaving the building were encased to ensure

"White-Black" criteria, a condition which precludes any magnetic inductance from emanating outside the building. After passing the teletype room, there are offices with doors closed. Further on the right, the wall becomes mostly glass, enclosing admin offices and behind those the commander's office. Further down the hall is a large room with several desks where I worked.

Our 509th group commander was a fine, older colonel whom I eventually learned, was also a chess player. A good chess player is always hard to find. In time I challenged him to a game of chess at the end of the day. I won the first round. The next day we came to an arrangement which enabled us to break up our 12-hour days with a little chess. He had a smallish chess set which he put on his desk. Sometime during the morning, at a coffee break, we would take a few minutes to begin a game. Thereafter, when I passed his office, I would glance through the office window to see if the little American flag in his pencil holder was up or down. If it were up, it would be my turn to move and if he were alone or away from his desk, I would step into his office and make my move, then continue with my work. It helped me get to know him and was a great way to break up the day. He played a good game of chess and I made sure he had the advantage of plenty of time to study each move, while, for the most part, my move was made in less than a minute. In chess, time is a great equalizer.

My job on the group staff was to handle special aviation matters, which I enjoyed. An important project, code-named Crazy Cat, was now coming together for me and I was fully immersed in that effort. Another action I was working on was a request from DA for a determination on whether the disappearance of one of our pilots should be carried as missing in action or deceased. I reviewed all the information available on the circumstance of his disappearance. His last radio transmission was made in bad weather on a heading which would take him directly into the side of Monkey Mountain. A search of that very precipitous mountain, north of Cam Ranh Bay, did not reveal any wreckage. I reasoned that he would not likely be found in that dense and inaccessible area. Further, my computations concluded that the impact at 130 MPH would have resulted in a G load greater than 50 G's, which would not be survivable. My return TWX (teletype message) to DA listed my findings and conclusions. A few days later I received a response that the pilot would be carried as missing in action. I later learned that, when there was no body found, the person was always carried as MIA for at least a year. This policy not only reduced the chance of a faulty conclusion of death but allowed any dependents to continue receiving full pay and allowances during the interim.

Our tours in Nam provided for a week of R&R (Rest & Recuperation) halfway through the assignment. My week was coming up in December and I had made plans to meet Barb in Hawaii. My anticipation of leaving the war zone for a Christmas week with Barbara grew day by day as I "Xed" out each day on my calendar. As the last day approached, my mind began to grapple with the fear of going down while flying over the Jungle. I knew from years of flying in various uncomfortable situations that these fears could be compartmentalized and shoved into a corner of the mind. To dwell on the unlikely serves no useful purpose and can only interfere with the mission. Nonetheless, as the day neared, I answered the urge to stop scheduling myself for missions.

Finally, the big day arrived. I packed a small suitcase and with high hopes headed for the airport. I boarded a "World Air" Boeing 727 for Hawaii. The plane was carrying a full load of soldiers and I breathed a sigh of relief as we steeply climbed out of Tan Son Nhut Airport into the safer skis above. In the seat next to me was a young soldier. We spoke briefly and I learned he was on his way to meet his fiancée for his R&R. It was about a 12-hour flight and seemed to last forever.

Barb's plane from San Francisco arrived at almost the same time as mine. Soon, after hugs and kisses, we made our way toward baggage pickup. On the way through the terminal, Barb spotted the young lady who had been her seatmate from San Francisco. She was sobbing heavily, and Barb went to her to see if we could help. She said her fiancé, had not shown and she was sure some calamity had befallen him before he left Viet Nam. Determined to help but not knowing how, I asked her the name of her soldier. To my great surprise, the name she gave me was the same as the name tag being worn by my young seatmate. I asked her to describe him and sure enough, we had a match. It seemed impossible that, of the hundred or so soldiers on my plane, I would be sitting next to her fiancé while on Barb's plane she was sitting next to his fiancée. What are the odds? It was almost like I had entered the "Twilight Zone"; like some divine hand had intervened on their behalf. I said to her, "Your young man is here. I was sitting next to him on my plane. Not to worry, we will find him." We escorted her back to the terminal where I had arrived and before long, like us, they were at last together again.

Barb had left the children with her parents in San Francisco which enabled a relaxing week for us at the Ill Akai Hotel on Waikiki beach. Of course, our time together flew by all too swiftly and we soon faced another heartrending goodbye for the second time.

—m—

It was April 1967 when we received word that our ground forces had recovered several Chinese Communist radios from a North Vietnamese base Camp we had overrun. The radios were to be sent back immediately to the Signal Center for detailed analysis. Enemy communications were our reason for being this was important stuff. It was significant enough that someone would need to accompany the radios to the U.S. in the same way a courier is used for highly classified documents. No doubt our chess relationship helped with my boss's decision to select me as the escort officer to bird dog the radios back to Fort Monmouth, New Jersey. Anything that would get me out of Nam for a while was a godsend. When the Colonel gave me the nod for this job, I took the opportunity to ask him if I could have a week of leave to visit my family in San Francisco on the way back to Nam. My request was granted. For several days I was walking on air.

Before leaving Saigon, I called the Pentagon and asked them where I would be assigned in June. Joe Kohler, an aviator I had met only a few weeks earlier in Saigon, was now one of the Infantry assignment officers and was glad to help someone he knew. He said, "Next week we will be looking at the June rotatee assignments. Where would you like to go?" I said, "How about the Presidio of San Francisco?" He said he would check it out and let me know. I told him I would call from the U.S. the following week to see what he had for me. When I got to Fort Monmouth, I again got ahold of Joe, who said, "Well, the only thing I have is a job as Peter Pilot in the Presidio Flight Detachment." A "Peter Pilot" is one who flies without accepting any other responsibilities, a non-career-enhancing activity. In the early days of aviation, we had only officer pilots (prior to the WO program) and many of them did not care about anything but flying and usually retired as captains. That was the very sort of job that could be a career killer for a major. After all, sitting in the cockpit of a light aircraft wasn't that much different from driving a truck but I was confident that once assigned to the Presidio I could work my way into a position of greater responsibility. With thoughts of returning to my beloved San Francisco, I said, "I'll take it." He said, "You've got it!" So, a few days later, after delivering the radios, Barb met me at SFO for our brief week together, we were both delighted with the news. San Francisco was our home, and our parents, brothers and friends were all in that area. This would be a rare opportunity for us all to be together again.

During our brief week in San Francisco, we decided to see if we could find a home to buy. There was a lovely home one block from where my mother lived and two blocks from where Barb had grown up and where her folks still lived. The only problem was that 380 Kensington Way was for sale for $60,000, far more than we could afford in 1967 when I was earning about $900 a month. The mortgage payments alone would be about 80 percent of my base pay with interest rates then at 7 percent, but we had been saving like crazy and plowing it into the stock market, which had more than doubled during the preceding ten years. I figured that, if we could get them down on their sale price, and I could borrow the money against my stocks at about 5 percent, we could do it. Our real estate agent said the couple who owned it were getting a divorce and we could possibly get it for less. We decided on an offer of $45,000, an unbelievable low-ball figure. They countered with $52,000 and I said to the agent, "Look, I'm going back to Vietnam in three days, so I will make a final offer of $47,500 and they have two days to accept or reject." I didn't have the time to screw around, and they knew it.

They accepted the offer and a down payment with the understanding that we wouldn't close until June when I got home. Before leaving for my return to duty in Saigon, I stopped by the Presidio of San Francisco to meet Colonel Lee, the Sixth Army Aviation Officer. Now, knowing I would be assigned there, I wanted to let my future boss know that I would like a job on his staff. This little visit would ultimately make the difference between my having a staff assignment at an Army Headquarters and being assigned as "Peter Pilot" in the Flight Detachment. We met in his office, and he was amenable to my request to be on his staff, saying he would see what he could do. My return trip to Vietnam was with light heart, knowing my next assignment would be in San Francisco. Once back in Nam, I returned to my Crazy Cat project involving arrangements for basing five Navy Neptune aircraft being reconfigured for Army use. Here is a photo of the P-2V Neptune.

Crazy Cat—RP2V Neptune Aircraft

The Neptune is a two engine, 80,000-pound, anti-submarine-warfare aircraft used by the Navy in the 1950s and early 1960s. Our five planes were at the General Dynamics factory being refitted with electronic stations which could acquisition enemy radio transmissions and jam them when appropriate. These large aircraft required runways with ten inches of homogenous concrete to withstand their landings, since their entire weight was concentrated on only two wheels. We had only two airfields in Nam which could handle that load. One was Tan Son Nhut Air Base in Saigon, the other the Naval Air Base at Cam Ranh Bay. My task was to arrange a home for this new unit and their aircraft. I decided on Cam Ranh Bay because the Navy already had P2Vs there, which meant there would be maintenance facilities available.

I had quite a time talking the folks At Cam Ranh into making space for us when I couldn't tell them about the high priority, super-secret mission the aircraft were designed for. Finally, the local commander pointed to a place on the tarmac and said we could park 'em there. I picked out some spots for locating our large GP tents and a place for the company personnel to sleep. At that point the Navy commander explained to me that Navy regs required that their pilots sleep in air-conditioned quarters and that we needed to comply with that. Wow, such a deal! Our chopper pilots flying in and out of the Jungle were told they couldn't carry their sleeping bags for overnighters because it used up space needed for ammo and resupply. Meanwhile the Navy was going air conditioned! Well, it was a strange war!

In early June of 1967 I was due to rotate home and our Crazy Cat unit, now designated the 1st Aviation Company (Radio Research), wasn't going to arrive until the following month. By that time, I really wanted to be in on the final phase of that operation but I wasn't going to spend a day longer in Nam than I had to.

Crazy Cat at Cam Ranh Bay, RVN

During the Vietnam War our days were long. We were usually on the job 12 or 13 hours a day, and mostly 7 days a week but as a major and an aviator, life for me in the war zone was strangely uncomplicated and not overly dangerous.

Not so for my old West Point roommate, Mit Shattuck. He was on his second tour in Nam, flying Hueys into hot spots, bringing in troops and taking out the wounded. He had been "in country" this time for about three months and had just brought a load of men into a hot LZ. Bullets were flying everywhere and as he rocked the ship forward and pulled pitch for a quick getaway, there in front of him a VC popped up out of the ground from what we called a "spider hole." With an AK47 automatic rifle, the VC raked the front of his chopper. Mit caught a round in his neck and one through his face. His copilot took the controls and brought them home.

Hueys lifting off from a hot zone in South RVN, 1966

Mit was patched up and returned Stateside for his recovery and next assignment. About 20 years ago I was able to locate Mit and arranged to get together with him for a few hours in Florida. Mit had always been somewhat tightly wound and when we got together, I could see that the Post Traumatic Stress Syndrome, I often wondered about, had truly taken its toll on him. This was nearly thirty years after Vietnam. He talked without a break in his sentences. His life was difficult. He was divorced, remarried for the third time and began to weep when the subject of Viet Nam was discussed. In recent years Mit seems to be totally recovered and has resumed a normal, productive life. War takes many forms, is selective of its victims and unpredictable in the human damage inflicted. I was unaffected, unaltered, except for being a bit hyper and short on patience when I got home. But that was short-lived.

Although I was a chopper pilot, my assignment to Nam was flying the relatively safer fixed-wing aircraft. Most of the chopper pilots had it rough and most had multiple tours of duty in Nam. Since war is a curious pursuit and one which most don't talk much about, I will insert a short treatment of the helicopter war in Vietnam from a more unsavory point of view than I experienced. Here is a poem by Michael Ryerson, USMC, a FAC (1966-1968):

The Man in the Door

They came in low and hot, close to the trees, and dropped their tails in a flare, rocked forward and we raced for the open doors. This was always the worst for us; we couldn't hear anything, and our backs were turned to the tree line. The best you could hope for was a sign on the face of the man in the doorway, leaning out waiting to help with a tug or to lay down some lead. Sometimes you could glance quickly at his face and pick up a clue as to what was about to happen. We would pitch ourselves in headfirst and tumble against the scuffed, riveted aluminum, grab for a handhold and will that son-of-a-bitch into the air. Sometimes the deck was slick with blood or worse, sometimes something had been left in the shadows under the web seats, and sometimes they landed in a shallow river to wash them out. Sometimes they were late, sometimes they were parked in some other LZ with their rotors turning a lazy arc, a ghost crew strapped in once too often, motionless, waiting for their own lift, their own bags, once too often into the margins.

The getting on and the getting off were the worst for us but this was all he knew, the man in the door, he was always standing there in the noise, watching, urging, swinging out with his gun, grabbing the black plastic and heaving, leaning out and spitting, spitting the taste away, as though it would go away.

"They came in low and hot, close to the trees, and dropped their tails in a flare, rocked forward and began to kick the boxes out, bouncing against the skids, piling up on each other, food and water, and bullets, a thousand pounds of C's, warm water and rounds, 7.62mm, half a ton of life and death. And when the deck was clear, we would pile the bags, swing them against their weight and throw them through the doorway, his doorway, onto his deck and nod and he'd speak into that little mike and they'd go nose down and lift into their last flight, their last extraction. Sometimes he'd raise a thumb or perhaps a fist or sometimes just a sly, knowing smile, knowing we were staying and he was going but also knowing he'd be back, he'd be back in a blink, standing in the swirling noise and the rotor wash, back to let us rush through his door and skid across his deck and will that son-of-a-bitch into the air.

They came in low and hot, close to the trees, and dropped their tails in a flare, rocked forward, kicked out the boxes and slipped the litter across the deck and sometimes he'd lean down and hold the IV and brush the dirt off of a bloodless face, or hold back the flailing arms and the tears, a thumbs-up to the right seat and you're only minutes away from the white sheets, the saws and the plasma. They came in low and hot, close to the trees and dropped their tails in a flare, rocked forward and we'd never hear that sound again without feeling our stomachs go just a bit weightless, listen just a bit closer for the gunfire and look up for the man in the door.

Loading wounded into a Huey—Vietnam, 1967

—⁂—

Finally, before leaving the topic of Vietnam, let me end with some words from John Steinbeck about helicopters. Steinbeck had a way with words. Only a handful of people have won both the Nobel and Pulitzer Prizes in literature. One of them was iconic American novelist John Steinbeck. His incredible body of work stretched from *Tortilla Flat* to *Of Mice and Men*, from *Grapes of Wrath* to *Cannery Row* to *East of Eden*. He had a gift for the language that few, before or since, have possessed.

Not widely known is the fact that in 1966-1967, a year before his death, Steinbeck went to Vietnam at the request of his friend Harry

F. Guggenheim, publisher of *Newsday*, to do a series of reports on the war. They took the form of letters to his dear friend Alicia Patterson, *Newsday*'s first editor and publisher. Those letters have since been published in a book edited by Thomas E. Barden, a Vietnam veteran and professor of English at the University of Toledo. The book is entitled *Steinbeck on Vietnam: Dispatches from the War.*

On 7 January 1967 Steinbeck was in Pleiku, flying with Shamrock Flight, D Troop, 10th Cavalry, and wrote the following home:

"Alicia,

I wish I could tell you about these pilots. They make me sick with envy. They ride their vehicles the way a man controls a fine, well-trained quarter horse. They weave along stream beds, rise like swallows to clear trees, they turn and twist and dip like swifts in the evening. I watch their hands and feet on the controls, the delicacy of the coordination reminds me of the sure and seeming slow hands of [Pablo] Casals on the cello. They are truly musicians' hands, and they play their controls like music, and they dance them like ballerinas, and they make me jealous because I want so much to do it. Remember your child night dream of perfect flight free and wonderful? It's like that, and sadly I know I never can. My hands are too old and forgetful to take orders from the command center, which speaks of updrafts and side winds, of drift and shift, or ground fire indicated by a tiny puff or flash, or a hit and all these commands must be obeyed by the musicians' hands instantly and automatically. I must take my longing out in admiration and the joy of seeing it.

Sorry about that leak of ecstasy, Alicia but I had to get it out or burst.

Love, John"

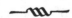

Before leaving Saigon, I finalized my arrangements for the arrival of the five Neptune aircraft to be located at Cam Ranh. I now had a little freer time in the evenings to plan my remodeling of the home in San

Francisco we would soon own. From photos I had of the place, I was able to derive some rough measurements and come up with drawings of what I wanted to accomplish. By our previous standards, this place was a mansion with its three floors and about 3500 square feet. But there were several deficiencies I would need to address. The original home, built in the late 1930's, had been damaged by differential settling with the help of earthquakes and construction of the Twin Peaks Tunnel, which ran under the property. It had been purchased several years earlier by a preacher who used the place as a church for his congregation. To this end, he had the main floor altered by removing the damaged fireplace and walls to create one very large room, perhaps70 feet long. At the end of the room there was yet another smaller room added on over the garage for use as an altar, with a stained-glass window on one side. When, after several years, the Church of God closed, it was sold to an artsy/dancey couple who used the "hall" for dancing lessons and art displays. Making it back into a home would be a challenge.

In April 1967 I heard from Mom that Grandmother Violette had died at age 87. Mother was leaving San Francisco for southern France to arrange her funeral and dispose of the chateau in Nice and the villa in Monte Carlo. There was a welter of problems to be solved and a lot of stuff in the old chateau which she needed to take care of. Mother asked if there were anything, I wanted from the Chateau. I replied that I had of course always admired the old oak clock on the mantle, which I re-membered from previous visits to Nice. I told her I would try to come home by way of Europe to see her and pick up the clock.

Material things are most meaningful when they carry with them past memories which may otherwise be forgotten. Now, when I hear Grandmother's clock ringing out its ancient chimes, it brings to mind the events surrounding my acquisition of that wonderful relic in June of 1967, shortly after leaving Vietnam.

I began my planning with Barb for me to come home via Europe, spend some time with Mother, arrange for shipping the clock to San Francisco and of major importance, pick up a new Porsche. With the German mark still at an unrealistic four marks to the dollar, the $6,000 price tag in Germany was a discount of nearly 40 percent from what a Porsche would cost in the States.

And the clock was important, too. It has a majestic appeal, large and stately with bronze ornamentations. The lion heads on the upper corners indicate the piece is of British origin. At its base, a bronze lion's foot is mounted at each corner. On the quarter hour the first four chimes sound, then eight chimes at the half hour and one loud "bong." The sixteen-chime tune it plays on the hour, followed by many resounding Bella Lugosi-type bongs, is what intrigued me most. I had to have that clock, which dates back to the mid-1800s. It is encased in a heavy oak frame with massive brass works inside. I would guess, although it is only about 18 inches wide and two feet tall, it must weigh 50 or more pounds.

The trick now would be to convince my boss that I should go home the slightly longer way through Europe. Nam is on the other side of the globe from the U.S. but the trip home to San Francisco would be more direct crossing the Pacific than the Atlantic. I think my old colonel really did like me, because right away he arranged for me to brief our V Corps headquarters in Frankfurt to assure the trip was properly funded and to provide a legitimate reason for sending me the longer way home.

There is something about leaving the war zone and going home that is unbelievably exhilarating. The calendar countdown had begun at about the 30-day point. Marking an x through each day heightened the anticipation. As my departure grew closer, the thought of going home filled every corner of my brain. Playfully lording it over the other guys that, in a few days, I'd be out of there was part of the game. During the last week, for the first time, I again began to feel some concern flying over the Jungles I knew were crawling with Viet Cong. The horror stories of the guys who bought the farm during their last few days before going home took on new meaning.

Yet, by the end of the week, there I was standing on the tarmac with one small bag waiting to board my Pan Am flight at Tan Son Nhut Air Base in Saigon. All my worldly possessions had been shipped the day before. If the plane wasn't hit on takeoff, in another several minutes I would be home free. For this trip I was headed east across Laos, Pakistan, and India, with a stop in Turkey to refuel. Then off again for the five-hour trip to Frankfurt's Rhein-Main Air Base.

Heading home seems to make watches run slower. Finally, I arrived in Frankfurt. The next day I made my way to V Corps headquarters and gave a two-hour update to the European ASA commander, covering details of what we were doing in Nam with Crazy Cat and airborne radio intelligence intercept . . . signal intelligence, SIGINT for short.

As planned, Mother met me in Frankfurt. And Herr Glebe, a Porsche dealer I had bought from previously, met us with the red 1967 Porsche 912 I had ordered. He invited us to join his family for dinner that evening. Mother was taken with the family and without discussing it with me, invited Herr Glebe's 16-year-old daughter to join us on the trip to Nice. We were traveling light and although the back seat of a 912 is nearly impossible for an adult, it worked fine for a wispy teenager.

Driving the new Porsche down the autobahns to Switzerland and over the Swiss Alps into France was a great trip, only slightly marred by the RPM restriction I needed to observe for the first 500 miles of break-in. Ninety miles per hour in fifth gear was OK but I really wanted to see what that thing could do at full throttle. I don't know if it was the bright German Racing Red color, or the fact that it was a Porsche, or perhaps that it was a German car but when I hit France every Citroen and Peugeot on the road was challenging me. Even my mother began to rise to the occasion and as I would close upon a slower vehicle, she would announce in her French accent, "Poosh heem out of ze way."

Returning to Nice brought back many memories. I had visited my grandmother there in 1953, after Plebe Year, with my best friend Bob Arnold. It was our first time in Europe. Every night we were out on the town. Now, as I entered the old chateau, I could still hear grandmother's words from when we would say good night to her before heading out for the evening: "You both look very handsome tonight. I am sure you will have many conquests." My second visit to Nice was three years later, in 1956, when after graduation Barb and I were there for three weeks on our honeymoon. Now, although it had been eleven years, nothing appeared to have changed. As my mind drifted back, time seemed to collapse.

Mother was busy trying to put Grandmother's affairs in order and close down the old chateau preparatory to selling it. Mother didn't drive, so my being with her was a big help. After about a week in Nice, it was time to leave and complete the rest of my journey. For my return trip to Franfurt, with the old clock and young teenager in tow, I decided I really needed to cover the nearly one thousand miles in one day to avoid an unseemly overnight somewhere with Herr Glebe's daughter. It was a long trip but this time without the speed limitations imposed by the break-in period. Once we were back on the autobahn the Porsche's speedometer easily pushed through 120 mph. It clung to the road like it was on rails. We made it back to Frankfurt in record time. After dropping off Fraulein Glebe and spending the night at the Frankfurt BOQ, I headed straight for the PX to have the old clock professionally packed and shipped to San Francisco. The next day, I boarded a commercial flight for the U.S. and home.

CHAPTER 27

PRESIDIO OF SAN FRANCISCO

Coming home from war creates a wonderful sense of anticipation and joy. After counting down the days for some time, the big day finally arrives and it's hard to believe. It was the second, long separation from my young family and now I was headed home again, home at last!

Unwinding from twelve months in Nam was an enjoyable unfolding of emotions: re-acquaintance with my family, the western world and San Francisco. The children were now ten and eight and had benefited from a year of living with grandparents while I was gone, though three generations living in one home was not always easy for Barbara, who had to balance the roles of mother and daughter.

During my last visit home in April, we had made a down payment on a home in San Francisco with the understanding we would move in in June. Now was the time. The home was a magnificent older Spanish-style, three-story, four-bedroom stucco building. It was impressive but inside it was apparent that it needed much help. It had structural flaws from thirty years of earthquakes and settling caused from its location directly over the Twin Peaks Tunnel. I remembered the house from ten years earlier, when it had been used as a church by its owners. They had removed the fireplace and wall from the living room, enlarging the room for an area large enough to seat their congregation. After several more years it was purchased by an artsy/crafty couple who used it to teach dance and display art. It was a $400,000 home with a view of the ocean which had been abused into a $247,000 bargain. Now it was again about to become a home, our home.

I was anxious to undertake the remodeling and reconstruction of the place myself and with 60 days leave was looking forward to the project. My overly ambitious plan required replacing the fireplace and wall, adding a bathroom and remodeling the kitchen. A load of 2x4's and sheet rock would take care of the walls but the bathroom was a real challenge requiring plumbing, electrical work and a built-in cabinet which would be created between two bedrooms. I had planned to build the bathroom cabinet from scratch but first needed to determine the layout of the bathroom. We had questions: what should go where, the bathtub, the shower, the door placements, and which way the doors should open. Barb thought we should hire an architect to flesh out our ideas . . . I gave way to wifely wisdom. In about two hours our architect had answered all our questions and given us some good ideas. I guess he recognized us as a struggling young couple, so to cover his fee he suggested that we give him the old wood-burning stove we were planning to dismantle and toss once the fireplace was in. We were delighted to exchange his services for the wood burner; and so was he.

The fireplace would also prove to be a project which would stretch my reconstruction skills. We bought a prefabricated fireplace called a "Heatalator," which had all the features of a regular fireplace without the structural requirements. My biggest challenge was getting the ten-inch, double insulated steel flue through the 20 feet of chimney which extended above the old fireplace. The fireplace box was intact, so all I needed to do was shove the five, four-foot steel sections up the chimney box, one at a time, until the first section came out the top. The first three sections were easy. I held them in place with a two by four and then, with the fourth section in place, forced all four of the sections up the chimney. Shoving that fifth section up was quite a challenge but with much sweat, up it went. Once that was accomplished, everything else fell into place.

There were an adequate number of rooms in the house that were habitable but for us to move in, Barb would need to endure my ten hours of construction work each day and the never-ending sawdust. She did and little by little it all came together, the bathroom, bedrooms, living room and fireplace as the architect had said to do. The bathroom was a bit tricky since the three-inch drain needed to find its way into the five-inch drainpipe in the basement. I found a plumber apprentice who handled the tricky part of breaking a hole in the five-inch cast iron pipe and then attaching a "saddle" to it. It was a very acceptable shortcut but not to code! When we had a Sears deliveryman bring in a new, larger water heater, he saw the saddle and reported it to the building inspector. There is nothing worse than a union bureaucrat throwing his authority around. He wanted the name of the apprentice (who would be sanctioned) and when it wasn't forthcoming, threatened to have the bathroom walls opened to inspect the plumbing inside. Eventually we gave up the name and to waylay any further bureaucratic action, Barb delivered two large potted flowering plants to his door.

Then there was the living room wall forming one side of a hallway that shouldn't be there. But I needed to put a wall between the master bedroom and the "altar." So, I cut the hallway wall out and with the help of my brother who had stopped by, moved it to where it was needed. With 90 percent of the remodeling done by mid-August, it was time to report for duty. The kitchen work would have to wait for later. It was perhaps the easiest part, since Sears made most of the decisions on the cabinets and what would go where, which left me enough time to be creative with the stove hood I wanted to build. On weekends, I began work on the hood. I initially constructed it from plywood with the idea of covering it with copper. I would need about 10 square feet of copper and found a place off Mission Street that handled sheet metal. During my lunch hour, I headed out to see the tinsmith I had called earlier. When he saw me in uniform, he wouldn't let me pay for the $80 sheet of copper. I insisted and he insisted . . . finally we agreed to let me pay for his costs. His appreciation for my being in the Army when we were at war was heartwarming and in stark contrast to the reception most vets were getting from San Francisco's flower children.

After covering my plywood stove hood with the copper, I used a ball peen hammer to texture it. We were pleased with the end result. It was the focal point of the kitchen and definitely one of a kind. The other major kitchen task was to tear down the wall between the kitchen and dinette, then divide the areas with cabinets to form a pass through. Since standard cabinets are not structurally sound enough to hang from the ceiling, I needed to devise a method to attach them. This sort of creative problem solving was the more enjoyable part of the effort. I decided to suspend the cabinets with a pair of cables just inside each end of the cabinets where they couldn't be seen. At this point of our marriage, Barb was still willing to trust my hare-brained ideas, so with a 4x8 beam across the top and a plank at the bottom of the cabinet, which looked like part of the structure, I was able to affix the cables to the plank for adequate support. The slight flexibility in the cables probably qualified it as the first earthquake-proof cabinets in San Francisco. Completing the rest of the kitchen was less exciting, with a vinyl floor professionally installed. With the addition of new appliances, the final product was a remarkable improvement. My second and last kitchen remodeling, which would come some 35 years later in Pebble Beach, was far more complex and is why my hair has since turned gray.

Duty at the Presidio was good. With all the Sixth Army staff either just back from Vietnam or on the way, no one was going to make life at that post difficult or unrewarding. I was pleased with my work and my boss in the aviation division of the Headquarters. In a few months a new colonel arrived to replace Colonel Lee. Colonel Ace Phillips was an improvement; he was one of those officers who was professional enough to be concerned about the career development of his junior officers. Before long he recommended me to our general, the chief of staff, to replace the departing Assistant Secretary of the General Staff (SGS) in the command group. The command group consisted of four generals who were in charge of Sixth Army, a command which covered an area of the twelve western states. As the Assistant SGS I would be specifically responsible for oversight of our protocol section, headed up by a captain with 27 NCOs and drivers and numerous staff cars.

The Chief of Staff, Major General Skeldon, had several officers from whom to choose for the job. I felt fortunate to have gotten the position, which was something akin to a "super aide." My duties were numerous and varied. Among other things, I was also something of a super gopher running down problems, arranging for the details of the Mexican Army generals' visit, planning a tour for the NATO commanders conference, and officer in charge of anything which might go wrong.

One of my miscellaneous tasks was assembling the staff in the command conference room each Tuesday morning for the chief of staff's conference in which the chief was brought up to date with ongoing actions. When all the heads of staff were present for the briefing, I would get the chief, call the room to attention when he entered, then keep notes for him during the conference. One day when I went to get General Skeldon for his meeting, I came into his office and stated with a bit of humor, "Sir, the staff is assembled and quivering in anticipation of your presence." Unbeknownst to me the other two-star, General Darnell, in charge of reserve affairs, was the ranking two-star and did not want to be subordinate to the chief of staff. But this was the chief's gathering, so General Skeldon replied to me, "Is General Darnell there yet?" I said, "No, Sir." He answered, "Then let them quiver." I went down the hall to get General Darnell. We never thought of General Darnell as a "real general." He was a reserve officer, without combat experience, brought on to active duty for a period of two years. When I would, on occasion, come into his office with an item for his in box, he was usually engaged in reading a newspaper or some other nonproductive activity.

I enjoyed my work greatly and though the hours were long; we had some interesting benefits such as when the commanding general needed some fillers on his yacht. Lieutenant General Stanley R. "Swede" Larsen, who had been a field force commander in Vietnam, was now our CG. Part of his job was to interface with key civilians in San Francisco. In this regard, Mr. Ben Swigg, owner of the Fairmont Hotel, was invited to join the CG on his Sixth Army yacht for a luncheon cruise on the Bay and a discussion of matters of interest to them both. For this occasion, General Larsen also included the aides and the officers of the SGS section and their wives as fillers on the yacht. It was a great day, a good cruise, and I enjoyed the hors d'oeuvres. We all met Ben Swigg and at the end of the cruise he invited us to come by the Fairmont the following day and take a tour of his penthouse, which we did. It was a once in a lifetime opportunity to see the way a zillionaire lives with the unbelievable views from the top of Nob Hill and unmatched elegance of the penthouse appointments. In his formal dining room was a 40-foot-long mahogany table flanked with high-backed chairs and completely set with candelabra, silver service and gold chargers. It was old wealth at its best.

The Heritage House

In June of 1968 we celebrated our twelfth anniversary with a trip to the Heritage House in Mendocino. At 8 and 10, the children were old enough that it wasn't a problem for Barb's folks to watch them. Mendocino has a great coastline, and the Heritage House cabins are advantageously perched on a bluff overlooking the Pacific. It was a good weekend made better by driving the Porsche home via Highway 1.

Our road was a two-lane highway with some remarkable views. It was a lovely day, and I was going a little fast but there wasn't any traffic to speak of. Driving the Porsche was always an exhilarating experience with five forward gears and a red line at 7,000 rpm. Dr. Ferdinand Porsche, who had been a professor of engineering, went through some extraordinary machinations at the planning board to make it a special handling roadster.

I was enjoying our ride home, appreciating the excellent handling quality of the Porsche and its ability to hold the road. Then, as we approached a long arching turn, a lesser car with an inferior driver accelerated sharply and passed me. I was surprised because I was doing about 65 at the time. As you may be aware, for a lesser car to pass a Porsche is an ultra-gauche exercise of arrogance and totally unacceptable. I had no choice but to accelerate and put this remarkably boorish-behaving clod in his proper place, i.e., behind me, sucking tailpipe.

There was ample road ahead and I could see for at least two miles, since the highway was arching to the left around flat marshland. I began to accelerate and was doing about 90 to catch him. At that speed I could feel the g's from the centrifugal force of the gradual turn. Although I knew that Professor Porsche had created a vehicle with the "unsprung weight" so close to the ground that the vehicle would cling to the turn as though it were on rails, it now became apparent from the voice in the right seat that my beloved was unaware of these attributes. She who must be obeyed was now insisting that I forget this puerile endeavor.

He, of course, was going faster now, but I knew that as the turn tightened, he would need to back off on his speed or risk losing it. Dropping it into fourth gear with a speed shift, I eased into the left lane and accelerated to pass (with visions of Juan Fangio). The right seat sounds became increasingly louder. Fortunately, Dr. Porsche had spent a great deal of time on the aerodynamics of this velocipede and now, as I reached about a hundred miles an hour, the air pressure kept me totally anchored to the road. I was gradually easing alongside of him and knew the longitudinal transverse links in the evolution of my McPherson struts would provide the superior road handling I needed to leave him behind. The voice in the right seat evidently, did not know this. Now a speed shift into fifth gear put the nose of the Porsche about three feet ahead of him and he could no longer accelerate and still hold the road. When I hit a hundred and ten, I knew he was beginning to sniff my exhaust and in a few more scant seconds it would be all over for him.

At that precise moment, with the scent of victory beginning to burn my nostrils, the risk averse one from Venus reached over, turned off the ignition, and snatched the keys out of my reach. It was horrible, like castration at the peak of exhilaration. We drifted to a stop in severe ignominy. The great contest indeed was over.

I had been in the SGS office for a little over a year when my name appeared on the selection list for the Command & General Staff College. I was fortunate. Every other aviator I knew had at least two tours in Vietnam and some had three, but about the time I would have been ordered back to Vietnam for a second tour, I was selected to attend the Army's Command & General Staff College at Fort Leavenworth, Kansas. In the Army, selection for advanced schooling usually takes priority over other assignments.

A couple of months before my departure, the Army had come up with an intermediate-level medal to be awarded for exceptional service "The Meritorious Service Medal". It would fill the gap between the Commendation Medal awarded to company grade officers and the Legion of Merit, usually reserved for officers serving in positions of great responsibility. And so it was that at the end of my SGS tour, General Skeldon recommended me for the newly conceived Meritorious Service Medal. The award was approved but since it was a recent creation, there were no medals yet in the system to award. However, at my award ceremony the general said some words and presented me with a certificate extolling my accomplishments, as is the custom for such occasions. Shortly before this gathering, in the hall I ran into General Darnell, who was not particularly fond of me, probably since I had often interrupted his newspaper readings with business. He said, "Major Hart, I want to congratulate you on your award of the Meritorious Service Medal. I can't think of any officer more deserving of a nonexistent medal!" This was followed by a resounding guffaw, indicating far more enjoyment on his part of this remark than on mine.

Award of the Meritorious Service Medal 1969

CHAPTER 28

FORT LEAVENWORTH

By 1969 I had been back from Vietnam for two years. Every Army aviator I knew had already received orders to return to Nam for a second tour, so I indeed felt fortunate to have yet another year ahead of me before the ax fell. The Army was graduating over a thousand pilots a month by then, but this airmobile war was sucking 'em in like a black hole. The aviator shortage was acute enough for the Pentagon to activate a retired lieutenant colonel to serve in my Vietnam unit, with the understanding that he would not be doing lieutenant colonel duties, just flying. While I was still in Nam, he told me he had been a mailman when recalled to active duty as a pilot. Vietnam was not only causing repetitive tours but adding much turbulence to assignments. The normal three-year permanent assignment was now shortened to two years in most cases and sometimes less.

So again, our family of four, plus cat, faced the proposition of moving after just two years. This move would be a little more difficult since we would need to rent or sell our home in San Francisco and decide which household items should go into storage and which we would take with us for the next year. Then there was the Porsche. Barb wanted me to get rid of it since it kept running into things, too many bad drivers on the road! The Porsche was sold for what I had paid for it in Germany and was replaced with a Buick station wagon. We took a couple of weeks leave to capture some of the enroute wonders such as Mount Rushmore and the Grand Canyon.

Our fur person (Justimere Cat) was half Siamese, and those cats seem to do better in cars than most. She was now a couple of years old and very much a part of the family, but she had an inauspicious beginning. I had told someone at the office in San Francisco that we were looking for a black kitten. A couple of days later a WAC soldier arrived in my office holding a paper bag. Inside was a six-week-old feral kitten, all teeth and claws. She said there was a litter of cats under the WAC barracks and the black one was captured for me. When I got her home and the cat was out of the bag, she zipped like greased lightning under the nearest sofa, where she remained until the third day, finally coaxed out by a bowl of milk. We named her Justimere; her last name was Cat. It took another couple of weeks before she lost the attitude. Now, two years later and in the back of the station wagon, she was not too happy. Siamese cats can be very talkative, and she let us know how she felt about this reassignment.

Our first stop was a motel in Elko, Nevada. About midnight Justimere got in bed with us and started a screaming routine like I've never heard before. Turning on the lights to see what the problem was, we found her in the midst of delivering her first litter of three. What a night that was! But the untimely arrival of the kittens turned out to be a blessing once we got Justimere situated in a well-padded cut-down cardboard box with her kittens. She was now delighted to be in the back of the station wagon, with her kittens away from everyone, and kept quietly busy doing what mother cats do.

Our arrival at Fort Leavenworth in late August was like old home week. We had about a hundred and fifty classmates and friends there at the same time, most of whom we hadn't seen for several years. I was particularly pleased to see my chess playing classmate, Jerry Grinstead, so we could resume our 18 years of chess competition. Jerry was also an aviator, so from time to time we would fly together to get our minimums. I remember well that night in Kansas when we scheduled a Beaver to get our night flying requirements done together. I brought a small peg chess board with me and while Jerry was flying, I set up the board and told him it was his move. There was plenty of room to put the board between us. We would trade off flying and pondering our next move. I would fly while he pondered. Then he would fly till I made my move. However, as the game wore on, it increasingly became more interesting than flying the plane. Pretty soon we were both pondering the board, with scant attention to the aircraft.

Fortunately, the Beaver is a very stable platform and once properly trimmed, will pretty much maintain its last heading and altitude. When the chess game ended, we looked up from the board without the slightest idea where we were. We had been grinding through the sky for nearly an hour and now had no concept of where we were or even what state we were over. It was too dark to discern any terrain features and we weren't in radio contact with anyone. Using our navigational equipment, Jerry began cycling through the nearest Omni stations. It wasn't long before he found a station that could give us a bearing from the station to our position. We had to find yet another Omni for another bearing to plot the intersection. The intersection of the bearings from the two Omnis would fix our position. Before long Jerry had our approximate location and a heading for us to get back to our airfield. We were about a hundred miles south and would be home in another 45 minutes. It was a great evening; we got to fly, completed our night minimums, and I won the chess game. It doesn't get any better than that.

A few months later, several of my classmates needed to get to Kansas City Airport and asked if I could fly them. There were four of them and the Beaver is a six-place aircraft, so no problem. When we got to the airport the tower put me in the number two position to land, but on final the guy landing first was slow to clear the runway, so the tower told me to "go around". I shoved the throttle forward to climb pack to traffic pattern altitude and as I climbed over the runway the tower said, "If you can still make it, you are clear to land." I chopped the power, put on full flaps, and dumped the nose. We were coming down faster than Marilyn Monroe's panties and all the guys in the back seat could see was the runway coming at 'em. They were sweating like a priest at a cub scout meeting. We landed without incident except for the white knuckles in the back seat.

Life at Fort Leavenworth for the nine months of the C&GSC course was good living. We had about a hundred classmates in school with us, so there was a great deal of socializing. All of us arrived as majors but were on the promotion list to lieutenant colonel (LTC). About ten classmates were higher on the list than the rest of us and would be promoted about six months early as a result of being selected "below the zone" for their outstanding performance. Before graduation, we had all been promoted to LTC with a little more than 13 years' service and were awaiting orders for our next assignment. The war in Vietnam was beginning to wind down, but a few classmates were selected to return there to take command of combat battalions. (Most of our classmates who commanded battalions in combat were eventually promoted to general officer rank.) Some received orders to command battalions in Germany or elsewhere. My orders were to the intelligence staff of a NATO headquarters, Central Army Group, in Germany, about halfway between Mannheim and Heidelberg. As far as I was concerned, any assignment other than Vietnam was a good assignment. The timing of my year at C&GSC coincided with the beginning of the drawdown of U.S. forces in Vietnam. And the promotion to lieutenant colonel also helped keep me out of a second Nam tour. There just wasn't that much demand for aviation LTC's in Vietnam anymore.

CHAPTER 29

GERMANY AGAIN - 1970

As the countdown for our departure to Germany began, our preparations included putting all our household goods into storage except for a few home accessories, some art, a TV, vases, toys, wardrobe and other personal items. Our home in Germany would be fully furnished, to include crystal glasses and kitchen appliances. We well knew the routine from our previous transition to Germany eight years earlier, so this second overseas assignment was much less stressful.

It was June of 1970 when we left Fort Leavenworth for San Francisco to spend some time with our folks before leaving for Europe. The kids were now 13 and 11 and were looking forward to our trip. They had moved often enough to be used to making these drastic changes in their lives and were taking it all in stride.

It was late June when our plane arrived in Frankfurt, complete with cat and baggage. Our car was still enroute, so the four of us boarded a local German train for Mannheim with plans to pick up a rental car upon arrival at the train station there. Our destination quarters in the local American Kaserne were available for immediate move-in upon arrival, which made for an easy transition.

In the Army, sponsors are designated to assist newly assigned officers. Contact is normally made several weeks ahead of time to coordinate details for transportation upon arrival and a smooth transition into your job and home life. Some sponsors go the extra mile, having the family over for dinner, loaning their second car, and helping in all aspects of assimilation into the local Army community. Our sponsor met us at the train station with keys to our house, which was a pleasant surprise.

Before long I was hard at my job in NATO intelligence, the kids were enrolled in our local American school, Barb was attending a class to improve her German, and we were into the swing of things. We had an active Boy Scout Troop on post which our son Lee had joined. In the course of life, a few months later, I was asked to take over as President of the Boy Scout Council. Army communities, especially overseas, are little cities unto themselves. There is much volunteer work necessary to keep things functioning and make the quality of life as good as possible.

As summer approached, the Boy Scout Council planned for their summer scouting events, including a camping trip to Camp Darby in Italy. Darby was a Boy Scout Kramp in the shadow of the Leaning Tower of Pisa. The challenge was to get our 35 lads there and back. I was not comfortable with having that project fall entirely on the shoulders of our enlisted scoutmaster, so I took on the role of "Officer in Charge of Unruly Scouts" for the purpose of getting us to and from Camp Darby.

Late in the afternoon of a pleasant June day, my 35 scouts and I boarded the German train at the Mannheim Bohnhoff. As life would have it, we had to change trains somewhere near the Italian border at about three o'clock in the morning. Can you imagine trying to wake up 35 scouts, ages 12 to 16, at three in the morning? Fortunately, I had been able to assign all the scouts to one car and the senior Scout leader and I were able to get our carload of boys, with all their packs and paraphernalia, off the train before too long. Once I got them assembled on the platform, I had the squad leaders check their squads and give me a head count. To my horror there were two boys missing. I had this panicky vision of the train leaving the station with my two scouts disappearing into the bowels of Europe . . . a tough situation to explain to their mothers.

I grabbed my senior Scout leader and the two of us got back on the train, heading in different directions to locate the missing boys. My vision now shifted from one of explaining to a mother, to the thought of the train leaving the station before we found the boys and could get ourselves off. I shouted to my Scout leader, "If this train starts to move, get off!" Unbeknownst to me, sometime during the night Sammy and his best buddy had gone exploring through the German train and finally parked themselves in an adjacent car for the night rather than returning to their assigned car. It was only a few minutes before we discovered them and herded them toward the exit, now clogged by anxious boarders trying to get on. With huge relief, we pushed them through the flow of bodies onto the platform before the train started rolling. As we settled into the seats of our next train for the final leg of our trip, I realized that this intense pain I felt in my head must be what people referred to as a "migraine." It was the first and fortunately last encounter I ever had with such a well-deserved affliction. Our week at Camp Darby passed quickly and to my great relief the trip home was uneventful.

I liked my compatriots at work. Our intelligence staff was comprised of an equal balance of German and U.S. officers. I suspect the nobility of Europe were all expected to serve in their country's armed forces, and it was reflected in the quality of their officer corps.

Speaking of nobility, as an aside, the portrait I have of grandfather shows a few medals he had been awarded, including one resembling our Legion of Merit, so I presume he also served.

Marquis Victorio De Ciccolini

Grandfather's portrait hangs on the wall in our San Francisco home. It tells something of the elderly gentleman's life. His gray double-breasted suit with European cut and the handlebar mustache indicates someone not of this country. In the corner of the portrait is his family crest. The talent of the artist (Jemimah Kahneman) is revealed in the quality of his work, the perfection of skin tone, and his capturing the striking hazel eyes typical of northern Italians. Grandfather's portrait shows a handsome man of dignity, perhaps in his late 40's, wearing a conservative blue-patterned tie. The painting shows that its artist was able to read beyond the obvious features of the full handlebar mustache and strong chin to uncover a strength of character seemingly radiating from these features. The family crest is lacking a bar sinister, which legitimizes his heritage. The six hills of the crest confirm his name, Ciccolini, which in old Italian means Six Hills which could be symbolic of the seven hills of Rome? It also may indicate that the family originated in Rome, since the early custom was to take the location of one's home as the family name. Thus. Victor de Ciccolini, Marquis of Rome.

Looking at this fine figure, I asked my mother, "How did Grandfather become a Marquis?" She said the title was bestowed on his great-grandfather for service to his country as a Roman senator and the title thereafter passed through the oldest living sons. "His heritage has been traced back to before Christ," she added. But I stray: Back to my NATO assignment in Mannheim.

All NATO Headquarters consisted of multinational representation. Our NATO element was CENTAG (Central Army Group), a headquarters in Secondheim, which was commanded by a U.S. major general with a German brigadier general under him. Each level of our staff alternated with German and US sections heads. Our G2 section was run by a German Colonel Glade with an American Colonel under him.

In my G2 Operations Division, my boss on the intelligence staff was a German Lieutenant Colonel who had served in the German Army during WW II. All staff in NATO was sandwiched that way with the host country officer and then a U S officer in alternating positions. LTC Dielitz was an older, dedicated, WW II veteran. He was very bright and knew his English better than I. He put me to work rewriting the CENTAG "Intelligence Estimate", a top-secret document of about a hundred pages which led to the conclusion that we would only have three days advance warning should the Soviet Block decide to attack.

It was worrisome because on the Soviet side of border separating the Cold War sides, the Russians had some 20 divisions with the East Germans and the 4ᵗʰ Polish Army, while NATO had about six divisions. Of course, our nuclear arsenal was something of an equalizer and they knew it.

As I worked my way through the NATO Intelligence Estimate it became apparent to me that it did not consider our COMINT (Communications Intelligence) capability since that was "close hold" U. S. intel. After about a year, considering all factors, I concluded that we would have about 8 days' notice of an impending attack. It took me nearly another year to finish the Estimate. It was gratifying, when about three years later while stationed at the Presidio of San Francisco, we received a top secret briefing from the Pentagon's DCSINT (Deputy Chief of Staff, Intelligence) which had incorporated my NATO findings.

Working with me in G2 Operations was Ober feldwebel (Sergeant Major) Bernd Sawatzki. Bernd spoke excellent English and held the highest enlisted rank in the German Army. He was also the youngest Ober feldwebel in his Army and I greatly benefited from our official association and enjoyed our office relationship. Twenty years after I left Germany and had retired from the Army, I received a phone call from Bernd. He had somehow tracked me down. In the emails and conversations which followed I learned that after I left NATO, Bernd was transferred in 1973 to the German Embassy in Islamabad to become the Office Manager and the Assistant of the German Military Attaché in Pakistan. After his 15 years of military service and a short stay in a civilian career in Germany, he was selected to become the General Manager and Vice President of a German Company in Toronto in 1981. Subsequently, Bernd formed his own companies (Import/Export and a Construction Company in 1986 with a Head Office in Toronto and extensive overseas operations. He was called to be an Advisor for Foreign Trade to the Canadian Prime Minister, Jean Chretien. Through continued contact we became good friends, visiting in San Diego and Canada. Bernd has now retired and lives at Lake Chapala/JAL, Mexico.

Army doctrine postulates a three-to-one advantage of an attacker over a defender to assure any degree of success in an offensive action.

The Warsaw Pact forces opposing NATO in East Germany, Poland and Czechoslovakia did indeed have that three-to-one advantage. Why would the Soviet coalition of forces maintain that level of offensive strength if they were only interested in defending? Our current intel estimate, which I was about to rewrite, concluded NATO would have a minimum of 14 days warning before an attack was imminent. That was based on the intelligence indicators of activity and build-up of those opposing forces. After two and a half years of working on this document, I concluded in the final "Estimate of the Situation" that our side would, in fact, only have 72 hours warning of an impending Soviet attack, not 14 days. My estimate was approved and eventually adopted as the official U.S and NATO Intelligence Estimate, which of course impacted our entire defensive posture throughout Europe in the Cold War. Fortunately, the imminence of an attack is no longer a major consideration.

And, so it was that, while serving in CENTAG headquarters near Heidelberg, I learned that one of the German majors in the operations section carried the title Graf. Titles of course are quite important to Europeans, and particularly in Germany, which has a very class-conscious society. Being an officer in the Army or Air Force is for them one of the few acceptable occupations for a European nobleman. Since I was working on intelligence plans that needed to be coordinated with Herr Major Graf von Falcon, I walked over to his office in another building to drop them off on my way to lunch one day and used the opportunity to discuss the documents. German officers are of course very proper, so I was a bit surprised when I entered his office that as the Junior officer (I was a lieutenant colonel and he was a major) he did not come to his feet as I greeted him in my very limited German, "Guten Morgen, Herr Major Graf von Falcon." Nor did he ask me to be seated. Perhaps, I thought, he was one of those rare individuals who after 20 years still objected to our having won the war! Only slightly bothered by his attitude, I said, "Tell me, Major Graff Von Falcon, which nobility carries a higher rank, a Graff or a Marquis?" He said, "That would be the Marquis, which is about the same in ranking as a Count." I said, "Thank you, in that case I shall be seated." Then, to put things in proper balance,

I explained the Marquis de Ciccolini and my heritage. After that, we always got along famously.

— ɱ —

Flying in Germany

Our three-year tour in Germany was a wonderful experience for the family. The children were old enough to enjoy and absorb much of the German culture, and I enjoyed my associations on the staff. In addition to my NATO duties at CENTAG, I was still maintaining my flying proficiency in both helicopters and fixed wing, This meant flying at least 4 hours a month, to include 6 hours of night flight every six months as well as 6 hours of instrument proficiency. In those days, the Army did not particularly care where you flew for this proficiency.

Bearing this in mind, one day I was called to our headquarters to find out if I wanted to join the NATO golf team. It didn't matter that my golf was lousy; the point was that we could use my required flying time to get the general to golf matches. Otherwise, NATO funds would need to be expended to provide such transportation and that was totally out of the question. So about once a month we would throw our clubs into the back of the plane and head for Belgium, Holland, or northern Germany for a golf match against another NATO headquarters, returning home that evening.

Flying in Europe was not much different than here but sometimes it was difficult to understand the controllers. We got away late one evening from a match in Holland and had some rough weather to negotiate, with a storm brewing that was tumbling us around badly. During those times, on instruments at night, it can get a little hairy in a light twin. Add to that the problem of sometimes having difficulty in understanding the controller. But eventually we cleared the storm area over Holland and got home in fine shape.

Some months later I made a helicopter flight to Brunson, Holland to visit our higher headquarters, AFCENT (Allied Forces Central), for a three-day conference. It was a good three-hour trip and when I arrived, I called their local airfield for landing instructions. The Brit in the tower had that heavy English accent that sounds like he is talking through a mouth full of potatoes. He answered, "Roger, Army 759, you are cleared to land runway "rouhen roff" (not understandable). I requested, "Say again active runway" and again it came through like "rouhen roff." There was just the one runway, and the winds were calm, so it wasn't possible to decide on the runway based on wind direction. Rather than have him do his "rouhen roff" for a third time, I turned right toward the end of the runway closest to me. This time he came back on the radio loud and clear, saying: "I SAY, YANK, YOU'RE GOING THE WRONG WIAY!" Of course, in a chopper it doesn't much matter which way you land but I reversed course to accept the protocol.

The AFCENT visit was more fun than work. Their headquarters, in the British sector of NATO, was commanded by a British three-star and staffed primarily with Brits, Dutch, and Americans. I planned to be at their office promptly at 7:30 the following morning but the Dutch officer who met me at the airfield said my counterpart at AFCENT did not want me to get there before 9:30 or there wouldn't be anyone around! I did as I was told, and the following morning was introduced around the office. When the social amenities were over, I expected we'd get down to business on the NATO Intelligence Estimate. But instead, at 10 AM, it was evidently time to break for "Tea." Tea of course is not something you sip at your desk. You go to a designated dining area with white tablecloths and are served a proper tea with all sorts of finger sandwiches and a great profusion of goodies.

It was a little after eleven AM before we got back to the office. But by the time we got our briefcases open and were about to settle in to get something done, my Dutch counterpart suggested that we wait until after lunch since we would need to walk to the Officers' Mess and would be stopping at the club first for a libation. So, twenty minutes later, we were again out the door. That afternoon was a repeat of the morning, coming back from lunch a little late and then the afternoon tea and breaking early in the afternoon to prepare for a formal gathering at the general's quarters. Consequently, we got absolutely nothing done all day. I could never be sure, but I always suspected that these efficient and effective officers were putting me through something of a scam because they knew our "Type A" American officers were always working too hard and too long.

I enjoyed being back in Germany with all the old familiar sights. I had fond memories of our times in Buedingen six years earlier and wanted to get back up to that village to revisit my old airfield and the local German chess club. Since I was required to have six hours of night flight each year, I decided to fly to Buedingen one evening to meet my night requirements and pay a visit to the old chess club. I was able get one of the local De Havilland Beavers available at Heidelberg Army Airfield and took off at dusk for the 40-minute flight to the little airfield I had commanded in 1966.

Buedingen is a lovely little town, tucked into a valley, snuggled against the foothills east of Frankfurt. It has a smallish medieval castle, surrounded by a moat which diverts the river around the ramparts. Its park-like grounds are open to the public and the castle is still, supposedly, owned by the Prince of Buedingen, though he has a more modern home on the outskirts of town.

The evening, I had planned for my flight to Buedingen was on a Friday, when I hoped their Chess Club would still be meeting at a local gashouse. It had been nearly six years since I had taken a table at the Buedingen Chess Club. I was confident they would still be meeting there, since routines in small European towns don't change much from year to year.

I landed just as the sun was setting and taxied to the operations area. The field was deserted except for the operations sergeant and a row of helicopters parked on the west edge of the runway. The sergeant told me that the squadron was in the field and he and the duty officer were the only ones left.

It was only about a mile walk into town, so fifteen minutes later I was reaching for the door of the gashouse. Several familiar members were still there, and I was delighted to be challenged to a game by the old attorney, Herr Arnold, who was the club's strongest player. It was amazing how the years had melted away since my last visit. Herr Arnold could hardly believe it had been six years, Vietnam and two other assignments since our last game. Three hours, one schnitzel and four games later, it was time to head back to the airfield.

When I got back to the plane, the operations NCO asked me to call the duty officer. A long phone conversation ensued in which the Duty Officer explained that Buedingen was no longer an airfield but had been redesignated a heliport and I would not be allowed to take off (Oops!). I explained to the duty officer that taking off on that short field wasn't nearly as challenging as landing there and since I was already on the ground, what was the problem? He said they couldn't take a chance on my wiping out the helicopters parked along the edge of the runway. We went back and forth on this for a while but since he was a captain and I was a lieutenant colonel, I had something of an advantage.

Of course, my landing at a "heliport" was a decent violation of sane flying practices and though perhaps justifiable under certain emergencies, it was my sensing that chess didn't qualify as an emergency. With this in mind, my rank advantage was somewhat neutralized. I finally said, with a note of authority, "Captain, I've got to get back but to keep you out of trouble, I'll begin my takeoff roll where the row of helicopters ends so there will be no possibility of damaging them." That was acceptable to him, but I had no idea if I could get off the ground with the six or seven hundred feet of runway left for my takeoff.

It was very dark and without the usual runway lights. As I lined up for takeoff, I was chagrined to see my landing lights revealed how little runway was in front of me. I put down full flaps and started pushing the throttle forward while standing on the brakes. As I reached full throttle the De Havilland was vibrating and jumping, fairly bursting to leap forward as the 450-horsepower radial engine throbbed to full power. I released the brakes and roared into the darkness, hoping this wouldn't be my final, career-ending takeoff. As the landing gear reached the end of the runway, I was pulling hard on the yoke, willing the plane into the air. Gravity finally gave way to the forces of lift and at last I was airborne as the runway turned to pasture. But there was still the perimeter fence somewhere ahead of me and the rising terrain of the hills at the end of the valley. I cleared the fence and began a gradual turn to the left to avoid the hills I knew were out there. As I exhaled, I realized I must have been holding my breath. Before long I arrived safely back at Heidelberg, the end of another routine day.

In the "old days" Army aviators flew both airplanes and helicopters without distinction. On this particular day I would be flying the Bell OH-6 with my boss to Kassel; about two hours north of Heidelberg. The OH-6 was the Army's version of the Bell Jet Ranger, a small 5-seat chopper that had only recently been included in the Army's inventory. It was a much-anticipated addition to the fleet, since it was far superior to the older reciprocating choppers we had been flying and word was that it carried four and a half hours of fuel, nearly twice that of its predecessor. I had been checked out in it the week before and found it a little trickier to land than its larger cousin the Huey. Every time I'd get it close to settling down, it'd get twitchy. It would take a little more time to master. I got in some additional practice in setting it down and a few days later, had a chance to make my first cross-country flight in this new chopper.

My boss, Colonel Davis, needed to make a visit to our strategic listening station near Kassel and I needed the chopper time. These stations were arrayed around the periphery of the USSR and could listen to transmissions deep within the Soviet Union as well as locate the transmission through triangulation. I presume they have long since been replaced by more sophisticated satellite snoopers, but they were very important then to our strategic intelligence collection effort.

The trip to Kassel would take about an hour and three quarters. I figured we would arrive home with about an hour of fuel remaining. We took off after lunch and a half hour out of Kassel, the fuel gauges were reading slightly less than half full. If accurate, this meant we would arrive at Heidelberg with less than the requisite 30-minute fuel reserve. Since the OH-6 was relatively new to me, I lacked the experience to know whether the fuel gauges were accurate or if the four-and-a-half-hour fuel capacity I had been expecting was something you only got when flying the bird at settings for minimum fuel burn. I pondered whether I should stop to refuel. That was my first mistake, pondering rather than stopping.

Another uneventful hour passed as we headed south through the Rhine Valley. But as the saying goes, flying is hours of boredom punctuated by moments of sheer terror. I was reminded of that saying now, as my 20-minute fuel warning light began to occasionally flash. That was not a moment of terror but certainly cause for a condition of "heightened concern." Un-fortunately my boss, sitting next to me, also noticed the flashing red light on the console and asked, "What's that?" Of course, it is important in a situation like this to be totally Joe Cool, so I nonchalantly turned my head toward him and announced that was merely an indication that the 20-minute fuel warning light was about to go from flashing to steady. Then, pretending total confidence and control, I explained that once the light became a steady red, I would punch the timing clock on the console to ensure we wouldn't exceed 20 more minutes of flight. In order to avoid any passenger angst, I pointed to the castle looming a few miles ahead on the left side of the valley, saying, "Sir, you see that castle a few miles ahead of us? That's the Heidelberg Castle." A few minutes later however, the expert in control went from "heightened concern" to "condition pre-pucker" as we neared the castle and found it was not the famed Heidelberg Castle, which displays the historic burned-out ramparts but just another picturesque Rhine valley castle. My landmark castle was still another ten minutes away.

By now the fuel warning light had been on steady red for eight minutes. I had 12 minutes of fuel left and from a cursory glance at the map, figured I was about 13 minutes out. I felt myself ratcheting up to "pucker level" but not yet at "sheer terror"; that would come a few minutes later.

There was scant relief as I confirmed we were now abeam of the actual Heidelberg Castle. I could see our airfield about five minutes distant but the second hand on the clock I had punched was now moving through 17 minutes. Fortunately, I was wearing my aviation crash helmet, so my boss couldn't see the sweat beading on my brow. I called the tower, announcing I was five minutes north and letting down for a straight-in to runway one eight. I began a very slow descent, hoping the reduced power required would stretch the clock just a bit. However, the lower I got, the fewer options I would have in the event the engine quit. It was a tradeoff which now carried me to the final level of "sheer terror." I was over the city of Heidelberg and rapidly running out of places for a successful autorotation. Now the red tile roofs of the German houses below were only a hundred feet beneath my skids; no sizable backyards, no options whatsoever. The clock passed through 22 minutes as my skids cleared the runway threshold. I hovered directly to the refueling point, twitched it down onto the tarmac and shut the engine off. As the line man refueled it, I was standing by to see how much fuel it would take. He topped it off and announced 88 gallons. I did not tell my boss that our chopper holds only 86 gallons of usable fuel or that, had I banked or changed the aircraft's attitude in the least, we would have fallen from the sky. As we got into the staff car he ventured, "That was a bit tight, wasn't it?" I said, "No, sir, just another routine flight." But of course, he knew better.

By 1973 we had been in Germany for three years and were closing in on our next assignment. I had completed the rewrite of the CENTAG

Intelligence Estimate which had involved a great deal of work. The revised estimate primarily concerned the amount of warning time NATO would have should the Soviets decide to attack the West. My new estimate significantly reduced the amount of time we would need to prepare for an attack. This was a significant accomplishment and I expected it would be reflected in a very good Officer Efficiency Report (OER). A good OER was important because in a couple years I would be closing in on competing for promotion to full colonel and only 25% of the Lieutenant Colonels who were qualified, would be selected for promotion.

My rating officer, Colonel Mat Gately, gave me an excellent OER but it ran counter to the Chief of Staff of the Army, General Abraham's instructions that commanders needed to deflate the army rating system. Ever since Vietnam, ratings had been creeping up to the point of "puffery". More and more officers who worked hard and did their best were rewarded with very high efficiency ratings. It was General Abraham's opinion that in any command the ratings needed to follow a bell curve with a small percentage of officers being rated in the highest category and the majority falling somewhere below that. In that regard, General Abraham sent a message to all his commanders telling them that it was time to "pull up our socks and get the rating system back to where it was more meaningful." Unfortunately, the new "Pull up your socks" concept, as it was now called, hit our command just when I was being rated. My iconoclastic boss was not about to be cowered with instructions to reduce the ratings on officers he believed did well and he gave me a rather high rating. When it arrived on the General's desk for his endorsement, he felt it should be adjusted down and sent it back to COL Gately for downward revision. My boss was a hard-ass, special forces colonel married to an ex-Israeli Major, and he wrote me a great report, disregarding the requirement to back off on good reports. The two-star (MG Downey) endorser was livid. He responded by filling out the written portion of his endorsement denigrating my rater and his evaluation of my performance. Then, somewhat as an afterthought, he added a separate page with a few good words about me with some decent numerical scores in keeping with the "pull up your socks" concept. Unless you read the report very carefully, it was not sufficiently apparent that the negative portion of his report was about my rater, rather than me.

The Army system provides an officer an opportunity to submit a "reclama" if the officer feels he received an unfair or invalid OER. So, I submitted a reclama on the basis that the OER endorsement was more about my rater than me. The reclama was not approved. I I tried once more, this time on the basis that the regs require the written portion be limited to the space on the OER for that purpose. But the DA nerds were not about to toss out a general's report on technicalities. They proceeded to rewrite the entire report using all manner of abbreviations to make the report fit in the space required. Again, my reclama # two was denied because the abbreviated rewrite now fit the space! I then submitted my third reclama noting that the Regs required the written portion to be "readily readable and understandable" and not only was their massive use of abbreviations far from readable and understandable, it also resulted in an ambiguity of meaning. Finally, after nine months of this, the third reclama was approved and all the negative portion about my rater was tossed. That nine month effort should never have been required but had I not persisted I could well have missed my next promotion to Colonel.

Our three years passed quickly with trips to northern Germany, Copenhagen, England Switzerland Italy and Spain. The kids became proficient skiers with lessons and downhill runs at the Zugspitze, the Matterhorn, Garmish and Berchtesgaden. About six months before the end of our tour I had completed a resident course (given at their local overseas facility) from Boston University for a Master of Science degree in Business Administration. There was quite a bit of rigmarole to go through for me to qualify for entry into the master's degree program. They needed transcripts of my grades at West Point and three letters of recommendation. Also, I had to take an SAT. With all that done, the Dean called me in to discuss my qualifications. Holding my application and the other documents, he said, "Your undergrad grades weren't too good, but I realize West Point is on a 3.0 system and it is hard to equate to a 4-point system. Your SAT scores were pretty good but what really turned the trick for you are these letters of recommendation." Of course, I didn't tell him I wrote the letters and got my boss and others to sign 'em.

So, anyway, in looking ahead to my next assignment I made a trip to Heidelberg to talk to the Seventh Army Personnel Officer, who happened to be my good friend and classmate Leroy Suddath. I asked Leroy what he thought I should do for my next assignment that would be career-enhancing. He said emphatically, "Ren, you need to command a battalion. I'll call the Pentagon and see if you are on the command-recommended list." That was a list of those lieutenant colonels recommended for command. The next day Leroy told me I was on the list, so a few days later I called Assignments Branch to request command of a battalion. They concurred and scheduled me for command of an Aviation Battalion in Frankfurt. but a few weeks later I was called by DA to change my assignment. In keeping with the Army's effort to stabilize assignments, after the turmoil of the Vietnam War, the current battalion commander in Frankfurt had his command extended. The assignments guy said, "We can get you a training battalion command at Fort Polk." Remembering Leroy's words, I said, "I'll take it". A few months later we were again getting ready for our return to the U.S., via a Month in San Francisco to see our parents; this time without our cat, which had been killed a few weeks earlier.

CHAPTER 30

FORT POLK, LOUISIANA

Fort Polk is a large sprawling base in Louisiana, which had a reputation from WW II days as being one of the more undesirable assignments in the Army. In the years before WW II, during the 1930s, Boise Cascade Lumber Company clear-cut the heavily forested lands that were to become Camp Polk. Photographs from that period show a desolate area of stumps and undulating hills, famous for the depth of its mud when it rained. In 1940 it came to life as a training base in preparation for the war. Our GI's who were assigned there quickly came up with the nickname of 'Camp Swampy'. In 1955 it was upgraded from "Camp" status to "Fort," which meant increased funding for improvements. In the 1960s it was decided that Fort Polk would be a major training facility with three training brigades of over 7,000 men each. By the early 1970s the trees had grown back, the roads were paved, and the old wooden WW II barracks began to come down and be replaced with permanent structures.

When we arrived in August of 1973 from our assignment in Germany and first drove through the outskirts on the way to post, we were disheartened by the appearance of what looked like "the trailer capital of the world." Barb shed a few tears over the scene and said, "Look where you've brought us now!" But once inside the gate you could see it was becoming a first-class installation. Improvement dollars were flowing and the Pentagon was pumping the command full of Regular Army officers to upgrade the quality of leadership and provide increased emphasis on training. Of the 23,000 officers and men then on post, there were only six West Point graduates. I was number seven but there were many more to follow. Fort Polk had been the land of meritocracy for decades, a place where the Army could relegate substandard officers until, like the old barracks ballad proclaimed, they'd "just fade away." The post was rife with entrenched incompetents who objected to the injection of hard chargers trying to change things for the better. In the civilian staff, there was also a culture of suspicion against those who didn't "talk south," I presume sort of a vaporous residual from the carpetbagger days. A culture shock awaited us.

Our arrival was difficult without adequate quarters and only the old wooden guest house at North Fort to live in until we could find a decent place. In August, temperatures are routinely near a hundred degrees, with matching humidity adding to the discomfort of settling in with teenage children. We had not yet received our household goods from Germany. They were in storage until we found a place to live. We moved into a temporary wooden building on post while we started house hunting. After a week, I reported to work, and Barb got Lee and Laura signed up for school. That afternoon the kids returned from school and explained there were not enough math books for everyone. The teacher said there would be dropouts soon and our kids could have their math books. We discussed the situation at dinner and Barbara said, "And who do you think the dropouts will be when our kids don't even have books?" We decided we would pull them out of that Leesville School and buy a home in nearby DeRidder, which would put them in a much better school district in a different county known as Beauregard Parish. (There, in the "Bible Belt," they didn't have counties; they had "parishes.")

In about ten days we found a great home and were amazed at what $40,000 could buy in that part of the country. It was a three-bedroom, three-bath home of about 2600 square feet in the "Country Club District" of DeRidder, about as good a community as you could find in that part of the country. A similar property in San Francisco would have cost about four times that amount. It did mean a 20-mile commute for me but that was certainly better than the alternative. And in this more affluent community, the schools were much better.

The old adage is that three moves are equivalent to one fire. This move to Louisiana certainly qualified. During our month in San Francisco our household goods from Germany had arrived at Fort Polk and were put into storage with a civilian firm. When we were finally ready to receive our shipment from storage the moving truck pulled up and three men began to offload and carry the items in. When they unrolled the Persian rugs, I was astounded to learn that they had been stored outdoors, in the rain and were now wet and mildewing. The French Vanity was carried in with the legs separate, having been broken off. And on it went. Of course, we submitted a claim against the moving company and received some level of compensation but with great resistance from the post transportation officer who was in part responsible for this disaster. I could never be sure whether it was a high level of incompetence or the long lasting, residual feelings against the arriving carpetbaggers? Barb felt that the dead animal left on our doorstep was indicative of the latter. In time I learned to cope with what was apparently Southern Discomfort. After three calls to various chimney repair people, which after a week of waiting, yielded only unkept promises to fix the problem, I made my fourth call using my best southern accent. I said, "Howdy, how y'all doin today. I gots a little problem with my "chimley" (south speak for chimney) I hope you can fix." It was taken care of that afternoon.

Lee was now 16 and entered DeRidder High as a sophomore. Laura was in Junior high, doing well in academics and popular with the other kids. Lee was doing well in school too but was unable to take Latin there, which he needed for college. After a year in DeRidder, we decided to enroll him in a private boarding school in North Carolina, The Ashville School for Boys. I planned to fly him to Ashville in one of the T-42s available through the Fort Polk Flying Club.

The T-42 is a 4-seat Cessna the Army had retired from its fleet. It was the same as a Cessna 172 but with a larger 220 horsepower engine and variable pitch prop. I picked up the plane from the flying club and few it to DeRidder to load Lee's stuff. We first removed the back seat, which made room for his bicycle, footlocker, go cart, skis and other sundry belongings. By the time we finished loading the plane, I joked that it appeared to be sagging in the middle. We took off the next morning with plans to stop at Knoxville, Tennessee, for gas and lunch but with the heavy overcast in the area when we got there I decided to just push on to Ashville since we had more than enough fuel on board. The airstrip at Ashville was a relatively short grass field that sloped downhill, but the T-42 had 10 degrees more flaps than its civilian counterpart to give it better short field performance. We landed and taxied to the gas pump, then rented a car and got Lee checked in to the Ashville School. It had a nice Campus with brick buildings in the old southern style. Lee fondly remembers his two years there and some of the capers they pulled. In particular, was the time several students slipped out of their dorm one night and carried Master Bate's VW up the stairs into the dining hall where it was discovered the following morning.

Having been selected for command was a quality gate which put me in the top 25 percent of eligible lieutenant colonels. At that time, there were three categories of command for Infantry officers. The most sought-after commands were combat units. The next level down were the training commands and at the third level were recruiting commands, referred to as "command equivalent." Originally, I had been in line to take command of an aviation battalion in Frankfurt, a combat command but missed out when its current commander extended his assignment to help stabilize the turmoil of Vietnam rotations. I was less content to have a second-tier command but as life would have it, commands in Germany, in the early 1970's turned into disasters for those commanders having to cope with a shortage of key officers and NCOs, who were now serving in Vietnam. So, it was fortunate for me that I didn't get command of the aviation battalion, as it was fraught with problems and eventually caused the other commander to be passed over for promotion to full colonel. During that difficult command period I had three classmates and a couple of other friends suffer career-ending experiences after taking command of battalions in Germany.

My initial position at Fort Polk was as executive officer in the Headquarters Command; an interesting job overseeing a couple companies of headquarters personnel and a WAC company. It was a transitional posting to ensure that I could handle the more demanding position of battalion commander and an interim spot to work until my command became available. Three months later I took command of an Advanced Infantry Training Battalion.

These battalions had about 1200 men organized into a Headquarters and five Infantry Training Companies. I reported to my new brigade commander, Colonel Diament. We talked he explained his philosophy of command saying, "When I pluck the strings of authority, I expect the vibrations to be felt to the last man in the command." My concept of leadership did not include being a "plucker of the strings of authority," so I was not real pleased with what I was facing. The most important thing for Diament was for the companies in his brigade to win first place at the monthly command parades. Winning parades was his method of determining his commander's attention to detail. He would watch to see if the hand swings were six inches to the front and three to the rear, the rifles were all aligned, slings tight, boots shined, ranks straight and so on through a 20-item check list.

I went to work on this. The five companies I inherited were mediocre in their drill and ceremony skills. I had my commanders schedule additional time for drill and held them responsible for their attention to detail. These soldiers were with us for ten weeks. Every month two companies would graduate, commemorated by a parade of about 2,000 men. So, as each new company of trainees came on board, I would have ten weeks' time to shape them up.

After three months I won my first parade but by then Colonel Diament had completed his command assignment and was moving on to greater things. Every parade after that was won by my battalion but my new commander, Colonel Henslick, wasn't much for parades. He was interested in the quality of the mess halls!

I had five mess halls in my battalion, one for each company. I made it a practice to eat a meal every day in a different mess hall. The quality of my mess halls began to improve, but it would be several weeks before I could win "Best Mess." However, as time went by, we started winning. Now I was winning all the mess awards and the parades, but I was again faced with a new brigade commander with different priorities. A few weeks before Colonel Henslick was to leave, he called me into his office and wanted to know why the Chief of Police had sent him a letter stating that I had received six tickets for speeding and was threatening suspension of my driver's license pending Henslick's recommendation. Evidently, more than four tickets a year was cause for suspension but since I had tickets on different cars and this was pre-computerization, they didn't put 'em together for many months. Now there were suddenly six. I don't think Henslick particularly cared, but he had to pretend he did, so I explained, and all was forgotten.

My third brigade commander was Colonel Spinks. He was primarily interested in the quality of our dayrooms. Again, I shifted gears and got to work on the dayrooms. Eventually those too began to come online with wins but alas I was nearing the end of my 18-month command tour. Fortunately, my last commander, Colonel Ray Spinks, was a great guy who had just completed the War College before taking command of the brigade. We got along well and my efforts with the dayrooms started paying off.

Most Friday evenings I would stay on post, inspect one of my company mess halls, have dinner in one of them and then go into Leesville to the local chess club, which met at one of the cafés in town. One Friday evening I visited a company mess hall I hadn't been to for a dinner meal. The mess sergeant wanted to have someone waiting on me (not for me) but that wasn't my leadership style. When the troops had all been through the line, I filled my tray and sat in the section reserved for officers and NCOs. The meal was fine except for the corn on the cob, which was very overcooked. The kernels had burst and imploded on the cob. I called the mess sergeant over and asked him how long he cooked his corn. He said, "About 20 minutes, sir." I knew corn only took two or three minutes to cook, so asked him to bring me the "menu card." Each mess hall had a file box of 3x5 cards. There was a card for every item and every card had all the recipe information and amount of time the item needed to be cooked. He gave me the card for the corn, and it said, "Boil for 3 minutes." As I looked at him for his response, he said, "Sir, we put the corn in when it is frozen, so it takes longer." I said, "OK but not that much longer." He said, "Well, sir, you know we are cooking on these old-World War Two stoves." I said, "Sergeant, do you know what temperature water boils at?" He said proudly, "Yes, sir, 212 degrees." I said, "That's right, and what temperature does the water boil at on an old-World War Two stove?" Of course, the old sergeants in those days thought they could BS their way out of any situation. I left for my chess gathering in town, saying, "Let me know the next time you are serving corn on the cob."

We usually had six or seven chess players show up for the Friday gathering. I would normally get a game going with the assistant Leesville DA, who was probably the strongest player there. Bill was also a decent tennis player, and we would occasionally get together during lunch hour at the courts near my office. Eventually I realized that, if

I challenged him for a chess game after he ordered his hamburger, he would be distracted by his burger when it arrived. On those occasions I normally won the game, but we were very close. At tennis, however, he always won except for the one occasion when I had just hit my famous "Polish Sewer Ball," a chop shot near the net with enough spin on it to bounce backwards when it landed. Bill launched off from his stance and somehow broke his toe in the effort. He dropped to the court, writhing in pain. I came around the net to see if I could help but first said to him, "Does this mean that you are going to forfeit the match?"

Anyway, after our chess one evening I headed back to DeRidder in the wind and rain and arrived home just as a tornado had ripped down our street and roared off, leaving the home next to ours with no roof and pulling apart the one across the street. For some reason our home remained untouched. I had heard the guttural roar of the funnel as I approached the house, and it was indeed impressive.

Since I was getting near the end of my command tour and would be reassigned in a few months, I called the assignment guy at the Pentagon to discuss what was available and where he felt I should be assigned. He said I needed high-level staff at the Pentagon, and he'd see if he could arrange such an assignment. A few days later he said there was a staff position in the office of the Deputy Chief of Staff for Intelligence (DCSINT) where he would assign me.

Two weeks later, Barb and I decided to take our family to Washington, DC, to see what sorts of schools were available there for the children. While Barb was taking Laura to an interview for her acceptance at the Madeira School, I was visiting the Pentagon to speak with the personnel guys at Infantry Branch, trying to get a feel for what my chances were for promotion to Colonel. The Colonel I spoke with pulled my file of efficiency reports and looked them over. After some time, he said, "You've got a pretty good file but we can't be certain you will be promoted; you are in the 'worry' zone." I was disappointed and asked him what I had to do to get out of the "worry zone."

Promotion to colonel is a toughie. Only 25 percent of the eligible lieutenant colonels were selected and most of them have had command and obtained a master's degree to enhance their chances of being selected, so it was very competitive. He said, "You need to have a high-level staff assignment to the Pentagon and a max report in command." I said, "OK, I'm slated to be assigned to DCSINT (Deputy Chief of

Staff for Intelligence) in July and I'll see what I can do about my OER (Officer Efficiency Report) when I get back to Fort Polk. When I got back, Colonel Spinks asked me what they had to say. I told him, "They said I need a max report in command and an assignment to the Pentagon." He indicated he could take care of the report and indeed he did!

A few weeks after that, I received a call from an officer in Assignments Branch at the Pentagon. He said, "Ren, I just saw them carrying your desk down the hall from the DCSINT. There has been a realignment of jobs and the position you were taking has been eliminated." I said, "OK but I need you to find me another spot so I can meet the high-level staff requirement." He said he would get back to me. In a few days, before he called back, the *Army Times* newspaper announced the promotion board for Colonel would be moved up six months to accommodate the government's fiscal year change from June to October. This meant the board considering me for promotion would convene in a few weeks; several months before I would ever receive an efficiency report as a Pentagon staff officer. There was no longer any advantage for me to be assigned to the gruel and grind of the Pentagon grist mill. Jobs there were famous for their 14-hour days and weekend staffing emergencies. I called my Pentagon contact and told him to forget the DC assignment; I was going to try to get assigned to the Presidio of San Francisco.

It was about that time I discussed with Barb whether I should have a vasectomy. We certainly weren't going to raise any more children and it was a rather simple procedure. We had a board-certified urologist at Fort Polk, so I figured I would be in good hands, so I made the appointment.

Throughout my career I had always felt there was some level of animosity between line officers and our military doctors, who had a hard time accepting a lower rank status than senior officers with less education. A typical confrontation occurred one day when I was on my way into the Officers' Club from the parking lot. I was a lieutenant colonel, battalion commander, responsible for the training and discipline of about a thousand soldiers and here comes a raggedy-ass captain (doctor) with his uniform jacket unbuttoned, hat off, hair way too long, and going past me without a salute! As he passed me, I stopped and called out, "YOU MAN, HALT!" I then proceeded to get him back into uniform, blouse buttoned, hat on and standing at attention. He was livid, so I began what we call an "Idiot Lesson," reemphasizing that which he most likely knew. I said, "In the Army the salute dates back to the early medieval days when one armored-clad knight would approach another, and they would lift their face shields so they might be recognized. Today, we similarly raise our arm in a salute as an action of friendship and camaraderie. And to emphasize the importance of order of rank, it is customary for the Junior officer to render the salute to the senior officer. Do you understand that?" He responded with a simple "yes," so I then explained the reason for saying "Sir" when addressing a senior officer. When I eventually turned him loose, I explained the importance of doing the right military thing on a post where we are trying to train thousands of soldiers in the customs and traditions of the service. He left without saluting, of course and of course I had to call him back.

About three or four weeks later, when I went to the hospital for my vasectomy, I stopped off to see my flight surgeon since I would need to be cleared for flight after the operation. The flight surgeon decided to go with me to observe the procedure. After a little simple prep with alcohol, the urologist explained the procedure of a small cut and then snipping and tying off the sperm source. As he took his scalpel in hand, he turned to my flight surgeon and asked, "This isn't one of those officers who harass our doctors, is it?" I didn't feel the remark was quite as funny as they did, and I was never sure whether that was his standard joke or if my name had indeed made its way through the halls of the hospital?

It was May and my 18-month command tour would end in June. I called my old secretary at the Presidio and asked her if there were any good jobs coming open. She had been promoted in the intervening years and was now secretary for General Salisbury, the chief of staff, so she knew everything that was going on. She said, "Yes, indeed, General Salisbury is looking over a list of names now to consider a replacement for his departing Secretary of the General Staff (SGS)." I said, "Great! I'd like to throw my hat into the ring. Could I speak to the general?"

This was a bold step for me but there was a lot riding on his decision. I told General Salisbury that I was coming off a battalion command assignment at Fort Polk, had been the Assistant SGS several years earlier and would like to be considered for the SGS job. About two days later our division commander, Major General Bob Haldane, came up to me when I was checking my troops at the range and said, "Hart, I got a call this morning from my old friend, General Salisbury, in San Francisco. He asked me if you could handle the job as SGS. Underplaying the moment, he said, "I told him I thought so." What great news! How lucky could I get? Not only Salisbury knew my bosses' boss, but he had also commanded a battalion at Fort Polk. And all three of us were West Point grads, which no doubt, helped. By the grace of the war gods, I was on my way back home.

Meanwhile, when it came time for my efficiency report, Colonel Spinks not only maxed me out with the numbers but used all the essential key phrases in the written portion, such as: "is sensitive to the needs of his subordinates, is recommended for immediate promotion to the next higher grade, should be considered for positions of greater responsibility," etc. After Colonel Spinks completed his report, it then went to General Bowen for an endorsement. General Bowen and his new wife Maureen were tennis players. Barb and I would often meet them on the courts. Maureen had been an airline attendant and knew absolutely nothing about the Army. She had joked that when she first was introduced to General Bowen (about a year earlier) she had remarked how unusual it was that his first name was General! So, Barb undertook to show her the ropes and told her that she could find her niche by taking charge of one of the volunteer programs on post, recommending the hospital Red Cross volunteers who did not have a titular head. Maureen was forever grateful and before we left saw to it that Barb received the Clara Barton Award, the highest award given by the Red Cross for service. And so it was that General Bowen was also disposed to giving me a great endorsement on my OER.

While digesting the good news of going home and delighting over my max OER, I was struck by yet another lucky bolt of lightning. Following my annual efficiency report I still had 18 days left in command before the brigade and battalion would be disbanded and replaced with a Mech Brigade. Because regulations require that every day in command be rated, another efficiency report was due for me two weeks later. My rater, Colonel Spinks, and endorser, Brigadier General Bowen, decided they would just Xerox their reports with a new date and signature. So then, when the promotion board met, they would find not one but two max command reports on the top of my file! I had hoped that, in spite of missing a Pentagon assignment, these reports would carry the day when the board met. Sometimes things seem to fall into place.

Before we left for San Francisco we had a truck load of details to settle. High on the list was selling our home. With the 5th Mech Division being formed at Fort Polk there were many officers inbound and I was able to contact another LTC who was interested in buying our home. I had an appraisal for $60,000 and told him that, if we could handle the sale without a real estate agent, we could split the $3,600 fee that would have been charged. He agreed and we settled the deal at the local bank. Next step, arrange for the movers and plan our trip home to San Francisco.

After those turbulent Vietnam-era moves, with a change of station every one or two years, our three years in Louisiana had been good for the family. Lee had his "Ashville School for Boys" experience and Laura was blossoming into a lovely sixteen-year-old with lots of attention from the boys and successful school experiences. At fourteen she got her driving permit and with three or four fender benders in her VW, took her place among the other aggressive family drivers! Now, with school over, the house sold, and our household goods packed, we headed west.

CHAPTER 31

BACK TO SAN FRANCISCO

The Presidio of San Francisco is a very old post by California standards. It was originally a fortress under the command of Captain Moraga of the Mexican Army in the early 1800s. The home that Captain Moraga had built still stands as part of the Officers' Club and is the oldest building in San Francisco. In later years, the Presidio became the headquarters for the Sixth U.S. Army. It has always been considered one of the finest posts at which to be stationed. Its picturesque location, with historic Fort Point at the foot of the Golden Gate Bridge, also provided the Presidio a strategic vantage point to oversee ship traffic entering the Bay. It remains one of the most valuable pieces of land in San Francisco, with its scenic overview of San Francisco Bay, the Golden Gate Bridge, Angel Island and the island of Alcatraz. During the occasions I was assigned there, it also proved to be a wonderful area in which to live and work.

In June, having loaded the Volvo, with Barb behind the wheel and pulling the ski boat, with me driving the Triumph and Lee following close behind in his VW, the family headed west, crossing Texas into New Mexico. We stopped in Gallup for lunch. There, while we were walking away from Lee's VW, the engine compartment (in the back) suddenly burst into flames. It seems it had developed a leaky fuel injector and when we stopped, the injector was dripping gas onto a very hot exhaust manifold. We ran to a nearby gas station for a fire extinguisher but by the time we got the fire out it had done irreparable damage to the fuel lines and wiring harness. We had to leave the stricken vehicle behind for a later retrieval.

In another two days we crossed into California and headed north to our beloved San Francisco. Barb's parents were living in the city, but my mother had recently moved to Sonoma, her final move. This would be my fourth west coast assignment and my second tour at Presidio of SF! My cup runneth over.

Now that we were back in San Francisco, it was our plan to find a home for our eventual retirement. I had 20 years' service in the Army at that time, not including my enlisted year and my four years at West Point. When I arrived and reported to General Salisbury, he told me he wanted me to live on post. I explained that I really needed to buy a home, since I would one day be retiring in San Francisco. He didn't like that much but approved my decision, so we began our search for the home we would live in the rest of our lives. We looked for a couple of weeks, searching everything on both sides of the Golden Gate Bridge. Marin County was great but the commute across the bridge would be tough. And California was in its third year of a severe drought, which was particularly felt in Marin County. Finally, we settled on a house in Forest Hill, at 88 Sotelo Avenue, within walking distance of where Barb's folks lived and near where I had been raised from 1940 to 1950. It was a special home, 3800 square feet, three-story, Spanish-style, sitting atop a hill overlooking Golden Gate Park and a view stretching from the Golden Gate Bridge east to Alcatraz. But the price was a problem: $179,000. We had sold an equivalent home in Louisiana for $60,000, so had enough cash for a down payment. We also still owned a home several blocks down the hill at 380 Kensington Way, but we were renting it and did not want to sell. We would find a way to own this special home with its arched doorways and rich features. We could sell stock, or perhaps our parents would help if needed. In the 20 years we had been married we had bought and sold five homes, so were no strangers to negotiating. On several occasions I had been successful in getting the sellers to come down on their asking price by about 15 percent, so we started with an offer of $150,000, finally closing at $160,000. The home was ours!

My job as SGS was like being an administrative aide to our generals, with the chief of staff as my boss. Also under my purview was the protocol office with its three officers, 27 enlisted men, and many vehicles. I interfaced with our three generals directly as necessary but was specifically responsive to and rated by the chief of staff. It was a power position, but I was careful not to take advantage of this in dealing with other, more senior officers. All staff actions requiring a general officer's signature were funneled through the SGS to ensure correctness. I enjoyed my work and seemed to do well at it. It was a very busy job, but it came with a highly competent secretary who had a separate office in front of mine, which limited interruptions. When I had a hot document that needed the attention and signature of one of our generals, I would usually walk it down the hall and put it in their in-basket. But I would seldom be able to make that trip without being stopped several times in route with questions and requests and often collected three or four actions needing to be added to my pile.

After about seven months as SGS, the promotion list to colonel arrived by teletype in my office. It was an anxious time for me. As noted above, I had reasons to wonder if I would make the cut. I leafed through the teletype pages, looking for my name. Promotion to colonel was a biggie. It meant the difference between a successful career and an acceptable career. It also meant a significant increase in pay and an upgrade of position and responsibility. Only 25 percent of the eligible lieutenant colonels considered would make the list. The qualified contenders were all highly competitive officers, most with master's degrees and combat experience. Promotion to colonel required completion of important assignments with excellence. For an Infantry officer, you would need to have been a battalion commander, completed the Command & General Staff College, have an advanced degree and an assignment to high-level staff. I met all the criteria but had not served in the Pentagon. My "high-level staff" had been on the NATO staff at CENTAG. That assignment met the criteria but was not as competitive as a Pentagon tour. Fortunately, my last two reports in command and award of the Legion of Merit in Vietnam would be a strong plus with the promotion board.

The teletype continued spewing out the pages in alphabetical order and there were hundreds of names on the list. My heart was pounding. Finally, the page with the H's started coming out of the machine. Holy mackerel! I had made the cut! I was absolutely delighted to see my name on the list. Taking the Sixth Army assignment last year, rather than a Pentagon position, had been a gamble which might have diminished my chances at promotion. Now I had not only made the promotion list but had the best assignment I could hope for - San Francisco. I was eating my proverbial cake. And as the saying goes, even a blind hog will every now and then root up a truffle. There was probably no other time in my career that circumstances aligned in my favor to this extent.

Promotion to colonel meant that I would now need to leave the SGS office but fortunately there was a job opening for an Infantry Aviator Colonel on the Region IX Staff in the very next building. It was also fortunate that one of the generals in the headquarters, Major General Jack Osteen, knew me and liked me since in addition to being the Deputy Sixth Army Commanding General he was also the Region IX Commander. That assured my remaining at the Presidio and being transferred to the next building as the Region IX Infantry Coordinator. Again, my luck ranneth over.

In my new assignment I had oversight of the training of all Army Reserve (USAR) and National Guard (ARNG) Infantry units in the eight western states. Reserve and National Guard units normally hold their drill periods on weekends. That meant that, without exception, I would be on the road every weekend of the month. Oftentimes I was able to rent an airplane from the Navy Flying Club at Alameda Naval Air Station to visit nearby California units. Flying not only added a dimension of enjoyment to my job but often enabled me to get home for at least part of the weekend. On other occasions, when I could visit several units in one weekend, it proved more expeditious to drive. That was the situation on one weekend in early May, a few weeks before my promotion to colonel.

The car I usually drove for these trips was the 1973 TR-6 we had picked up in England at the Coventry factory. The Triumph is a great car and is almost as much fun to drive as an airplane. Ours, is a lively red roadster with wire wheels and a big engine. With its electric overdrive it has six forward gears and at 60 mph the engine lopes along at a high idle of about 2000 RPM while getting 30 miles to the gallon. The RPM redlined at 6,000, so there was plenty of oomph left for the heavy-footed. The TR 6 is now 50 years old and remains in our possession today.

On this weekend I had visited a unit in San Jose and another one training at Fort Ord. Planning to drive to Camp Roberts on Sunday, after spending the night at Ord, I left about 9 AM. It was a beautiful day, which demanded I make the trip with the top down. I was decked out in my starched fatigues, bloused over highly shined Corcorans and enjoying the thought of the eagle insignia soon to be sewn to my collar. Still flushed with self-satisfaction and the purr of a highly maintained roadster belted under me, I was entirely unable to resist the urge to go a bit faster on the long stretch of freeway ahead. In 1977 the California speed limit had been reduced to an unrealistic 55 mph in a national effort to save gas. However, since this was done without anyone consulting me, it therefore was not a law which I felt obligated to abide by. And as most of you know, after traveling for some time at 60 or 70 mph it no longer feels very fast. There wasn't much traffic at that time of the morning in the Salinas Valley so, sensing the roadster was crying out to stretch its legs, I let the speed creep upward. For a while 80 mph was adequate but before long, the roar of those six cylinders, the beauty of the day, and the wind ruffling my hair called out. At 90 mph the car felt great as its engine was at last developing some torque at 3000 RPM.

Roaring past lesser vehicles and their plebeian drivers was just exhilarating enough to spur me on to the century mark. However, even at a hundred miles an hour, the RPM needle had not yet reached 4,000. I began to wonder just how fast this baby could go. I answered this primal need by pushing through a hundred and ten when suddenly I saw a CHP heading in the opposite direction. It is odd how, at that speed, eyeballs can lock on each other across the freeway divide. In fact, his head snapped in my direction. There was not the slightest doubt in my mind that he knew that I knew. This was not a radar area, so I had figured I was safe. I had about 30 miles left before reaching Camp Roberts. I wondered how long it would take for the CHP to get slowed down, find an adequate crossover, and then try to catch me. I figured that, if I took this baby up another notch or two, perhaps to 130 MPH, there was no way he could ever close on me before I reached Camp Roberts in about 13 minutes. I began to accelerate but as I hit 120 there was a transient flash of rational thinking that I was not used to. It was sort of a voice of reason trying to creep in and screw up my fun. It was saying something like, "Wait a minute, Ren, do you really want to do this? In nine days you will be wearing eagles. If this guy catches up with you, he's going to put you behind bars. Tomorrow's headlines will read: *Colonel arrested doing a hundred and thirty miles an hour!*" But he'll never catch up with me, my true self retorted. The voice said, "Think what you are risking here!"

My heavy foot reluctantly lifted from the accelerator; not because there was a chance, he would catch me but because the risk was just too great. The Red Blur began to again take the shape of a car as the RPM needle unwound. I hated to stop soaring like an eagle and join the turkeys, but I let her unwind all the way to 55. And then, ugh, kept it there!

Instead of 13 minutes to destination I was now looking at 26 minutes. The countryside was moving past at a snail's pace. I could hardly stand it; 55 mph after an hour of really moving, was ridiculous. After about 15 sluggish minutes I was closing on a truck and needed to pass. I accelerated to 60 and pulled into the passing lane. Suddenly there was a red light flashing behind me and a "Black and White" blur closing fast with siren blaring. I pulled onto the shoulder and stopped. He pulled up behind me. *Where in hell did he come from?*

As the officer got out of his cruiser, it was like that James Bond movie when that redneck cop swaggers up to the perp. He whipped out his pad with something of a flare and said, "You were doing about 90 miles an hour when I passed you in the other direction, weren't you?" Not wanting to tell a lie, I said, "No, sir, I was going a little fast, but it wasn't ninety." (Which was true because I was doing close to a hundred.) He then proceeded to read me the riot act, eventually slipping in the fact that he had been following me for the last 15 minutes and I had on two occasions hit 60 miles an hour. I humbly mumbled my excuses, showing my great contrition. Finally, he slapped his ticket book closed and shouted, "I'm not going to give you a ticket, but I'll be watching you from now on." Sometimes, in great nostalgia, I still wonder if he could have caught up with me at 130 mph? I doubt it!

When I returned to work Monday, I learned I had a new boss, an old cantankerous colonel who had come up through the ranks the hard way and really had it in for West Point officers. He and my old roommate from West Point, Ernie Wilson, had many a falling out. Ever since Ernie joined Rgion IX, they were literally at each other's throats. Ernie had missed the promotion, but he was a proud guy with a silver star from Viet Nam and having made the All Eastern, middle heavyweight boxing championship list, was not about to take a lot of crap from Colonel Kamp (I referred to him as Colonel Kramp). Once he learned that Ernie had been a best friend and roommate of mine, after Ernie left, he immediately transferred his residual spleen onto me! Our relationship was doomed. However, there was another old colonel in the chain of command who was to be my rater. Kramp would be my endorsing officer. Ratings were required annually or upon change of rater, which meant that a year from now Kramp would be writing the endorsement on my efficiency report. However, it was my good fortune that would be retiring a few weeks ahead of my rating officer, so there would be no change of rater and no rating before he left. In my eyes he was a lame duck that was of no concern to my career or job. He harassed me; I paid no attention. When he ordered me to do things which were not in the best interest of my job or the organization, or if the orders ran counter to what I felt should be done, I ignored the Kramp and did it my way. This of course infuriated him. Tough shit, I was about to be a colonel and would do it my way.

When I first arrived at the Presidio, in 1976, I decided that I needed to complete the U S Army War College course to enhance my promotion chances. I had missed the top ten percent selection rate for attendance to the War College but if I qualified for the correspondence course I would have "War College" on my record. After a few weeks of applying, I received my acceptance and a stack of papers outlining the curriculum. It was a tough course requiring hours of reading, followed by a requirement every six weeks to write comprehensive answers to the questions provided. In June of 1977 I received orders for temporary duty at the Army War College, in Carlisle, Pennsylvania, for the resident phase of instruction. During those two weeks the orders promoting me to colonel were published and the Deputy Commandant, Brigadier General Joe Kohler, pinned on my eagles, the same ones my Father had worn during the 15 years I was growing up.

In those days, the law required that promotions to colonel be initially carried as "temporary" so in the event of a reduction in force the Army could readily return temporary colonels to the rank of lieutenant colonel. After about three years in that rank, a promotion board would meet to determine if you should be given the permanent rank of colonel. Not only was this another quality gate which I wanted to pass through, but it meant I would be guaranteed tenure for 30 years' service rather than being forced to retire at 28 years. It was with this in mind that after returning from the War College, I learned the shocking news of an organizational change which would place Colonel Kramp as my rating officer and not my endorsing officer! This meant, in fact, he would be able to get to me! This change in raters was the result of General Osteen's decision that there were too many colonels rating colonels and by taking my previous rater out of the chain, Osteen would now be my reviewing officer and Kramp my rating officer. Kramp was not to be denied his revenge. He called me into his office and announced, "Hart, I am now your rating officer, and I am going to zero you out." Then he thought a minute and said with malice and delight, "No, I won't zero you out because that may provide grounds for you to reclama the rating. What

I'll do is rate you one notch higher than zero to make sure the rating will stick." This was the first time in my long career that I had run into a superior who was dedicated to doing me in. But, as life would have it, Kramp somehow managed to dig his own grave. About three weeks before his retirement he wrote his denigrating report of my performance and passed it to the endorsing officer. The endorsing officer, Sam Smith, was a fine officer but he was obliged to back his subordinate Kramp, who was running things while Smith was working on his master's degree prior to retirement. So, he wrote an endorsement which backed Kramp's rating. The report was passed to me for my signature. I was not about to let this malice go forward without a fight. I wrote an excellent two-page rebuttal, noting that Kramp's rating was contrary to regulation in that he had predetermined my rating on that first day, prior to ever judging my performance during the rating period. My rebuttal and the report went forward to General Osteen. Osteen knew and liked me, and we had some history together when I organized and ran the West Point Founder's Day arrangements for him. So, he was in something of a quandary, as the Reviewing Officer. On the one hand a commander needs to support his subordinates in their decisions. On the other hand, he knew me as a capable officer so was very much at sea in deciding just what to do with this negative report.

It sat in his "hold box" for a couple of weeks. While the report was "marinating", the weekend of Kramp's retirement party was upon us. At the party, Kramp was seated at the head table next to Mrs. Osteen. Wine was consumed, the dance band played and soon Kramp, with too much to drink (I was delighted to later learn), began to dissemble to Pat Osteen while under the influence of his heavy drinking. The first thing he told the general's wife was that he didn't know why he was sitting at the head table next to an old prune instead of over there with those pretty ladies. He then proceeded to tell her what a lousy officer her husband the general, was and how much better a job he could have done. Mrs. Osteen, finally reduced to tears, left the table. The following Monday the general called Kramp into his office, gave him a royal reaming and relieved him of his position in the headquarters. He then turned his attention to his hold box and began writing his review of my efficiency report. He noted that Kramp and Smith lacked objectivity, had a personality conflict with Colonel Hart and in no way should their remarks be considered valid! His review continued through two typewritten pages extolling my quality and virtues! Wow! What a turnaround!

It was about a year later that the promotion board announced their results in promoting temporary colonels to permanent colonels. There were 12 of us at the Presidio being considered. There was one selected. It was me! But I was not yet to "live happily ever after." General Osteen was retiring, and a new general was arriving.

Our new two-star general's arrival was preceded by his reputation as a severe hard ass. Stories had floated across the Pacific ahead of him: As chief of staff in Korea he put out the word that all personnel were required to always wear their dog tags. During this period the general was recovering from a broken leg and was wearing a cast. He was gimping along on crutches when an off-duty sergeant in civilian clothes, driving his own auto, stopped to ask if could give him a ride. The general said, "No, thank you and do you have your dog tags on?" He did not. The upshot was, for his offer of a ride, the sergeant ended up with a court martial and a reduction in rank. Good grief!!

It is difficult to make general, particularly during periods of prolonged peace. Normally only college graduates are commissioned, most of whom will make captain if they stay in a few years. But only 56 percent of our year group (those commissioned in 1956 from all sources, including ROTC and OCS) were promoted to major and perhaps three-quarters of those made lieutenant colonel. The pyramid narrows! There is a large gulf from lieutenant colonel to colonel, with only 25 percent going on to the rank of colonel. Five to 10 percent of the colonels can expect to make general. Those who are chosen for this exalted rank are usually delightful people who have worked hard, displayed sensitivity towards the needs of their subordinates and have the ability to get along with others. This general did not qualify by any of those measures, and he was about to become our commander.

Shortly before his arrival I received a call from the Pentagon to announce that they had an assignment for me as a defense attaché overseas. In that position I would have the Army, Navy and Air Force attachés working for me. The assignments officer said I would have a twin engine "King Air" turboprop aircraft assigned for me to fly. It sounded like a great assignment. Before I could ask where it was, he added, "Your quarters come with three servants and a swimming pool. By the way, do you speak French?" With visions of Paris or Geneva, I replied, "Mais certainment." He said, "Great, are you any good?" I said, "Magnifique. Where is the assignment?" He said, "It is in the old Belgian Congo, North Africa—Kinshasa, Zaire." I said, "Vas ist das?" Of course, he was pretending I had a choice, and I was pretending I believed him but as negotiations continued it became apparent, I was going to have to take this assignment or submit a letter of intent to retire. By now our kids were in college, we were making payments on our home, and both of our aging parents were living in the area. There was no way at this point of our lives we could go to Africa for three years. I explained to the assignment officer that it wouldn't work for me. He said, "Ren, I have a hard requirement to meet. There are only three colonel, aviator, War College graduates who qualify for this position. One is overseas and I can't reassign him to another overseas assignment, the other is about to retire. You are it!" Knowing my choice was to accept or retire, I told him I would get back to him in a couple of days. I pondered my options. It suddenly occurred to me that attaché positions require wives! I called him back and told him, "Fine, I am sure the job will be both rewarding and challenging (using a bit of Pentagonese) but my wife will not be accompanying me." They could not have an attaché without "portfolio" so I was dropped from consideration.

In a few months I had to refuse another assignment to Germany, and this meant I would now have to retire within six months. However, a few months later, in October, Congress passed a significant increase in our pay which would go into effect on the first of the new year. That pay raise was going to affect the amount of my retirement earnings for the rest of my life. I would need to delay my retirement one month. I submitted a request to remain on active duty for an additional month, until January 1982. True to his colors, our new General Dahlman disapproved my request. I called the Pentagon and spoke with my classmate, Bill Roll, who was chief of assignments. He said, "Dalman can't stop you from staying another month, he can only recommend; by law you can remain, you have 30 years tenure."

I went to the general to explain why I intended to remain on active duty for another month. He was furious and said, "You signed a letter of intent to get out in December and I am holding you to it. If you don't do as you said you would, I will consider it a matter of honor and it will be reflected in your efficiency report. Furthermore, there will be no retirement ceremony or award." I said, "General, that was a letter of *intent*, and it was exactly what I intended at the time but now the situation has changed, and I *intend* to retire in January instead." He was livid. When I left his office, I again called Bill at the Pentagon and told him what had transpired. He said, "Not to worry, we can take the heat."

By January my immediate boss submitted a recommendation that I be awarded a Legion of Merit, the second highest award that can be received for service to our country. Dahlan recommended disapproval and sent it forward. Some days later I was told that our three-star Army commander had called the two-star troublemaker into his office and explained that we don't deny retirement awards to officers who have served their country in combat and with honor for 30 years. My retirement parade was scheduled for the last week of January 1981, so the thwarted two-star departed on leave that week to avoid being a party to my ceremony. I was awarded the Legion of Merit, the band played on, and I lived happily ever after!

Following the retirement ceremony we held a reception at the Presidio Officers Club with friends, neighbors, relatives and associates to conclude a career which began over 30 years earlier in June 1951.

CHAPTER 32

MY SECOND LIFE BEGINS – TO THE ORIENT

The next day, following my retirement reception at the Presidio and with three days of terminal leave left to complete my service, we drove to Travis AFB to catch a military flight to Japan. Catching a space available flight to the Orient was much easier while I was still on active duty. It was important to me that Barb to see the Orient, since I had spent many months in Japan as a teenager and a year each in Korea and Vietnam.

At the Travis terminal, while waiting in the VIP lounge (available to full colonels and above) for our flight, we met a fun Navy couple, Larry and Lea Marsolais. Larry was a retired Navy captain, a submariner, who had graduated from Annapolis about ten years before I was commissioned. After several hours of conversation in the lounge, we were notified that our flight was scheduled for a two AM boarding. We were heading to Tokyo, then on to Korea the next day. Later we were able to link up with the Marsolais in Seoul, which made our wanderings there much more enjoyable as we toured the many points of interest.

In about ten hours the plane landed at Tachikawa Air Force Base, not far from Tokyo. We had planned to meet with a classmate (Zuke Day) and his wife (Lucy), who were assigned to the base. He had arranged for us to spend the night at the Distinguished Visitors Quarters, a privilege reserved for ranks of colonel and above. We had dinner that evening with Zuke and Lucy, then the following morning again boarded our plane for Seoul Korea. It was about a two-hour flight, with the plane landing at Osan Air Force Base a few miles south of Seoul.

It had been 20 years since I was last in Korea. What a change! Seoul City had grown to ten million people. The only sign of what life may have been like during my 1960 assignment was their Korean Folk Village, a walk-through village depicting the way life had been at about the time I was there. In the ensuing twenty years Korea had changed from a place where my clothes were washed in the river by "mamasans" beating our fatigues against the rocks to a modern, throbbing city. Gone were the days of the cooking fire at one end of the clay hut with the chimney vented under the floor for heat. Seoul was now a vibrant city, with a subway and bustling traffic. Our drive, to the Yongsan section of Seoul, revealed dozens of 20-story apartment buildings to house the city's population.

Eighth Army Headquarters at Yongsan was relatively unchanged. We decided to stay at the Naisa Hotel, a military facility off post. We checked in there in what was a civilian hotel under contract to the Army. As I took off my uniform, I suddenly realized this was the last day I would ever be in uniform. My terminal leave would end at midnight, and I would then be officially retired. The Army had been my life since I first donned the uniform 31 years earlier, now for the first time the total change in my life began to hit home. It was a strange sensation knowing that I was now a civilian, never to wear the uniform again. It was not a good feeling. Our plan was to stay as long as necessary to see the sights and visit points of interest.

Barbara, having studied to be an interior decorator and having an eye for value and for what would look good in a home, was astounded by the very low prices of Korea's arts, crafts and home furnishings. At that time, in 1981, the typical Korean worker earned a dollar an hour, worked ten hours a day, and got one day off a month! The merchandise we were looking at in Itaewon, the primary shopping district in Seoul, was selling for about one-fifth of what it would sell for in the U.S. Barbara decided we really should be importing these things and selling them in the U.S. market. I was less enthused, being only a few days into my retirement. But Barbara's conviction was strong enough that she started buying things with her own funds. I finally came on board with her idea.

Shopping with the idea of selling it when we got home added a lot more interest and meaning to our travels. We spent about two weeks and several thousand dollars in Korea, then shipped the items to San Francisco before catching an Air Force flight back to Japan for a few days.

I had returned to Japan in 1961 on R&R from Korea and at that time was amazed at the post-war recovery there since my high school days in Osaka in 1949. Now, in 1982, it had emerged from a Japanese society to a western nation with all the western comforts, while still retaining most of the old-world customs and traditions. We visited the local tourist highlights: the Ginza with its Times Square appearance; the Tokyo Tower, erected to be 10 feet higher than the Eiffel Tower in Paris; and the Imperial Palace. Prices in Tokyo were even higher than what you would pay in New York.

We had been staying at the Hakone Hotel, an armed forces facility. After three days in Tokyo, we ventured on to Nagasaki and Hiroshima by bullet train. The bullet train was indeed impressive, moving at speeds of nearly 200 kilometers per hour. Our first stop was Nagasaki. At the train station we hired a cab to show us the city but decided to first drop our bags at some local "ryokan", the Japanese version of a bed and breakfast lodging but very different indeed. Our tour driver, who spoke passable English, suggested the Ryokan Fukara, then took us there to check in and drop our bags.

Not really noticing the name of the place, we set off on a tour of the city and to visit the famous Nagasaki Atomic Bomb Museum with its photographs and artifacts from the 1945 atomic bombing. I was 12 years old in 1945, when atomic bombs dropped on Hiroshima and Nagasaki totally leveled the cities, so I was quite interested to see what these cities looked like in 1982. It was absolutely amazing how modern and functional everything was.

We had turned our driver loose when we went to the museum. By the time we were ready to head back to our ryokan, neither of us could remember the name of the place! Good grief, a city of a million people and we didn't know where we had left our bags! Barb came up with a suggestion which led to our salvation. We went into the lobby of a nearby hotel and asked them for a phone book, hoping to recognize the name. Fortunately, their "yellow pages" were in both print and the language characters hieroglyphics the Japanese use. What a relief when

Barb recognized the name Ryokan Fukara among the several ryokans listed and with an address and phone number.

We caught a cab back to our ryokan and shared a relaxing hot tub before dinner. That night we slept on the tatami mats for a night's sleep which was better than we expected. After a short trip to Hiroshima on the "Shinkansen" rail system, we made a taxi tour of their impressive city and were greatly impressed with the "roll on, roll off" automobile loading of ships at the port and the attractive city which had arisen from the rubble of the A-bomb 35 years earlier. After returning to our ryokan and packing out, it was back to the bullet train. At two hundred kilometers an hour we were soon back in Tokyo readying ourselves for a commercial flight to Hong Kong.

Hong Kong is a mind blow! A vibrant, throbbing island city where commerce is so much in vogue that the shop owners stand in front of their shops and leave no stone unturned to entice you to come in and shop. It is also an expensive city. The best choices for our stay were found on Kowloon, on the mainland a bridge away. In Kowloon we found yet more bargains to buy. Then, after about ten days of shopping, we headed home on a commercial flight to San Francisco. Our new fledgling business was about to get started and we would return to Hong Kong in a few years for some serious shopping.

CHAPTER 33

SAN FRANCISCO IMPORTS

We were home again after five weeks of touring and buying in Seoul, Hong Kong and Japan. It was now mid-March and the merchandise we had purchased started arriving. It wasn't clear to us just what we would do with it as we faced the reality of how we should market all this good stuff. We investigated the possibility of being wholesalers, which meant operating a booth at the wholesale markets. I decided that for that to work we needed the ability to take orders and have the merchandise drop-shipped from the country of origin to the customer. Our primary country of interest was Korea, where in early 1980 their production of chests, art, brass and porcelain (primarily Celadon) was still a cottage industry. Most of their merchandise was put together and produced in a garage or barn. It was clear that we did not have the exporting skills or reliability we needed to deal with that. We were starting from ground zero, with no experience and limited knowledge of that which we were about to do, and without an agent in country.

By the end of May, I was unconvinced that the business of importing, and merchandising was a direction we should move in. We headed to our Tahoe place for the summer and busied ourselves with the needs of the house there, also playing tennis, golf and enjoying the lake and mountain activities. It was a great vacation but after several weeks I began to realize that, at 49 years young, there really weren't many playmates my age. Everyone else went back to work after the weekend was over. So, six weeks of that was about enough and we decided it was time to build some sort of importing business.

In September we learned that the Officer's Wives Club at the Presidio would be holding a Christmas bazaar in November. We signed up for a table to see if our merchandise had any appeal. We were rather surprised at how well our things sold and when the bazaar ended, learned we were responsible for the vast majority of its sales, having sold more than all the other tables put together. We walked away with a couple thousand dollars.

Encouraged from this moderate success, which validated Barb's choice of merchandise, we were casting about for a retail operation we could run. The Presidio had several concession shops in a small mall outside the PX facility. One of the shops, which wasn't doing so well, had a "Going Out of Business" sale. Knowing my way around the Army, I found the person in charge of the concessions to discuss the possibility of taking over the soon to be defunct shop in the mall. It turned out he was going to take bids for a new video rental shop and the procedure would take a few months. He asked, "Would you like to rent the space for a few months until we have a new lessee?" As with many retail operations, the rental price would be a percentage of sales. That was perfect for us. If the stuff didn't sell, there would be no rent! At the end of May of 1982, we took over the shop, calling our new business "San Francisco Imports." All those boxes and crates of stuff which had arrived from the Orient now filled the shelves of our new shop. The four of us started running the business. It wasn't long before Lee and Laura, out of school for the summer, were able to take over on their own.

We agreed that we would name our new business "San Francisco Imports" and I set about designing a logo and getting it patented. We had a sign made and hung it in front of the little store at the PX mall. We were in business!

In those years, brass decorations had become very popular and Korea was one of the best exporters of brass. We carried brass deer of every size, a large variety of brass candelabra, brass boxes, saucers, and animals of every sort. The shop also included various oriental chests, boxes, paintings, celadon, and perhaps thirty other different items of home décor. It all sold well but I still had hopes for finding a way to move the merchandise wholesale. In our travels around California, I carried several items of brass I hoped would interest retail stores. In Carmel, we found a brass shop at The Barnyard, an upscale shopping center in the mouth of the Carmel Valley. I showed the proprietor the brass merchandise we carried. He was impressed with the price and quality but said he was going out of business. We then went to see the owner of The Barnyard to ask if we could take over the brass shop when it closed. The owner of the Barnyard, John Waldrop, was interested. We decided on a date when he could come to San Francisco to see what we were selling.

As it turned out, John had another agenda in addition to filling the soon to be vacant shop. His wife had let a friend take over one of the store fronts to sell Oriental merchandise and because she was a good friend, they were not charging her rent. When John saw our Presidio shop and the prices of our merchandise, he decided that we would be undercutting the competing Oriental shop sufficiently that it would probably drive them out of business in the Barnyard. Then he could again collect rent for that space! We took over the now vacant brass shop in September 1983. Three weeks later the other Oriental shop closed their doors!

We were in an entirely new realm of activity; hiring employees, going to trade shows, getting our merchandise through customs, dealing with payrolls, inventory control, taxes, and nonstop government requirements. Little by little we overcame a myriad of obstacles. Sales were increasing nearly every month and we would soon need to start making trips back to the Orient and increase our purchases to contain size shipments. We could not do this and man the shop ourselves. Fortunately, nearby Fort Ord provided a plethora of Army Officers' wives; a great source of honest, capable, educated women and of course Army Wives can do anything! One of these special wives had been a head nurse before her husband's assignment to Fort Ord and she became our manager. Many of her several bridge club wives were interested in spending a day or two a week in our upscale shop, selling, meeting people, and earning some extra dollars. So, our new manager had a great source of employees who were friends and social equals, doing something they enjoyed.

To fund our business inventory and buy a place to live in Carmel, we sold our four-unit apartment building in San Francisco. West Coast real estate doesn't provide much rental profit with taxes, repairs, mortgage costs etc. But it nearly always will do great in appreciation, particularly in San Francisco where there is no more room to build. So, we had the benefit of capital gains from that investment which enabled us to begin our business debt free.

During the next 12 years of growing our business we opened another shop in a newly established shopping center in East Bay, in the community of Black Hawk. It no sooner had increasing sales than the economy turned south in a rather bad recession. The Black Hawk shopping center was very impressive and upscale, with lots of marble and fountains and a pianist in Tux with tails, playing a grand piano in the supermarket! With the economy headed for a tailspin, customers were now shopping at Walmart's and the buying traffic at Black Hawk was rapidly drying up. A year after we opened the store we had to back out of our contract and close. We pretty much broke even on that venture.

The Carmel Store continued to make money but the month to month increase in sales went flat. Perhaps it was the anti-oriental feelings following the 1989 Tiananmen Square debacle in Peking, when Chinese troops open fired on protesting students, killing hundreds. Or perhaps the increased costs of merchandise from Korea after their Summer Olympics, made the difference in decreased sales? At any rate, by the end of 1993 we were no longer making a profit and decided it was time for a second retirement. Initially, I took steps to sell the business and received a few offers from young families whom I felt would not be able to survive a new venture in a down economy. So, following a major discount sale, we closed our doors (and lived happily ever after!).

CHAPTER 34

I FLY AGAIN

Retirement at age 48, after 30 years of a hyper, type A, pressurized life, is like stepping into a vacuum; you think you are having fun, but your nature abhors it. The good people we had running San Francisco Imports, ably handled the retail and our importing only got active about every six months. So, after the first few years of making San Francisco Imports work, I found there was a bit of time on my hands. Also, about that time, one of my childhood friends, Bob Anderson, asked me to join his Society of Forensic Engineers and Scientists (SFES). Bob was a Ph.D. in Material Science and a Professor at San Jose State. He said their Society had experts in nearly every field except aviation and they needed me. Bob knew I had been an air safety investigator in the Army and had graduated from the aircraft accident investigation course at USC. I joined up. A few months later Dave Yoshida, another member, referred me to an attorney he had worked for in Hawaii. I soon started my first case; a helicopter accident involving a wrongful death that had taken place off the coast of Maui.

Evidently, a ship had gone aground on the coral reef about a mile offshore. A commercial helicopter taking a Lloyd's of London insurance agent and a shipping line executive to the ship ran into trouble trying to land on the deck of the reefed ship. The tide was coming in and the ship was at a pretty good angle on the reef, so the chopper pilot had to try to hold the bird steady with one skid on the deck for the passengers to exit. There was a stiff offshore breeze, and the sea was fairly rough, with waves occasionally breaking across the deck. Between large waves, the pilot would attempt to hold the chopper on the deck long enough for the passengers to get out. After a couple of tries the first passenger made it on deck. The pilot lifted off as another wave hit. He then tried again to get the second passenger off-loaded but the guy was hesitant, and the pilot waited too long to lift off before the next large wave hit. As he began lift-off, the wave barely caught the tail rotor and it disintegrated. The purpose of the tail rotor is to counteract the torque of the main rotor blade, so once he lost his tail rotor the chopper began spinning. At this point, all you can do is chop the throttle to eliminate the torque. Then down you go. The pilot and passenger were able to get out of the chopper after it hit the water but by the time the Coast Guard rescue helicopter arrived the passenger had drowned. The pilot started swimming and was plucked from the water about a quarter mile offshore.

I told the attorney that the commercial helicopter crew was in violation of an FAA regulation requiring aircraft, beyond gliding distance of shore, to carry flotation devices and a Very Pistol with signal flares. That was all he needed. My first case was over before it really got started but I decided then if I were going to be rendering expert aviation opinion I had better get back into flying. I joined the Navy Flying Club at Monterey and was surprised to find that eight years without flying had left me way behind in airspace know-ledge and communications. When I last flew in the Army, we would contact the tower for taxi, takeoff, and departure instructions, all on the same frequency. Now there was a different frequency for airport information (wind direction and active runway), then taxi instructions and a third frequency for takeoff. After climbing out there was yet another frequency for in route instructions. Also, the technical complexity of the radios and navigation instruments had increased. I was amazed at how my flying skills had deteriorated, not in controlling the airplane but in orchestrating the entire flight. My lack of proficiency in radio procedures, changes in regulations, airspace and instrument flying all needed work. Thirty-five hours of instrument training later, I was ready to take the practical exam and demonstrate my proficiency to an FAA examiner.

The next step was to get current in multi-engine aircraft. The Navy Club had an old Army Beech Baron, B-55. My 500 hours of experience in the Baron was now twenty years stale but it was slowly coming back. The tough part was that I would need to take another practical instrument exam before being able to fly the Baron under instrument conditions. That would be a difficult exam since it not only involved flying instrument approaches to different airports but also at some point in the flight I would have to make an approach with one engine out.

The check ride had been going well, with all climbs and descents at 500 feet per minute, turns at 3 degrees per second and altitude variations at less than a hundred feet. The controller had cleared us for a VOR approach to Salinas and I was turning onto the final approach heading when suddenly the engine out "gotcha" hit as he shut down my left engine. This immediately throws you into a one-armed paper hanger routine with five things needing to be completed at once. The first requirement is to add power to stay in the air, then identify the dead engine from the yaw. The second immediate action is to feather the prop on the dead engine to reduce drag. A dead, unfeathered prop creates as much drag as a parachute of the same diameter hanging off the wing. So, with half the power gone, it's just a matter of minutes before you can get into serious trouble.

I shoved the throttles full forward, the plane yawed left, and I identified the left engine was out and feathered the prop. That's the real pucker point, if you shut down the wrong engine, you fail the check ride. Since I had already began my decent for the approach and reduced power on both engines, the dead engine was more difficult to identify. All the while this is going on, I am still under the hood and needing to fly the plane on instruments, maintaining heading and attitude. Finally, back under control, I completed my approach and landed. Now on the ground, I noticed that the good engine had been running on only one magneto. My knee had evidently bumped the magneto switch and turned off one row of spark plugs. Good grief! I had nearly made a no-engine landing. The examiner didn't see it and I didn't tell him.

I passed and was now fully qualified to fly all the planes available in the club under all conditions. It had taken me about a year to finally requalify in every aspect of flying and I made it a point to fly at least four hours a month to maintain my proficiency.

As noted in the first chapter, although the forced landing event on a tank trail ended happily, the Navy Flying club blamed the incident on me. I blamed it on the condition of the plane they rented me. The aftermath of that was the Navy Flying Club charged me for the cost of getting the plane from the tank trail back to the airfield. I felt that the chain of events leading to the forced landing could be traced back to the Flying Club's renting an aircraft to me which had flown a hundred hours + beyond the usual engine overhaul time and had faulty gas gauges.

A few weeks later I bought into a 1974 Cessna 182 with two partners. It was a great plane that I flew for the next 22 years. Since I was now occasionally involved in investigating aircraft and helicopter accidents and testifying as an expert in that field, I was often able to use the 182 for travel in that regard. I would be commissioned for that purpose only occasionally, perhaps once every year and a half. The accidents were always interesting and the process of fact finding, investigating and litigation would often go on for over a year. Many of the accidents involved failure of parts that simply had worn out, but the airplane manufacturer was still held responsible regardless of how old the airplane was. By the mid 1990's, litigation became so expensive for the makers of Cessna, Piper and Beach Aircraft that congress acted to correct this unfair situation. The result of their action was known as "The Statute of Repose" which provides that the manufacturers of aircraft are not responsible for any parts more than 18 years old. That was a much-needed statute, but it tended to reduce aircraft accident litigation and dry up my consulting activities. Consequently, the ratio of accident suits to available experts caused most of my consulting to shift to helicopter investigations since rotary wing accident experts were a scarce commodity. Most of my consulting experiences were very interesting so I have included a few in the following chapter.

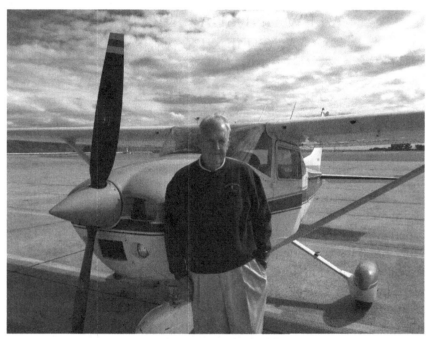

My 1974 Cessna 182

CHAPTER 35

A FEW UNUSUAL AIRCRAFT ACCIDENT CASES

PIPER CRASH AT PINE MOUNTAIN LAKE, CA

Attorney Larry Ince found my name in one of the legal publications which list experts and evidently read in my Vitae Curricula (VC) that I also handled "Case Management". He had little if any aviation accident experience, so when an associate and friend of his was killed in a Piper 180 crash, he no doubt went looking for someone who could help manage his wrongful death case. His attorney friend, Charlie, was killed when piloting his Piper home to Pine Mountain Lake for the weekend,

It was late November and the weather in the Sierras was getting scuzzy, low clouds and multiple layers. But it was Friday and Charlie, whose office was down the hall from Larry's, would leave San Jose a bit early to fly home to Pine Mountain Lake. He had a longstanding travel arrangement with a lady attorney, who also lived at Pine Mountain Lake. They would fly together to San Jose on Mondays and return to Pine Mountain Lake on Fridays. He picked up Mary at 4 PM and headed to the airfield. By the time they got to Pine Mountain Lake 45 minutes later, it was getting dark, and the little airfield was obscured by a low overcast. Charlie pulled out his cell and called a pilot buddy who, also lived at Pine Mountain Lake, and asked him how the weather looked from on the ground. His friend told him it seemed to be getting worse but there were occasional holes in the cloud layer. That was the last anyone heard from Charlie. His plane augured into the top of a ridge.

About three weeks later, I was to meet Larry Ince at the Pine Mountain Lake Airport to visit the accident site. The weather was still occasional overcast, but I was flying my Cessna 182 below the overcast using the GPS to fly up the valleys, and after several turns, wended my way to the airport. A local, who knew his way around that area and had driven to the crash site earlier, took us up the mountain in his Jeep.

It was about a 45-minute ride over muddy dirt roads to a ridge at about the 4,000-foot level. The pine tree that the Piper first impacted was snapped off about 50 feet up the trunk. It bothered me to think that had Charlie been 20 feet higher, he and his lady lawyer passenger may still be alive. Aside from the broken tree limbs and impact scar, there was little to see since the NTSB (National Transportation Safety Board) had long since hauled away the wreckage for further examination.

A few weeks later, I was to meet Larry at Woodland Airport (not far from Sacramento) to view the wreckage which had been released by the NTSB and was located at a "dead plane" facility a couple miles from Woodland. Since this "wrongful death" suit was to provide compensation to the lawyerette's husband, it would involve several million dollars. Typically, in a case like this, a finance expert would also be hired to determine the amount of income foregone by the deceased. She was the primary family support and earning about $150,000 a year, with about 30 years of earning left (do the math!). I suspect that this large sum of money, with about a third of it going to Larry, was cause for him to bring in another aviation expert (with PhD). His appearance at the wreckage site surprise me and I was a bit annoyed that Larry had not discussed that decision with me.

With the help of a worker, the four of us reassembled the airplane pieces to learn what we could from this Gestalt ("The sum of the parts is greater than the whole."). I needed to explain to the PhD, the meaning of those aircraft instruments which were frozen in place from the impact, and how the markings on the control surfaces indicated the position of the controls when the collision with the ground occurred. It was apparent that his expertise was not in aviation. I was surprised that he (let's call him Jim, I can't remember his name) was also not aware that when the tips of the propeller were bent forward, it is indicative that the plane was under power at impact. When we finished with the wreckage it was time to discuss what we had learned. We repaired to a nearby country store that had a table and chairs with coffee available. It was my opinion that this was a straightforward case of pilot error in that he was flying in marginal conditions at night and while trying to talk on his cell he lost enough altitude to clip the trees on the ridge. At this point, Jim propounded his theory that since the lawyerette also held a private pilot's license, she may have been the one flying the plane. I countered that since she was a low time pilot, it was highly unlikely that the owner of the plane would have turned over the controls to her under those conditions. Additionally, I sniped, had he read the autopsy report, he might have noticed that the pilot's thumbs were broken indicating he was gripping the controls at impact. At this point, unabashed, Jim pompously opened his briefcase, pulled out his papers and a chart depicting the conditions necessary to induce carburetor ice. Under the proper conditions of temperature and humidity, the air flowing through the carburetor compresses as it enters and expands as it leaves on its way to the cylinders. This "venturi" action reduces the temperature of the air and freezes the moisture coming out of the flowing air. Under proper conditions, ice will rapidly form in the carburetor throat, shutting off air to the engine. Jim gave a short explanation of how carb ice is formed and noted that on the evening of the crash, all of the conditions for carb ice were present. He ended his diatribe with a pompous, "…and this sir, was the cause of the accident". At that point, I took great pleasure in announcing, "Jim, the problem with that theory is, this Piper did not have a normally aspirated engine, it was fuel injected and THEREFORE DID NOT HAVE A CARBURETOR!" He returned to Indiana the next day. After a final judgement on the case was made and the insurance paid, Larry retired!

A "FOXTROT-4" KIT PLANE KILLS
TWO AT ABILENE TEXAS

Rick Shafer, Major USAF, was a 35-year-old, Air Force rated Senior Pilot assigned on active flight status as a military instructor pilot with 2,600 hours of flight time. He was a 2002 graduate of the Air Force's elite Military Academy. Rick had been working on his Foxtrot-4, kit-built plane for over three years. More than half the people who buy kit planes never get them completed and the Foxtrot 4 was indeed a difficult project. Nevertheless, after three years, and some help from the manufacturer, Rick had finally completed the task and to celebrate he loaded his wife and two children on board for his first cross country flight. The four-place Foxtrot 4 was a great looking, fiberglass aircraft, which had the large, optional, fuel injected, 300 hp Lycoming 540 engine. With a cruise speed of 180 knots, Rick arranged to leave Columbus, Mississippi Friday morning and arrive in San Marcos, Texas in about four hours. His parents met him at the airport. Before leaving the airfield, he had his aircraft topped off with 67 gallons of 100 Octane, low lead Av gas. Rick was with the aircraft when it was refueled and hangered. Two days later, on Sunday afternoon, his parents brought him and his family back to the airfield for the next leg of his trip to Abilene, which was about an hour's flight east of San Marcos. He preflighted his aircraft, loaded his family and headed for Abilene to visit his brother and show off his new Foxtrot 4. Upon his arrival, Rick's brother, wife and baby met him at the airfield and the two families switched places in the aircraft. With Rick's brother now in the front seat and his sister-in-law with baby in the back seat he taxied for takeoff.

One minute after takeoff, at 400 feet AGL, the Foxtrot 4 engine quit! A witness on a nearby golf course said he looked up when he heard the engine sputter and saw the plane in a steep left turn before diving to earth. Three minutes after the crash, the first responder, an Abilene Police Officer cruising nearby, arrived at the scene. Officer Paynor had been driving his patrol car on a road that paralleled the airfield when he heard the emergency call from the tower. When he arrived, within three minutes of the crash, he could see the two bodies against a tree. He was less than a mile away when he heard and saw the plane go in. The wreckage was visible, about a hundred yards from the road, as he parked his patrol car and ran toward the crumpled aircraft remains. Aware that that most aircraft accidents of this sort result in fire, he was surprised that there was no aroma of gasoline but still he approached the aircraft cautiously. He heard cries coming from the broken fuselage and immediately helped the lady and her two-year-old son from the back seat of the plane. She was badly hurt and somewhat hysterical. Her son had some strap bruises from the car seat which had been strapped in. About that time the ambulance and fire department arrived on the scene and she and her son were rushed to the hospital. Concerned with the possibility of fire, the Airport Fire Department deployed their fire hoses, secured the scene, and photographed the area to include the two male bodies and aircraft wreckage. The airport police secured the scene and contacted the NTSB. The next day, the Flight Standards District Office (FISDO in pilot speak) in Dallas, sent an investigator to the scene. An additional NTSB investigator arrived from Washington DC in a few more days.

It was about four months later that a Texas Law firm contacted me and asked if I could manage the case. My contact, Jeff, seemed knowledgeable and capable as we discussed the accident on the phone. I thought I was talking to an attorney but eventually learned he was the chief investigator for the law firm. We exchanged more information by email and a week later I flew to Dallas. Before boarding at SFO, I had contacted Super Shuttle to get a ride from the Dallas Airport to a motel in a nearby town where I was to meet Jeff for dinner. Of course, the plane was late, Supper Shuttle was nowhere to be found, and when I finally met up with Jeff three hours later in the village of Nowheresville, 25 miles south of Dallas, we were both starved. Jeff was a big man, about 50 years old and with a strong Texas accent. Like many Texans, he was carrying. Perhaps he meant to impress the California city boy? Texas is a great state with likable people, but what impressed me most was the excellent steak we had for dinner. Perhaps I was in cattle country like in the old TV series, "Dallas"?

The following morning, we boarded Jeff's 800 hp pickup truck. Well, maybe not 800 hp but it was definitely a big mother. We found our way to the warehouse that was devoted to storing airplane wreckages. The Foxtrot 4 wreckage was stored in a bin and the warehouse minions were busily unloading the bin and spreading the pieces out on the concrete floor. There were several reps from an opposing law firm milling around and a couple photographers. Jeff and I helped offload the fiberglass pieces and put them in their appropriate positions relative to the fuselage, wings, and tail section. Both fuel tanks had ruptured at impact with the trees and ground. We took several photographs: me with my iPhone, he with his 32-megapixel Nikon. When we were through placing the wings and broken sections where they belonged, it looked something like a plane and provided us with some perspective of what happened at impact. As usual, the NTSB investigators had taken all the critical parts away. In this case, the fuel lines, fuel pump, fuel filter, instrument panel, engine, and everything else of importance needed for further investigation and testing (which left little for me to examine other than the airframe). After about four hours we were back in the truck headed for Abilene; a three-hour (and probably a 20-gallon) trip. Jeff had scheduled an interview for me with the Schafer brother's widow. She was still on the mend from several broken bones. I spent about an hour talking to her. As is most often the case in a fatal accident of this nature, she had totally blacked out every detail of the flight other than the takeoff.

The following morning, we made the short drive to the accident scene. At impact, the engine had separated and traveled through a barbed wire fence and across the road we were parked. The oil track from the ground scar to where the engine had come to rest, was still apparent, though the engine was long gone with the NTSB for further examination. The impact ground scar was about a hundred yards from the road. When I stood at the ground scar, looking up to the broken Mesquite branches, it was apparent that the plane had crashed through the mesquite at about a 45-degree angle. It struck the hard, baked, Texas earth with such force that the pilot and front seat passenger were ejected from the cockpit. There were still a few small pieces of fiberglass and broken tree limbs scattered about.

After returning home, I spent some time trying to piece together why a well-trained, active-duty instructor pilot with 2,600 hours flight time, would commit the unforgivable sin of trying to return to the airfield when his engine quit. There is unquestionably a strong urge to do so, but a professional pilot with Rick Schafer's level of training, would never succumb to that error of judgement. Over the next several months, the law firms took depositions from everyone who was even remotely involved. The NTSB, and a Lycoming engine rep, examined the engine and associated fuel system parts, and found nothing which would cause engine failure. Then, why did the engine quit when the Foxtrot 4 had (supposedly) about 100 gallons of fuel remaining after the short flight from San Marcos?

As the case entered the "discovery phase" the opposing law firm provided depositions and proof that the aircraft had been topped off when Shaffer arrived at San Marcos. A photograph taken by the back-seat passenger as the plane taxied for take-off to Abilene, revealed that the fuel indicator showed full. The NTSB in their "Factual Report of Accident" stated that the crash site showed signs of "fuel blight" on the Mesquite leaves and noted that the pilot had the option of landing in open fields straight ahead and was therefore responsible for the multiple deaths. In this regard, let me interject Wiener's Law:

> *"In aviation, there is no problem so great or so complex that it cannot be blamed on the pilot."*

However, it was my conclusion that the accident was caused by fuel exhaustion because there was insufficient fuel to sustain flight. When the opposing law firm received my expert opinion that the cause of the accident was fuel exhaustion, they requested that I provide them sworn testimony in a deposition that was to be taken in Houston. Prior to the planned deposition I returned to Dallas again for a final viewing of the wreckage which now included many of the items that the NTSB had returned which were not available on my first trip to Dallas. On examination of the now available parts, I was astounded to see the inadequacy of the NTSB's investigation that lacked the following actions: -No soil sample was taken at the crash site to detect fuel residue.

- The oil filter had not been cut open to check for metal particles or residue.
- The fuel pump had not been opened to determine if fuel was present.
- The incased fuel filter was not checked for fuel presence.
- The opposing law firm had scheduled my deposition for 10 AM the following morning.

I suspected it would be over by noon. At 9 AM, my attorney and I briefly discussed the conduct of the deposition, which is sworn testimony, video recorded and written down by a court reporter. I would be represented by my attorney who could, for the record, object to any question or procedure if they were not appropriate. The "attack attorney" conducting the depo was very good! During the questions and answers which followed, I presented the following rationale for my opinion of "fuel exhaustion":

1. The NTSB could find nothing wrong with the engine or fuel system.

2. If Rick had taken off with minimal fuel in each tank, his angle of climb would cause the fuel to be unported shortly after takeoff, which is what happened. Although Foxtrot 4 gas tanks would hold 60 gallons in each of the wing tanks, typically 4 or 5 gallons are considered "unusable" since at steep angles the last few gallons of fuel cannot reach the fuel port.

3. If a competent pilot has an engine failure on takeoff, he will lower the nose of the plane and look for a landing area ahead. Attempting to return to the airfield is a fully understood no-no. So, why would Rick, an experienced, proficient instructor pilot, attempt a steep turn to return to the field? Because, when the engine failed and he lowered the nose of his plane to level flight, the unusable fuel could then reach the fuel port, was suddenly useable and the engine momentarily sputtered to life (as noted by the golf course witness). At that instant, Rick had hope of making it back to the airfield and executed a steep left turn. Again, the engine quit and with the wings in a near vertical angle he was out of options and his aircraft took on the aerodynamic characteristics of a rock! With the left wing down and the right wing up, what little fuel was left in the right wing could now reach the port. However, the fuel in the left wing could not reach the port. Guess which fuel tank the fuel selector was set on? Correct, it was set to the left wing which would cause the engine to again quit!

At this point in the depo, the attack attorney said, "How could he have been out of fuel when the photograph taken by the backseat occupant showed he had taken off from San Marcos with 55 gallons in each tank?" The fuel indicator was a high-tech instrument made by Dynamics. Fortunately, I had previously contacted the company to enquire how that instrument functioned. I learned that the amount of fuel is inputted by the pilot during his preflight check. The amount shown on the photo was not the 60 gallons that each tank held, because Rick had correctly inputted the USABLE amount of fuel, not the full tank! Although, he had watched the plane being refueled the Dynamic's gauge reading was based on what the pilot inputted when preflighted not what was in the tank! I explained this to the attack attorney and added: "With the plane in the hangar for two nights after it was refueled, was it possible that the kid who sweeps out the hangar in the evening for $7 an hour saw an opportunity to off load $500 worth of Av Gas?"

That question hung for a few seconds, and she said, "Then how do you explain the fuel blight on the Mesquite leaves at the crash site?" I told her that when the fuel tanks ruptured upon contact with the Mesquite trees, the few gallons of unusable fuel left got on the tree leaves. At that point she very much surprised me by stating, "In your book you said that when the helicopter blade ruptured the fuel tank, the Av Gas was atomized!" She did not give me a chance to respond that in that accident the atomized fuel caused an explosion and fire. There was no explosion or fire in this accident. None-the-less, I was impressed by the fact that in preparation for the depo, the attack attorney had Googled my name, found the book and read it! After four and a half hours, the depo finally came to a close.

In conclusion, I felt that my scenario of the sequence of events satisfied the big questions of, "why did the engine quit?", "why did the experienced pilot commit the unforgivable sin of attempting to return to the field?", "why was there no post-crash fire or any aroma if 100 gallons of av gas were dumped on the ground?". Although my "expert opinion" was not shared by the NTSB's conclusion, this was not the first time I've found them to be wrong.

Unfortunately, this case was never resolved by going to court. There was no way to prove that the Av Gas had been off loaded while the plane was in the hangar, so the deep pockets of the FBO (Fixed Bas Operator) would not be accessible even if a jury agreed with my findings. So, dear reader, it is now up to you to decide.

CHAPTER 36

DEEP RETIREMENT

Ren & Barb at our Pebble Beach Home, 2002

With our shop now closed and the $30,000 of merchandise in our warehouse having been given to the Cancer Society (for tax deductions), we were free and I retired again at age 60. I had also been consulting in aircraft accidents for a few years and so continued that but with increased time on the golf course. Now, in recent months, I found the pleasure of sinking deep into retirement. At first, giving up the vitality of being involved and making a difference didn't feel right. But with my last aviation case closed and my West Point Society Board involvement much diminished after stepping down as president, I felt well kicked back. I decided the trick now is to flow down the river of life without causing too many ripples. It's important not to inflict discomfort or unhappiness on others and even more important, not tolerate those who do. After all, we are here but once and now was the time to feel comfortable with each day. There will always be those around us whose personalities reveal the detritus of a wounded psych, but they are not hard to avoid.

When a younger friend asked me how I liked retirement. I thought about it and decided that retirement is a gift. We work and work and move toward that day when, for the first time in our lives, we can become the person we have always wanted to be and do what we want to do.

Barbara was on a different but parallel routine, enjoying more reading. We allowed ourselves and each other this indulging of self as a great way to begin our day. Truly "Deeeep Retirement" is best defined by the length of time one spends in bed and then proceeds to do what is most enjoyable. Most days, after a light breakfast, we found our way to the fitness club at Spanish Bay. Usually, we were even able to get through the coffee and polite conversation with friends in time to actually exercise. However, guilt-free, deep retirement also requires a modicum of accomplishment to prevent the moss of the mind from growing in potentially fertile fields. For me, this means spending some time on home improvement projects and, ugh, cleaning up and putting away.

In this regard, a final home improvement project loomed large. We really needed to do something about our 50-year-old kitchen. For a year we planned, discussed, and argued over the kitchen design we wanted. We concluded that we would enlarge the kitchen about a foot into the family room and do away with the utility room on the other side. Granite counter tops, new appliances, hardwood floors, beamed ceiling with sky lights and a bay window completed the concept. There was a half bath off the utility room which also needed help.

The project was huge, and it would be entirely done by me over a period of several months. The ugly, old cabinets were ripped out and new, "divided light", multi-paned windows were ordered. I left the sink and electric stove for last so we could continue to use the remains of the kitchen. I hired a couple of guys to rip out the ceiling up to the roof and paid an engineer to tell me what structural modification was necessary to replace the roof supports with beams.

The beauty of taking on the tasks of plumbing, rewiring, and restructuring by myself, was that we could make changes as we went along, without regard to what would have cost big dollars had a contractor been involved. We decided to cut a hole in the wall to the garage so the fridge could be shoved nearly flush with the wall. The washer and dryer were moved into the garage, and I rerouted the plumbing and 240-volt wires to make that work. It was enjoyable for me to solve the problems this involved and use the carpentry skills I had developed over the years. Putting down the hardwood floors was a chance to develop a new skill as was cutting and laying the granite tiles on the new cabinets I installed. Eventually, there was a period when we had no stove, sink or refrigerator, so for a few weeks it was best for Barb to return to our San Francisco home while I lived on TV dinners and sawdust. Finally, after nearly two years, the project was finished, and we were highly pleased with the results. Over the years, I found there was a cost, in addition to lost dollars, for allowing free time to be nonproductive. If I were not getting something accomplished during nonworking hours, it didn't feel right. And it was probably harmful to my psych.

As I was preparing to retire again, I received an email from New Jersey from an attorney seeking my assistance on a helicopter accident. Evidently, there are far fewer experts in helicopter accidents than for fixed wing aircraft. This turned out to be a very interesting accident case which lasted for two years. The details of that investigation and others are below in Appendix II under "Aircraft Accident Investigations".

PART III

A COLLECTION OF PERTINENT EVENTS AND VIGNETTES

APPENDIX I

A VISIT WITH AUNT SARAH

by Eliza Lee Flynn

Sarah Margaret Johnson Lee was nearing her 83rd birthday in 1928 when I visited her in Clarinda, Iowa. The weather was variable, sometimes sunshine and sometime snowflakes were struggling for recognition. Sitting in her comfortable living room, we listened to the wind as it speeded onward heralding the approach of March and looking at the scurrying snowflakes falling thicker and ever thicker. She said, "It is like the day your Uncle James first came to see me... but that was in the month of December."

It was then I asked her to tell me of her courtship with the eldest brother of my own dear Father, William Lee...both men long since gone to their eternal home. "Well," said Aunt Sarah, "I hardly know where to begin. As I hearken back in my memory, it seems but a short time ago that I heard his knock on the door of the little log school at Tarkio Creek, seven or eight miles from College Springs in Page County, Buchanan Township, Iowa. Yes, it was when I was teaching there that I met your uncle James Lee. It may interest you to know how I happened to be in the frontier district, having been born on a farm in the central part of Ohio. My Father's name was Samuel Johnson and my mother's name was Eliza Jane Carson. When I was in my teens, father traded our farm for a two-thirds interest in a Collegiate Institute in Urbana, Ohio in Champagne County, becoming the president of the school. (His father

305

was Nathaniel Johnson and according to the Chillicothe Court records in 1837, his will lists his seven children as James, Henry, Nancy, Jane, Margaret, John and my Father Samuel.)

Nathaniel died in 1839. I have sent you a little story of his life written by Rufus Johnson, brother of Sarah Johnson Lee. He and Mother, together with the teachers required, constituted the faculty. For one year all went well but then Father had been a farmer living close to nature, a tiller of the soil, a student of land development of broad acres, and he began to yearn for the big open spaces. He scarcely admitted to himself that the call of the West he had heard and was responding to the magical "Go West, young man" of Horace Greeley. He contracted to exchange his thirty-thousand-dollar equity in the Ohio college for one thousand and eighty acres of wild, unbroken land in Iowa.

It was shortly before the close of the Civil War in 1864 when Father told us of his plans. There was not much in those days that would appeal to the modern flapper. Silken hose and short skirts would have been but scant protection in an open wagon or prairie schooner and compared with our traveling outfit of Civil War days, would place us in the cave man days. Mother and Father were seeking buffalo robes to wrap their children in.

Knowing full well that the climate of the western territory would mean additional clothing, we chose clothes for warmth rather than for style. As I was a young lady, my Father thought I would not care to accompany the family over the plains to the young state of Iowa. I did, for a brief time, consider remaining in Urbana, where all my college friends were. My parents encouraged this decision through great, unselfish love. Father said to me, "Your Mother and I are not asking you to accompany us west; you will miss your school friends and besides, the country we are going to is unsettled, rough and has very few young people your age. We fear you will be lonesome." I agreed that this was so until I saw active preparations being made for the emigration to Iowa; then I had a change of heart. I wondered what I would do when they all left, how I could be happy without my parents, sisters, and brothers. For in our family there were eight children, which meant that there never was a dull moment., Brother Rufus, who afterward was a minister in the United Presbyterian Church, and Carson, who became a farmer, Nanny, my invalid sister; how sadly she would miss me. I was the fourth child, then came Etta and Lizzie; brother Nathaniel was at this time fifteen

Once A Soldier

years of age and a student at the institute; Samuel was our youngest. The world of Urbana would indeed be a big empty place were these dear ones to drop out of it. Oh no, I never could let them go without me. So, I speedily resolved to go whithersoever my people went.

We traveled from Urbana by way of St. Louis to St. Joe, Missouri, thence to St. Mary's, Iowa, where we stayed for ten days, this being the nearest point to Glenwood, Iowa, the county seat of Mills County where Father had to go to pay taxes on our new Iowa land.

These days of the fast trains, fast automobiles, fast airships, rapid transit generally, it would be difficult to make you understand the hardships and fatigue we experienced on that journey. The regular order of our daily lives was completely upset. Often since have I wondered at the patience of my dear mother and how much more was meant in pioneer days, when the marriage service was read to the bride and she responded, "I will" and meant what she said. "Wither thou goest, I will go." This was her creed and right well and cheerfully did Mother follow and train her little flock, not only to obey but also to respect our father and the provider of our family. In those days, women did not talk about careers. There was only one career for a wife and mother and that was to be a real helpmate to the father of her children . . . her husband "till death do us part." We meant it when we said those solemn words "for better or for worse."

During that tedious travel I learned a never to be forgotten lesson in fortitude, in the example set by my mother. This lesson was a great help to me in later life when caring for my own family of eight children.

It was during the few days at St. Mary's that father became acquainted with a man from Mills County at a place on the Missouri River, eight miles south of Council Bluffs. He was interested when Father told him where we were from and of the trade of the college for the farmland in Iowa. When Father mentioned that his daughters were with him, the man told Father of the lack of teachers in his district and suggested that, if Father's daughters would care to teach, we would have no difficulty getting a school. When father returned from paying his taxes, he recounted all the conversation he had with the man from Mills County.

Teaching school on the plain would be another adventure; why not apply for this school? Besides, I had heard Father say that it had taken a

307

great deal of money to take care of the taxes and other necessary expenses pertaining to the new land.

I knew from remarks father made that our financial resources were low, so it did not take me long to decide to try to get the school and add to our bank account, if only a little. My application was quickly acted on and I signed a contract to teach three months. It was late in the summer when school closed, and I joined my family near Clarinda on the new farm.

I would have rather stayed on there with them, as I had found the children on the plains hard to restrain. They were part of the big open west, full of originality and initiative, and did not yield readily to discipline, while I was the product of a conventional, well-disciplined college. Naturally, we merged about as easily as oil and water. But I wanted to do my bit to help and during the next three years, I continued teaching in Iowa, the last school being the one on Tarkio Creek where your uncle first rapped on my door!

I will tell you how he happened to find the trail to my little log schoolhouse. At College Springs, seven or eight miles distant, there was a church raising and among the church elders was a visiting young bachelor, James Lee from the territory of Nebraska. The last day of the meeting there was to be a social gathering and for miles around the settlers planned to go. The Galligan's, with whom I made my home, their neighbors and everyone hastened to the merry making.

This was the first time I saw James Lee, who was a distinguished-looking man of quiet demeanor...perhaps 12 or 14 years older than I. Not once during the day did anyone present him to me, for even then, as now, there were jealous maidens and young men were scarce by reason of the Civil War. Just as we were to start back to the Galligan Farm, a neighbor by the name of Manzingo met Mr. Lee and as he approached our wagon to bid us "goodbye," James followed and was introduced to us. It was not until eighteen months later, in December, that I saw him again. During those intervening months I became very restless and discouraged. I could not get home very often; the roads were frequently impassable because of the rains and snow. Iowa roads, if not paved, can be as impassable now as they were then.

To be sure, we had our occasional gatherings of neighbors and would enjoy the big picnic dinner or dance in the big room at the home of a settler's log cabin. My real trouble lay in recognizing the unwelcome truth that I was not intended to be a schoolteacher. I was popular enough with the few young men of the neighborhood but herein lay another thorn; eligible young men were scarce, as I have said before, and the result was inevitable, and jealousy entered our small district. Fortunately for me my sister, Henrietta, was now teaching school nearby and we frequently saw one another. Having been raised in Ohio near a city, we had enjoyed many privileges superior to our frontier associates and the atmosphere of our college home had put a stamp upon us so that we were different in many respects from the girls of the district.

In the school room, too, I had the misfortune of attracting the biggest boy in school, Zack Montgomery. He fell desperately in love with me and this made it difficult for me to keep order. The younger pupils were alert to every glance of Zach's and ready to couple my name with his at every opportunity. It seems like a joke now but then it was a real tragedy and the cause of abundant tears. Often, in the solitude of my room, I would ask myself, "Why did we ever leave Urbana? Why did Father ever join the army of home seekers?" But later in life the pioneer spirit entered me, and I could see the lure of it, which is not easily explained.

Now as I travel over Iowa and try to find some of the old familiar places, I am bewildered and lost. When I try to realize that so many changes have taken place in one short lifetime, it is inconceivable. Where there was the trail, there is now a graded highway. We have traded the Indian pony and the prairie schooner for automobiles. Where we once camped with our buffalo robe and frying pan, there now stands a splendid hotel surrounded by all the luxuries that a railroad bringsthe prosperous farms, the people and the wonderful works of art and architecture that we call school buildings. I have seen it all come; only a pioneer can understand.

But I shall return to the school on Tarkio Creek. There I was deluged with what I considered a big problem. I was approaching my twenty-fourth birthday, old enough to have a home of my own and thoroughly convinced that I was not intended for a schoolteacher. Yet, I had seen no young man that I would care to marry (I had my ideal prince visualized). I wanted a real man like my own Father, a man temperate and of goodly habit, one I could respect and love, one of my own religious beliefs. Consequently, I did as I had been taught do; I took my burden to the Lord in prayer. For the period of a week or more, I made the same prayer, that the Heavenly Father would send me a worthy husband. After leaving all in His hands, I returned to my schoolwork afresh. I would await the answer to my prayer.

My heart was light once more and I began to look forward to a visit home when the Presbytery of our church would meet at Clarinda, fourteen miles distant. I knew my parents would be expecting me and too, that James Lee might come to the meeting.

During the next two weeks I could see a great improvement in the schoolwork. Zach Montgomery had accepted the inevitable and had ceased to annoy me with his attentions. Yes, I was making progress and reported this to the Galligan's, thrift farmers from Missouri with whom I made my home. My own people could not have treated me with greater consideration; the comfort I received in their society leavened many of my grievances and put a silver lining to many a cloud on my sky. It is a pleasure to recall the time I spent in their home and it was a great disappointment to me when Mrs. Galligan told me the great secret of the visit of the stork and said that the Montgomery's wanted me to stay with them until she would again be able to have me with them. To be sure, I rejoiced with her that she was soon to be so blessed, although I did not want to go to the Montgomery's, even though it was but a quarter of a mile from the schoolhouse.

When Zach heard of the possibility of my coming to live at his house, he foolishly broke out again, so much to my disgust that I resolved to return to my people in two weeks, attend the meeting of the Presbytery, and resign the school at Tarkio Creek. But Fate willed otherwise. Severe weather coming on made the trip to Clarinda impossible. I must bravely carry one . . . perhaps there may have been rebellion in my soul and a wandering wave length transmitted it as strength to the pupils for, from then on, they seemed to be possessed with the very imp of Satan. They were so mischievous that I was unable to control them. Sport was the master of their being, their desire to create a ridiculous situation at recitation time ...to plan something to embarrass me ... all of course in the spirit of fun ...occupied the time that should have been given to the lesson. It was one of these days when the conviction was upon me that I was working in the wrong vineyard, on which a lone horseman rode down the path to our schoolhouse and loudly knocked on the door.

Visitors were scarce in those days. Instantly, the pupils were all aglow with curiosity to see who it might be. When the tall young man entered the room, a pin could have been heard to drop, so suddenly was noise changed to silence. Then, the caller asked if I were Miss Johnson, knowing full well I was, as he afterwards confessed and asked me if I remembered the day at the church raising when Manzingo had introduced us. He added that he had been looking forward to meeting me at the united Presbyterian Presbytery a short time back in Clarinda.

The tall young man was James Lee, as you have guessed. I was glad to meet him again and asked him how he had found me. He replied, "I called on your parents while in Clarinda and they directed me to your school." By this time, he had found a bench and was seating himself upon it, with the remark that he had wanted to get better acquainted with me and would enjoy visiting the school while in the district. He gave me one message from my mother and when I again turned my attention to the pupils, my heart suddenly skipped a beat they were grinning in a suggestive way that I so well knew meant a Waterloo for me. The older boys, led by Zach Montgomery, had started activities to embarrass me and I could scarcely wait for recess to come and hope James Lee would not tarry.

But he stayed on, and the noon hour came when we all took out our dinner pails and boxes. The children gathered in one end of the room while my visitor and I shared the lunch put for me by Mrs. Galligan. James seemed happy and contented, and quite at home with the rest of us, and I must confess I was enjoying the relaxation too. It seems as if we had always known each other. However, I hoped he would terminate his visit when the noon hour ended but not he. We sang our opening song, in which James joined us. Before calling the class to order, I suggested that his pony would be getting hungry. He did not seem to agree with me. Again, later in the afternoon, I ventured the information that it was snowing, and he might have difficulty getting back to Clarinda. My caller was not in the least disturbed by what I said, and I can assure you that the pupils were glad to have him stay, as they knew I would not interfere with their mischief or insist on anything while he was there. I had tried that before, and never again would I give those big boys a chance to worst me before company. I prepared not to notice their activities.

It would soon be time now to excuse school for the day and again I essayed to point his way from whence he came and to sympathize with the little Indian pony tied to the post outside. He replied that he could visit better after school was dismissed. No use. The children would soon go home and tell their parents of the visitor at the school, which would occasion much speculation by the district.

By four o'clock the last child had disappeared, leaving us alone in the shadows of that December afternoon. We talked of the latest war news, of the new political party principles just beginning to reach the ears of the people in our part of the country, of General Grant, of the terrible deeds the Ku Klux Klan was doing to the families of the south who dared approve the platform of the new political party, and we expressed our admiration for the policy of our great President Lincoln. The December afternoons are short, and the snow was falling heavier. James rose to go, remarking, "It will be a long ride back." Then, to my amazement, he asked me to let him kiss me goodbye. I was shocked ...he must have seen my sudden resentment as I rose in all the dignity I could command and told him that he had insulted me and that I never wanted to see him again. I had supposed that he was a gentleman and a Christian. I said many other things that I have forgotten, for this was the climax to a very trying and unusual day and my patience was worn to the extremity.

When he saw the attitude I had taken, he was completely amazed and was almost as indignant as I had been, assuring me that he had no intention of insulting me but on the contrary, had a most excellent opinion of me and would as soon think of insulting his own mother as to insult me. I could see that I had hurt him, and the sincerity of his defense convinced me that he was speaking the truth. He told me that he had wanted to get better acquainted with me ever since the church raising, and that he knew me better than I thought, as he had inquired about me and had made the acquaintance of my people and had their approval to visit me, and that he had come to my school for the purpose of seeing me again. He added that he had also seen me at the church raising as I arrived, but he had no means of meeting me until Manzingo had introduced him to me. He finished by saying, "I have admired you since I first saw you and I ask you to marry me. We are old enough to marry and we are of the same religious faith." To his proposal I turned a deaf ear and told him I would not consider his proposal, as I was too astonished to think and besides, I did not know him well enough to give it serious thought.

It was past the supper hour when I reached the Galligan's. The first thing Mrs. Galligan said was, "Where is Mr. Lee?" She added, "We expected him to eat with us." When I told her he had returned to Clarinda she said, "Did you not ask him to stay the night here?" I replied that I had not even thought of such a thing. Then my words brought forth the first rebuke ever spoken to me by my friend. I was promptly told that I had violated the rule of hospitality of the district to allow him to return at that hour, a distance of fourteen miles in a heavy snowstorm, and not even offer him or his pony any refreshment. She said, "We knew he had spent the day at the school, and we looked forward with pleasure to an evening with him. He is a most excellent gentleman, and his people are greatly respected in the territory adjoining us. It was a compliment to you that so fine a man as he would come in over rough roads in weather like this to see you. He is the finest young man that has come to these parts since we settled here and as good a man as your own Father."

When Mrs. Galligan spoke these words, I remembered the prayers I had made for a week, that the Lord would send me a good husband of my own faith, "a man such as my own Father."

Without making any reply, I hastened to my own chamber and throwing myself on my knees, I asked God to forgive me for not recognizing the answer to my prayers, for such a one as I had prayed for had visited me that very day.

Humiliated and thoroughly awakened to my blindness, I wept bitterly and again asked the Lord to give me another chance. Gloomy days passed. Mrs. Galligan, seeing my confusion, consoled me with the suggestion that I would hear again from Mr. Lee and that he would understand that I had not meant to give offense. Sure enough, during the Christmas holidays a letter came from James informing me that he had reached home without any encounters with the red men and was planning to join the company of the Indian fighters who were protecting the settlers farther west, as word had been received of the killing of five soldiers who had been defending the mail. A call had been sent out for assistance. He might leave any time and later, if men were needed in the big war, he would join the United States troops if I continued to refuse to marry him. But if I would marry him, he would cultivate the new land his people had acquired in the territory of Nebraska and continue in the work of protecting the settlers from the violence of the unwelcome Indians. He asked that I write him soon and give him a little encouragement. No more would I disregard the answer to my petition. Yes, I would write to him; it would be a friendly letter and I would tell him, too, that the next time he came to Tarkio Creek he was to stay the night with the Galligan's. But how could I marry him? I was contracted to teach the spring term of school.

This friendly letter went astray and, in the meantime, a Mormon girl, Sara Gallen by name, met James and did all she could to attract his notice, even to writing him expressing her admiration for him. As days went by, they saw much of one another but when he was absent on one occasion, she wrote him a very bold letter which fell into the hands of his pious mother, who did not look with favor on this Mormon girl. The letter was promptly destroyed. Soon after my letter to the second proposal from James Lee, which had been delayed, reached him.

And why was I not hearing from him? Was he trifling with me after all? Who can know my many misgivings during the interval between writing to James and the day he again appeared to claim me as his future bride?

There were many explanations of his looking in vain so many days for the answer to his letter. It was finally delivered to him by a friendly Indian who had found it after the stagecoach had been held up and robbed by a band of Sioux. He had told his people about me, and they were asking too that I would come into their family.

I explained that I had contracted to teach another term but James persuaded me that it was more necessary that I marry him. He advised me to resign, since there was another girl in the settlement who would be glad to get my school. Even now, his brother John was waiting to meet me. The two brothers had driven in a one-seated buggy with a span of young horses from the valley of the Platte and would not return without me. So, I cancelled my contract to teach the spring term, returned to my parents near Clarinda and shortly after, we were married there. James and I had a short courtship, but the times were such that long courtships were not thought of. Neighbors were few and far between and young people married and learned to know each other later. Besides, in those days' men were scarce and if a girl had a vocation for the married state, she could not be too slow in deciding or she might lose out altogether. But in my case, I knew now that it was God who had sent me my husband. I was convinced of this and have never doubted it to this day. James was all I had asked for as my ideal life partner and was always a kind and considerate companion. He was temperate in his habits and industrious in his life, respected by the best people in the territory, and I was satisfied.

After the wedding breakfast, we prepared to start to the new home. My trunk was placed in the back of the buggy on which sat brother John Lee, our chaperon. However, in those days it was wiser to travel in numbers as there were often stray Indians and three was few enough, even so.

By evening, we came to a log house. James said it would be best to stay there all night if we could be taken care of. We went to the door and a very queer woman asked us in. She put some food on the table and told us that she had but one spare bed and did not like to violate the text of the scripture by separating husband and wife but that the brothers could have the spare room and I could sleep with her.

This plan did not please me at all. I was not favorably impressed by her appearance. John must have read my thoughts, for he spoke up and said, "Let the husband and wife have your spare room. I have my buffalo robe and will lie outside their door for the rest of the night. We will be leaving at daybreak."

Next day, after an early breakfast, we continued our journey to the Lee farm in Nebraska, close to the town of Fremont which the Lees had helped settle. It was nearing evening when we drew in sight of the place and for the first time since leaving home, I realized that I was beginning a new life. Here I was to remain indefinitely, and a flood of tears and weeping seized me.

In front of the cabin, James stopped the horses to let John jump out. Then James kindly said, "We will take a little drive around the place, and you can get acquainted with the farm." Many times since, I have thought of this considerate action of my young husband. All through my married life the same thoughtfulness of me has been evident.

When I composed myself, he said, "We will go in to meet Mother, as she will be waiting for us." I was greeted with the greatest cordiality and warmly welcomed by the members of the family. Afterwards we all sat down to a splendid meal which had been prepared especially for us.

Before bidding one another good night, we had family worship. I felt instantly at home with my husband's people. We were now, in truth, one family.

It was a matter of weeks before James and I settled in a home of our own. And to that home the next year came our firstborn whom we named after my father, Samuel, and my youngest brother, Samuel.

There were no lonesome days now. We felt greatly enriched by our lovely baby. Soon after leaving Dodge County to establish our home in Saunders County, our second son was born in December 1869. Him we named after the first of the Covenanter martyrs in Scotland, James Renwick. Since we were the ones to start the town of Yahoo, there was no one to assist me at the time of Ren's birth. James took us back to Fremont, where the baby was born.

In the newly organized town which we named first Leesville and later Yahoo we finally built our first frame house where William was born ...our third child. He had the distinction of being the first white child born in Yahoo on March 20, 1871. Our next child was a daughter whom we named Annabel, born May 29, 1872. She was the first white girl born in Yahoo. In 1893, daughter Annabel married Harry Caley Hart and moved to the state of New York.

END

Note from Trudy (Gertrude Lee, youngest daughter of Ren Lee):

At this point, Eliza Lee Flynn sent what she had written to Grandmother (Sarah?) Lee for additional material. Grandmother Lee thought the tale was too sentimental and too personal. I was told she threw the first one in the fire. I also remember reading one account that told that before she and James went in the house in Fremont, while she was "composing" herself, that we said the psalms. This doesn't seem to be in this copy.

Anyhow, as you know, the next child was Rufus, then Mary Alice (who had a tumor and died at sixteen months), then Walter, Bessie and Sadie.

Please excuse all the errors. This is a labor of love. I have never had typing and have done this by the hunt and peck method.

Grandmother's sister, Henrietta, was married at the same time as Grandmother (double wedding). She doesn't mention it. She married Frank Graham. Not long ago I had quite a correspondence with one of her great grandchildren who was working at Cape Canaveral. She sounded lovely and highly educated.

/s/ Trudy Lee, 1969

APPENDIX II

THE SECOND HALF OF MY LIFE: VIGNETTES

1. East Europe Tour

1991 I received an invitation from Retired Admiral Don Engen, who was heading up the Aviation Safety Foundation, to join a group of aviators on a "People to People" tour of four eastern European capitals. Incidently, Admiral Engen, WW II, was famous for sinking the first Japanese Battleship when he managed to drop a bomb down its stack,

There were many interesting people on the tour, but particularly memorable was our interaction with one of the New Zealand aviators.

He stood apart from our group, a nice-looking gentleman with a graying crew cut, perhaps two or three years my Junior, trim and nearly my height. When I saw him the next day, standing nearby but again somehow not among us, I took the opportunity to introduce myself. I guess I have always been a collector of strays, be it people or puppies. Shaking hands, he said his name was John. "John Spencer," he added, with something of a British accent. I tried to figure out the accent - it wasn't quite British but could be South African or perhaps Australian? John had joined the group a few days late when we were in Moscow.

"Where are you from, John?" I queried. "My home is New Zealand, but I have just come here from South America. It was 1991, just a few months before the Cold War officially ended, and our tour included Mocow, Kiev, Prague and Warsaw, ostensibly to brief the aviation ministries in those capitals.

"Why South America, John?" "I was sailing the west coast in my yacht." he said. "Nice," I replied. "What kind of yacht do you have?" "It's a 120-foot motor launch," he said innocently. "Wow, something like that must be worth a few mil," I replied. "Well, actually, I have it up for sale for 6 million," he continued. "Isn't that a little expensive?" I asked, hoping to appear knowledgeable. "Well," he explained, "it has an all-metal hull." "Where did you find a yacht like that?" "I had it made in my shipyards," he replied. It was becoming apparent that each question was revealing an ever-expanding cornucopia of wealth. I asked, "Do you find shipbuilding profitable these days?" John replied, "Well, I don't really know, we only build ships for me." I thought to myself, this is getting a little deep for me, but I had one last inquiry. "What is it you do, John?" (Besides counting your money, I was thinking). He said, "I have about 35 people who work for me full-time, locating investments." At that point, I changed the subject and we began to discuss flying.

John's associate, Barry, had arrived earlier. Barry was a helicopter pilot and after our chopper discussion ended, I took the opportunity to ask him if John was for real? He said, "Oh yes! He is the wealthiest man in New Zealand, worth about 300 million." Doing some rough calculations in my head, I said, "Good grief, at a 5 percent return, that's an income of about $40,000 a day!"

The following week, when we arrived at our hotel in Prague, I went to check on the baggage while Barb checked out the lobby shops. When I next saw her she told me of having remarked to a lady friend in one of the shops that our daughter would really like a necklace she saw there but it didn't have a price marked on it and was probably more than she should spend. Evidently John had overheard her and when she left, he bought the necklace! He gave it to her a short time later, when we were in the cocktail lounge, saying, "This is for your daughter!" We were both taken back by his generosity.

That evening after dinner I asked if he could join us for coffee. In the course of the conversation, when Barb had left the table briefly, I expressed my gratitude for his generosity. It was then he said, "You must promise not to tell Barbara" and he then confided that when he told the boutique clerk he wanted that necklace he was surprised to learn it cost $500. My eyes must have gotten big, because he added, "You know, that isn't an awful lot of money for me and I wasn't going to back down just because of the price." I stumbled through a few more thank yous and when Barb returned, we called it a night. On the way up in the elevator I told Barb that I had made a solemn promise to John that I would not mention he paid $500 for the necklace, so please don't ask me.

The next day Barb went back to the shop and reported to me later that she bought another of the same necklace for $15. I was absolutely astounded by that. It was a mind blow. Why would the richest man in all of New Zealand be lying to me? He must have been mistaken, or in the translation of New Zealand dollars to U.S., to Czechoslovakian kapoltepecks (or whatever they were) had the math gotten screwed up?

That evening my head was swimming with the problem of whether I should tell John he had been bilked or just be quiet? The Norwegian general and the retired Navy admiral with whom we were having dinner, both agreed that nothing should be said. Of course, this haunted Barb and me for the rest of the trip, not knowing if we had incurred a debt or were the butt of some strange wealthy jokester.

A few days before the tour ended, John's wife, Tutie, left for her home in Finland and John said he would be staying in Prague to determine if he should buy a Mig production facility that was going out of business. By this time, Barb had visited the necklace factory and ordered a couple hundred different types for our shops. In quantity, the price came down to about $5 per necklace. One of her newly acquired necklaces from the factory was identical to the one John had gotten her but had some different colors in it. She got it wrapped up and in a stroke of brilliance presented the little box to John to give to his wife when next he saw her. The loop was at last closed, the debt repaid, and if it were a bad joke the last laugh would be on him.

As a postscript to this story, for years I wondered if John Spencer were really the wealthiest man in New Zealand or if he and Barry had just set us up. Then, several years ago, I was at a party in Carmel on Race Weekend and had a chance to meet Sir Sidney Hume, New Zealand's great racing champion, knighted for his accomplishments on the track. I said to him, "Sir Sidney, do you know John Spencer?" He responded, "Do you mean the wealthiest man in New Zealand?" I said, "Yes, that's him." He continued, "He is a strange one. He owns nearly half the North Island and once each year, he will close the state highway to impose his right of eminent domain."

—✳—

2. Night Flight

As I lifted off from the little Marin County airstrip, the sun was slipping into the horizon, beginning the glow of evening. There was an undefined calm that seemed to settle across the sky…indeed across the land there seemed a certain quietus which is not easily explained. Perhaps it was a calmness of mind and spirit. It is a period that is officially known by aviators as "Before Evening Nautical Twilight," or BENT. It is a special time in the sky as the lights below begin to come alive and twilight fades into darkness. It takes perhaps an hour of BENT before the black ink of night chases the last hue of light from the sky. When it is truly dark, one's senses begin to come alive. The eyes adapt to the night and contrasts of light and darkness begin to appear. The engine's drone becomes a more distinctive beat as you listen closely for anything it might tell you. The engine instruments seem more important now and are routinely checked with a visual instrument scan. Climbing to 3,000 feet, I called Bay Approach controller to give him our location and request permission to transition through the San Francisco Control Area. It was an unusually clear and quiet night, with hardly any aircraft traffic in the are.

Below me were a hundred thousand points of light. It was rushhour and the major freeways leading to and from the city were lit by a cascade of headlights; like a river of gold. It reminded me of gazing at Yosemite's "Fire Falls" years ago when the Park Service would astound viewers by dumping huge quantities of burning wood and embers into the headwaters at the top of the falls.

To my left, three bridges stretched to join key points of the Bay like strings of pearls against the totally black water. In the west, a half-moon hung low over the Pacific, providing that classic moonlight glimmer on the water. It was one of the great scenes in life and at 135 knots, it was constantly changing. Sixty miles ahead, the sky was aglow with the lights from San Jose and further in the distance, the horizon held an aura from the lights of Monterey.

As I crossed the Santa Cruz Mountains, my mind involuntarily returned to the long, creepy nights over the Jungles of Vietnam. Then there were hardly any lights below and the threat of engine failure over an enemy-controlled Jungle dominated my thoughts.

Now I checked my altimeter to make certain I was higher than the highest peaks in the area to avoid any unpleasantness. Soon I passed over Santa Cruz and could see the coastal town lights delineating a 40-mile arc stretching all the way thru Monterey Bay to Pacific Grove. I tuned the frequency for airport information and then called Monterey Approach control. I was almost home and it had been another memorable experience. I flicked on my landing lights so the tower would have me visually and was cleared to enter the flight pattern for landing.

But, turning onto final, my landing light flickered out and toggling the switch did not solve the problem. I thought to myself, "Landing lights are nice but I've made some of my best landings without "em." With that positive thought, a few seconds later I flared the plane for landing and was greeted with the comforting squeak of the main gear making contact with the runway. With another greaser in my logbook, I taxied to my hangar, vowing to get back into that velvet darkness very soon again.

3. Precautionary Landing

Many years ago, at West Point, my English professor proffered the story of an unusual event he survived during the Korean War. He was traveling down a dirt road in his jeep when suddenly he hit a land mine. He said the detonation threw the jeep into the air and he landed several feet away in the dirt. To his amazement, he was uninjured. He looks back on the occasion as the most exciting event in his life and said, "You know, there are very few things in life that are really exciting. Where else can you get that kind of excitement?"

I agree it's nice to have a little excitement in our lives, as long as the situation doesn't go beyond exciting. That is where I was last month on takeoff from a smallish strip in Davis, California. I was just leaving the runway at full power, looking forward to the flight ahead. One of the best moments in flying is when you shove the throttle full forward and feel the engines' power surging through the airframe as your aircraft comes alive. It wants to fly; you want to fly and together the great experience begins. Within seconds the speed hits 75 knots and you ease back on the aileron control to point the craft skyward. But just as I was lifting off the runway, the needle on my RPM indicator blew past the red line. ARRGRH! What a way to start the day.

I figured I had a "runaway prop" with a failed governor. I pulled the power back and put the props in high pitch to reduce RPM. The plane really wasn't very pleased to fly that way., but I had visions of pistons coming through the cowl or prop blades flying loose if the RPM stayed above red line—which it didn't.

Strange how these things happen just after you run out of enough runway to put it back on the ground, yet not enough altitude for any decent options. Ahead of me there was too little runway to abort and a small river with trees if I didn't get off the ground by the end of the runway. Thankfully, with less power, the "over-red-line" needle stabilized in the green and I was able to continue a slow climb that way. I kept messing with the power and prop lever to squeeze a little more gumption out of the climb and still stay below red line. This seemed to work, and I nursed the beast higher. Of course, it was our usual cloudless California weather, so I was able to climb to 5,000 feet, where I began to breathe a little easier. In that plane, at 5,000 feet, you can glide ten miles; that's over two hundred square miles (Pi R squared) to find a good spot for an emergency landing. Not really very scary. If you can't find a decent place to set down in two hundred square miles, you shouldn't be flying. At least that's what I told myself, seeking scant comfort.

I limped along that way for over an hour, wondering if I could make it home to Montery. The low power and low pitch had my speed down to about 100 knots and the situation was well below my comfort level. I wondered if I should put down at the first airport. To do so would mean mucho (my gardener's been teaching me Spanish) time and trouble. It was Sunday, so even if there was a facility at Podunk International which could fix the problem, there wouldn't be anyone there on Sunday. And how do you get home a hundred miles from "Nowheresville"? Then eventually you need to get back to pick up the plane. That whole drill sounded worse than to just keep limping along and hoping. The only part really bothering me was flying over the Santa Cruz Mountains. The choices for a good emergency landing would be greatly reduced during those ten minutes. Still doable but with hairs.

After I cleared the mountains, I called the controller and told him I was gimping along with an uncontrollable prop and wanted him to be aware of the sitch. The propeller must have sensed my lack of confidence, because almost immediately it began acting up. Again, it was over red line and to get it back in the green, I had to pull off so much power that I would lose attitude. At that point I was approaching Watsonville Airport, which I knew had a decent maintenance facility and was only about 40 miles from home, so decided to pack it in. I chopped the power, informed the controller of my intentions and glided into the traffic pattern. On downwind I went through the normal landing procedures, dropped full flaps on final and touched down without incident. I taxied to the restaurant parking, called Barb and since she was only about a half hour away, asked her to join me there for dinner. BTW, my inspection of the left seat did not reveal any pucker marks. I checked with the local repair facility and dropped off the keys to the plane.

The next day the mechanic called me with the news of what was wrong. Evidently the RPM indicator had reached the end of its natural life and started twitching up to a higher RPM indication. Interestingly, my low tech airplane, commissioned in 1974, had a dying RPM indicator but my high tech, noise-cancelling headset kept me from recognizing there wasn't any increase in engine RPM. There was no problem with the prop or engine; it was the instrument. Without the headset, I would have known from the steady hum of the engine that I could have happily flown on for hours. The unexpected is never expected. As life would have it, the plane needed to be delivered to Watsonville the following week anyway for a GPS upgrade. So, I saved a trip, got it there a week early and had a little extra excitement to boot.

—⟁—

4. The Traffic Expediter

At a cocktail party in San Francisco some years ago, my neighbor Ralph approached me and asked, "Did I not see you going through a stop sign on the way home today?" "I hope so," I quipped. "I think it's important to clear an intersection as quickly as possible so that those who approach after you don't need to wait." "What do you mean?" he asked. "Well," I responded, "at a four-way stop intersection, whoever gets there first is the one who should proceed first. FIFO, the accountants call it, first in first out. Have you ever been at a four-way intersection and there are four cars at the four stop signs, and none of them knows who should go first, so the cars start piling up behind them? So, when approaching an intersection, an on the ball attentive driver can almost always easily determine if there are other cars approaching and whether they will get there before you. If they get there first, or are destined to arrive before you, then of course you must either slow or stop to give them the right of way. But if you are obviously the first or only one to arrive, the most polite thing you can do is take your foot off the brake and get through the intersection as quickly as possible so the next guy won't need to wait for you to go first. Four-way traffic stops in San Francisco, in times of congestion, can be a problem, so I like to think of myself as a Traffic Expediter."

The concept made Ralph uncomfortable, and he retorted, "I think of you as a traffic violator." "Ralph, me lad, that's because you have trouble thinking out of the box," I said. "For 60 years you, and those of your ilk, have been stopping at stop signs unthinkingly. All you must do is stop without engaging brain. It's safe, easy and brainless and in your total unawareness, you can even feel good about yourself while the traffic is stacking up behind you. Have you ever considered that expediting through the intersection is not only considerate but saves gas, saves brakes, reduces pollution, and saves time?"

Now, becoming a little angry, Ralph falls back to his only defensible position and stammers, "It's the law! You are a scofflaw!" "True, Ralph but laws are continually changing with the times and laws that require you to do what a sign says, whether it is applicable to the situation or not, are not going to last." "Yes, he admits but until the law changes good citizens must obey." "Even to the detriment of others?" I ask. "Have you ever considered that obeying a sign in a non-pertinent situation is tantamount to admitting the sign knows more about the situation than you do? Isn't that sort of like being dumber than a signpost?"

I continued, "Several years ago in Germany, about 1971, my wife and I were returning from a party very late, about two in the morning. There was absolutely no traffic. The light was red, and I stopped. There were no cars as far as the eye could see and I began to wonder if the light was ever going to change. Finally, I said 'the heck with this' and as I went through the intersection, there was a flash. A couple of days later I received a ticket in the mail that had a picture of the back of my car, the license plate, and the back of my head. I mailed in my 20 marks." Germany was about 20 years ahead of us with traffic cameras.

"Ralph," I said, "there are many situations such as this in which laws are broken without having a negative impact on anyone …these are victimless violations. On the other hand, there are some laws such as "Slower Traffic Keep Right" which, if not obeyed, will impact all those people in the fast lane who are behind the violator. Yet the "Keep Right" law is seldom enforced, while the victimless rolling through a stop sign or exceeding the speed limit will catch a ticket every time. The problem is that predetermining what is happening at the four-way stop in front of you, as you approach the intersection, requires a higher level of expertise and alertness than just rolling to a stop in a semi-somnambulant state."

"Not everyone has the ability to successfully expedite traffic. But just because you can't handle it is no reason to knock it. And by the way, Ralph, on my way through the desert from Barstow to Fort Irwin there is one stop light. As you approach it across the barren sands, you can see about twenty miles in every direction. Given that situation, suppose you come to that traffic light, and it is red. So, you come to a stop, even though there isn't a car in sight for twenty miles. Now suppose the light is broken and unbeknownst to you, it will never change. How long are you going to wait in front of that red light before you become a violator?" Ralph left.

—⟨⟨⟨—

5. On Getting Even

In the late 90's, after we had closed our Carmel business, I would occasionally handle an aircraft accident case. On this occasion I had received a call from an Arizona Attorney. As an aviation accident consultant, I was charging $175 an hour but I was "between commissions," you might say. So, when the attorney called to see if I could manage the case, I was glad to discuss the nature of the accident with her by way of engendering a possible client relationship.

Over the years I have had many a call from an out of state attorney which did not blossom into a consulting fee. Usually it is a small case and the attorney is looking for an expert's vita to scare the opposing counsel into a settlement. Perhaps the lawyerette who called me from Arizona was after just that, or perhaps she was hoping to gain some insight into whether or not she had a decent case. She called back a couple of more times until after I had faxed her my vitae and fee schedule, then suddenly no more calls. When I tried to get a hold of her, she would not take my call or return it. It was obvious I was being stiffed and in a very unprofessional manner.

With emails and conversations, I had spent a couple hours of time for which I would normally bill. This sudden severing of our relationship was truly rude and uncalled for and left me feeling angry and used. Time, of course is money, and that was part of the problem. The other part, the part which really bothered me, was that she had treated me shabbily.

Thus, it was that I began to ponder just what I could do to get even. I had the time and proclivity. In this state of mind, it wasn't long before I arrived at a convoluted concept for revenge. There are many ways to be creative, whether it is the execution of a detailed series of chess moves leading to the opponent's annihilation or devising a name-logo for our new business (San Francisco Imports). On this occasion, my challenge was to plot creative revenge. My scheme was to create someone who could offer a lucrative case to this law firm, and then withdraw the offer due to the manner in which the lawyerette had treated me.

To do this I used my favorite alias, Hugh De Shawn, and sent an email to her law firm in Tucson, under his name, explaining that (my) Hugh's sister's husband had recently been killed in an aircraft accident and we would like to consider their firm to handle a wrongful death suit. I am sure my mention of the two-million-dollar insurance coverage stimulated the great interest that her senior partner's return email expressed. As Hugh De Shawn and the senior partner further explored the potential suit, Hugh explained that the only thing he would like to request in this matter was that the law firm utilize his dearest friend, Ren Hart, as the aviation expert in the case. This of course was acceptable to the senior partner, and Hugh De Shawn hastened to add that Ren Hart was not only a highly regarded aircraft accident consultant but currently was investigating an air crash off Cape Cod, from which he was expected to return in a few days.

Now of course the bait had been taken and the two-million-dollar pot was causing some degree of salivation in the law firm. Hugh then sent Ren Hart an email requesting his participation in the case as the aviation expert, with a copy to the law firm. Ren Hart responded to Hugh De Shawn's email, noting that he believed this was the same law firm of Huber, Wilson and Berger whose lawyerette had recently caused him such angst. His email further inquired if this firm was from Tucson and had a lawyerette by the name of Magritte Solar. Hugh De Shawn then passed this email on to the law firm, which responded that they did indeed have an attorney by that name.

At this Juncture, by return email, Ren Hart then explained to his best buddy Hugh that he had been treated very shabbily and unprofessionally by that lady and he suggested that he find another firm to do business with.

Of course, the senior partner was very upset to learn that Margaret had treated Ren Hart so poorly that it caused him to lose this client and a chance at 35 percent of two million dollars.

6. Touching the Face of God

One of the truly great poems about flying lives on through the years with its young author, an American who joined the Royal Canadian Air Force during WW II, then died in an air crash at age 19. It is the story of flight the way it was intended to be.

High Flight
by
RCAF Flight-Lieutenant John Gillespie Magee Jr.

Oh, I have slipped the surly bonds of earth
And danced the skies on laughter-silvered wings;
Sunward I've climbed, and joined the tumbling mirth
Of sun-split clouds—and done a hundred things
You have not dreamed of—wheeled and soared and swung
High in the sunlit silence. Hovering there,
I've chased the shouting wind along, and flung
My eager craft through footless halls of air.
Up, up the long delirious, burning blue
I've topped the windswept heights with easy grace
Where never lark, or even eagle flew.
And while with silent, lifting mind I've trod
The high, untrespassed sanctity of space,
Put out my hand and touched the face of God.

John Gillespie McGee Jr. was an 18-year-old American who went to Britain in October 1940, during World War II, and joined the Royal Canadian Air Force. He flew in a Spitfire squadron and was killed at age 19 on December 11, 1941, during a training flight from the airfield near Sopwick, Lincolnshire. Written on the back of a letter to his parents he said, "I am enclosing a verse I wrote the other day. I started it at 30,000 feet and finished soon after I landed."

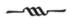

7. Aircraft Accident Investigation 1992

It was Thanksgiving and the Cessna 182 had just taken off from Pismo

Beach but now it was hurtling towards the ocean below. It impacted the waves at a hundred and fifty miles an hour, crushing the aluminum fuselage and decapitating the pilot. In the right seat, his lady friend was also killed instantly. The impact sound could be heard from shore, less than a mile away, and one witness described it as "an explosion." Another witness said the plane was on fire. In the morning, the sea began to give up its secrets as the bodies floated ashore, along with several parts of the plane which hadn't sunk.

By the time I was called in to develop an expert opinion of exactly what had happened that night, the NTSB had long since finished its investigation but had reached no conclusions. The children of the passenger, the plaintiffs, were suing the estate of the pilot for $3 million in a wrongful death suit contending pilot error. I was hired by the plaintiffs. The opposing side was the insurance company, contending it was a problem with the plane, not the pilot. I carefully went through the NTSB report and the autopsy to learn all I could. Aircraft accident investigators need to gather all the information they can about the pilot, the aircraft and the weather. These three M's (man, machine, medium) conveniently break out the elements of every aircraft accident.

The man was my age, with a similar 4,000+ hours' flying experience, but he lacked instrument qualification and was what we refer to as a "VFR only" pilot. He required visual reference to the ground to fly and was not qualified to fly on instruments. He and his lady friend had flown to Pismo, along with two other aircraft, to join a friend for Thanksgiving. After dark they said their goodbyes and stated they would over fly the beach by way of a farewell.

My review of the pathology report indicated no alcohol or drugs in the pilot's blood. However, I noted a high concentration of nicotine at a level associated with the deceased having smoked several cigarettes prior to the accident. This was of interest to me because of the deleterious effects of nicotine on night vision. I went through the pilot's log books carefully and spoke to other pilots who had flown with him recently. When I had exhausted all information available on the pilot I turned to the machine.

Aircraft records are by law detailed and comprehensive and are normally available at the local maintenance facility. These records went back to 1974, the date of the aircraft's manufacture. I was interested in recent maintenance activities, and specifically anything which would indicate the condition of the engine. Everything was essentially in order.

After studying the available documents, I needed to fly to Pismo to see what I could learn. I asked my artistic daughter to come with me so she could make a schematic drawing of the runway relative to the ocean and accident scene. My C 182 was identical to the accident aircraft which would be a plus when I duplicated the flight.

Parts of the wreckage had floated ashore and were available for examination. I reassembled the parts, laying out the fuselage pieces where they should be relative to the wings, cockpit, and tail section. I was able to rule out fire and found no indication of control problems. Lastly, I checked for the weather at the time of takeoff. On November 18th, the sun had set at 4:52. By the time the pilot took off it was totally dark. I talked to other pilots who had departed Pismo at about that time. They said that on takeoff it was like flying into a black hole. The Pacific Ocean is only a few hundred yards off the end of the runway, so that almost immediately after takeoff any lights or ground references pass behind the airplane. With the evening mist forming over the water, all reference to the ground would be lost. I now began to develop a scenario of what had happened.

I was aware of a little-known phenomenon called "Somatagravic Illusion" which may have played a part in this accident. This phenomenon came to light during WW II when naval pilots would take off from carriers at night, or into weather conditions in which the horizon was obscured by haze. Unless they were using instruments, it was learned, the pilots would confuse the sensation of acceleration with that of climbing, thus misinterpreting what was taking place. After climbing a short distance, the pilot would unknowingly fly a gradual arc back down into the sea. I suspected that this was at least part of the problem that had occurred at Pismo Beach that evening. Today, when being catapulted from a carrier, the pilot is told to take his hands of the controls during the high acceleration period.

My next step would be to duplicate the "Death Flight" as nearly as possible. The thought of flying that same flight, which had already killed two, gave me a creepy feeling but it had to be done. I flew to Pismo in my Cessna 182, landed and waited for dark. It takes about 20 minutes for one's eyes to night adapt but most pilots will not wait around for that to happen. So after a few minutes of checking my plane I jumped in and took off.

As I cleared the runway and then the beach, I was enveloped in a truly dark sky with absolutely no surface reference lights to help me avoid vertigo. I immediately reverted to instrument flight to assure that I was still climbing and would not lose my sense of what the aircraft was doing. When there is no reference to a horizon, as in the case of the Kennedy crash, an aircraft can get into a dangerous attitude without the pilot realizing it. This is because the hair-like cilia in the canals of the middle ear will not register any motion or change of attitude which occurs at less than three degrees per second.

It was now apparent what had happened on that Thanksgiving evening over Pismo Beach. The pilot wanted to fly low over the beach in his goodbye "buzz". To do that he needed to make his turn early and not get too high. Without ground or instrument reference, he attempted a turn in total blackness and somatagravically began a shallow decent. As he steepened his turn, his wing hit the ocean, cartwheeling him and his passenger to their death. The passenger's children each received a million dollars (less fees!).

8. Never Again

After fifty years and four thousand hours of flying light aircraft, I suppose one should expect an occasional bit of excitement. Most of us can handle excitement but unfettered pig-headedness from the left seat can be a real problem.

It was April and we had just completed a three-day seminar with our Forensic Society in Tucson. My Skylane was undergoing an annual inspection at Santa Maria, so I asked a fellow "forensicator" (my name for our members), who was headed back to the Bay Area in his Cessna, if I could bum a ride with him. I of course insisted on paying for half the gas. Bill was an M.D, had owned his Skylane for a couple of years and had about 300 hours and a recent instrument ticket. He was glad to drop me off at Santa Maria enroute and I was looking forward to the flight back and picking up my Cessna.

At the airport we checked weather, completed an IFR flight plan, and went out to preflight the aircraft. I expected to split the flying time and controls with him, my usual experience when flying with one of my buddies. If both pilots were qualified, one would usually fly as safety pilot while the other was under the hood. It was a symbiotic thing which benefited both in the shared experience and knowledge. So, when Bill started his preflight on the pilot's side and I said "I'll catch the right side," I was somewhat taken aback when he insisted on doing the entire preflight himself! Was this a vote of no confidence, or was he somehow intimidated with my having so much more experience in the air? In fact, my C-182 time alone was three times his total time.

I shrugged off the insult and strapped in. Bill had recently installed a three-axis STEC Auto Pilot with altitude hold and ILS, coupled so at 8,000 feet the plane leveled off without his input. I asked him if he would like me to handle the radios and nav instruments. He said he would prefer to do it. I was surprised, since in my many years of experience flying Army aircraft we completely shared all crew duties. It not only unloaded the pilot but out of mutual respect, gave the right-seater something to do. When we flew De Havilland Beavers in the Army, I would jokingly refer to my copilot as "The Carb Heat Control Officer," since there was so little for him to do on long flights. But our copilots were always assigned duties of navigation and communication, whether or not it was something we could handle ourselves, to take advantage of all crew resources. It was the smart and courteous thing to do.

When the aircraft was trimmed, Bill adjusted the mixture to about 100 degrees below peak on the EGT indicator. I moved the red line indicator on the instrument to indicate our current setting and reached for the cowl flap lever, since it is on my side of the cockpit. At that point he became quite agitated and excited, saying he didn't want me touching anything. Wow! Talk about crew management and utilizing your assets! What a departure this was from what I was used to.

As we approached the Palm Springs area SOCAL Approach cleared us to 14,000 feet. Our headwinds were already about 20 knots and at 14 thousand I expected we would be closer to 30. I said "Bill, why don't we cancel IFR and continue at a lower altitude to avoid the higher headwinds?" Of course, sharing good ideas is another benefit of a two-pilot cockpit. My suggestion fell on totally deaf ears as we bored higher and prepared to use the oxygen equipment. We were now about three hours into our flight and would need another two and a half hours to get to Santa Maria. Since Bill's wife was in the back seat and I was already about 30 minutes into my reserve bladder time, I made a last stab by suggesting we make a stop at Banning and continue on under the now scattered layer. This time there was not even a reply from the left seat. On we bored.

I figured with our 80 gallons usable and sipping gas at this altitude, we probably had at least seven hours of fuel available, so arriving at SMX after five and a half hours meant plenty of reserve in my book. Not so Bill. He now decided we should divert to Camarillo for more fuel. I said, "Bill, with 16 inches of manifold pressure, getting to SMX with plenty of fuel is a non-event. It's only 30 minutes more than Camarillo but if we divert at this point, we'll add nearly an hour to our flight." He said emphatically, "We're diverting to Camarillo." Well, at least that would save me about 20 minutes of bladder pressure, so I grimaced my agreement and he called SOCAL.

Camarillo doesn't have an ILS, so approach vectored us to intercept the VOR and we began our let down. We had a couple thousand feet of coastal undercast to let down through but the ceiling was close to a thousand feet, so the whole thing should have been a piece of cake, right? Wrong! Almost immediately Bill began to screw up the approach, since he was evidently used to coupling to an ILS and letting the auto pilot do the flying. By the time we got into the soup I was giving him heading corrections and he was telling me to be quiet. He was totally incapable of handling the radios and aircraft on instruments. In a disgusted tone, control told him to execute a missed approach. I said, "Bill, let me handle the radios for you so you can concentrate on the approach." He reached up to the console, flipped a switch and shut off the intercom. My mike was dead. I was beginning to get concerned. Here I am in the soup with this incompetent whose god complex is keeping him from accepting any help AND HE IS THE PILOT IN COMMAND! Part 91.3(a) clearly mandates that the Pilot in Command is the final authority for the operation of the aircraft!

This posed a real dilemma. As a passenger I am powerless. Was I to just sit there and hope to live through the experience? After pondering for a few seconds, I reached over and flipped the intercom back on, saying sternly, "Listen up, Bill! This is my life you are screwing with and I'm not going to sit over hear wondering if we're going to survive the crash. What I want you to do is tune your STEC to intercept the VOR, put it on autopilot and control your decent with power." Somehow that message got through to him and the rest of the approach was uneventful.

Of course the moral to the story is you need to know who you are flying with before you commit to his care.

—⚊—

9. Fiftieth Reunion West Point, May 2006

Planning to attend our 50th reunion was a big deal. We included a trip to Vermont for a time-share week at Smugglers Notch and a cruise to Bermuda following our reunion to celebrate our 50th Anniversary; three separate events, miles apart, with disparate venues and climate.

The reunion was great but the first leg of the trip to our New Jersey hotel was awful. Somehow there was just too much to get packed, what with our plans for a week in New England a week at West Point (with golf and reunion activities) and our Bermuda cruise, all with widely differing climates. We intended to leave Pebble for San Francisco the evening before our flight but finally left the following morning rather than fight the exhaustion of that evening. It was a mad rush to get out of our home and make the two hours plus, trip to SF in the less than two hours we then had left. In loading the car, I somehow managed to leave my "hang up" bag in our hallway at Pebble Beach, which went unnoticed until checking the bags at SFO. This was a major disaster in that all my dress clothes for the reunion and the Bermuda cruise were in that bag.

Fortunately we had left the key to our home under the matt for daughter Laura, who would be spending a few days there. This meant our neighbor could gain access to our home and possibly ship the missing bag to rendezvous with me in New Jersey. Through the miracle of the cell phone, which had our neighbor's phone number listed, I was able to get a hold of Mary and beg her help in UPS-ing the bag to me. Mary is one of those highly efficient, reliable persons who had been an Army wife long enough to be able to cope with any situation. By the time our flight had climbed to altitude, Mary had the errant bag boxed and on its way by UPS overnight! We had been unable to secure First Class tickets but had a decent nonstop flight from SFO. Business class is not what it used to be but certainly more comfortable than in cattle class.

We arrived at Newark Airport in early evening, while it was still light. Newark has got to be one of the worst experiences of many years. Perhaps not as bad as a colonoscopy but a close second. I was expecting a smallish airport on the edge of town. It was anything but. We arrived with our three carry-on items and headed to baggage claim for the other three pieces. It was quite a walk to the baggage claim before we could wrestle our luggage off the carousel, but our exercise had just begun. Next, we needed to find our way up elevators, down escalators and through long connecting halls to the monorail. It was the first time I've tried taking one of those two-dollar luggage carts up an escalator. Eventually we found the monorail station and waited for the train. The "air train," as we called it, carried us several miles to the rental car shuttle . . . more luggage transfer, this time having to leave our cart behind.

Finally, we off-loaded from the shuttle and re-load at the rental car. But getting out of Newark is where the real fun begins. In spite of my MapQuest instructions (or perhaps because of them), it was impossible to find my way out of Newark and the maze of parkways, thruways, freeways. I even paid tolls at the same gate twice, going around and around and was just getting to know the toll lady when I finally got it right and we escaped the concrete Jungle. We made our way north to the Hilton (our reunion hotel) at Woodcliff Lake, New Jersey. Good accommodations. Probably 400 of us there. Every time I turned around there was another classmate to greet. It was great fun seeing the guys again and running into old friends unexpectedly.

Thursday, we drove another classmate to golf at the Garrison course after having lunch together first. The old town of Garrison is across the Hudson River from West Point and provides a wonderful view of the Military Academy and the river. Our lunch there, preceding the golf, was at an ancient home/restaurant called The Plumb Bush, very special, good food but had to hurry to make our tee times. Twenty-two classmates and four wives played golf. My foursome was with two company-mates and a son. Golf was followed by an indoor BBQ which started about the same time as some late spring rains. Some got a little wet going from car to BBQ area, but our spirits remained un- dampened.

Our Friday golf at the West Point course was a bit of a disaster, as the rains began in earnest. I quit after the first couple of holes and got a ride back to NJ with other classmates. That evening we joined another couple and headed for a nearby restaurant. Wandering the back roads convinced me I needed to get a GPS to take on these trips.

Saturday was the beginning of the early bird activities for the 200+ of us who arrived early. We boarded buses midmorning, crossed to New York through the Holland Tunnel and first toured the aircraft carrier *Intrepid*. That WW II vessel served prominently in the Pacific and sustained two Kamikaze attacks at the Battle of Midway. It is docked permanently in New York harbor as a monument to those who gave their lives serving on that ship.

On board the Aircraft Carrier Intrepid, NYC, 2006

Following the *Intrepid* tour, we boarded a tour boat for a harbor cruise that took nearly four hours, a very enjoyable tour around Manhattan Island and up the Hudson River. Dinner followed at Harbor Lights Restaurant, not far from the infamous 9-11 site of the World Trade Center's Twin Towers, where we had lunched ten years earlier during a previous reunion.

The reunion planning and scheduled events were terrific, if semi-hectic, with a series of activities and events, breakfasts, luncheons, tours, mostly coat and tie, ending with a formal banquet. We had

246 classmates in attendance, a little over 500 people counting wives, etc. Our West Point experience of 50 years earlier was unique enough that lifetime relationships had formed, links that don't happen at other universities or fraternities. Of the 480 who graduated in the Class of 1956, 376 were still living. Of those, nearly two-thirds came for the reunion. Every day was filled with activities at West Point, which involved about an hour of busing.

On our first day, we met at the Officers' Club. It was our time to be together again. We gathered now, after 50 years. A few had not been together since the Jungles of Vietnam. We came from all over the country, patriots finding our way back to Mecca, to be where it all began, to be with each other and to remember the good times. A few came with the scars of battle; all came with the scars of life. For some it was a life too long and this would be their last pilgrimage, their souls grown fragile. For now, we were again at the place where it all began.

Here at the bend of the Hudson River, this stone fortress, which served as our crucible of discipline, is where we first learned to let Duty, Honor and Country take priority over self. This was the place where we had come as boys and left as men. This was the place where most would be put to rest. For us, it began mid centaury with 790 young, disparate, lads traveling by train, plane and car. We melded and molded until only 480 remained to graduate. Fifty years later our numbers had dwindled to 376. Of those no longer with us, who had passed to the other side, most were lost through natural causes and some, like the ballade said, "had found a soldier's resting place, beneath a soldier's blow."

Greetings rang out from across the room. Hands now wrinkled and bent grasped one another. We embraced without the shame of youth. A thousand memories flowed from the past, eyes moistened, and fifty years melted to yesterday. We spoke of familiar times in the air or when the cannon roared and where we had last met, was it Frankfurt, Saigon or Seoul? Together, we were as one. An indefinable bonding had drawn us together again, a bonding unlike any at other schools or fraternity groups.

Fiftieth Reunion—West Point, May 2006

Soon it was time to gather on the Plain where we had first formed to take the oath of allegiance so many years before. That vast spread of lawn, stretching from the massive stone structure of Washington Hall to Trophy Point and the River, was familiar territory. We had marched a hundred parades together on the Plain, and finally our Graduation Parade. Now we would form once more for the last time as the Corps of Cadets passed in review to pay their respects. We old grads positioned ourselves in a line three deep. Some shuffled into place, some limped but we all stood shoulder to shoulder, as we did of yore, erect, proud, and effused with memories. Today our presence would be honored as the band played a special march written and dedicated in our honor, a march we had commissioned entitled *Steadfast Leadership*.

As the band began with the oldest favorite, *The Colonel Bogey March*, our backs stiffened and the commands from the cadet leaders rang out to pass in review. In our mind's eye we were back to our beginnings, fallen comrades were with us again in ghostly assemblage, moving among us, yet apart. We stood together in this long gray line, which now seemed to stretch from our past to our future. The spirit of those who had gone before joined the line behind them and stretched through two centuries. It was a line without beginning, a line without end.

When the Corps passed in review the band struck up the strains of *Steadfast Leadership*, commemorating the fifty years that carried our class from the Korean War (when we were still cadets) through the Cold War, Vietnam, and finally Desert Storm.

Too soon it was time to leave, partings were sad. We shook one another's hands. Our eyes locked with the understanding that this was our last hurrah. We said goodbye with hugs and bravado but also with the quiet understanding that our era had ended.

Following this event, we walked across the Plain to Washington Hall, the humongous building where nearly 4,000 cadets are fed three meals a day. Our 500 + occupied a portion of one wing. After lunch Barb relaxed while I wandered off to see the nearby new gymnasium and to look at the old barracks where I had lived for four years. At about four PM we again boarded the buses to return to our New Jersey hotel to get ready for the evening's final banquet on Tuesday, 23 May.

The reunion ended with a brunch the following morning, including remarks by the class president. Once that was over, we checked out with several final goodbyes and drove an hour north to Poughkeepsie for a follow-on event . . . a tour and dinner at the Culinary Institute of America (CIA), a mile from Poughkeepsie. We checked into the Poughkeepsie Grand Hotel and joined about 70 couples from the class for a two-hour tour of the culinary college, followed by a wine tasting and dinner. Poughkeepsie is also home to Vassar College, and nearby is Hyde Park where Roosevelt (FDR) had his home and Vanderbilt had his mansion on the Hudson River.

Thursday AM, we checked out of the Poughkeepsie Hotel and on our way further north toured the Roosevelt Library. We altered our route a bit through the back country to pass by the Old Rhinebeck Aerodrome. There wasn't anything happening there but it was interesting to see what a grass strip airfield looked like 70 years ago, with old wooden structures and a couple of 1910 French airplanes (without engines) sitting in an old hangar. It was a picturesque setting with a stream running nearby.

By 5 PM we had come 160 miles and were driving a two-lane road in Massachusetts, on the outskirts of Williamstown. That far north it was late spring, with lots of new green on the trees. To our right, along a tree-lined rocky stream, we passed a nice-looking inn called the 1896 House and decided to stop for the night. After checking in, we explored Williamstown, a college town with a very impressive Campus (Williams College) rambling over the southern part of the town. When we returned to the 1896 house, which oddly enough was built in 1896, we decided to dine at another inn across the road from our motel. We were served a great meal in a lovely dining room and felt we had landed well. By late morning the next day, we were on our way again for the last 160 miles to Smugglers' Notch in Vermont.

It was Friday, 25 May 2006 when we arrived at Smugglers' Notch; primarily a ski resort in the hills above Stowe, Vermont. At the pass above Stowe is Smugglers' Notch State Park. Although only 2,500 feet high at the pass, the terrain rises rapidly on both sides and is a popular spot for bikers and hikers. The time-share unit we traded into was a very nice two-bedroom apartment overlooking the hills of northern Vermont. It was a great spot to unwind after our hectic reunion schedule at West Point. We enjoyed late breakfasts and quiet evenings. Most days we would visit a nearby village, shop at their country store, and find a local restaurant for lunch or dinner. After six days of relative quiet in that peaceful setting, we felt well recovered from the hectic overload of our travel and reunion week.

On Thursday, June first, we checked out a day early to make our 360-mile drive back to Bayonne, New Jersey, a more relaxing two-day trip. I pondered whether we should take the more expeditious freeway route down the eastern side of Vermont or the back roads which would avoid the heavily traveled area through Hartford and New York. As we neared Hartford the traffic became very heavy, made worse by thunderstorms so strong that some towns along the route lost their electricity. About 6:30 PM we called it quits and pulled of into a motel on the southern side of Hartford.

With plans to stay at the Sheraton Newark Hotel Friday night, we had only 150 miles to drive that day so were in no hurry to get on the road. That was a mistake, as the increasing rain and heavy Friday traffic resulted in about a hundred miles of stop and go slow driving for nearly six hours. Finally, we checked into our hotel. The following morning, I turned in our rental car and returned to the hotel to pack us out and get a cab to our cruise ship. That vessel, the *Zenith*, was standing by at the Port of Bayonne, New Jersey, only five miles as the crow flies but 30 minutes by cab. Our baggage was loaded, and we went through an expedited processing available to cabin class passengers. In a few minutes we were shown to our cabin and were definitely ready for the fun to begin.

Celebrity Cruise Lines has an alternating schedule of formal dining, informal dining, and casual. But if you don't want to dress up, there are other places on board you can eat. The ship was fully booked with about 1500 passengers, larger than the Princess ship we took to Alaska some15 years earlier. After that many years between cruises, the biggest difference I noticed was the present-day proclivity to make money from passengers in every way possible. Particularly noticeable was the price of drinks and a restriction against bringing any alcohol on board.

After unpacking and enjoying a great buffet lunch, we went to the forward lounge to watch the castoff and departure from the New Jersey mainland. It was a great beginning as we sailed off into the sunset with our seven-dollar Manhattans, before relaxing over dinner at the six o'clock seating.

Dinner that evening was informal (coat and tie). I long ago learned that many people confuse "informal" with casual, so I wondered if the other two couples at our table of six that evening would be properly dressed. They were both from New Jersey, life-long friends, and appropriately attired. Evidently this Bermuda cruise was very popular on the east coast and folks from California were an anomaly. Initially we were good company but after several meals we decided it might be more enjoyable at another table and requested we be switched.

Our ship was cutting through the water at about 20 knots with relatively smooth sailing. We would arrive at the port of Hamilton (the capital of Bermuda) on our third morning, the night before our arrival.

was the 5th of June, our 50th anniversary. I had checked the day before to buy flowers for the occasion and was surprised to learn there was quite an array of arrangements available. I made my selection and arranged to have them placed on our dinner table that evening. I had expected the cruise line would do something special to recognize the occasion— dinner at the captain's table, a bottle of wine, something? But evidently there are many anniversaries celebrated on that cruise and the only recognition is to gather the "anniversarians," on the second afternoon out, in one of the cocktail lounges with dance music, champagne and a ship's officer to offer congratulations to the group. We probably numbered about 50 of us. One couple was celebrating their 60th, several their 50th, and the rest, all various numbers from their first anniversary on.

On the morning of June 6th, we awakened at the Port of Hamilton. I had been to Bermuda some 50 years earlier on my return flight from our honeymoon in Europe. I was flying in a military transport which landed to refuel at Kindly Air Force Base, now known as Bermuda International Airport. At that time Bermuda was a British protectorate and was claimed by the British as a place to house their fleet in the late 1700's after they lost their American ports in the Revolutionary War of 1776. At my first arrival, in 1956, there was very little to see at that end of the island and the only memory I carried away from my two hours there was that Bermuda was a place of sandy beaches.

As to be expected, the trip home was a bit anticlimactic, but it was a great three weeks to remember.

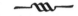

10. Desert Song

The desert is a strange place. In the winter and early spring, the first signs of life appear when the morning dew offers the desert flowers a chance to bloom. The evenings are crisp and clear and when the sun sets, there is a glow across the horizon which provides an orange backdrop to the darkening hills. Sometimes there are winter rains which cause the eggs of prehistoric shrimp to begin to hatch in the dry, cracked lake beds, yet another sign of life. The desert has its own beauty which can grow on you over time. But by the end of March the sun becomes harsh and the foreboding heat of the summer with its furnace-like atmosphere gives new meaning to such local names as Dead Man's Hollow and Furnace Creek. This is the Mohave Desert.

In 2003 I had the opportunity to visit the Desert Training Center at Fort Irwin, California, to witness a "Desert Battle." It was about a three- hour flight from Monterey, and of course no transportation on the other end. My son Lee was flying down with me, and I asked a friend, Lt General McEnery. to join us since he is good company, had commanded the same unit now operating as the Opposition Force, and as a retired general officer would receive some courtesy assistance. I informed Fort Irwin of our planned arrival so that their protocol section could provide a staff car (for the visiting general). Here is my short review of our experience.

It was a place where men came together to do battle, set on a vast stage in the desert. This barren desert is where it would begin and where it would end. The landscape was lunar with a sand dirt surface and rocky substrata which in places ruptured the earth with ugly outcrop-pings of dark shale and strangely flattened boulders. The rounded hills were more like folds in the earth than what we usually think of as hills. For the most part, it was totally inhospitable terrain racked by summer temperatures as high as 130 degrees in the shade but of course in this land where there are no trees there is no shade.

It was here that the battlefield had been prepared, here in Hell's furnace where the modern-day Centurions would clash with their tanks, armored carriers and weaponry. Each soldier had been instructed in individual survival skills and the value of a full canteen. They learned how to protect their weapons and equipment from the wind-driven sand which etched the paint on their Humvees. Their officers had studied the desert tactics of Rommel and Patton and taken their knowledge further, much further. They would control their tanks, armored personnel carriers, and subordinates by satellite, computers, and radios imbedded in their helmets. This was the final test, created to instruct as well as determine if the unit was combat ready. The battleground was deep in the Mohave Desert. It was an electronic battlefield using Global Positioning Satellites, computers, and laser beams instead of bullets, rockets or tank guns. The combatants and their tanks, vehicles, trucks, and armored personnel carriers were all equipped with laser sensors which, if activated by a laser hit, would make a noise, send a signal to the controllers, and emit red smoke.

The blue force (good guys) comprised a battalion or squadron of 1200 to 1500 soldiers. They fight the Red Force, comprised of a smaller more agile armored cavalry squadron. From the air-conditioned command center we watch the battle unfold on a large projected computer screen. It shows all the movement on the battlefield in real time and which tanks, or vehicles have been hit. We watch the action from the briefing room as our modern-day Centurions maneuver their forces into the killing zones which will turn the course of the battle. Huge clouds of dust and sand fill the air as the battle rages for three days and although the combatants would fight to the last man standing, the exercise is brought to a halt by the controllers as battlefield losses reduce one unit after another to a status of "Combat Ineffective." Soon the dust settles, and key players gather for their critique and a determination of whether their unit is combat ready. Next stop—Iraq.

11. Letters to my Grandchildren

Will there be time to tell our grandchildren or great grandchildren all we think they need to know? Is what we believe to be important really meaningful in their lives, or is it two generations passé? Is there some knowledge we have that could pass for wisdom?

March 14, 2006

Dear grandchildren—

As we go through life, we all find we have done things that we later regret. Sometimes we can fix them but much of the time we just have to live with it. In this regard, the other day I read an ad in the newspaper in which a church offered to pay for the removal 222of gang-affiliated tattoos, tattoos which young people had done to themselves earlier in their lives which marked that immature phase of life but no longer expressed who they were today. Tattoo removal is not much fun. It involves injecting skin-colored ink into the area that has the tattoo. There are other methods, such as skin grafting, that are even worse.

This article was interesting to me because I recall a prayer with the words: "… help us to do those things which we ought to have done and not do those things which ought not to have done." Those words go back probably a couple of centuries. So here we are, two hundred years later, trying to undo the tattoo "which we ought not to have done!" Of course, it is human nature to do things which we later regret and there is nothing that anyone can say or do to change that aspect of life.

People change as they grow older (and we hope wiser). The boy or girl you have a crush on at age ten you wouldn't want to come near at age 15. The loss of a baby you had to give up for adoption at age 16 may really start to bother you ten years later. The marijuana you tried at 19 creeps out during your background check 20 years later, when you can't qualify for a government job or miss a promotion and wonder why. The list goes on forever. But there is a secret I can pass on to you that you may find useful if you are smart enough to take advantage of it. I have never told it to anyone else because it has only been in the past few years that I discovered this wonderful secret and thought that perhaps I should keep it for myself. Now that you are getting older, I think it is time to share it with you, so here it is.

Believe it or not, old people can look into the future and see what is going to happen! It is a little like knowing the sun is most likely going to come up again tomorrow because you have seen it happen so many times. Even at a very young age one begins to develop the ability to glimpse the future in some simple ways. You learn that walking in the rain will get you wet and uncomfortable.

Your efforts to get good grades in high school may be why you did so well in college and why you now have a great job. Do you think the scientist who hated to do his multiplication tables at age seven had any idea how that building block enabled him to achieve greatness? When you are 10 or 11 you know if the two-year-old touches that hot iron he will be burned. You are able to see future consequences for some actions taken. Can you imagine how well you will be able to predict future consequences by the time you have lived 80 years? That is why old people can see into the future. So, when your Father or mother tries to guide you away from touching something they know could burn you, it may well be time to listen. I'm sure you know the wisdom in their words is born of years of experience and their love and concern for your happiness. Of course, if you ever want a really brilliant view of how what you do today will affect your tomorrow, just ask your grandparents. There's a reason why we call 'em "grand"!

June 20, 2006

Dear Granddaughters,

It seems to me that the entirety of the dating exercise is to find someone with whom you will want to spend the rest of your life and have fun with now and in the future. Of course, you want that someone to also be as free as possible of mental and physical defects. However, until one reaches the threshold of wisdom (which begins at about age 25 for most), what you need as a life's mate may not be entirely clear. The attention and feel good aspects of a loving relationship can easily mask the flaws in a partner. Over time, as the relationship stales, the flaws become apparent, and things fall apart.

Adding to the burden of a badly matched relationship is the fact that we are continually changing, rapidly in the early years, less so in the later years. So, the trick is to find someone who shares similar life goals so that you increase the chance of you both changing together and growing closer. When one partner moves too far ahead of the other partner in education, self-improvement and aspirations for greater self-fulfillment, the disparity becomes destructive to the relationship. The opposite is also true. If you share the same goals and work towards them, the relationship strengthens as the goals are reached. It becomes a case of having built too much together to throw asunder.

Some young men have a hard time finding a direction in life which suits them. This is not unusual for young people and most will find their way if they have a strong supporting family and have been brought up with the right values. However, if your young man is drifting without positioning himself for a future life through education or learning a skill, it does not bode well. It is one thing to not have direction, however it is quite another to consistently avoid any forward motion.

For a lovely and talented college student I would suspect that you are at the cusp of eligibility in what a male partner would be seeking. I also suspect, of those who are seeking a quality mate, there are probably 22,974 who have promise and could meet your eligibility requirements. So it is important that you do not use up your "high eligibility" years linked to someone who will not fit into your future. Every day spent with a "non-eligible" is a day lost in the quest for Mr. Right. And while you are spending time with Mr. Wrong your own eligibility will begin to diminish. OK, so how do you find Mr. Right? Here is my theory on that:

I suspect that the best place to meet a garbage collector would be at the annual Garbage Collectors Ball. Right? This is also true at the other end of the spectrum. It is just as easy to meet and fall in love with a professional or person of promise as it is with someone who is at a dead end. So why not target your activities in those areas where you will increase your opportunity of meeting higher quality individuals?

Higher quality people are found at institutions of higher learning and professional organizations. People in college have made it through the first quality gate. Those who graduate have passed through the second quality gate (college graduate) and have demonstrated that they have the ability, initiative and drive to succeed. That's where you are now, headed toward the second gate.

So, for your final grade in Sociology, tell me why on earth anyone would want to cling to someone who has demonstrated he is unable to pass through even the first quality gate?

TG F

—⟋⟋⟍—

2008

Dear Grandchild—

Now that you are an adult, I want to offer you the gift of wisdom. Wisdom 101 for young adults may be quite useful for you, so let me start at the beginning. Every adult freedom you now enjoy carries with it an adult responsibility. The responsibility of relationships is perhaps the most complex responsibility, so I will begin there. You may already know this intuitively, because you are intuitive, but it is worth a minute or two.

All adult relationships (and I do mean ALL!) are "quid pro quo" (tit for tat); they are like contracts between individuals. Your friends are there for you only if you are there for them, in the same way, to the same degree, your friends do for you only if you do for them. If one side or the other becomes more of a taker than a giver, the relationship falls apart. Self-interest is the overriding factor. If you examine any one of your relationships closely you will be able to identify why it exists, what you are getting out of it and what they are getting out of it. If one of you fails to get out of it what you expect, the relationship dies. That is a fact of life; I first learned it from my college readings and though skeptical then, later found it to be true in life.

Family is a little different. Your parents will always give more than they get from their children and so children are unaware of this give and take; or perhaps I should say they understand the "take" much better than the "give." The parental relationship is special, and I won't get into that here. But relationships with extended family are more like relationships with friends. If not nurtured, they won't do well. As a child, the grandparent relationship is pretty much a one-way affair; the older relation or grandparent gives and the child takes but when you are an

349

adult, the relationship needs to move closer to quid pro quo. As an adult, there are many things you can do and should do to support a family relationship, because the family is the greatest support group you will ever have. It is worth supporting!

Communicating is one way of strengthening your support group. You can give by calling other family members to wish them a Happy Birthday, or Happy Mother's Day or Father's Day, or just to find out how they are doing. You can meet the still expected and accepted standard of sending a thank you note or email for a gift or dinner. Also, as an adult, when you receive an email, a card, a gift or any giving from anyone who has spent time, money, or effort on you, you need to return the effort or expect the relationship to suffer. That doesn't mean you need to respond in kind but rather in quality. If your parents spend $200 on you, as an adult, you need to think what you can do for them in return, not just soak it up and forget about it.

On the social side, there are also some obligations which, as an adult, you will want to be aware of. When you go to a party, be it family birthdays, friends, or Christmas dinner, there are obligations incurred. It is the hosts' responsibility to provide the party (the place, the food and drink and decorations or ambiance). It is the guests' responsibility to make the party go. You may not sit in a corner reading your favorite book or texting a boyfriend. You must make an effort to speak to everyone at the party, be upbeat and fun. This is the adult way of the upper class. That is how you transition to adulthood. Also, you will enjoy yourself more and so will everyone else. However, your responsibility does not end there. You also incur an obligation to your host/hostess to return their kindness. When you are earning a living or have become a person of means, you should expect to return an invitation with one of your own.

But how does this play out now? Here's the scenario: you remember the boyfriend or girlfriend you love, or your best friend's birthday, by getting them a small gift but when a few months later, on your birthday, you receive nothing from them, no phone call, no remembrance? How would you feel? Would that end the relationship? How would a parent or grandparent feel? Is the parent or grandparent, who you will have for life, less important than the girlfriend or boyfriend that you will shed a couple of years later? As a child your disregard is perhaps understandable but now you are an adult! As a starving student, you cannot be expected to return a gift from a parent or a grandparent in kind. But as an adult, you are expected to show some remembrance of other family members on their special days and if you can't be bothered, neither will they!

Remember, "There is no free lunch". When someone does something for you there is an obligation incurred. When someone asks you to dinner you may not be able to respond in kind but much of the obligation you incur can be discharged by being a big help to the hostess: pass the hors d'oeuvres, bring the empty glasses or plates to the kitchen, help with the cleanup after. Asking if you can help is not enough, because the polite hostess will not want to "put upon you." You must find ways to be an asset if you care about the relationship and want to fulfill your social obligation.

Years ago, when a new general and his wife arrived at Fort Polk, he made the effort of having small dinner parties for all of his staff and commanders so that he could get to know them and also to create an upbeat organization in which people enjoyed each other.

After about six months, when he had long completed his entertaining effort of several dinner parties, he called his staff together and said, "Gentlemen, I have been here six months now and have had every key member of this organization to my home for dinner. But I have yet to receive my first return invitation. I do not expect you to entertain at the same level as I do, and I am perfectly happy if you have me over for spaghetti and not steak but I do expect you to meet your social obligations."

Now is the time for you to know this, not when you are 35 and wondering why your relationships are not fruitful.

Love, TGF (The GrandFather)

August 2013

Cadets Lily and Chloe Forlini
PO Box 1125 & 1136
USAF Academy, CO 80841

Dear Cadets Forlini:

Congratulations for all you have been and all you have done to arrive at the AFA. As you probably know, about 20,000 apply, 10,000 qualify but only 1,200 are admitted and about 900+ graduate, so there is still a little work ahead of you.

June went by too fast and I regret that I didn't push harder to get you both into the air! Flying is something almost everyone dreams of doing. Yet only a fraction of us are fortunate enough to translate that dream into reality. As pilots, occasionally we are given the unique privilege—and responsibility—of facilitating the realization of this dream by someone else. Few things are more exciting and validating than giving another their first flying experience. It was my responsibility to make sure that your first exposure to aviation was both positive and memorable and I hope that opportunity will be with us when I see you next.

Please know that you may encounter some uncomfortable times, partly because you are entering something of a man's world which is manifested by less emotionalism, more directness and less sensitivity. Do not take this personally, keep a sense of humor, gut it out and let them see you roar! BCT is a period of intense indoctrination into the military and is partially intended to thrust you into adulthood. When you have finished your 4th Class year, you will be light years ahead of your friends and contemporaries, who went to Podunk U, in both maturity and a readiness, to accept responsibility. Remember, any sacrifice and deprivation you go through builds character!

Of course, you know we are all pulling for you and love you as you find your way through the obstacles and challenges ahead. You go girls!

Love, TGF

12. Abduction

Some years ago, I received an email from the membership chairman of our local chapter of SIR, an acronym for Sons in Retirement. Our SIR organization has no dues, no agenda, no affiliations, and no rules except that you must attend six of the twelve monthly luncheons each year. It is a men's luncheon group which exists only for the amusement and fellowship of the members and is organized so that the members can participate in golf, tennis, bridge and other retirement activities.

Well, evidently, I had failed to meet the requirement of six luncheons, so the membership chairman found this to be a good occasion to send the following letter:

August 16, 2004

Dear Sir:

Just wanted to give you a reminder about the need to attend six SIR meetings in a twelve-month period. The attendance chairman informs me that you are barely meeting this requirement.

Perhaps a significant reason exists that has prevented you from attending the meetings. If so, I would sincerely appreciate hearing from you. As you know, we have a category of membership in SIR called "Inactive Membership." Acceptable reasons for requesting inactive status are health and extended travel. If either or both reasons apply, perhaps you may want to request a change to Inactive. As an inactive member you can still attend the meetings and participate in SIR #115 activities. At the present time we have 7 prospective members on our waiting list, and we cannot induct any of them into Active membership until a vacancy occurs, since our membership is limited to a maximum of 150 members.

Sincerely, Membership Chairman

To ensure that he did not take himself too seriously, I sent him the following reply:

August 20, 2004

My Dear Membership Chairman:

I read with alarm your recent missive of the 20th instant. It is of course my fervent desire to attend every luncheon, not only to savor the suculations of the day but to be in the company of greatness. However, as you can undoubtedly understand there does arise from time-to-time events over which we have little or no control. Such an event occurred only recently while I was in fact on my way to a SIR Luncheon.

Until now, I was careful not to mention a most unusual event which unfolded the day of our last SIR Luncheon but as I am now faced with expulsion, I will reveal the whole story, strange as it may seem.

As I was stepping out of my velocipede to enter the sacred Lodge of the Pebbles, in great anticipation of our luncheon, I was momentarily distracted by a faint whirring sound and looked up to encounter a brilliant, translucent, circular form, shaped generally along the lines of a saucer but with an ethereal effervescence, the likes of which I can hardly describe. As I pondered the magnificence of this vision, a light bluish conical haze came from the apparition above me.

Suddenly, I was enveloped in the haze and seemingly became weightless. Evidently, I was instantaneously transferred to the object in the sky, because when I regained consciousness, I was in what appeared to be a hospital room but unlike any earthly facility I have ever seen.

As the strange-looking attendant in the room left I looked up at the mirror above the gurney on which I was lying and noticed in the reflection that there was a very small incision-like mark on my forehead. I could also see in the mirror that there was a manila folder just within reach and I picked it up. Quickly I read the doctor's instructions, which said in part, "…earth patient to receive a reduced memory chip by use of insertion gun." At that moment the door swung open, and several attendants entered the room. The last thing I remember was an odd buzzing and then I found myself again standing by my car in the parking lot next to the bank. But it was no longer 11 AM, it was 2:30 PM. I had missed the SIR meeting!

I dared not mention the incident until now because there are so few people who would believe such a strange story. I must therefore prostrate myself before the board and hope that there is one among you who will accept this rather bizarre-sounding story as true and indisputable.

Realizing that I am not worthy to be among those of you who have been able to attend on a regular basis, I beg your understanding of my peculiar circumstance.

I remain your humble servant,

R. Renwick Hart

13. Lake Tahoe Summer 2006

It was a great day for fishing. With temperatures in the high 70's and the deep blue of Lake Tahoe a slightly darker shade than the sky. The air was still and across the lake the snow-capped mountain peaks attested to a heavy winter now past.

Chuck, our guide, pulled away from the pier while saying, "We'll be headed out toward mid-lake where the Mackinaw schools are the heaviest. I've been fishing this lake for 40 years and if there's any fish out there we'll find 'em'." Chuck was a gregarious and garrulous type and it wasn't long before we became "friends for life."

After the hooks were baited and the lines lowered to the proper "Mackinaw depth," he offered an interesting tale, saying, "Do you remember in the early 70's when Cousteau's son, Jean Cousteau, was commissioned by the Feds to examine the lower depths of the lake to map its contour and determine its depth?" I nodded yes, though I wasn't sure Zif indeed I did remember that occasion but the mention of it did seem to stir some neural pathways.

He continued, "The reason he was commissioned by the Feds is the lake is bisected by the California—Nevada border, so it is a federal matter to conduct the survey. At some expense, Cousteau had his submersible brought to the lake and prepared for the many dives it would take to complete his contract. No one had ever reached anywhere near the depths he planned for his descents. The first day he went down to about 100 feet to make sure all systems were go. The next day, again descending alone, he reached the 168-foot level beneath the surface and began to encounter thumps occurring every few seconds but at irregular intervals." Chuck suddenly paused, looking at grandson Drew, and asked if it was OK to reveal the unsavory details he was getting to. As I was replying in the affirmative, wife was responding in the negative. Chuck then backed off on his tale and said he would tell me another time. Of course, 14-year-old Drew was not about to let this particularly interesting story go untold and the two of us eventually out prevailed his grandmother.

"Well," Chuck continued, "Cousteau wasn't going to go any deeper until he could figure out what was thumping against the sub. He leveled the vessel, locking the controls to remain at the 168-foot level. He then climbed into the viewing bubble to see what was going on. Turning on the lights, he saw a continuing stream of heavy objects coming at him. As the next one rammed into the bubble, to his absolute amazement he could see it was a stream of human bodies impacting the sub."

"You see," said Chuck, "at the 168-foot level the water is a constant temperature of 38 degrees all year long. At that temperature, the bodies are perfectly preserved, and the water density and density of a human body are in balance, so the bodies won't sink or rise to the surface, They just stay at that level and move about the lake with the current. I have heard estimates that over one-third of the lake, at that level, is covered with these bodies. It's too deep and cold for the fish to feed at that level, so over the last hundreds of years the number of bodies has continued to increase. There are Indian bodies from the 1700's, when they would use one area of the lake as a burial ground. There are also bodies from all those Chinese workers who died putting in the railroad. Add to that the fishing accidents, the Mafia killings, etc., and the estimate is there are over 3,000 bodies moving around at the 168-foot level."

Drew swallowed and looked to me for verification. I shrugged. Chuck picked up on this exchange of body language. He said sternly, "I didn't want to mention this but on two occasions, not far from where we are now, when I was fishing 'the shelf' over the past many years, I somehow managed to reel up pieces of human skin."

I asked, "How is it there never was any action taken to clean it up?" He replied, "When the Feds heard the details from Cousteau the next day, they immediately paid him off and closed his contract, which already included provisions preventing him from making the results of his survey public. There was no way anyone wanted to deal with that situation and had we begun a determined effort to recover the bodies, the damage to the tourist industry would be only the least of the fallout. Can you imagine the resources to recover and identify the bodies, notify next of kin, reopen cold case files etc.? It would be horrible and the cost horrendous."

14. We Fly to Banffffff

Labor Day weekend, Y2K, was coming up and the Society of Forensic Engineers and Scientists would be meeting in Banff, Canada. It would be a great opportunity for Lee and me to catch some meaningful cross-country flying in the Cessna 182 and do a bit of bonding. It was about a thirteen-hundred-mile trip, so we would need to spend one night somewhere in route. We left early Friday morning, planning to have lunch at Sun River, Oregon, spend the night at Kalispell and arrive in Banff early Saturday morning. But flying is adventuresome and as Robert Frost said, "The best laid plans o' mice an' men aft gang agley" (often go astray).

We chose Sun River as our lunch stop because it was about halfway to Kalispell and their runway along the Des Chutes River is only a couple hundred feet from the lodge. We landed at noon, made the short walk across the small, river bridge, and found a sandwich at the lodge. But in the short interval between sandwich and takeoff a beautifully restored C-45 had landed and collapsed a landing gear while taxiing from the runway. It looked very much like this photo of a C-45, but not the wounded one.

Beech C-45

They had closed the airfield and were working on finding some method of getting the plane off the runway. If we didn't get away soon our schedule of arriving Banff in time for my meeting would need to be scrapped.

At the little terminal building I asked the person in charge whom I could speak to for permission to take off on the remaining two-thirds of the runway. I was told I would need to talk to the airport manager, who was not there but would be calling in shortly. We waited. A few minutes later the phone rang and I was able to speak with the man in charge. He said I could take off as long as it was away from the crippled aircraft on the runway. I had planned a takeoff in the opposite direction, into the wind and downhill. Uphill with a tail wind was going to make our departure just a little more challenging, since we were at about 4,000 feet altitude.

I used standard short-field technique, adding full power, a few degrees of flap and then releasing the brakes. With a full load of fuel, we cleared the runway with only a few feet remaining. It was tighter than I had anticipated, and the rising terrain ahead added to our discomfort. As we followed the Des Chutes River through the lower part of the valley, we slowly gained speed and altitude and were eventually able to reach our cruise altitude of 7,500 feet. A bit of a sweat, not unlike my takeoff from Buedingen in a Beaver, years ago.

Our flight path to Kalispell headed us across the magnificent Montana land-scape but a huge forest fire which was devastating the countryside that year required us to divert our flight path south. There are two airports at Kalispell. The one to the north side of town is the gateway to Glacier National Park. The other is on the south side of the city, which is where we landed. It was a small, rural airport and there on the south side of the city, the town seemed rather basic, but it did have a couple of motels and we walked from the airport to the nearest one.

The following morning the clouds were hanging low over the Canadian Rockies, which we needed to cross to get to Banff but first we would need to stop at Springbank, an airfield a couple miles west of Calgary, to clear Canadian customs. We checked with the airport operator to buy the IFR Nav charts we would need to fly on instruments to Springbank. None were available; we were on our own. Although it would be a short flight of less than an hour, the 11,000-foot Canadian Rockies, we needed to cross, were not something we wanted to tackle in marginal weather.

As we readied for takeoff the sun was high enough to shine through an area between two peaks where there were no clouds. We headed toward that opening in the Elk Lake area at an altitude of about 12,000 feet. The unbelievably sheer mountain cliffs passed beneath our wings and in a few more minutes we were able to drop down into Turner Valley at about 7,500 feet and head directly to Springbank.

Crossing the Canadian Border

After landing, the tower directed us to park in a space painted yellow and marked "CUSTOMS" near the operations building. We were required to stay parked in the box until we had been inspected. After shutting down the engine we remained on the radio as directed. Eventually customs began asking us questions concerning our cargo and purpose and after a while we were told to come to the operations building and pick up our customs approval.

Next stop to Banff was the airport at Calgary, about a 45-minute hop from Springbank, due west. We left the plane there to be refueled and have the oil changed and were able to arrange for a rental car. After a half hour drive through Banff National Park, we checked in at the opulent Fairmont Hotel. We finally got to my meeting about four hours later than planned.

Crossing the Canadian Border

The trip home was something of a reverse, again needing to fly about 20 minutes off course to cross the border back into the U.S. with a stop at Cutbank, this time for U.S. Customs. Evidently the customs official had to drive about 30 minutes to the airport, so we again had to wait for that bit of officialdom. We were flying with a hand-held Garmin and were able to pretty much fly directly to Klamath Falls for our next refueling stop. As we neared the airport after about four hours of flight, a heavy thunderstorm was dumping sheets of rain on us to the extent that we couldn't see the airport until about the last mile before landing.

Inside the operations building we checked the weather and learned that Klamath Falls was under a stationary front, and we could be there a matter of days before getting better weather. We were of course qualified to fly in bad weather but to get on top of the cloud layer we might be forced to encounter icing conditions, which can be a real killer. The freezing level was at about 6,000 feet and we needed to get to 9,000 to get on top of the overcast. We were in a bit of a tight situation since Lee needed to be back at work and I had things scheduled at home. Bearing in mind that "get-home-itus" had killed many a good aviator, we gave the weather careful consideration. After finding a sandwich, we decided to file IFR and head home. Above 6,000 feet there was forecasted light rime ice which, although undesirable, is not nearly as dangerous as clear ice. The biggest danger for a light plane in icing conditions is that the stuff will form on the leading edge of the wings and decrease lift. And if it forms on the prop, it greatly decreases the efficiency of the propeller.

We entered the overcast at 6,000 feet and sure enough, the rime ice began to form on the struts where it is most visible. At 7,000 feet we had about a quarter inch of rhyme ice buildup, and I needed to add full power to keep the aircraft climbing. Finally, when I began to get concerned at 8,000 feet, we started coming out of the overcast. The windshield was frosting over, and I pulled on full defrost air and noticed our airspeed had dropped off drastically. Although I had turned on the pitot heat to keep the pitot tube from icing over, the de-icer evidently didn't work. I could tell from the control response and the feel of the aircraft that there was no aerodynamic change to our flight condition but the inoperative air speed indicator was a source of distraction.

As we continued to climb there were scattered cumulous clouds which towered above us, but we were able to avoid them as we leveled at 9,000 feet. Mount Shasta was now behind us, and the weather conditions began to improve as we left the coastal range. The ice on our wings and struts began to dissipate through sublimation and eventually we were able to cancel IFR (Instrument Flight Rules) and descend to an altitude where the temperature was above freezing. In time, our airspeed indicator came alive again and the remainder of our flight home was uneventful.

APPENDIX III

WHAT I LEARNED IN MY FIRST 90 YEARS

After 90 years, a thousand experiences, a hundred mistakes and many misjudgments, there must be something I know that you don't— something which would be of value? On the other hand one of the things I have learned is that one cannot pass wisdom to one's progeny. But this is only true in life and may not be true in death? After all, when one is gone, do not their words seem to take on a smidgen more validity? So, I will continue this segment only with the explicit belief that one day my final condition will empower my words... just a little. Here are six things I have learned the hard way:

Item I Character

Character is the be all and end all of what you are and who you are. It encompasses integrity, honesty, diligence, truthfulness, and trust. It is achieved through trial and error. When I was 12, I broke a knob on my father's hi-fi set and when questioned, stated I hadn't done it. My stepmother didn't believe me but Father chimed in and said, "If he said he didn't do it, then he didn't do it." He put his trust in me when I didn't deserve it and the impact was profound. I never lied again. Your character will be tested in many ways on many occasions. As an act reaps a deed and the deed reaps a habit, the habit will reap your character! Always be on the alert to avoid slippage into poor character traits. Poor character will affect your life negatively in many ways. A simple character failing is not doing what you say you will do. A glaring example is when I gave a granddaughter $200 to do some editing. The money got spent, the editing never happened. Before you commit, consider what you are committing to and make sure it happens.

Item II Love

You and the person you love at age 17 or 18 are in a continuing state of change and will not be the same persons at age 25. The ability of the maturing mind to reach proper decisions is a function of the cerebral cortex which is not fully developed until age 25. Change is a product of growing older but over time the change takes place more slowly. In your twenties you may be fortunate enough to find your true love. When this happens and you go forward through life as one, there will be rough spots, disagreements. and arguments. It is important that you do not let these inevitable blips in your relationship affect your long-term happiness together. In this regard, when angry, avoid saying hurtful things that will damage the relationship. The things you say are said, and once said cannot be erased. As Omar Kayin wrote, "The moving finger having writ moves on. And all your tears, nor all your piety can err change a word of it." So, be careful lest they erode your love for each other. Love is the byproduct of admiration. If ever you stop being admirable in your partner's eyes, love will suffer.

Item III The Workplace

After I graduated from West Point and finished my early training, it was time to be productive. I believed the primary objective on the job is to work hard and be effective in your accomplishments. That is the primary objective, but the most important aspect of any job is getting along with your boss and coworkers. That doesn't mean you sniff after them, it means you impress them with your honesty, dedication and loyalty. If you don't like them and they don't like you, game's over. You've lost, no matter how well you perform.

It is easier to be ignorant than responsible and informed! Responsibility is power. As a staff officer there were always new requirements cropping up. For example, a document would come floating into the office requesting our analysis of the "air space requirements" at Camp

Roberts. The boss says to us, "Whose responsibility is this?" Silence! Then I say, "I'll handle it, sir." No one knew beans about military "air space." So, along with my other tasks, I became the air space expert! After that, I was the only one with the answers and the knowledge. After taking on a few more of those projects, you begin to stand out because you know more stuff about more stuff than anyone else. And remember, if you want to get ahead, there is no substitute for hard work and an affable personality.

Item IV Being on Time

With friends or at work, being on time is probably the single most important aspect of your job or relationship. If you show up late for work or meeting someone there can be only one reason…the person or event wasn't important enough for you to be on time and that is a terrible message to send! Also, it is an obvious evaluator of whether you have your act together. If you don't have sufficient control of your life to orchestrate what needs to be done to arrive to work on time, what does this say to your boss? Being on time is easy…you backward plan. E.g., I need to be there at 9, therefore, I'll need to leave at 8:40, so I need to fix breakfast at 7:30, get up at 7 and finish shower and dressing by 8:10, etc. After a while you will learn exactly how long each phase takes. Until then, it is a good idea to add 15 minutes of buffer time. It is very difficult to accurately estimate how long it will take you to complete any particular task, so you need to add about 20 percent more time than you think it will take you. Unless you give "being on time" a high priority in all your activities, your lateness will continue to negatively impact your life.

Item V On Being Gracious

Being gracious is so easy, yet it is becoming a rarity. Graciousness is pretty well encompassed by the "Golden Rule". Step one to being gracious is to learn to say "THANK YOU." Most of us could say thank you and mean it if we were given a new iPhone. But if you were expecting to get a new car for your birthday and only received an iPhone, "thank you" might be more difficult. That's when you begin to understand the meaning of gracious. I like to say thank you three times when someone gives me something or does something special for me like taking me out to dinner. The first thank you is at the event or occasion. The second thank you is with an email, note, or phone call. The third thank you is the next time you see the person . . . "Charlie, I sure had a nice time at your home the other night...thanks much." Or "I sure appreciated that $100 for my birthday. I was able to buy a new gismonometer, which I enjoy." It's easy. They say George Bush made it to the White House on the quality of his thank you notes!

Item VI Money

As a depression baby I was raised with rather limited goodies. Mother had very little disposable income after her divorce ($30 per child per month child support and $60 for her). In the European manner, she was careful in her spending. So, when I was able to save a few dollars from my paper route, it provided a level of comfort knowing I had some purchasing power. When it was Mother's birthday in October 1945, I took my six saved dollars, walked down to the streetcar at West Portal in San Francisco and went downtown looking for a gift for her. The first shop I came to on Market Street, had glittery stuff in the window. I found a gold colored, ladies compact for $5.95 but with tax I didn't quite have enough money. A sailor shopping there overheard my plight and came up with the extra 12 cents. And so it was I learned the value of a dollar early on and over the years finally figured out how not to be poor. It is very simple. Here is my FOUR-step formula:

1. Save at least ten percent of every dollar you earn. It is easy to do and adds up rapidly. Once you start, you will never miss it. At age 23 we began saving 15 percent of my paycheck and that $50 went into the stock market each month to buy shares of Lorillard Tobacco Company. In one year that $600 had doubled to three months' pay!
2. Never, ever spend money you don't have (credit cards) to buy things you can do without. If it is important for you to have it, start saving for it; do without other goodies until you can afford it.
3. Never, ever invade your invested capital to own goodies you would like to have but don't NEED to have. That is like killing the goose which lays the golden eggs!
4. Take advantage of your nonproductive time to be productive. When I was 12, my mother asked me to fix her "Mangle". The

mangle was a mechanical device to iron items like napkins or pillowcases. It was my first repair effort. After spending some time taking it apart, I put it back together and plugged it in. Nothing! On closer examination, I could see the problem was the plug. An easy fix. As I grew older there was never a "fix it" that I wasn't willing to undertake. As a youngster, I couldn't afford much, so at age 17, I undertook a major repair to my '39 Plymouth which in later years led to overhauling my SJ 6 Jag engine. As you get better at something, fixing it is enjoyable and provides a sense of accomplishment. But most importantly it saves a ton of money and provides some level of convenience if you can do it yourself. Eventually, I had enough confidence to undertake plumbing, carpentry, and electrical problems. I still found time for tennis and golf, but when something in the home didn't work it took priority. The alternative is sitting in front of the TV!

By 1962, when we arrived at Camp Wolters, Texas, for helicopter school, we were investing all of my $120-a-month flight pay in the stock market. If other, non-flying, classmates could get by without flight pay, we could too. One of my classmates, who also arrived at Camp Wolters at the same time, was enjoying a new car, his third since graduation but come to find out, he had no investments. We were still driving our 1956 Chevy but had nearly a hundred thousand invested in the stock market. Going without, early on, was beginning to pay big dividends. When you go without something so that you can save (self-discipline), the dollars you have saved become more important because they represent all those goodies you have gone without and you are less likely to blow it on something over time. And of course, the power of compounding was an important factor. When the money you've invested begins to earn money and the earned money is earning money, compounding becomes very powerful!

Item VII Alcohol

Why I quit drinking 20 years ago:

It is expensive; there are so many other things I rather spend for.
Any amount of alcohol kills brain cells and I need to hold on to whatever I have left.

Alcohol is addictive.. The more you drink the more you need it.
The consequences of drinking are always negative.
It slows your metabolism so losing weight becomes dificult.
Drinking has no benefits and no redeeming features. So why do it?

Item VIII Nine Rules to live by

1. Never be content with a half truth, when the whole can be won.
2. The way you do anything is the way you do everything.
3. In life, as in the game of chess, there is always one best move. The trick is to look far enough into the future to determine which move you should make.
4. Seek efficiency in everything you do. For example, when you are finished with an item put it back where it belongs, it requires no more time, only a bit of thought.
5. Never diminish your character by going back on your word or your agreements.
6. Possessions clog life. Buy only what you need not what you want in case you will need it.
7. There are three easy ways to achieve long life: moderation, exercise and what you eat.
8. Intellectual honesty. Sometimes there is something that you may have done wrong or are not proud of. But you are the only one who knows what is in your head so you can pretend otherwise, conversationally, to make your point or win your argument. However most often this intellectual dishonesty will be recognized and serve to discredit you. Strive for honesty in thought, word and deed, it will result in transparency and will build a reputation for you as a straight shooter.
9. Live your life with grace and good cheer. Like a good boy scout:
   A Scout is ... prepared, trustworthy, loyal, helpful, friendly, courteous, kind, cheerful, thrifty, and brave.

APPENDIX IV

CHRONOLOGICAL LISTING
OF WHERE I LIVED

Born in Columbus, Ohio April 3, 1933

Summer 1935	Royal Circle, Kahala, Honolulu
Summer 1938	Van Ness Avenue, San Francisco
1940	Fort Mcdowell, Angel Island San Francisco, 1st Grade
1941	Fort Lewis, WA & 31st Ave, San Francisco, 2nd Grade
1942	San Francisco, Grades 3-10
Dec 1948	Ashia, Japan, 10th Grade
Summer 1949	New Cumberland Depot, PA, Grades 11-12
Dec 1950	Washington, DC, Last Semester 12th Grade
11 Jun 1951	Entered US Army, Fort Meade, MD Basic Training, Fort Belvoir, VA
Sep 1951	USMA Prep School, Stewart AFB, Newburgh, NY
Jul 1952	Entered U.S. Military Academy, West Point, NY
5 Jun 1956	Graduated, commissioned 2nd Lieutenant, Married Barbara
3 Aug 1956	Reported Fort Benning, GA for Basic Infantry Officer Course and Airborne/Jump School

Jun 1957	Lee was born, Drive to Camp Gary, TX for Flight School in August
Dec 1957	Completed Phase I Flight Training, Departed for Fort Rucker, AL via San Francisco
Jun 1958	Graduated as US Army Aviator, Departed for Fort Lewis, WA via San Francisco
Jun 1960	Moved family to San Francisco, Departed for Korea
Summer 1961	Returned from Korea, Drove to Fort Benning, GA
Summer 1962	Fort Wolters, TX for Rotary Wing Qualification
Aug 1962	Ford Ord, CA via San Francisco
Dec 1964	Buedingen, Germany, D Troop, 3/12th Cav Squadron
Jun 1966	Depart Germany for Vietnam via San Francisco
Jun 1967	Depart Vietnam for Assignment to Presidio of San Francisco
Aug 1969	Attend Command & General Staff College, Ft Leavenworth, KS
Jun 1970	Assigned NATO Central Army Group, Mannheim, Germany
Jun 1973	Assigned Fort Polk, LA as Battalion Commander
Jun 1976	Assigned Sixth Army, Presidio of San Francisco, as Secretary of the General Staff
Feb 1982	Retired from US Army to live in San Francisco.
Jun 1982	Opened San Francisco Imports with shops at Presidio of San Francisco and Carmel, CA
Summer 1987	Moved to Carmel, CA part-time.
Summer 1990	Changed permanent residence to Pebble Beach, CA.
June 2022	Moved to Roseville, CA and lived happily ever after.

APPENDIX V

OUR HERITAGE

On my mother's side, it is interesting to note Grandfather Ciccolini was an Italian Marquis, so part of our heritage is from European nobility. Victorio de Ciccolini was from Northern Italy. He was born 28 May 1860 and died 1 June 1933, two months after I was born. His father was a Roman Senator. His mother was from Arnhem, Holland with the good Dutch name of Von Fronhauser. My maternal grandmother (Violet Brown Prichard, Marquise de Ciccolini) was born 1 February 1880 in London and married at the turn of the century. After she married the Marquis, they lived first in Monte Carlo, then in Nice, France until she was 90. She died 10 June 1970 in a rest home in Grass and was buried in Nice, at the Caucade Cemetery. Records show that her husband had earlier purchased a mausoleum for 121,434 francs (about $25,000). A classmate, Gene Fox, visited the Cemetery in 2014 and sent me a photo of her grave. It was not in a mausoleum!

Grandmother's Father (my great-grandfather Prichard) was from England, but his wife was Hungarian. They lived in Budapest, where her family owned a large (110 units) apartment building. There were also properties in Arnhem, Holland a villa in Monte Carlo, and a chateau on 20 acres in Nice, France, at 9 Route de Billet. In about 1900 Grandfather Victorio de Ciccolini married my grandmother, Violette, in Budapest. Later they moved to his villa in Monte Carlo, Monaco. Grandmother said her family traced back to before Christ. This abbreviated family tree will help clarify the lineage on my mother's side, starting with my Grandmother Violette:

- Violette Pritchard—marries Victorio de Ciccolini in 1900. (Two children, Sacha & Lilly—Lilly dies at age seven).
- Alexandra (Sacha) de Ciccolini—marries Harry Lee Hart in 1931. (Two children, Ren, & Harry. Harry marries Anita in 1956).
- R. Renwick Hart—marries Barbara Jean Rising in 1956.
- (Two children—Lee & Laura).
- Lee Renwick Hart—marries Ellen Morgan in 1986.
- (Two children—Janine Alexandra & Allison Karoline).
- Laura S. Hart—marries J. Todd Forlini in 1991.
- (Three children—Drew Hart, Lilly and Chloe).

Father's side of the family traces back to William Carson, born 10 May 1727 in Clontinaglare, Kilmore Parish, County Down, Northern Ireland. In 1743 he married Anna McCord, age 21. Their son (my great-great-great-great grandfather) William Carson Jr., born 5 October 1745, was married in January 1771. He and his wife Isabella emigrated to America in 1773, settling in Colerain Township, Lancaster County, Pennsylvania. In 1776 he served as a soldier in the American War of Independence. This is of interest, since my daughter and all our granddaughters and great-granddaughters qualify as "Daughters of the American Revolution" (DAR's). But wife Barbara, who is a Colonial Dame, has traced her heritage to over a hundred years before the Revolutionary War, which means all female progeny to follow are potential "Colonial Dames."

In June 1806 William Carson moved his family to Ross County, Ohio, where he bought a large tract of land. His daughter Elizabeth (Betsy) Carson (born 1775) was one of 13 children and among the 8 who survived to raise families in Ohio. In 1808 she married James Johnson and raised 8 children, one of whom was Samuel Johnson, my great-great-grandfather. In about 1860, Samuel traded his Ohio farm for a two-thirds interest in a college in Urbana, Ohio, where he served as president. Shortly afterward his daughter Sarah Margaret Johnson (my great-grandmother, born in 1843) graduated from that college, her

Father, Samuel, sold his interest in the college to buy land in the new frontier of Iowa. In 1865, as the Civil War was winding down, he moved his family to Iowa. Sarah's story of traveling by covered wagon to Iowa and finding the man she married (James Lee) is at Appendix 1. Sarah and James Lee had 9 children—5 boys and 4 girls. The first girl born was my grandmother, Annabel Lee, in 1872 in Yahoo, Nebraska. She was also the first white girl to be born in that town, which the Lees had founded.

Two of Annabel's daughters died before the age of 18 but her son Harry Lee Hart (my Father) and his sister Helen lived to raise families. Today the Lee name is carried on by my son Lee Renwick Hart and my half-sister Nancy Lee. Father's sister, Helen, married Dr. John S. Sinning and spent most of her life in Iowa. Their sons, John and Jim, my cousins, resided in Iowa. John became an orthopedic surgeon, married Beverly, and had four children and many grandchildren. Jim married Kay, adopted two sons and lived in Marshalltown, Iowa, on the family farm until his death in 2008.

Appendix VI

THE LAST HURRAH

And so it came to past, that my active days were over. I had my stent and "pig valve" installed, and even a mild stroke when they stopped my heart to insert the valve. As a result, I tell my friends, that when I make my semi-annual visit to my primary care guy and he pulls out his stethoscope, what he hears is "oink, oink". Fortunately, the stroke didn't affect my fine mind, but my balance suffered.

So, at age 89, it was time to leave Pebble Beach. Since we had already left our San Francisco home to our son, daughter would get the Pebble home.

About 25 years earlier, Barb bought a home in Sun City Roseville with her inheritance since it was near our five grandchildren. That was great, we could spend seasonal time there and it was a nice stopover when driving to Lake Tahoe. But, as time would have it, the grandkids grew up, went to college, and 0ur 5 wonderful grandchillins scattered to the four winds.

Our daughter Laura also graduated from UC Berkeley and has had a long and successful career as a Business Analyst. Laura was a stay-at-home Mom prior to her career and produced 3 awesome children. Her first-born child Drew graduated with a double major in Food Science and Biochemistry and minor in Microbiology. He very much enjoys his work as a research scientist and his executive status. His twin sisters graduated from the Air Force Academy in Colorado and are completing their respective commitments in service to their country. Lily Alexandra (named for my mother and my mother's sister) married her classmate and

USAFA Quarterback Nate and is a Command Pilot at Travis AFB where she is close enough for me to continue to exert grandfatherly influence. Chloe is enjoying her residency in Family Practice and has just completed her intern year at the beach at Florida's Eglin AFB hospital where she lives with 2 feline support staff. The academy experience they went through was like my West Point experience and gives us a special link.

Of daughter Laura's three children, Drew is now in Logan, Utah and very much enjoys his work in research and his executive status. His twin sisters graduated from the Air Force Academy in Colorado and are committed to spending a few years in that service. Lily is a Command Pilot at Travis and married her classmate Nate. Chloe completed medical school and is working hard at her residency in Family Practice at the Eglin AFB hospital. The academy experience they went through was like my West Point experience and gives us a special link.

Our son, Lee got married after graduating from UC Berkeley and also has two special granddaughters. Jay married a computer whiz (like her father) and has given us our first two great grandchildren. She is very much involved in caring for her daughter and her recently arrived son. Her younger sister, Allie (middle name Alexandria after my mother) has just completed her master's degree in psychology and is working in that field while handling her newborn son.

Meanwhile, Barb and I have figured out how to extend our 66-year marriage another 20 years! The secret is to find space in one's day-to-day activities. In retirement the husband finds he is no longer in charge of his office environment because he is now living in his wife's environment; 24 hours a day! To survive this, he must have a man cave. My man cave is less than a mile away from Barb's Roseville home and is a 1,600-foot unit in a lovely area named Eskaton. Eskaton was modeled after a French village with much landscaping and winding paths to the homes. It is a small, nonprofit, elder community with an activity center and a care facility for those in need of help. Barb and I talk on the phone daily and get together a couple times a week for a luncheon date. It is what I consider a perfect way to grow old!

"And when our day is won, may it be said, "Well done, be thou at peace."

THE END

Printed in the United States
by Baker & Taylor Publisher Services